THE COMPLETE GUIDE TO

UNDERSTANDING AND CARING FOR YOUR HOME

A Practical Handbook
for Knowledgeable Homeowners

JAMES MADORMA

BETTERWAY PUBLICATIONS, INC.
WHITE HALL, VIRGINIA

Also by the same author
The Home Buyer's Inspection Guide

Published by Betterway Publications, Inc.
P.O. Box 219
Crozet, VA 22932
(804) 823-5661

Cover photograph by Timothy Sams
Illustrations by James Madorma
Typography by Park Lane Associates

Library of Congress Cataloging-in-Publication Data

Madorma, James
   The complete guide to understanding and caring for your home : a
practical handbook for knowledgeable homeowners / James Madorma.
      p. cm.
   Includes index.
   ISBN 1-55870-210-5 (pbk.) : $18.95
   1. Dwellings--Maintenance and repair. 2. Dwellings--Remodeling.
3. Room layout (Dwellings) I. Title.
TH4817.M33 1991
643'.7--dc20

91-19203
CIP

Printed in the United States of America
0 9 8 7 6 5 4 3 2

This book is dedicated to my parents, Jimmie and Lena Madorma,
for their encouragement and love,
and to my wife, Marie Avona Madorma,
whose editorial expertise made this second book possible.

Contents

ACKNOWLEDGMENTS

Special thanks to the following manufacturers, suppliers, professionals, government agencies, and associations whose assistance was invaluable in the preparation of this book:

American Gas Association
American Plywood Association
American Society of Heating, Refrigeration, Air Conditioning Engineers
American Society of Mechanical Engineers' Boiler and Pressure Vessel Code
American Society of Testing Materials
American Wire Gauge System
Andersen Corporation Inc.
A.O. Smith Water Products Company
Berner Air Products Incorporated
Bionaire Corporation
Bossaire, Inc.
Carrier Corporation (United Technologies Carrier)
Cedar Shake & Shingle Bureau
Coalition for Container Safety
Conservation Energy Systems
The d-CON Company
Devcon Corporation
Jim Dunn Company, Inc.
Fibermesh Company
Four Seasons Design & Remodeling Centers
Goodwin Lumber Company
The Home Depot
Honeywell Inc.
Honeywell Residential and Building Controls
Hydrotherm Inc.
Innovis Interactive Technologies
Institute of Boiler and Radiator Manufacturers
International Association of Plumbing and Mechanical Officials
Jacuzzi Inc.
Lennox Industries Inc.
Lindal Cedar Homes
Marvin Windows
Masonite Corporation, Building Products Group
Massachusetts Historical Commission

The Maytag Company
National Chimney Sweep Guild
National Electrical Code (NFPA)
National Fire Protection Association
National Kitchen & Bath Association
National Pest Control Association
National Safety Council
National Wood Window & Door Association
NORCO Windows, Inc.
Owens-Corning Fiberglas Corp.
Pease Industries, Inc.
Pella/Rolscreen Company
Season-All Industries, Inc.
Shakertown Corporation
Simpson Door Company
Slant/Fin Corporation
Steamist
Steel Boilers Institute
Thoro System Products
3G Mermet Corp.
Underwriters Laboratories, Inc. (UL)
Uniform Building Code
Uniform Plumbing Code
United Technologies Carrier (Carrier Corporation)
U.S. Consumer Product Safety Commission
U.S. Department of Agriculture Forest Service
U.S. Department of Energy
U.S. Department of Housing and Urban Development
U.S. Environmental Protection Agency
U.S. General Services Administration (Consumer Information Center)
USS, a Division of USX Corporation
VELUX-AMERICA INC.
Weil-McLain, a division of The Marley Company
Western Spruce, Pine and Fir Association
Western Wood Products Association
Wood Moulding & Millwork Producers Association

Introduction

There are basically two types of homeowners: those who understand and know how to live with and care for their homes, and those who do not. Knowledgeable homeowners tend to enjoy their homes, while the others often find their homes to be sources of irritation and unwanted expense. This guide, therefore, has been written to help you live comfortably and happily in your home. To do this, it asks you to decide what you like and don't like about your house. This is done by examining the house first as a single unit and then by breaking its components down to individual units. These evaluations will help you decide what you want to keep, what you want to change, what you want to add and, yes, what you have to live with that is unfixable. Such an endeavor is an enormous one but well worth the effort because once you have accomplished it, this guide provides you with the information needed to fulfill your family's essential needs as well as their many individual desires.

As part of this assessment, suggestions are made to show you how the same space can be altered to accommodate several possible alternatives. This is done by using a typical one-family, two-story structure and by demonstrating the possible variations of the original layouts on a floor-by-floor basis. Detailed illustrations are used in conjunction with the text to explain these various possible alterations. Some of these variations actually have been done, others are conjecture; however, all are possible within the limits of the original spaces. These ideas for conversion and renovation are not intended to be copied, rather they are meant to suggest ways that additions and alterations can be made in a simple, single

framework. By studying the illustrations and reading the text, you can create other ideas to accommodate the changes and improvements you have been contemplating but did not know how to undertake.

A thorough explanation of all the components in a house follows this assessment. Using simple language and numerous photographs and illustrations throughout, this guide explains the complexities of the structure and the systems in it. It does not do this in the way that a "how-to" book would. In fact, there are many times when it specifically tells you not to do a certain repair or replacement job on your own. Instead, it reviews and clarifies the components of a house so that you can intelligently decide what to maintain or upgrade as the need or opportunity arises to do so. Further, it provides information about the products and materials used in a house, discussing such relevant subjects as manufacturing standards, grading systems, production methods, application prcedures, and other details so that you can make decisions based on comprehensive, factual data. Whether you do any of the work yourself or decide to have someone do it for you, you will know what you should be getting in terms of quality of materials as well as degree of craftsmanship.

This guide also teaches you how to prioritize the maintenance and renovation projects in your home so that, for example, you don't decide to have new electrical wiring installed throughout your house after the kitchen and bathrooms have been renovated. As you read this book, you will see that much of this information has been culled from the actual experiences of homeowners who have faced these same problems in the past and learned how to deal with them the hard way. Some of these firsthand lessons are also the result of the author's personal experiences as a homeowner and renovator for almost three decades.

Since the subject of this guide is so broad, it is fair to say that each topic in it could only be reviewed briefly. It does, however, include more than adequate information for you to be able to make a decision, answer a question, or resolve a problem. Although many of the topics included here are technical in nature, they have been explained as simply as possible so that you can easily comprehend them. Where some component or detail of a topic has been excluded, it was done only when your comprehension of the subject would not be compromised, or when the additional data would be confusing. You can be sure that what the typical homeowner needs to know about each subject has been fully covered.

As a result of the preparation of this book, the author has two suggestions to make. First, before making any drastic decisions or changes in your house, take the time to research each topic extensively. Manufacturers, suppliers, and professional associations can provide you with enough material to make your research as current and complete as possible. Technological advances and scientific breakthroughs affect the quality and characteristics of products and materials almost on a daily basis, or so it seems, so be sure that the product you are buying does the most it can do to meet your specific requirements.

The second suggestion follows logically after the first; don't be afraid to ask for more assistance and information. For the most part, information and help are available, but you will have to ask for it or you will not get it. It is always preferable to have to sort through too much information than not to have enough data to make an informed choice. For example, the list of suppliers, manufacturers, government agencies, and associations at the end of this guide mentions only a few of the manufacturers and suppliers that could have been listed with similar products or services. The same is true of the associations and government agencies. Non-profit organizations as well as government agencies are formed not only at the national level, but also at state, city, and other local levels. These organizations and agencies offer free brochures and advice. Some associations also make referrals to professionals who must meet the standards of quality and workmanship set by the group. And, if you have a problem with one of their recommended vendors or professionals, you can go back to the association to tell them about it. Therefore, if you are about to embark on a repair, replacement, or improvement project, take some time first to do a little research, to consider what you want to accomplish, and to ask for more information and assistance before you make your final choice. You can begin, however, by reading and referring to this guide.

PART I
Analyzing Your Options

1
Deciding What You Like About Your Home

HOW DOES YOUR HOME MEET YOUR NEEDS?

Your home is very much a reflection of who and what you are, so when you look at it to decide what you like and do not like about it, you are going to have to take into account what you feel is important to the lifestyles of each of the members of your family. Your house will need as many rooms in it, for instance, as the size of your family dictates. But that is not all there is to consider. If you like to have guests stay over for a weekend on a fairly regular basis, you will need space to accommodate those visitors. If you are an avid woodworker, you will need space for a workshop. If you are especially fond of good clothes, you will need space in which to store them neatly. If you like to sew, you will need space for your sewing machine and a large cutting table. If you like to exercise, you will need space for your exercise equipment. If your family takes lots of showers as a result of all of these activities, you will need extra bathrooms. If you like to cook, you will need a large kitchen with lots of counter space, and if you are very enthusiastic, space enough in it for a commercial stove. If you are an avid reader who likes to keep the books you read, you will need space for a library or den with plenty of bookcases. If you like to host large dinner parties, you will need a large dining room in which to serve them. If your children like to have their friends over for frequent visits, you will need a large family room to give them playing space and keep them out of the rest of the family's way.

What all of these suppositions add up to is that before you can analyze your house, you must take the time to analyze your family's likes and dislikes. Make a list and in it include your basic needs, such as the number of bedrooms and bathrooms, and also your hobbies and recreational activities. Decide how you do these things and how you could do them more easily and enjoyably with a home that better suits your family's lifestyle. Find out what is important to you and your family as well as what is superfluous, or what is done because you cannot do something you would prefer to do. In other words, make a list of your needs as well as a "wish list" with "if onlys" on it because after you have read this book, you might determine ways to accommodate some if not all of them. With this list in hand, you are ready to start to analyze your house.

EVALUATING THE OVERALL LAYOUT

With your busy schedule you may often feel that all you do at home these days is sleep there. In fact, a house is used for three main functions — working, sleeping, and entertaining. A house provides space to prepare your meals, to accommodate your bathing and other sanitary needs, and to provide for the things that amuse you, whether they are the TV and VCR or a group of close friends and some conversation. Therefore, the house's overall floor plan should be able to deal effectively and efficiently with these three major uses.

1. Sliding doors and elliptical transoms bring the outdoors into this kitchen. Courtesy of Marvin Windows.

3. This compact kitchen was redesigned to make a "socializing" kitchen and to provide added work space. Courtesy of The Maytag Company.

2. Solid cedar accents this kitchen in a log-style house. Courtesy of Lindal Cedar Homes.

4. The working area in this kitchen is uninterrupted by cross-traffic from the dining area of this dual-purpose room. Courtesy of The Maytag Company.

5. *Skylights and lots of windows provide plenty of natural light in this kitchen. Courtesy of VELUX-AMERICA INC.*

6. *The sink and surrounding countertop are full of natural light in this kitchen, coming from windows above and along surrounding walls. Courtesy of VELUX-AMERICA INC.*

For instance, work spaces, which are usually the noisiest, should be located far away from the rooms where quiet is essential. If you like to entertain and you have small children, you will want to keep your entertainment area and your children's play area in spaces that are not located near each other. If you live in a city, it is a good idea to keep your bedrooms in the rear of the house, or at least as far away as possible from the noises in the street such as sanitation pickups, delivery trucks, and the like. Bedrooms need to be as near to a bathroom as possible, and each bedroom should have as much privacy as possible. If you have a house that is more than one story high, you will need a bathroom, or at least a toilet facility, on the main level as well as one located near the bedrooms. And if you have a finished basement, you will want to have at least a toilet facility on that level as well, with a water closet and sink in it.

Usually it is a good idea to have some kind of buffer area at all entrances to your house. These foyers, or mud rooms, not only prevent heat loss in the winter

and the loss of air conditioned air in the summer, they offer privacy for those in the house from those outside. The secondary entrance is not for guests. Guests should come into your house at the front entrance, or wherever the primary entrance is located. The secondary entrance usually is more functional, while the primary entrance is meant to be inviting, or even dramatic, for visitors as well as for those who live in the house. The secondary entrance most often leads into the kitchen, one of your house's working areas, so that groceries and the baby's stroller can be brought into it easily. Some houses allow you to enter the kitchen directly from the garage; a nice touch, but one that is not always possible, especially in older houses. Most of these design details were considered when your house was being built and many may already be in place. If they are not, do not despair, because later in this chapter we will show you ways to get more use out of the space you have. Some sacrifices or compromises may be necessary, but ultimately you will be left with what you really want and need, and that will surely please you and your family.

ASSESSING THE ROOMS: THEIR NUMBER AND SIZES

Are there ever enough rooms in a house? Not by a long shot. Are they ever large enough to fit your furniture and other possessions in just the way you would like? Never in a million years. Despite these two unrelenting facts of life as a homeowner, let's discuss the subject anyway by examining each and every room in terms of its size and all of the rooms in terms of their number. The kitchen is an excellent place to start.

The kitchen can be compact but quite functional in minimal terms, or it can be spacious and airy yet still functional in expansive terms (Figures 1 and 2). Which of these extremes it ought to be depends entirely on how you use it, how big your family is, and how often you like to be in it. It does not have to be large to be functional but it does have to be large if you want to use it as a family eating area as well as a working kitchen (Figures 3 and 4). It should have plenty of ventilation and natural light, no matter what size it is, and the secondary entrance should lead into it from outside (Figures 5 and 6).

The bedrooms need space for large pieces of furniture such as a queen- or king-sized bed, dressers, bunk beds, maybe even a desk for correspondence. You need privacy in the bedrooms, but also windows for ventilation and natural light. These rooms should have easy access to the bathroom, dressing room, and any closets. Because the furniture in these rooms is so large, you need a couple of uninterrupted walls, that is, walls without windows or doors in them. You want to have a master bedroom as well as one for each child. Children like to play in their rooms and often do their homework there, so their bedrooms need to have ample space for these activities as well as for sleeping. Children can easily double up in bedrooms while they are very young, but they will each quickly need their own private rooms as they mature. If you can, plan initially to buy a house with one bedroom for each child you have, no matter what their ages are when you are buying it. You also are going to need extra bedrooms for guests, grandparents among them, who will stay overnight. Extra bedrooms can be used in

years to come as offices, dens, or exercise rooms. They will never be idle or wasted space, that is certain.

Bathrooms are another type of room that you cannot have enough of in a house. Generally you need at least one full bathroom and one toilet facility in a house, but a larger family, five or more individuals, could use at least two full bathrooms and one toilet facility. The full bathroom should be nearest to the bedrooms, preferably adjacent to the master bedroom. Ideally, since this is a "wish list" after all, the full bathroom should be located so that it can be entered privately from the master bedroom, although this is not always possible in older houses. Again, you need ventilation and natural light from a window in the bathroom, but the window must allow for privacy. Also, the window should not be placed where it will cause drafts into the shower stall or bathtub. Mechanical venting systems are readily available as an alternative to having a window in the bathroom or toilet facility, where they are most commonly used, but a window is always preferable for better ventilation. Lately, skylights are being used to provide ventilation in bathrooms, particularly where outside walls are not available for the installation of a window.

With the major rooms considered, it is time to decide what other rooms are needed in a house. The living room needs to be large enough to accommodate comfortable sofas and chairs, the stereo and TV, some bookcases, table and floor lamps, and other such items essential to your relaxation. The dining room needs to be fairly large as well for your dining room table and chairs, the hutch, dry sink, or other similarly useful types of furniture placed in it. If your dining room table lengthens as extensions are added to it, then your dining room has to be large enough to accommodate the table's longest possible length. Also remember that the room must have space for chairs filled with guests so that they can move freely around the table while others are still seated at it. The windows in this room need to supply adequate light and, if there are enough of them, they can make the room appear to be spacious despite its smaller size (Figures 7 and 8).

Less formal spaces also have to be examined. The family room needs space for chairs, desks, the TV and VCR, and maybe a personal computer as well

7. *Numerous skylights and spacious doors brighten this dining area. Courtesy of VELUX-AMERICA INC.*

8. *A generous amount of natural light in this dining room comes from large windows, doors, and skylights. Courtesy of VELUX-AMERICA INC.*

as space for a card table or a table to do homework on after playing is done. Your den needs lots of space for bookcases or built-in bookshelves and a desk, perhaps your pc, and for chairs, lamps, and plenty of privacy for contemplation as well as reading. If you run a small business from your home, your office at home will need plenty of natural and artificial light and space for your desk, chairs, a drafting table, copy machine, fax machine, and a pc workstation, among other possibilities. Here, too, privacy is essential for creating ideas as well as reading.

Children need space for special uses too. A child's room needs a window for natural light and ventilation as well as space to change the baby, or for the children to play, often with a few friends around. Older children need space for a desk for homework and school projects, to play video games, or to ex-

ercise. Let them practice their jump shots and baseball swings outdoors, though, because no room in a house is large enough to practice these kinds of games without causing damage or an accident or both.

Besides all of these rooms for all of their various possible uses, be sure that there is enough closet and storage space, especially in the bedrooms and kitchen and in, or adjacent to, the bathrooms. Walk-in closets are wonderful, but they are not always in place. Instead, there are usually many smaller closets throughout the house to compensate for one or two big ones. Closets that have been built into a house sometimes have more uses than the obvious one of storage. Often a closet has been placed in a specific location in the house to act as a sound barrier, so do not immediately consider removing one someday unless you are sure that it is serving no other function, or unless you intend to muffle the sound in another way. A utility room, mud room, or dressing room also may have been placed to prevent noise from moving from one space to the next. If you have any of these kinds of rooms or closets and you are considering removing them, be aware of the effect of their loss in terms of noise as well as lost storage space. For instance, do not decide to eliminate the utility room until you have decided where you are going to put the washer and dryer currently in use there. You will still need these appliances, even if you do not need a room in which to place them exclusively. Also, bear in mind that you need electrical power, water, and drainage in the new location, just as you did in the old utility room, so choose the new spot carefully.

Staircases are another item to consider carefully. Although their function is obvious, in many houses they have been designed so that they are barely wide enough for furniture and other large objects to fit through them. Sometimes a staircase also has been situated poorly, drastically reducing the size of the room in which it has been placed. For instance, they are often placed in a dining room, where they reduce the width of the room, a critical loss when the dining room table is filled with guests. You may want to consider relocating your staircase, if it is in an inconvenient location, but remember that staircases also are used to muffle noise from one space to the next, or even to define an area. If you are thinking of moving a staircase, building a wider one, or installing one for access to a newly finished level, consider it in terms of all of its possible uses before making any final plans.

STUDYING THE TRAFFIC PATTERNS

Traffic patterns in urban streets and highways were designed for much the same reason as those in the house, namely, for easy access to and from various areas. Generally it is necessary to be able to move easily from one room to the next, from one space to another, without obstructions or barriers preventing an easy flow of movement in and around the space. For instance, an obvious example is that the kitchen should be adjacent to the dining room and breakfast room. If you have to walk through a long corridor to go from the kitchen to either or both of these

rooms, it can be a problem. At first glance, this corridor may look easy to walk through, but it is a long trip when you are balancing a large turkey on a platter to serve for Thanksgiving dinner, or when your hands are filled with heavy dishes to be carried to the dishwasher from the dining room. This precarious trip becomes even more difficult when another person tries to pass by as you walk along with dishes in your hands. This is an accident waiting to happen, as well as an example of poor traffic flow in a house.

Doors and doorway openings, or archways, also should be wide. The reason for this is obvious since moving furniture through any narrow opening is going to be difficult. You may have been made painfully aware of this when you first moved into your home, when you moved furniture from one room to another, or when you had new furniture arrive only to find getting it carried into your house and into its appropriate room was very difficult. If the furniture kept hitting the door frames, it may not have been because of inept movers, or because the furniture was too large, but rather because the door openings are too narrow. This is particularly true in houses that are very old because, when they were built, furnishings were much smaller than they are today. People also were shorter a century ago than they are today and the king-sized bed, for example, was unheard of when the house was being constructed.

A sensible way to check traffic patterns in your house is to do a walk-through; that is, to try actually bringing in your "groceries" from the car in the garage to the kitchen, or to answer your "doorbell" at the primary entrance, starting from a point at the rear of your house. Make believe you are going to wash your clothes, or that you are about to serve dinner guests seated in the dining room, and take note of what, if any, obstacles you encounter along the way. You will probably find that, overall, there are few problems associated with these various chores since the architect who designed your house considered them when he planned interior spaces. On the other hand, you will also find a few obstacles that cannot be missed as you act out these routine daily tasks.

There are a few rules of thumb to consider as you analyze the traffic patterns in your house. For instance, you should be able to enter any room (usually the living room) from the main entrance

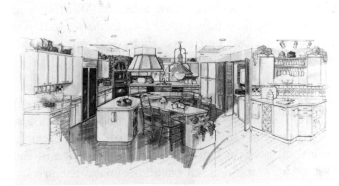

9. *The hexagonal design of this kitchen provides space for guests to gather or to help the cook while the meal is being prepared. First place, 1985 Maytag CKD Excellence in Kitchen Design Competition, Dean Ingram, CKD, Lebanon, NJ. Courtesy of The Maytag Company.*

10. *First place, 1986 Maytag CKD Excellence in Kitchen Design Competition, Michael B. Laido, CKD, Franklin Lakes, NJ. Courtesy of The Maytag Company.*

without having to walk through any other rooms in the house. If your kitchen is close but not necessarily adjacent to the main entrance, that is even more convenient for you. Your kitchen is most conveniently and most commonly entered from the secondary entrance. If you have a mud room, utility room, or just a space for coats, boots, etc. between the kitchen and the secondary entrance, you will probably not have to wash the kitchen floor as often as if you did not.

Ideally, you want access to your kitchen from your garage; however, that is not usually the case, especially if you have an older house. As explained earlier, your kitchen and dining room should be adjacent to each other, and your deck or patio should be accessible from the kitchen. If you have small children, visibility from the kitchen is essential so you can watch them outdoors as well as in another room, so that you can move quickly to end battles between siblings or to bring the ice and bandages to care for those predictable accidents. Today's kitchen has again become what it used to be decades ago, the focus of the family's activities, therefore, movement to and from it is not just for food preparation and serving, but also for homework, bill paying, family discussions, informal dining, and a host of other activities. As a result of all these activities, the kitchen has several traffic patterns to accommodate and they all must be considered simultaneously to determine how best to use the space to place furniture and appliances in it strategically. This room

all by itself will take a great deal of time to analyze and then to reconsider after you think your analysis is complete. It is worth the extra effort, however, because it can be the most useful and pleasant room in your house (Figures 9 and 10).

LOOKING AT THE ATTIC AND BASEMENT FOR SPACE

Now that you have studied your house as a single unit and room by room, it is time to look at it in an entirely different way. You are now looking for flexibility in the spaces you have, for opportunities for change. If your house has an attic or basement or both, then these spaces offer opportunities for expansion as your family increases in number and as your children mature to adulthood. These spaces also make it possible for you to invite aging parents or a widowed aunt to live with you. This extra space enables you to offer your oldest child a place of his or her own while preserving your privacy. Now that so many people are operating small businesses at home, these spaces can provide for an office area that is out of the family's way, separated from its regular traffic flow, and that distinctly demarcates your workspace from your home space. Perhaps even more important, these spaces can let your imagination run wild for a change. For instance, you might like to have a larger master bedroom with a private bath, walk-in closet, and a dressing room, but the space you would have to expand into is one of your children's bedrooms, so the idea could not be realized. Not true. The attic could offer you space in which to move their bedrooms so that you and your spouse can have that ideal master bedroom after all.

Possibilities for expansion and conversion also exist just because you have a basement. As a rule of thumb, basements do not make good living spaces, but they can be useful and are quite flexible nonetheless. You can put your home office in the basement, since it is an excellent space for privacy and it is nicely separated from the rest of the house. You also can make a family room in the basement where you and your children can watch TV, or they can do their homework without being distracted by other activities taking place in the house. If you add a bar and install a pool table, you could use the basement for socializing with family and friends until dinner finishes cooking and the young children get to sleep. In other words, the basement gives you space for options that you probably thought you did not have, just as the attic does, but only if you look at these spaces from a very broad perspective. Let your imagination go to work for you here and you will find that your options are practically endless.

CONSIDERING OTHER OPTIONS FOR THE GARAGE AND GARDEN

After having sought space for additions and conversions inside your house, it is time for you to look outside as well. Your garage and garden present numerous opportunities for growth, but only if you take the time to consider them creatively. An interior garage, for instance, can easily serve as an extra bedroom or guest room, a family room, a home office or, depending on its placement, as space in which to expand your kitchen. An exterior garage, one that is not attached to your house, has many different options for its use. It can be converted into a storeroom, a workshop, or a gardening center. This means, of course, that you have to be willing and able to park your car in the driveway, but it is a

small price to pay for the added convenience of any of these alternate uses. Be sure the local ordinances allow you to park your car in the driveway, however, before you convert the garage, or you will have to look for an empty garage on your block after completing the conversion. Be certain that the garage is structurally sound, rot and termite-free, and able to be satisfactorily converted for use. The engineer, architect, or contractor you hire can help you determine these factors.

You may not have thought of your garden as space that offers you much of an opportunity for alternate use, but it does. First, your garden is land on which you can build a structure, such as a storage room or a garage, if you do not have one but would like one. It is also space on which to expand your house with a room, porch, deck, or patio, for example. Again, you must be sure that local building codes permit you to enlarge your existing structure, or to build a free-standing structure on your property, before you proceed to do it. If you learn later that the new structure violates local codes, it may have to be torn down and your time, money, and effort will have been wasted.

The additions suggested may not seem to be much of an advantage, but they really are. Just consider building a patio, the easiest and most inexpensive suggestion, to comprehend its impact. The patio provides you with more space to entertain guests, or to relax with your family, or to enjoy the summer's sun and a cool evening's breeze. And you do not have to sacrifice your whole garden to do this, or any of the alternate uses, since even a portion of a small garden used for a small patio is better than no patio at all. With thoughtful planning of this space, your garden can serve a variety of your family's needs while it enhances your lifestyle. That is why it is so important for you to be imaginative as you consider your home's advantages as well as its potential for more of them. Do not just look at what you have, consider what you could have and look for space in which to create these possibilities.

2
Deciding What You Don't Like About Your Home

WISHING YOU HAD A LARGER KITCHEN

Most of you probably prefer a large kitchen, in fact, the larger, the better. That does not mean that you want one so poorly planned in terms of its size that it adds time and effort to the work you must do in it. First and foremost, the kitchen is designed for preparing the family's meals, therefore, the three objects essential to this work — the sink, range, and refrigerator — must be in close proximity to each other for an efficient performance of this task. Their proximity to each other reduces the number of steps you need to take to get the work accomplished while also keeping external traffic flow out of this work area. Along with these three main objects is the need for counter space adjacent to each of them to complete the tasks they entail easily and efficiently. You need as much counter space in your kitchen as can be incorporated into its design, especially near the basic work area.

After the primary use of the kitchen has been accommodated, you want to consider the other ways in which the space is used, or at least the ways in which you would like it to be used. For instance, your guests may enjoy sitting at your kitchen table to chat with you as you prepare the salad, or your children may like to do their homework there so they can quickly ask any questions they have about it. You may even like to read the daily newspaper there or answer your mail while sitting at the table. If your kitchen faces out onto a deck or patio, you may enjoy serving informal family meals there, or doing some of your kitchen tasks there. In other words, consider all of the ways in which you and your family use the kitchen. After you have done this, you will know exactly why you need a larger one.

Once you know what you want your kitchen to be able to accommodate, you can decide how to enlarge it for all of these uses. Your kitchen should reflect your personality, lifestyle, and design preferences. Wood cabinets are appropriate if you like the look of wood. If not, consider plastic laminates, commercial shelving, or other options more suitable to your taste. Be practical but also creative when you consider how your kitchen could look and work for you. Use spindles, for instance, to create an illusion of spaciousness when nothing else is possible. Get as much natural light into your kitchen as you can. Make up for what you cannot get from nature by installing plenty of artificial lighting strategically around the room for maximum visibility. Do not be afraid to change what is already in place to add features you feel are important to your own and your family's lifestyle. Cut away a closet, open or eliminate a wall, add or enlarge windows, install skylights. One homeowner renovated his kitchen four times in fifteen years before he felt that he had what he really wanted. He changed it as its use changed to accommodate each new need. This may sound excessive, but he is quite happy with what he has, so excess does not really matter.

To enlarge the kitchen you have, look in every direction for more space. Often the space is available;

however, it may have other uses, ones that you do not mind sacrificing for the sake of a larger kitchen. You may need to add space onto your kitchen by eliminating a portion of your garden, or by converting the adjacent interior garage. Remember that the best kitchens are those that have been thoroughly planned, so spend as much time as you need talking about it not only with family members but also with kitchen renovation experts and interior designers, all of whom will be more than helpful. Assistance also is available from such organizations as the National Kitchen and Bath Association as well as from your local home centers. For instance, The Home Depot, a national home improvement center chain, has computerized kitchen design centers that allow homeowners to experiment with numerous design options so that they can see the actual results of their ideas before doing the work. Later in this chapter, some other alternatives will be presented to assist you in getting the kind of kitchen that works well, looks good, and enhances your lifestyle.

ESTIMATING THE NEED FOR ADDITIONAL BATHROOMS

Everyone who sells real estate knows that as the number of bathrooms increases in your home, its selling price also goes up. This is because bathrooms are so important for today's active, busy lifestyles. Most often you and your spouse are dressing to go to work while your children are getting ready to go to school. As a result, all of you need to use the bathroom simultaneously. Thus, the more bathrooms you have, the easier it is to get cleaned, dressed, and out the door on time. The ritual changes somewhat in the evenings, but bathrooms are still essential for cleanups after work, Little League games, aerobics classes, cleaning the car, sweeping the leaves and, of course, washing all of those bathrooms.

Based on the modern lifestyle, you should figure that you need one bathroom on each floor in your house, or a minimum of one full bathroom and one toilet facility or half-bathroom as it is also called. A toilet facility or half-bathroom has a water closet and a sink, and sometimes a shower, while a full bathroom also has a bathtub. One bathroom on each floor also eliminates the need to climb up and down stairs, thereby reducing traffic flow while

adding convenience. As the number of adults in your family increases, such as if your parents come to live with you and as your children reach adulthood, bathrooms should be added. If you convert the attic or basement into living space, you should install a bathroom on that level, if it is not already there, to accommodate those living or working in the new rooms. In other words, do not plan any expansion without also considering its impact on existing facilities. Add another bathroom or half-bathroom in or near the converted space. If you do not, the strain on the existing facilities will make living in your home troublesome and will diminish what little privacy you had.

When you decide to add a bathroom, remember to consider the essentials such as where water will come from and where it will go after use. Locate new bathrooms not only near existing plumbing and heating systems to make installations fairly easy and inexpensive, but also along exterior walls to provide natural light and ventilation. And, as you did in the kitchen, you will need plenty of artificial light and storage space in any bathroom or toilet facility. After considering the essentials, think about the amenities you would like in your bathroom such as a makeup vanity with special lighting, a second sink, separate enclosures for the tub and shower, and maybe a whirlpool bath or spa, or a small washer/dryer arrangement (Figure 11).

If you want to enlarge an existing bathroom, make a full bathroom out of a half-bathroom, or accommodate extra features, look in all directions for additional space. Perhaps an existing closet can be eliminated, or an adjacent room can be made a little smaller without detracting from its usefulness, to add space to the bathroom. Remember that if you decide to relocate the bathroom, in most cases, it will be difficult because the plumbing and heating systems cannot be moved or extended easily. The better way is to enlarge what you have, or to add a bathroom above or below an existing one. Like the kitchen, a bathroom is an expensive room to renovate, relocate, or install. The final cost will depend largely on your taste. For instance, tiles are beautiful, but the prettiest ones are very expensive as are all of the bathroom fixtures. The simpler you keep this room, the less expensive it will be. To undertake a bathroom project correctly, first find out what all of your costs will be before proceeding with any of the work. Some compromises may be necessary to make the job affordable, but the benefits as an investment and in terms of comfort are invaluable just as they are in the kitchen.

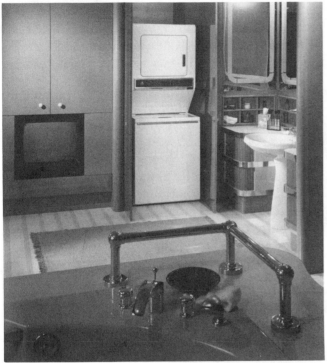

11. Full-sized stacked washer/dryer unit fits almost anywhere, such as in a corner of a bathroom, for easy use and installation. Courtesy of The Maytag Company.

SEEKING MORE NATURAL LIGHT

Windows have two major functions: they provide natural light, and they allow for ventilation, two essential elements in any house. The glass's transparency also is able to link the indoor setting to the outdoor landscape, a significant contribution to the comfort and beauty of any home. Although cost is the only reason for you not to want to add windows to your house, there are many considerations to make before you attempt to do so. For instance, you should consider how a new window is going to look from the outside of your house as well as from the inside before adding one anywhere in the house. When you choose the style of the window, be certain that it complements the house's architectural style, not just its furnishings. For example, grids in double-hung windows are appropriate for traditional style houses, but not for contemporary ones. Conversely, large, undivided sections of glass en-

hance a modern home, but they are not appropriate on a typical Colonial-style house. The wrong choice of window style can ruin a house's outward appearance, even though it adds generous amounts of natural light indoors.

Placement of windows also is very important. For example, the most pleasant lighting effect is achieved from windows that have been located on two walls in a room, leaving the other two walls uninterrupted for the placement of furniture. You should also consider where you want the natural light to come from, which landscapes offer a pleasant view, and where you need or would prefer privacy. Bathrooms and bedrooms tend to need more privacy than the kitchen, living room, dining room, and family room, but you still need windows in them too. A skylight in a bathroom or bedroom, for instance, can add light and ventilation while maintaining your privacy (Figure 12). An extravagant use of windows along one exterior wall in the master bedroom can provide for a dramatic view of your property that can easily be hidden by a drape or blind when privacy is needed. There are many beautiful yet practical ways to cover a window when privacy is needed, so do not be hesitant to add them where you think they will be pleasing and attractive. Just be sure to make a careful study of the location since placement is important for many reasons.

For example, when you think about adding windows, you should be aware of the fact that light varies in intensity and brightness, depending on its direction. Light from the north is pleasing, soft, and very enjoyable; however, windows that face north could cause heat to be lost from the house during the winter. Therefore, be sure to have energy-efficient windows installed on the north side of the house. A western sunset is a magnificent sight, but windows facing west need to be shaded from the heat of the sun during the summer. Windows on the south side also need to be covered during the summer, not only to keep the heat out of the house, but to prevent the sun's ultraviolet rays from bleaching colors in upholstered fabrics and in rugs, a problem that can occur after lengthy exposure. These problems, however, do not mean that you should not install windows around your house, nor that you should eliminate existing windows. Instead, they are reasons to carefully plan the size and location of windows as well as if and how they will be covered after they have been installed. If you have any intention of using passive solar energy for heating your house, remember that the southern sun will be the best for this purpose. Later in the book the various types and styles of windows will be reviewed as well their energy-efficiencies, etc. Suffice it to say that generally windows add beauty and enjoyment to your home in addition to natural light and ventilation. Therefore, there are many beneficial reasons to consider their potential in your home.

12. Skylights brighten this bedroom. Courtesy of VELUX-AMERICA INC.

WISHING THERE WERE MORE ROOMS

As you are no doubt well aware, families have a tendency to grow. What you might not already know is that houses can be coaxed into growing too. There are many ways that this can be done. If you need another room on the first floor level, consider enclosing and finishing the screened porch at the front or side of your house, or enclosing the deck at the back of it. Another idea is to add an addition at the rear or side of your house, wherever there is some extra property you can call your own. If there is no room for expansion left or right, front or back, consider going up or down to add another level to your house, or even a partial level. If you already have a second floor level but it is not the full width or length of the first floor level, enlarge it to the same dimensions as the first floor. You also can finish an existing basement, or if it is only a partial

basement, you might want to have it excavated to the full width or length of the first floor level above it. A closet can be converted into a toilet facility, or a full bathroom into a small, compact home office. You also might want to switch the uses of two existing rooms to make your small kitchen into a breakfast room and your informal dining area into a larger kitchen. This kind of switch is a good idea for the cook whose family gets small as children marry or leave home to pursue their careers. It is also good for childless couples or for families with one child.

There are still other ways to find space for additional rooms. For instance, you could add a sunroom, preferably near the kitchen (Figure 13). This sunroom can be used as the dining room to free the existing dining room for another use, or it can be your new kitchen or just enlarge the one you have, thereby either freeing up space or adding to existing space, depending on what is best for your needs. This new sunroom also could be used as a living room or family room, again freeing an existing room for a new purpose, or just creating a room that you wanted all along. Additional information about sunrooms follows later in the book, but is it important to be aware of such an option and to know that today's sunrooms are much more versatile and beautiful than the old greenhouses they evolved from in years past. Design and technological advances have made them an excellent option.

As you look around your house, ask yourself what each room can do to make living in your house more comfortable and enjoyable. A large master bedroom may be nice; however, as your children grow older, it may be more important to divide that room in half so that each child can enjoy his or her privacy in their own smaller bedrooms. Only one partition may be necessary to accomplish this significant change in the way all of you live. You may find as you examine each room that a smaller bedroom can be made large with the removal of a walk-in closet, a small sacrifice to make to create a spacious bedroom. In short, you must study the rooms you have, their number and sizes, reevaluate their uses, and consider how your family uses them now and how they could utilize the same space differently or even better (Figure 14). The next chapter expands on this idea, so forge ahead as you seek new and better ways to make the space in your house work for you.

13. The addition of this sunroom adds space for dining while enlarging and brightening the kitchen. Courtesy of the Pella/Rolscreen Company.

14. A full-sized washer and dryer need twice the space of this stacked unit, which leaves space for a combination storage center/home office area. Courtesy of The Maytag Company.

3
Determining Your Options

USING WHAT YOU HAVE — ONLY BETTER

For the sake of this discussion, let's presume that you are willing to make some minor alterations to the house to meet your family's growing and/or changing needs but, for the most part, you want to stay within the limits of the existing structure. You know what you like and do not like about your house and you want to deal with the latter without disturbing the former to any significant degree. To help you think about this, it is best for us to look at a house plan, level by level, to see what is in place that we like, what we want to change, and how we can make these changes.

ILLUSTRATING HOW THE SAME SPACE CAN BE USED MANY WAYS

The house that we are about to study is a two-story, three-bedroom structure with a large, unfinished basement and a large attic that was not meant to be lived in when the house was constructed almost fifty years ago. It has an exterior garage and small gardens in the front and at the rear of the building. There is nothing particularly special about it architectural design, its structure, or its framing. Since it is not a modern home (that is, it was not built less than twenty-five years ago), it was not designed to accommodate many of today's new technologies, devices, or lifestyles. It is a house that poses many problems for today's living, yet it simultaneously of-

fers numerous opportunities. In that respect, it is quite typical of the houses built before and after it, for that matter, typical of many houses everywhere in the country, which is why it was chosen for this study. The other reason is that the house is a real one, not a hypothetical case, therefore, the problems discussed are real problems and the alternatives presented for their solution also are real. Some of the variations presented were actually done in this house or in houses built like it that needed to serve different purposes. Still other ideas presented here have not actually been executed by anyone, but they are legitimate alternatives, worthy of consideration by you and your family. Naturally, we cannot include all of the possible variations that could be presented; but there is a sufficient variety here to stir your imagination and to help you develop original solutions of your own. Dimensions in this house have not been included so that you can concentrate on the concepts rather than try to calculate the square footage. The idea is to unleash your imagination, not your mathematical prowess. The quest for the perfect house begins with the main floor — the first floor plan.

FIRST FLOOR PLAN — ORIGINAL LAYOUT

The first floor consists of five rooms: porch, living room, dining room, kitchen, and breakfast room (Figure 15). There are a small foyer and a closet in

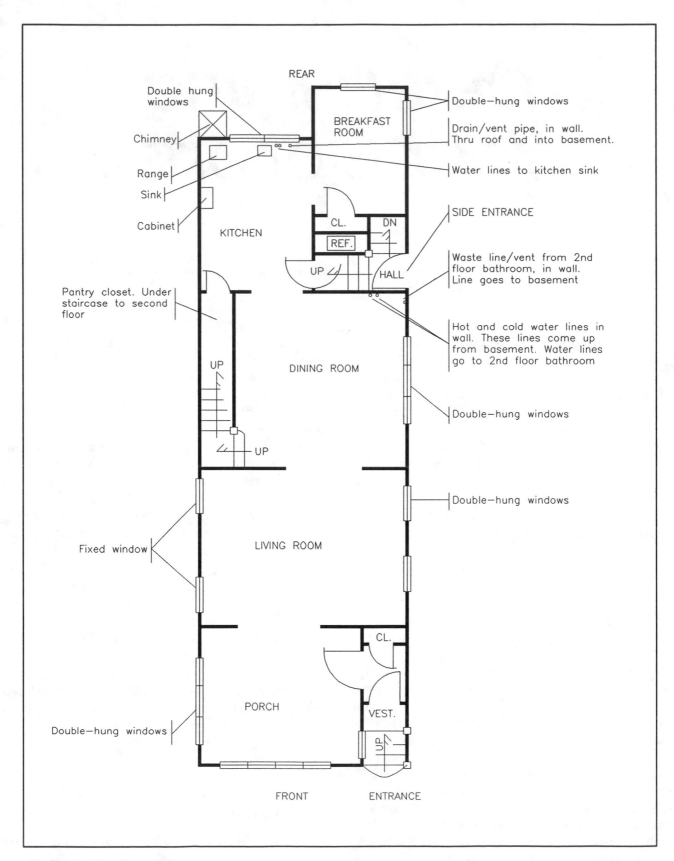

15. Original first floor plan

front of the house, a pantry closet under the only be used to prepare meals. The breakfast room can comfortably seat two adults and two small children. Once the children are six or seven years old, this room is too small for this average-size family to dine in. The staircase leading to the second floor starts in the dining room. The stairs leading to the basement are split into two parts, one goes up into the kitchen, the other down from the side (secondary) entrance. Usable space in the kitchen is lost due to this hall at the side entrance and to a closet that opens into the breakfast room. The dining room is made rectangular due to space lost for the pantry closet and the staircase leading to the second floor. There are double-hung windows on the front, back, and right side of the house on the first floor level. Two small stained-glass windows that cannot be opened are in the left side wall, adorning the living room.

FIRST FLOOR PLAN — SOME VARIATIONS FOR USE

In terms of their size and usefulness, the foyer and porch work well. The only alteration you might want to make is changing the porch windows. The old wood windows do not provide enough light and ventilation and they are not very energy-efficient since they are the original ones installed when the house was built. Although double-hung windows that are double-glazed could be used, casement windows are a better choice because their narrow frames allow for more natural light and their ability to open completely provides greater ventilation. Windows with insulating glass keep the porch warm in the winter and cool in the summer, perfect for enjoying this room all year long.

The living room works well too, except for a few minor changes. Storm windows installed on the exterior side of the stained-glass windows keep drafts out of the room while protecting the old leaded glass and wood frame from further damage due to exposure to the weather. New double-glazed, double-hung windows replace the old ones for greater energy-efficiency. The only other change is the addition of a fireplace in this room. There had been a non-functioning, brick-constructed fireplace between the two stained-glass windows, but a previous owner removed it. The wall looked as if something

was missing from it which, of course, was true. A carved-wood fireplace, also non-functioning, put against this wall again makes it look complete. A working fireplace could be installed, but only if it is properly vented. The construction of a brick fireplace would be nice but costly. A zero clearance fireplace can be installed at a fairly reasonable price, and it can be vented easily so it also is a good alternative. For now, the wood non-functioning fireplace works well to complete the wall and make the room look cozy.

In truth, it would be nice if the dining room did not lose space because of the placement of the staircase, but it has been placed in the most common location and the room is still fairly large so there is little to do here. Again, old wood windows are replaced with double-glazed, double-hung wood windows for more natural light and greater energy-efficiency. And, since the staircase has to stay, it might as well be dramatic and beautiful, so the old one is replaced with a new oak staircase. This is an expensive job to have done if you cannot do it yourself, but it works wonders to enhance the dining room.

The major problem in terms of the use of space on the first floor level is with the rooms at the back of the house. The kitchen is very small, even just for preparing meals. The breakfast room is so enclosed that it seems to be worlds apart from the kitchen even though it is actually adjacent to it. The first suggestions for conversion, therefore, are to eliminate the closet, the door opening into the kitchen, and all partitions separating the kitchen from the side entrance and the breakfast room (Figure 16). To make the space in the kitchen even more useful, the pantry door that opens into it is closed, and a new door for access to the pantry closet is installed in the dining room. This idea may not please an architect's sense of design, but it is sure to please you. Now that there is an L-shaped section in the kitchen, the three main objects for working there, the range, sink, and refrigerator, can be placed in it. The two narrow double-hung windows over the sink in the kitchen can be replaced with a casement window, which opens easily and lets in more natural light by reducing the size of the window frames (Figure 17).

The kitchen and the breakfast room appear larger than they are with the removal of a double-hung

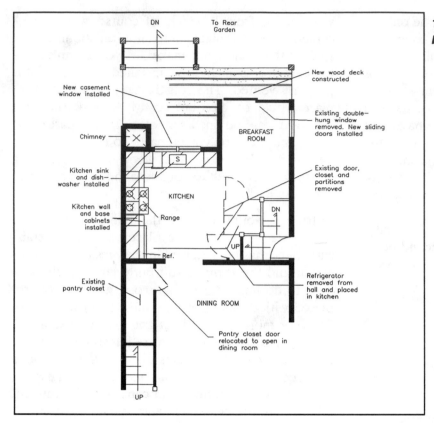

16. Renovation of kitchen and breakfast room

DN

To Rear Garden

New casement window installed

Chimney

Kitchen sink and dish-washer installed

Kitchen wall and base cabinets installed

BREAKFAST ROOM

S

KITCHEN

Range

Ref.

DN

UP

New wood deck constructed

Existing double-hung window removed. New sliding doors installed

Existing door, closet and partitions removed

Refrigerator removed from hall and placed in kitchen

Existing pantry closet

DINING ROOM

Pantry closet door relocated to open in dining room

UP

17. Sample kitchen layout

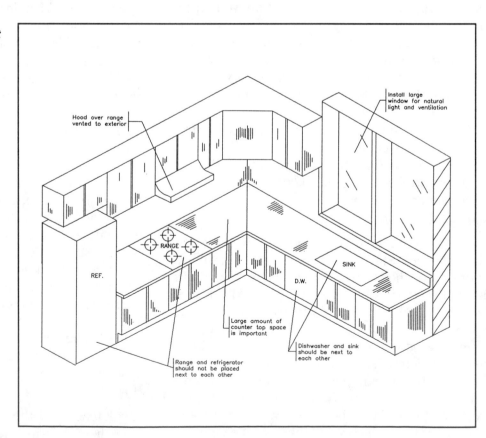

Hood over range vented to exterior

Install large window for natural light and ventilation

RANGE

REF.

SINK

D.W.

Large amount of counter top space is important

Range and refrigerator should not be placed next to each other

Dishwasher and sink should be next to each other

window in the breakfast room and the installation of a sliding glass door with a fixed round-top window over it. The rear of the first floor level is now airy and spacious, yet it has remained within the restrictions of the existing space. To make the rooms appear even larger, a deck can be added at the rear of the house on the first floor level, providing more space for eating, reading, potting plants, etc. Even if the square footage of the deck is minimal, the effect of its addition is enormous.

If you want to increase the square footage of the kitchen, you could extend it so that it aligns with the rear wall of the breakfast room; that is, the rear of the house could be squared off rather than left in its original "Z" shape (Figure 18). This conversion lengthens the "L" shape of the working area of the kitchen, hides the existing chimney in the longer part of the "L", and provides for more counter space. The addition of a rear deck in this conversion also makes the space in these rear rooms more comfortable and versatile. Instead of a deck, a sunroom could be added at the rear to be used as a dining area, family room, or greenhouse (Figure 19). With the addition of this fully enclosed, weatherproofed space, you can make the breakfast room part of your kitchen and use the sunroom as a breakfast room. Such a conversion easily doubles the size of your kitchen. Some of this added space can be used to accommodate a toilet facility, which would be helpful on this floor. This toilet facility can be placed where the closet used to be next to the stairs. Since it is not located along an exterior wall, it must be vented mechanically. The door for this new toilet facility opens into the stairway, not into the kitchen which, of course, you do not want it to do.

There are still more changes that can be made in this same space. For instance, you can close the side entrance completely, since you have a rear entrance, and remove the stairs at the side of the house that lead down to the basement. In this way, the kitchen can be made into a square. The stairs descending to the basement can be placed where the pantry closet is located, which means you have to sacrifice that closet, but it is not a severe loss since you now have plenty of cabinets in the kitchen for storage. A new toilet facility can be installed where the stairs and side entrance were located. Since it is placed along an exterior wall, a window can be used instead of a mechanical vent to provide

natural light and ventilation. If you are willing to live without a toilet facility on the first floor, an idea not recommended by most architects and homeowners, you can add counter space and cabinets in what is now a second L-shaped section of the kitchen. With plenty of storage space in the new cabinets, the loss of the pantry closet is no longer critical. If you do not feel that you need more cabinets or counter space, you could use that corner of the kitchen for your table and chairs to create an informal dining area for family meals. In other words, the possibilities are endless, once you have increased the amount of space that can be used.

SECOND FLOOR PLAN — ORIGINAL LAYOUT

The second floor consists of four rooms: the master bedroom, two smaller bedrooms, and a bathroom (Figure 20). It is slightly smaller than the first floor level because it ends before the porch in front and before the breakfast room in the rear. There are closets in each of the rooms and a linen closet near the bathroom. The bathroom opens into the hall near the second story landing of the staircase. The master bedroom is the largest, and it is at the front of the house. The middle bedroom is the smallest bedroom. The rear bedroom is made narrower than the master bedroom because there are two built-in closets in it on the left wall. Without these closets, it would be as large as the master bedroom. Space in the bathroom is also lost to built-in closets, one that opens into the middle bedroom and the linen closet that opens into the hall adjacent to the bathroom. The built-in closet in the master bedroom is long and narrow because it has been constructed over the staircase that ascends to the second floor. Windows on all four sides of the house are wood, double-hung. All of the bedroom doors open into the hallway as well as the doors for the bathroom and the linen closet.

SECOND FLOOR PLAN — SOME VARIATIONS FOR USE

The major problem on the second floor is the location of the master bedroom at the front of the house. The house faces onto a busy street with lots of noise from traffic as well as from regular visits by

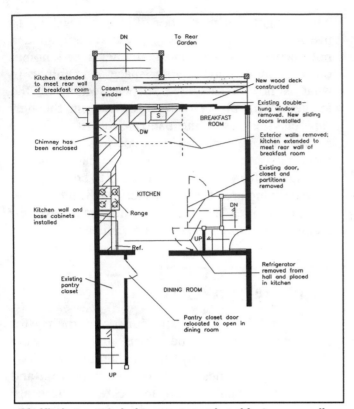

18. Kitchen extended to meet rear breakfast room wall

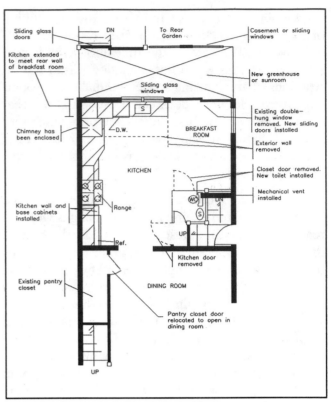

19. Kitchen extended and greenhouse or sunroom added

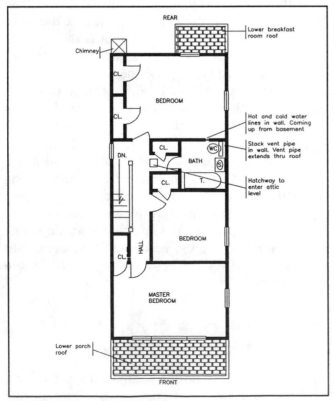

20. Original second floor plan

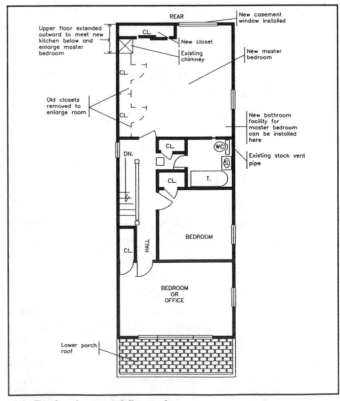

21. Revised second floor plan

sanitation workers, landscapers, and other maintenance contractors. As a result, the master bedroom needs to be moved to the rear of the house for quiet and privacy. The rear bedroom, however, is smaller, making it hard to accommodate the same amount of furniture in it. There is no space on this floor to use as the master bedroom other than the rear bedroom. The problem is easily resolved, however, with the removal of the two closets in the rear bedroom. You can make the room even larger by extending the second floor level of the house at the rear (Figure 21). To do this, you have to square off the kitchen in the rear at the first floor level. This conversion is particularly beneficial because the extra space provides for some diverse options.

For instance, you can now install a closet in this room at the rear of the house, which helps to offset the loss of the two built-in closets that had been on the side of the room. Another idea is to install a private bathroom for the exclusive use of the occupants of the master bedroom. It can be installed fairly easily as long as it is located adjacent to the existing bathroom. This location makes the plumbing installation much simpler and less expensive to do than it ordinarily would be. An additional bathroom on this floor eases the burden of use on the single existing bathroom. There is one last change to make in this room and that is to replace the double-hung window with a larger casement window for better ventilation and more natural light.

With the master bedroom moved to the rear of the house, the front bedroom can now be used in any one of a variety of ways. It can be your home office, the family room, or your child's bedroom, presuming your child is like most who can sleep through just about any racket. No matter how it is used, this room is comfortable and spacious. Another large casement window can be installed to replace the old double-hung windows to improve ventilation and increase the availability of natural lighting. As you must have realized by now, casement windows are excellent alternatives to double-hung windows so they are recommended for use here often. That is because casement windows are easy to use, open completely for maximum ventilation, and are appropriate for almost any style house. The addition of rectangular or diamond grids enables them to match most architectural styles. Naturally, the final choice is entirely up to you.

There are not too many options available in the middle bedroom since there is no way to expand its size without obstructing other spaces, but its coziness makes it an ideal room for a baby, or for a sewing room, playroom, home office, etc., depending on your family's needs. It could even be used simply as a large walk-in closet and storeroom, as would be appropriate for a family of two or three. A larger family could use it in one of these ways, if you decide to find more space for bedrooms in the attic, for example. Again, the final decision is based on your needs.

The bathroom on the second floor level can be enlarged by eliminating the two closets next to it, specifically, the linen closet and the closet that opens up into the middle bedroom. The plumbing can easily be extended or angled to accommodate the enlarged space. With the added space, you can have an extra sink, increase your storage space, or even install a larger vanity so that shaving and applying makeup can be done simultaneously. Once you have this additional space, there is no doubt that you will find many uses for it.

There is one other change you can make that will not add space but can definitely add to your convenience. The closet that opens into the front room, which is narrow and quite deep, is not readily accessible from the existing door. That door can be removed, the opening sealed, and a sliding or louvered door can be installed in the hallway. This gives you greater access to items stored in it, not to mention better visibility. It is a relatively simple alteration compared to some of the others suggested, but one that you are sure to appreciate. Also, by removing the door, you create more wall space where furniture, file cabinets, bookcases, or whatever else you want in the room can be placed.

For the sake of this discussion, assume that you have made several of the suggested conversions on the second floor, thereby eliminating one or possibly two bedrooms. As time passes, you find that you need more bedrooms. Now is the time to look up, into the attic, for space.

ATTIC PLAN — ORIGINAL LAYOUT

The attic is unfinished because when the house was built, the attic was not intended to be occupied

22. Unfinished attic area

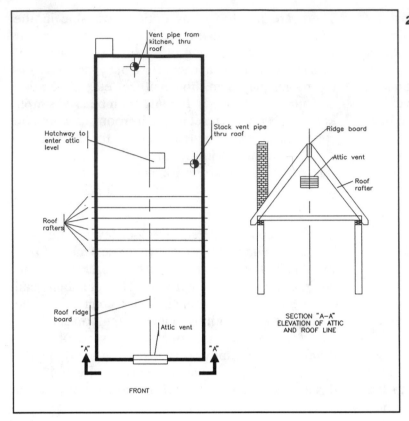

Vent pipe from kitchen, thru roof

Stack vent pipe thru roof

Hatchway to enter attic level

Roof rafters

Roof ridge board

Attic vent

FRONT

Ridge board

Attic vent

Roof rafter

SECTION "A–A"
ELEVATION OF ATTIC
AND ROOF LINE

23. Attic area converted to living area

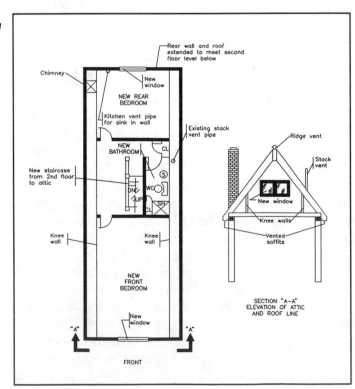

Rear wall and roof extended to meet second floor level below

Chimney

New window

NEW REAR BEDROOM

Kitchen vent pipe for sink in wall

Existing stack vent pipe

New staircase from 2nd floor to attic

NEW BATHROOM

CL

S

DN

WC

UP

SH

CL

Knee wall

Knee wall

NEW FRONT BEDROOM

New window

FRONT

Ridge vent

Stack vent

New window

Knee walls

Vented soffits

SECTION "A–A"
ELEVATION OF ATTIC
AND ROOF LINE

(Figure 22). It is only accessible through a hatch located in the hall ceiling in front of the bathroom. There are no stairs ascending to this hatch, nor are there stairs that unfold down from the attic. An 8-foot ladder is needed to climb up through the hatch to enter the attic. There is a partial floor in place, running from the front to the back of the attic, for access to the vent at the front of the house. Insulation is visible between the ceiling joists, except where the partial floor has been installed. The roof has a very high pitch so you can easily walk in the attic while standing upright throughout most of the space. The height narrows on the left and right sides where the roof rafters meet the top plate. The overall space is large, running the full width and length of the second floor level.

ATTIC PLAN — SOME VARIATIONS FOR USE

A great deal of work has to be done to make the attic livable (Figure 23). Rooms can be defined by installing knee walls and drywall, and a dormer can be added to increase headroom. Of course, the heating and electrical systems have to be extended to service this new living space, although they can be zoned separately if that is preferable. Windows can be added at the front and in the rear of the house for ventilation and natural light in the front and back rooms. Also, a bathroom can be added to service these rooms or as a convenience to those living in them and to prevent putting an additional burden on existing facilities on the second floor level. The bathroom should be installed above the existing second floor bathroom so that the plumbing installation can be done as efficiently and inexpensively as possible. Finally, a staircase can be installed for easy access to and from this new level (Figure 24). Bedroom and bathroom doors can open into the hallway that is created when the staircase is installed.

Both of these new rooms are large, but the front room is larger than the rear one because space is not lost to accommodate the staircase, hallway, and bathroom. Built-in closets can be constructed in each of the rooms. Although these rooms can be used as bedrooms, there are many other options for their use. The front room, for instance, makes an excellent location for a home office because it is spacious yet private, eliminating disturbances from activities taking place elsewhere in the house. For the same reason, it also can serve as a den, a family room, or even a library. The smaller room also has many possible uses. It can be a computer room, TV room, sewing room, etc., whatever you want or need it to be and, of course, its uses can be altered as your family's size and interests change.

To install the new staircase to the third floor level, one small sacrifice of space on the second floor level has to be made, namely, the elimination of the two closets near the bathroom. This is probably the most efficient way to make this addition without losing essential space in existing rooms on the second floor level (Figure 24). Even the existing bathroom does not have to be touched in any way except to move the door from the center of the room to the left, a minor alteration, but one that causes no problems in terms of the space's utility. Remember that you do not want to destroy space in one room, or on one level, to enhance space in another; such conversions are self-defeating. Before you make any spatial sacrifices, consider what you are going to do to the existing space and the use of the space very carefully. If you think the trade-off is going to be worthwhile, then go ahead with your conversion. If not, look for another option; there always is another one.

Now that you have found and used as much space as there is at the top of the house, it is time to look down, into the basement. Although no one should have to live there, the space in a basement can be used for many family activities. With some work and careful planning, the basement can be converted into a finished basement that is quite comfortable to be in now and then.

BASEMENT PLAN — ORIGINAL LAYOUT

The basement, like the attic, is unfinished because it was not intended for use as a living area when the house was built a half-century ago. It is a large, open area except for the toilet facility that is located at the right side of the house near the rear. The concrete foundation walls are visible, as are the first floor joists. There is a laundry area with a slop sink located in the area under the breakfast room, and

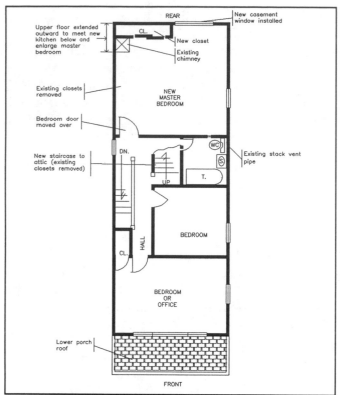

24. Second floor plan showing staircase to attic and extension of rear wall

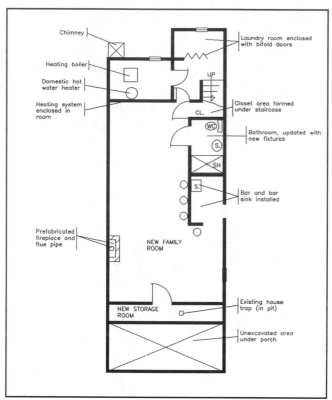

25. Development of basement area

the boiler is installed nearby. Very small windows, installed only for ventilation, are along the left side of the house and in the rear near the boiler and laundry areas. The house cleanout traps are located in small pits at the front and in the rear of the house. Lighting is minimal in the basement, consisting of a few bare bulbs placed in strategic locations. Entry to the basement is made via narrow steps at the right side of the house descending from the side door. A second section of these stairs ascends from the side door into the kitchen.

BASEMENT PLAN — SOME VARIATIONS FOR USE

A great deal of work has to be done to make the basement into a finished basement with livable space. First, the foundation walls have to be waterproofed, then the walls and floor joists have to be insulated, framed, and covered with drywall. As part of the framing process, decisions have to be made about what areas need to be defined for specific purposes (Figure 25). For instance, the laundry area can be enclosed with bifold doors after the slop sink

has been removed or moved to make space for the installation of the washing machine and dryer. A boiler room can be created to enclose the furnace and the domestic hot water heater. In most cases, the enclosed boiler room will have to incorporate one of the windows to provide ventilation for these units. A closet can be created by enclosing the staircase that leads down to the basement, and the toilet facility can be enlarged to include a shower stall, which will be needed when the basement is in frequent use.

The remainder of the space, which is slightly shortened at the front by the formation of a storeroom to hide the utility connections there, can be used as a spacious family room, playroom, exercise room, home office, etc. If you use the space as a family room, you might want to install a bar with a bar sink in it, but if you do, be sure to locate the bar near the existing bathroom to make plumbing connections fairly simple and inexpensive. One final touch might be to install a prefabricated fireplace such as a zero clearance fireplace in this new room. This type of installation can heat the room while creating a cozy atmosphere. If you live in an area where temperatures get extremely cold during the winter, some type of heating system will have to be installed, such as baseboard heating units. Additional lighting also has to be installed since very little natural light can enter the basement from the small windows there, and larger windows cannot fit in the existing space. Lights can be installed over the bar, near sitting areas or gym equipment, in closets, in the laundry and boiler rooms, and in the front storeroom. Remember that this type of space is dark unless you add artificial lighting to it, and it is cold and damp unless you install some type of heating system, so plan the conversion accordingly. A thoughtfully planned conversion in the basement can free space in the floors above for new uses, or give you additional space to expand into as your family's activities increase.

Now that all of the spaces in the house have been exhausted for possible use, it is time to look at the more unusual spaces — the garage and garden — for more living space. Keep your mind open and your imagination at work as you go outdoors.

GARDEN/GARAGE PLAN — ORIGINAL LAYOUT

The backyard of this typical house handles two functions: storing the car, and offering some hints of greenery in its urban setting. Half of the space is filled with the exterior garage, a nondescript block structure on a concrete slab with old wooden doors to enclose it at the front. The other half of the backyard is soil partially covered with weed-infested grass and a single pine tree, and filled with a few perennials that have been left to grow wild. The soil nearest to the house is covered with concrete slabs that extend about 6 feet away from the structure to where the grass begins. There is little room for much else in the backyard since the lot on which the house sits has not been parceled with any extravagance. If it had been, of course, few urban dwellers could have afforded to purchase it anyway.

GARDEN/GARAGE PLAN — SOME VARIATIONS FOR USE

Since space is so limited here, it is critical to decide what is most enjoyable to you when you are out-

doors. For example, if you like to putter around in the garden, then you will want to keep as much of the soil intact as possible. On the other hand, if you can be content with a small border of flowers along the perimeter of your backyard, then you will have some new space to think about in terms of alternate uses. The same can be said of the garage. If you are one of those people who thinks it is important to keep your car in a garage, then it will not have any other possible use. Conversely, if you do not care where you park your car, then the garage will present new possibilities. If you decide to use your garage for other things, however, be sure that local building and fire codes permit you to leave your car out of the garage overnight, in the driveway or street, for instance. Some local codes, usually in suburban areas as opposed to urban areas, require your car be parked in its garage overnight, so determine what is permissible in your area first before proceeding to use your garage for other purposes.

If you decide that you want to put a deck or patio at the rear of your house, you may have to sacrifice some portion of your garden. Such an addition, however, can create new spaces for entertaining as well as for everyday living. A deck or patio can dramatically enhance the existing living space by adding to its total square footage. An enclosed porch also is a pleasant addition and one that can prove to be very useful by adding space to your living area. Again, before proceeding with these types of additions, you must determine what type of construction is permissible by local building codes as well as what size it can be and how far it can extend into the backyard. You may also need to obtain a building permit before the work can begin. This usually means that you will need to have architectural drawings made to submit for prior approval and that you will have to pay some sort of fee. Just be sure to determine what needs to be done before you buy any materials or start any construction. Local contractors usually know what is involved, so this is only a problem for the uninformed do-it-yourselfer.

The garage offers an interesting alternative. Even a one-car garage, as is the case with this house, can make quite a generous-sized workshop, although a larger garage would be better. It also can be an excellent storeroom for items that are used infrequently during the year, such as patio chairs and snow blowers. You can combine the storeroom with the workshop by increasing the size of the garage to accommodate both uses. Another way to do this is to build a storeroom adjacent to the existing garage; however, that means you will have to sacrifice a portion of your garden, so this is a good idea only if you are willing to make the garden smaller. If you convert your garage into a workshop, be sure to add electrical power in it to accommodate additional lights and power tools. The best way to do this is to install a circuit breaker panel box, as well as additional receptacles, in the workshop for its exclusive use. You also will need additional electrical lights and receptacles if you build a deck or patio at the back of the house. If it is not already in place, a water source also will be needed, so make it part of your renovation plans.

At this point, we have exhausted all of the space in this house while offering many different uses. Your house may have more or fewer of these levels and they may be larger or smaller, but the concepts presented here stay the same. Other possibilities for

accommodating your needs depend on how creative you can be after studying the variations presented here. With a thorough understanding of space and how it can be manipulated for a variety of uses, you can learn to use the space you have for maximum flexibility and usefulness. Remember that whenever an extension, addition, conversion, or other exterior change is being anticipated, it must conform with state and local building and fire codes, so do not proceed with it until permits have been obtained, fees paid, etc. This is particularly important if you are planning to do the work yourself, since a contractor or architect would already be aware of code requirements.

The use of space is not all you need to know to live with and care for your home. Each topic covered briefly in this part of the book, as well as others not reviewed, now must be studied in detail to expand your knowledge and enhance your enjoyment of your home. Part II looks at the exterior components of a house, which is where you can begin.

PART II
Examining Exterior Components of a House

4
Roof Coverings and Their Care

THE IMPORTANCE OF YOUR ROOF COVERING

Since water can destroy just about any building material given sufficient time to do so, it is essential to keep it out. One of the best ways to do this is to have a waterproof roof covering installed so that it is watertight and to maintain it so that water cannot enter the house through it. In addition, any damaged or old roof covering should be repaired or replaced before any other renovation project is done, to prevent rainwater and melting snow from entering the house through it, where it can damage the newly remodeled rooms as well as other rooms.

Materials used as roof coverings include asphalt, fiberglass, slate, and wood shingles, rolled roofing felt, terra cotta tiles, and metal roofing. Roofing materials are sold in a measure called a "square," which equals 100 square feet of that material. The number of squares in a package of roofing material is printed on the wrapper or box in which the material is sold, and the weight of a square varies depending on the material used. For instance, a square, or 100 square feet, of fiberglass shingles weighs 225 pounds while a square of asphalt shingles weighs 240 pounds. Roofing contractors base their estimates on the number of squares needed to cover the roof along with the costs of other materials and labor. Since the characteristics and application technique of each roofing material vary greatly, the homeowner should become familiar with many of them.

ASPHALT AND FIBERGLASS SHINGLES

Asphalt and fiberglass shingles are the most frequently used roofing materials. They cost less than slate and wood shingles and terra cotta tiles, and they are more fire-resistant than wood shingles. Asphalt shingles differ from fiberglass shingles only in that the materials used to manufacture the base sheets are not the same. The base sheet used in the production of asphalt shingles is an organic one that looks like a type of felt covering. This organic base is composed of cellulose fibers that have been saturated with asphalt. As its name implies, the base for the fiberglass shingle is composed of glass fibers. Beyond the difference in the composition of the base sheets, there is little difference in how these two roofing materials are manufactured. In both cases, the two sides of the base sheet are coated with asphalt, then mineral granules are applied to each side. These granules shield the asphalt from the sun's ultraviolet rays and improve the fire-resistance of the shingles while adding color to them. Asphalt or fiberglass shingles will last from fifteen to twenty-five years, depending on the weather conditions in the area where the house is located.

An asphalt or fiberglass shingle is manufactured with cutouts along its width. Notches are made at 6-inch intervals at the top edge of each shingle. A sealing strip is applied along the width of the shingle just above the cutouts in the shingle. When heat from the sun warms these shingles, the sealing strip on the overlapping shingles seals itself to the shingle below it to make the roof covering watertight. Some manufacturers make the notches at 3-inch intervals on the shingles instead of 6 inches. The only difference this makes is that when the shingles are installed on the roof, the pattern of the shingles repeats itself every third row instead of every sixth row.

Asphalt and fiberglass shingles are installed on top of a layer of roofing felt that covers the roof sheathing (Figure 26). Roofing felt is available in 15 and 30 pound weights; that is, 100 square feet of felt either weighs 15 pounds if it is lighter in weight, or 30 pounds if it is heavier. The roofing felt protects the roof sheathing from exposure to the weather, insulates the roof, and prevents water entry from the shingles. It also helps to prevent rain, ice, and snow from backing up under the shingles where water can enter the roof.

A house that has eaves overhanging its exterior walls is likely to be prone to a condition called "ice damming." Ice damming occurs when melting snow backs up under the roof shingles in the location of the overhanging eaves, and water enters the house from this section of the roof (Figure 27). To prevent ice damming, a 36-inch wide strip of flashing, called an ice shield, is nailed along the length of the eave. The tacky side of this membrane-like ice shield faces down toward the roof sheathing so that the ice shield can seal tightly around the nails to prevent water seepage. Since the ice shield can be damaged by the sun's ultraviolet rays, only the square footage that can be covered with shingles in a day is installed so that it is not exposed to the sun for any length of time.

Sealing and flashing is installed around vent pipes, skylights, stack vents, and chimneys to prevent water entry from any roof covering. This work also is done in critical areas on the roof such as in an area called a "valley." A valley is formed wherever two sloping sections of roof intersect at a single point. An open valley is lined with metal flashing, and the shingles are installed so that they overlap the flashing. Metal flashings are made of copper, aluminum, or galvanized metal. Metal flashings are not used in a "closed" or "woven valley." In a closed valley, the shingles from one side of the roof run across the valley and overlap the shingles from the other side

of the roof. These shingles are trimmed at the center of the valley. In a woven valley, the shingles from both sides of the roof are overlapped alternately.

Galvanized-coated roofing nails are used to attach the shingles and the metal flashing to the roof because they are rust-resistant. Nails that rust will eventually stain the shingles. If the rusted nails are left on the roof for an extended period of time, the nails will deteriorate and the shingles will loosen and become damaged. Rusted nails also may loosen and fall away, leaving the shingles and metal flashing susceptible to water entry.

A new layer of asphalt or fiberglass shingles should not be installed on a roof that already has two layers of roof covering on it for several important reasons. First, the third layer can add so much weight to the roof that the roof rafters may not be able to support it structurally. The second reason is that long nails would have to be used to attach the third layer of shingles to the roof sheathing under the existing two layers, which would make this a difficult nailing job. In addition, the different expansion for each layer of roofing material would cause stress on the shingles. This is visible as a wavy effect on the roof, and it creates an opportunity for water entry (Figure 28). The fourth and final reason not to apply a third layer of roofing material is that securing the metal flashing through three layers of shingles can be difficult, and some of the flashing may be left loose on the roof. For all of these reasons, it is best to remove the two old layers already on the roof, and to install a new roof covering directly onto the roof sheathing after it has been covered with new roofing felt. This will make the roof watertight when the installation has been completed, and it will keep it that way for a long time thereafter.

The homeowner can determine if the asphalt or fiberglass shingles on the roof are starting to wear when the shingles are badly discolored, when they are broken in some sections, and when they are blistered (Figure 29). These conditions are indications that a new roof covering needs to be installed.

SLATE ROOF SHINGLES

A house with an old slate roof covering may have patches in it that are covering areas where shingles

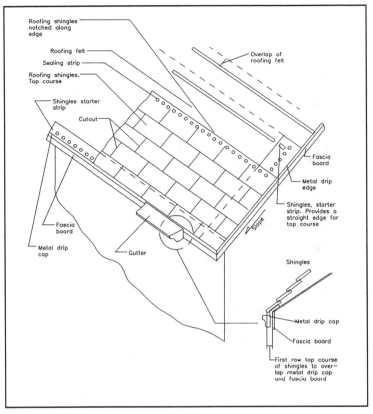

Roofing shingles notched along edge

Roofing felt

Sealing strip

Roofing shingles. Top course

Shingles starter strip

Cutout

Overlap of roofing felt

Fascia board

Metal drip edge

Shingles, starter strip. Provides a straight edge for top course

Fascia board

Metal drip cap

Gutter

Slope

Shingles

Metal drip cap

Fascia board

First row top course of shingles to over-lap metal drip cap and fascia board

26. Asphalt or fiberglass roofing shingles

27. Ice damming

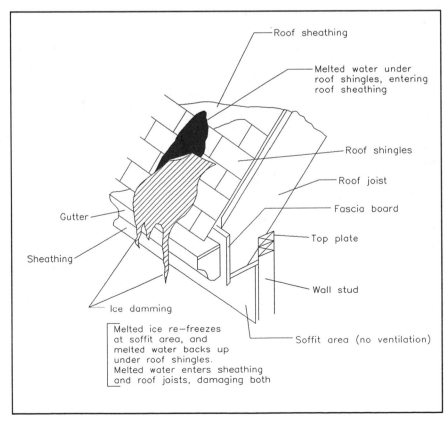

Roof sheathing

Melted water under roof shingles, entering roof sheathing

Roof shingles

Roof joist

Fascia board

Top plate

Wall stud

Soffit area (no ventilation)

Gutter

Sheathing

Ice damming

Melted ice re-freezes at soffit area, and melted water backs up under roof shingles. Melted water enters sheathing and roof joists, damaging both

28. Wavy effect on shingles is due to the differing expansion of the previous layers. Photo by the author.

29. Blistered roof shingles are aging and wearing, and they will need to be replaced. Photo by the author.

are missing. These patches may be made with tar or pieces of metal. These attempts at patching the slate roof covering usually are not very successful, and they were probably done to avoid the installation of a new slate roof, which is a very expensive project. Although the life expectancy of a slate roof is long, ranging anywhere from 50 to 100 years, it can vary greatly, depending on the weather conditions in the area where the house is located.

Slate roof shingles are available in three tones: gray, red, and green. Gray-toned slate is found in eastern Pennsylvania; red and green-toned slate in Vermont and New York. These slates, which also include a dark gray-toned slate, are available at most roofing supply centers. As with wood shingles, slate roof shingles are rated for their durability. Slate roof shingles that are rated as "clear" usually will last longer than those that are not. The tone of these shingles also is categorized as either "unfading" or "weathering." As its name implies, the tone of the unfading slate will not change as it is exposed to the elements, while the tone of the weathering type will be altered. Slate roof shingles, which are approximately 3/16 inch thick, are available in 6-inch and 10-inch squares and in 14" x 24" rectangles. Usually the holes for nailing the slate roof shingles to the roof sheathing are made in the shingles while they are being manufactured so they are ready for installation as soon as they are purchased.

There are two types of slate-covered roofs: the textured slate roof and the graduated slate roof. On the textured slate roof, the shingles vary in thickness only, while on the graduated slate roof, the shingles vary in both size and thickness. Either type of slate roof can only be installed on a house with a roof framing structure that is strong enough to hold the extreme weight of these heavy slate roof shingles. A house with a slate roof already installed on it probably has roof framing members that have been sized to hold the weight of the slate roof shingles. If a slate roof is going to replace a roof covering made of a material other than slate, or terra cotta tiles, the homeowner should consult a roofing contractor to be sure that the existing roof framing structure can hold the extra weight of the slate roof shingles. If it cannot support the additional weight, then the homeowner should replace the old roof covering with a new one made of the same or a similar roofing material of about equal weight. The homeowner who is determined to install a slate roof will have to reinforce the roof framing structure, which will prove to be a costly preference.

When a slate roof reaches the end of its life expectancy, telltale signs are visible. One homeowner learned about this when he saw stains on the slate roof shingles on his house. He also noticed that the shingles were soft and that they crumbled easily when he touched them. The homeowner knew that the slate roof was at least fifty years old, and he soon learned that all of these conditions were evidence that the roof had aged and worn after exposure to the weather for all of those years. The slate roof had experienced numerous freeze/thaw cycles over the years, which had caused the shingles to delaminate. As a result, cracks had opened in the

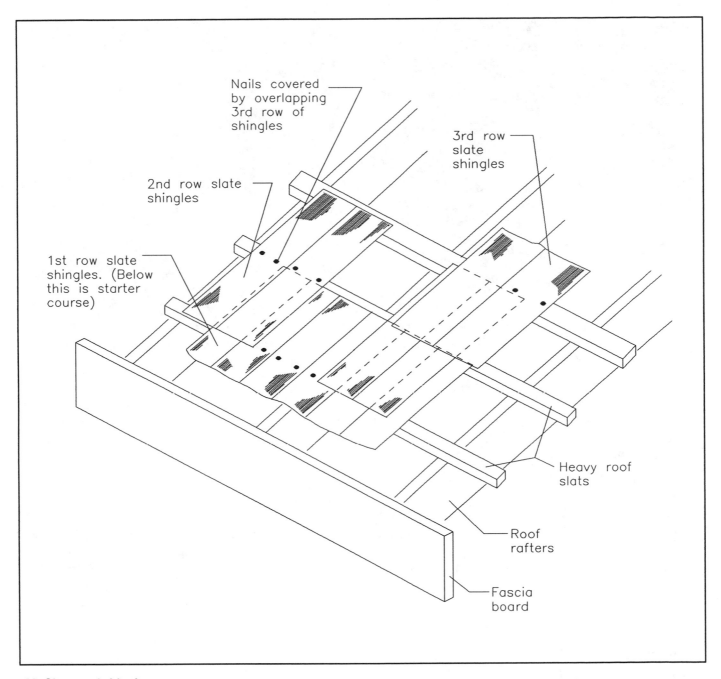

Nails covered by overlapping 3rd row of shingles

3rd row slate shingles

2nd row slate shingles

1st row slate shingles. (Below this is starter course)

Heavy roof slats

Roof rafters

Fascia board

30. Slate roof shingles

31. *Cedar shakes have a natural oil in the wood that enables water to drain off quickly. Courtesy of the Cedar Shake & Shingle Bureau.*

32. *Wood shingles are installed over roofing felt and plywood sheathing. Courtesy of the Cedar Shake & Shingle Bureau.*

surface of the shingles, and spalling and white stains were visible on them. This white staining, which is also referred to as a chalky deposit, forms around the edges and on the face of the shingles. These blemishes and cracks were clear indications to this homeowner that he needed to have a new roof installed.

Before the new slate roof shingles are installed, it is important to check the condition of the roof sheathing or the slats, whichever happens to be under the old shingles. Any cracked or damaged sections will have to be replaced to make the new installation secure and watertight. On many older houses, slate roof shingles have been fastened to wooden roof slats. These slats are similar to but heavier than firring strips (Figure 30). Some roofing contractors use plywood as a roof sheathing under the slate roof shingles, while others attach slats to the roof rafters and then nail the slate roof shingles to these slats. The latter method is preferable because spaces are left between the slats, and these spaces allow air to circulate under the slate roof shingles. This circulating air enables the shingles to dry quickly and thoroughly after each rainfall or snowfall. When the slate roof shingles are installed over plywood, the plywood is first covered with overlapping layers of roofing felt. This felt protects the plywood sheathing while it cushions the slate roof shingles. Galvanized-coated or copper roofing nails are used to install the slate roof shingles. The galvanized-coated nails are preferred because they are much less expensive than copper; however, the copper nails are more durable.

WOOD SHINGLES

As with all roof coverings, wood shingles have their advantages and disadvantages. On the negative side, for instance, is the fact that wood shingles cost much more than asphalt or fiberglass shingles. This additional expense is somewhat offset, however, because the life expectancy of wood shingles, which is approximately forty years, is much longer than that of asphalt or fiberglass shingles. Another advantage is that a house with a roof covered with wood shingles stays cooler during the summer than those with other types of roofing materials. What was once a major disadvantage, specifically that wood shingles are very flammable, recently has been resolved because they are now chemically treated to minimize their flammability. Finally, many homeowners prefer wood shingles because their textured look gives the house a cozy appearance. Some local codes prohibit the use of wood shingles as a roofing material, however, so it is necessary to consider local requirements before deciding to install wood roof shingles.

Wood shingles, which are tapered lengthwise, are available in several different lengths and styles as well as in three grades. The No. 1 grade is used for roofing. It is made of 100% clear heart wood species. The No. 2 and 3 grades are made from sapwood and they have knots in them, which make their life expectancies shorter than that of the No. 1 grade. Wood shingles are made from a variety of species including redwood, Western red cedar, cypress, and pine. Western red cedar shingles, which are called cedar shakes (Figures 31 and 32), are preferable because the natural oil in the cedar enables water to drain off them so quickly that it does not have time to be absorbed. This natural oil also helps to prevent the cedar shingles from splitting, especially when used in areas where the humidity levels and temperatures vary greatly during the year. Cedar shingles are quite brittle, so they have to be installed carefully to prevent the roofing nails from damaging them during their installation.

Before installing new wood shingles on a roof, it is important to check the roof sheathing for any damage. Those sections that are damaged should be repaired to make the installation watertight after it has been completed. Depending on the age of the house, the wood shingles are either attached to open slats or to a plywood sheathing. As was the case with slate roof shingles, it is preferable to install wood shingles onto open slats so that air can circulate freely under them. Wood shingles installed on slats dry faster than those attached to plywood sheathing (Figure 33), and this will extend the life expectancy of the wood shingles. Since recovering a roof of this type is very expensive, this is an important consideration for any homeowner.

ROLLED ROOFING FELT

A house with a flat roof, or one that slopes very slightly, generally is covered with rolled roofing felt. This type of roof covering has about a ten-year life expectancy. There are several visible signs to indicate when this roof covering is aging, such as blisters and cracks as well as areas where the granules have separated from the surface of the felt. The metal flashing and felt flashing around the skylights, chimneys, vent pipes, and parapet walls also have to be replaced when this new roofing material is installed, especially if the flashing is already damaged

or corroded. The new roof covering will not be watertight if all of this work is not done simultaneously.

Rolled roofing felt, which is manufactured in 3 feet wide by 36 feet long rolls, is available in 50 and 90 pound weights. Rolled roofing felt is an asphalt sheeting material that is impregnated with wood and rag fibers during its manufacture. One side of the felt also is covered with mineral granules that protect it from the sun's ultraviolet rays. It is available in two colors, black and gray. Rolled roofing felt is not only the least expensive roofing material, it also is the fastest to install. In addition, since the roof it is going to be installed on is flat or almost flat, it is the one roofing installation that can be done by the homeowner, so long as he does it correctly. A proper installation is essential in this case because the roof is flat and, therefore, more susceptible to leaks than any other style of roof.

The most effective way to install rolled roofing felt is to remove the existing roof covering completely. Since this is not an easy task, some roofing contractors prefer to install it on top of the old roof covering. Such a procedure, though not preferable, is acceptable, but only if there are no more than two coverings already installed on the roof. If three roof coverings have already been installed, then the contractor should remove all of the old roofing materials and start from the roof sheathing to prevent water entry. Any blisters or damaged sections in the old roof coverings also must be removed from the existing layer or layers before the new roof covering is installed. Loose material must be removed, or resecured if it has not been damaged, before the new rolled roofing felt is installed. To be certain that the new roof covering is watertight when the installation has been completed, each length of rolled roofing felt should overlap the previously applied piece allowing at least 3 to 4 inches to be covered.

Before installing rolled roofing felt, it is important to take note of the pitch, or slope, of the existing roof covering. The new roof covering must pitch or slope toward the drain installed on the roof for proper drainage of rainwater and melting snow and ice. The pitch or slope can be observed immediately after a rainfall when the roof is still quite wet. Naturally, this is not the time to start work on the new roof installation, only the right moment for observation.

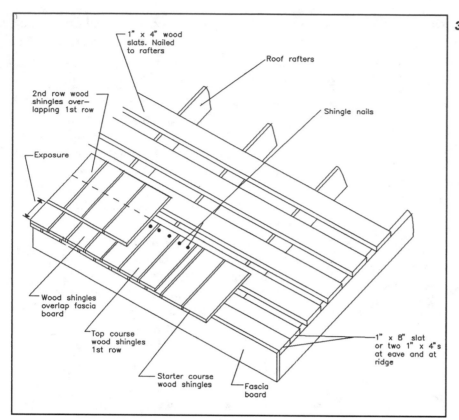

33. Wood roof shingling

1" x 4" wood slats. Nailed to rafters

Roof rafters

2nd row wood shingles over-lapping 1st row

Shingle nails

Exposure

Wood shingles overlap fascia board

Top course wood shingles 1st row

Starter course wood shingles

Fascia board

1" x 8" slat or two 1" x 4"s at eave and at ridge

34. Barrel tile (terra cotta) roofing

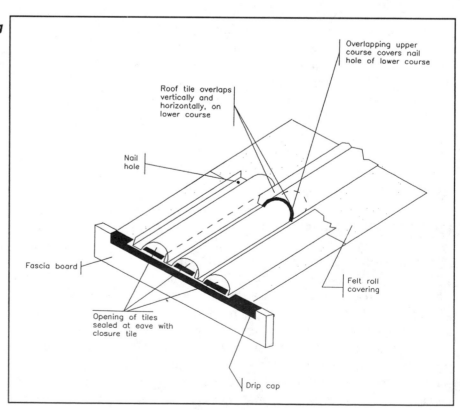

Overlapping upper course covers nail hole of lower course

Roof tile overlaps vertically and horizontally, on lower course

Nail hole

Fascia board

Felt roll covering

Opening of tiles sealed at eave with closure tile

Drip cap

If rainwater collects on the roof in a "pond" or in numerous puddles, then the pitch of the roof will have to be increased before the new roof covering can be installed. This adjustment can be done in several ways, depending on the extent of the correction to be made. If the pitch has to be increased greatly, it is done by nailing plywood onto the existing roof structure so that the roof slopes toward the drain. If the pitch only has to be increased slightly, then several layers of rolled roofing felt can be used to do this. When a flat roof has the correct pitch or slope, rainwater drains off it completely as soon as the rainfall has ceased. If rainwater is allowed to puddle or pond on a flat roof, it will cause the roof covering to deteriorate. Over an extended period of time, if left uncorrected, the roof sheathing and framing also will be damaged.

The best time to install rolled roofing felt is when the roof is completely dry and the weather is warm. This type of installation should not begin unless the outside temperature is at least 50° F. If the metal flashing that overlaps the existing roof covering is not going to be removed, then the flashing should be lifted carefully to insert the new rolled roofing felt under it. If the flashing breaks as a result of being lifted, then new metal flashing will have to be installed to be sure the covering is watertight after the work has been completed. Metal flashings made of copper, aluminum, or galvanized-coated metal can be used effectively as long as they are installed correctly. The copper flashing is the most expensive of these three materials.

TERRA COTTA TILES

A roof covered with terra cotta tiles has the same life expectancy as one covered with slate roof shingles, anywhere from 50 to 100 years. Terra cotta tiles are available in many different sizes and shapes, including the barrel tile, which is the one most commonly used on older houses (Figure 34). They are available in several colors such as red, terra cotta, and brown. A roof covered with terra cotta tiles needs to be repaired or recovered when the tiles are cracked and missing, or when tar has been used to patch many broken and missing tiles. A patch made with tar can only be effective as a temporary measure to protect the roof from water entry until it can be permanently repaired or recovered.

To install terra cotta tiles correctly, the tiles must overlap each other horizontally and vertically. As with slate roof shingles, terra cotta tiles are very heavy, and the roof framing structure must be strong enough to support their weight. These tiles are very fire-resistant and quite brittle, as are slate roof shingles, and they are quite expensive to repair or replace. The installation of terra cotta tiles differs from slate roof shingles, however, in that the tiles are installed from right to left instead of the more familiar left to right, as is done with slate shingles.

METAL ROOFINGS

Modern metal roofing materials should not be confused with the metal roofing materials used many years ago. The old corrugated and galvanized sheet metal sections rusted after many years of exposure to the elements, while high winds were able to pull them apart, ripping them off roofs and exposing the roof sheathing to rain and snow. Today's metal roofing materials are quite weatherproof, and they are available in a variety of materials, patterns, and colors, so they offer many advantages when installed on homes. For instance, a metal roof covering is very strong, yet it is also lighter weight than many of the other conventional coverings available. Metal roofing is not brittle as other roofing materials such as slate and terra cotta tiles, and it is not flammable. With the development of improved fabrication techniques, metal roofings are manufactured in larger sheets than they used to be and, as a result, fewer joints are needed for their installation. This means that there are fewer opportunities for water entry through them.

As with any roofing material, there also are some disadvantages to metal roofing. For example, since a metal roof expands and contracts as temperatures fluctuate, the installation must be done so that the roof covering will remain watertight as it moves. In addition, as with any metal material, metal roofing materials are subject to corrosion and some materials corrode faster than others. This problem requires constant maintenance to prevent corrosion. Although the cost of some metal roofing is comparable to that of a shingle roofing material, the installation of a metal roof can be much more expensive than that of a conventional roof covering, depending on the material and pattern chosen. For obvious reasons, the cost of a metal roof covering increases as its resistance to corrosion also increases or, to put it another way, the longer the metal roofing material will last, the more the initial cost for its installation is going to be.

Materials Used for Metal Roofings

Among others, and there are many more that could be mentioned, common materials used for roofing include stainless steel, copper, galvanized steel, aluminized steel, a type of steel called COR-TEN®, and aluminum alloys. Each has different characteristics, installation requirements, and maintenance procedures, so it is important for the homeowner to know something about them to care properly for the type of covering on his roof.

Stainless Steel

The stainless steel used for metal roofing is called Type 304, and it is highly resistant to corrosion and rust. It is also known as an 18/8 material, which means that it contains 18% chromium and 8% nickel. Chromium helps the stainless steel resist corrosion while nickel improves its corrosive and mechanical properties, such as increasing its durability. Nonetheless, stainless steel will eventually corrode. When it does, the roof covering will have a pitted appearance. The pitted roof actually has many small holes, allowing water entry into the roof sheathing below it. Stainless steel roofing should not be used in a salt-water environment, such as along a coastline, because the chlorides in this type of environment will corrode the covering more quickly than it would in other environments.

Copper

Copper is the best metal available for use as a metal roof covering because it can last a lifetime. In old cities, many older public and private buildings have copper roofs on them. Although the copper has turned greenish by now, this is not a problem because the "green" is actually a surface layer of corrosion that is protecting the copper below it from further corrosion. Despite its long life expectancy, copper's use as a roofing material has been limited because it is very expensive. Additionally, when copper comes into contact with other metals, it causes those metals to corrode, so its use is not always appropriate in all types of installations.

Plated Steels and COR-TEN

Galvanized steel, aluminized steel, and COR-TEN are also quite popular roofing materials. Since steel cannot resist corrosion very well, it is plated with zinc, which makes it more corrosion-resistant. In this form, the steel roofing is available as hot-dipped galvanized roofing. Aluminum also is used as a plating material for this same purpose and the result is called aluminized steel. Galvanized steel is the least expensive of the metal roofings available; however, it must be painted to extend its life expectancy. When galvanized steel roofing is not painted, the plating material wears off the steel and it eventually rusts and corrodes. Before any type of metal roofing material is painted, it must first be cleaned thoroughly and coated with a primer. The roofing manufacturer's instructions regarding the correct type of materials and procedures should be followed for lasting results.

COR-TEN, which is made by USS (U.S. Steel), forms a layer of rust to protect it from corrosion. COR-TEN is thicker than the other roofing materials discussed here, so it also is heavier than other metal roofings. The disadvantage associated with its use is that COR-TEN's protective layer of rust drips from the roof onto the siding, gutters, etc., when it is raining, and this rust stains them as well as the nearby soil, streetwalk, driveway, etc.

Aluminum Alloys

Aluminum in its pure form is too weak to be used as a roofing material, so alloy compositions are added to it to increase its strength. Aluminum alloy roofing resists corrosion very well, making it preferable for use in coastal environments. As the aluminum alloy roofing is exposed to the weather for an extended period, it oxidizes, and a coating forms on its surface. This coating helps the covering resist corrosion. Aluminum alloy roofing also can be painted to protect it further from corrosion or it can be immersed in a hot bath of aluminum and zinc. One disadvantage of aluminum alloy roofing is that it has a tendency to expand and contract excessively. As a consequence, the installation of this type of roofing material must be designed to compensate for this movement. As was the case with copper, when aluminum alloy roofing comes into contact with certain other metals, corrosion occurs due to the presence of the dissimilar metals.

Patterns Available

Metal roofing patterns include corrugated and ribbed panels as well as a combination of corrugated and straight-lined panels. The length of the panel depends on the pattern that is being fabricated, while the thickness and weight depend on the material being used. The width and length of the panel also are determined by the insulation requirements as well as the manufacturing process being used. Most metal roof panels are fastened to the roof sheathing with nails or screws that are put into the face of each panel. Screws are preferred, especially when a great deal of expansion and contraction of the roofing material is anticipated. Neoprene washers are used to seal the holes made in the panels by the fasteners, to keep the roof watertight after the installation is complete.

OTHER ROOF CARE TIPS

Immediately after a heavy rainstorm is an opportune time to examine the attic or cockloft for evidence of water entry from the roof covering, vent pipes, chimneys, etc. Water entry from around the vent pipes or chimney indicates that the flashing is loose or damaged, and that it will have to be repaired. Water entering through the roof covering may mean that a section of the roof covering needs to be repaired or, if the covering is quite old, that the roof needs to be recovered completely. As a rule, it is not a good idea to patch a roof, except as a temporary measure or when the damage is very small, because patches generally are not very effective at preventing water entry. The most effective and efficient way to handle a leaky roof is to have it recovered immediately.

Unfortunately, a roof cannot always be repaired or replaced when the need arises. For instance, cold temperatures are not very favorable for such repairs or replacements. This is especially true if asphalt shingles, fiberglass shingles, or rolled roofing felt will be installed because warm temperatures assist the sealing process that makes the roof covering watertight. In fact, no matter what material is going to be used, it is simply easier to recover a roof when the weather is mild.

Any roof repair or replacement also should encompass the repair and/or replacement of the roof flashing, chimney step flashing, roof vents, stack vent flashing, skylights, etc. Even a brand new roof covering will not be watertight unless all of this work was done at the same time. They are all parts of a complete roofing system, and if they are maintained and replaced as needed along with the roof covering, they will prevent water from entering for many years.

Unless the homeowner is a roofing contractor, it is best to have any repairs or replacements done by a professional. For the most part, this simply is not do-it-yourself work. For instance, it is especially difficult for the homeowner to work on a roof with a severe slope or pitch. And even though a flat roof is easy to stand on, if the installation is not done properly, the roof will not be watertight. The average homeowner may find that he has made a futile attempt to save money if the roof leaks shortly after he has completed its installation, or worse, if he is injured while attempting to recover or repair it. The homeowner's time is best spent getting estimates from roofing contractors and checking recommendations so that he can choose the best professional at the most reasonable price to do the job correctly. He also should be sure that he is getting what he paid for in terms of quality of materials as well as workmanship. In addition, the homeowner should be certain that the contractor's workers are insured in case of any injury during the job, to protect himself from any liability.

5
Getting to Know Gutters

THE HOWS AND WHYS OF GUTTERS

Gutters are installed around the perimeter of the main roof as well as any secondary roofs to catch rainwater or melting snow as it drains from them and to carry it into the house's sewer line or out into the municipality's sewer system. Downspouts connected to the gutters bring the water from the roof to the drain lines that are connected to the sewer lines. When there is no sewer system, the downspouts allow the water to drain into the soil. By collecting the rainwater and melting snow from the roof, the gutters and downspouts prevent seepage into the house's exterior walls, the structure, and the foundation, and the damage to these areas that this seepage would cause. Therefore, gutters and downspouts are essential parts of a house that should be repaired or replaced as the need arises.

Several materials are used to make gutters and downspouts, and each has special characteristics while giving a house a unique architectural appearance. Gutters and downspouts are made of wood, molded-vinyl, and several metals. Wood gutters are used mostly on old houses to preserve their historic architectural styles. For today's modern houses, molded-vinyl and metal gutters are preferred. Molded-vinyl gutters and downspouts, which are available in brown and white, do not rust; therefore, holes cannot develop in them as a result of damage from rust. When installed on houses in areas where

there are four seasonal changes, the molded-vinyl type is strong enough to withstand the extreme temperature fluctuations. Molded-vinyl type also does not crack or dent as metal gutters tend to do. Sections of the molded-vinyl gutters and downspouts are attached by snapping them together by hand. The downspout fits into the gutter with the use of male/ female fittings. Silicone rubber gaskets are installed at each joint in a molded-vinyl system to leave space for expansion and contraction. The gasket is part of a slip joint that connects the ends of each length of gutter together.

Metal gutters are made of steel, aluminum, or copper, and their installation is different from the method used for the molded-vinyl type. End caps, outlets, and butyl caulk are used to connect metal gutters at the corners as well as along the lengths of the gutters to prevent them from leaking. Instead of gaskets, elbows and other metal fittings are snapped into place by hand to connect the various parts of a metal gutter system. Steel gutters rust as a result of constant exposure to the weather. This rust shortens their life expectancy. Steel gutters and downspouts are available with a galvanized coating or a baked enamel finish, both of which extend their life expectancy. Steel gutters are warrantied to last about fifteen years while aluminum gutters are expected to last a maximum of forty years. Aluminum gutters do not rust, so they last longer than steel gutters when used on houses in coastal areas. This is due to the fact that the salt water environment in

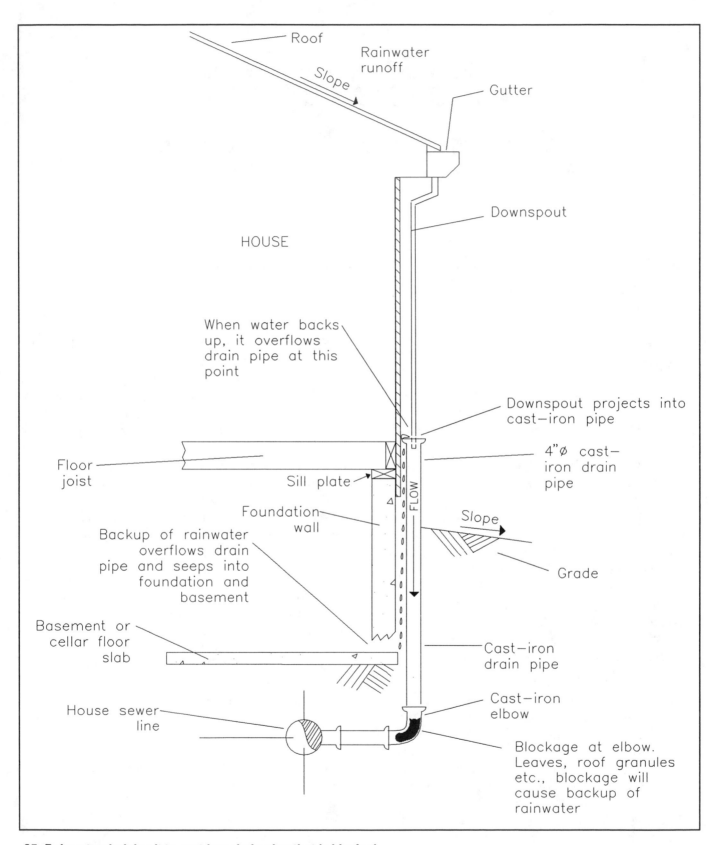

Roof

Rainwater runoff

Slope

Gutter

Downspout

HOUSE

When water backs up, it overflows drain pipe at this point

Downspout projects into cast–iron pipe

4"ø cast–iron drain pipe

Floor joist

Sill plate

FLOW

Foundation wall

Slope

Grade

Backup of rainwater overflows drain pipe and seeps into foundation and basement

Basement or cellar floor slab

Cast–iron drain pipe

House sewer line

Cast–iron elbow

Blockage at elbow. Leaves, roof granules etc., blockage will cause backup of rainwater

35. Rainwater draining into cast-iron drain pipe that is blocked

these areas is very destructive to steel. Aluminum gutters, however, are more susceptible to being dented than steel. Aluminum gutters are available with a baked enamel finish in brown or white. Copper gutters last much longer than aluminum or steel gutters, but they are much more expensive than aluminum or steel, which is why they are not used frequently today. Although aluminum gutters are more expensive than steel, they are preferred because of their durability.

Steel gutters with a galvanized coating can be painted to extend their life expectancy as well as to match a house's color scheme. Before painting, they should be left unpainted for six to twelve months after installation to allow the surfaces to weather. If the surfaces are not going to be given sufficient time to weather, then the metal should be washed with vinegar and rinsed thoroughly before the steel gutters are primed and painted. When steel gutters are going to be repainted, the peeling paint should be removed completely. Then these gutters can be reprimed and/or repainted, depending on what type of paint is going to be used (see Chapter 15 for more information on exterior finishes).

When gutters are going to be installed on a house that is surrounded by trees, a screen mesh should be placed over them to prevent falling leaves from collecting in the gutters. These leaves eventually will clog the downspouts or the drain line, causing water to back up in them and into the house. When a downspout in an installation is going to accept water from an upper roof, it should be installed so that it connects into a lower gutter, or it should continue all the way down to the grade level. This downspout should not end on a secondary roof level because as the draining water continues to fall onto this one area of the roof covering, it will wear out the roof covering prematurely in this location.

BASEMENT SEEPAGE FROM THE GUTTERS

It is not uncommon to find a seepage problem in the cellar or basement coming from the gutters or downspouts, so it is a good idea for the homeowner to know how to recognize and deal with this type of problem. One homeowner's seepage problem was due to a blockage located in the drain line that is connected to the downspout. The blockage was caused by dead leaves that had collected in it along with granules that had loosened from the old asphalt shingles on the roof. This debris had clogged the drain line at the first underground elbow, the most common location for this type of blockage (Figure 35). Water draining into the downspout during a heavy rainstorm could not pass through the drain line. Instead, it was backing up and overflowing at the connection between the downspout and the drain line located near the house's foundation wall. From there, the rainwater had worked its way down through an open void or small crack in the waterproofing on the foundation wall and in the wall itself, where it eventually seeped into the basement.

For the most part, this problem can be solved inexpensively, even if the homeowner calls for professional help. A sewer cleaning service breaks the blockage with a sewer cleaning machine. The homeowner can break this blockage himself, but it will take time and patience to do it. The homeowner must first remove the downspout to pour a small amount of drain cleaner into the clogged drain pipe. He should be absolutely sure that the drain cleaner he uses states specifically that it will not damage this piping material, since any damage it causes is going to be costly to repair. He also should read the directions for use on the drain cleaner to prevent personal injury from the chemicals in the cleaner.

After the drain cleaner has been in the pipe for the amount of time stated in the manufacturer's instructions, the homeowner can insert the garden hose nozzle into the clogged drain pipe and open the water valve to get maximum pressure in the hose. The drain cleaner, working in conjunction with the water pressure, will break the blockage, but only after these steps have been repeated several times. Leave the hose in the drain line with the water running for several minutes after the blockage has broken to make sure that all of the debris is flushed out of the drain line. To prevent debris from collecting in the drain lines, the homeowner should remove the downspouts once a year, preferably in the fall, to flush the drain lines with the garden hose at its maximum water pressure. This also is a good time to remove the area drain cover at the rear or in the front of the house, wherever it may be, to flush

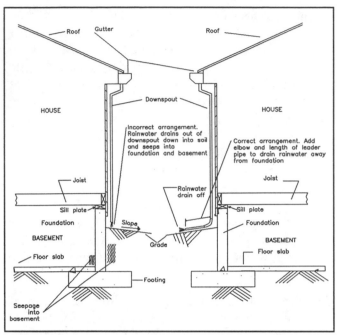

36. Incorrect and correct downspout arrangement for rainwater drainage

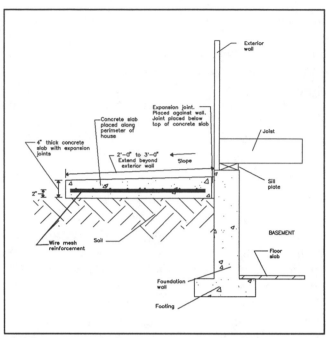

37. Concrete slab at base of exterior wall to protect foundation wall and basement

it with water from the garden hose. These simple, inexpensive maintenance procedures, if done once a year by the homeowner, will prevent serious seepage problems from occurring that could destroy the foundation or damage the basement or cellar.

A seepage problem in the basement also can be caused by rainwater that is allowed to drain constantly from the end of a downspout onto the soil near the foundation wall. This problem occurs when the downspout is not attached to the drain line. For instance, on many of today's modern houses, the downspouts end approximately 1 foot above grade where a 1-foot square piece of concrete is placed to disperse the rainwater pouring from them. This piece of concrete, which is called a splash block, inevitably disappears sooner or later, allowing the water to drain directly onto the soil. Eventually the rainwater makes its own path through the foundation wall, causing a seepage problem in the basement.

There are two ways to remedy this problem, and

one costs much more than the other. The less expensive solution is to add a section of downspout to the end of the existing one to carry the rainwater farther away from the foundation wall as it drains from the downspout (Figure 36). This can only be done if there is space at the end of the downspout for an additional section. Therefore, this solution is not always possible. The second solution is very costly because it involves building a concrete streetwalk or walkway at the location of the downspout that extends at least 2 to 3 feet away from the house. This concrete must slope away from the house so that the rainwater can drain away from it. The concrete will have to be reinforced with wire-mesh and expansion joints, if temperatures in the area vary greatly (Figure 37). This method will remain very effective if cracks do not develop in the concrete. The first solution also is quite effective, so the choice depends on the location of the downspouts as well as how much the homeowner can or is willing to spend to resolve it.

6
Exterior Sidings and Coverings Explored

EXTERIOR MATERIALS

The exterior facade of a house can be made of a variety of materials including masonry, stucco, asphalt shingles, asbestos shingles, aluminum siding, vinyl siding, and various wood siding products. The qualities and characteristics of each vary greatly as do the procedures for their installation and care. Any one of these materials can be used on a house to protect it from the weather while helping to define its particular architectural style. That is why this discussion is extensive. Let's begin with masonry.

EXTERIOR MASONRY

Exterior walls constructed of masonry may be made of brick, stucco, limestone, sandstone, which also is called brownstone, granite, or marble. Since brick is the most common material used, this section focuses on it; however, much of what is covered applies generally to all types of masonry, particularly in terms of repair, replacement, and general maintenance. The other materials are briefly covered at the end of this section.

Types and Characteristics of Bricks

Clay is used for the manufacture of bricks. There are different types of clay available and each is used to make a specific type of brick. Bricks used in commercial and residential construction are called face bricks and common bricks, and they are manufactured from surface clays and shale. Bricks used in

fire boxes in boilers, in chimneys, and around fireplaces are called refractory bricks. Fire clay is used in the manufacture of these bricks, and they are installed for high-temperature applications only. Face bricks are used for exterior and interior construction. These bricks are fired at very high temperatures during their manufacture so that the surface of each brick is not porous. As a result of this firing process, face bricks do not absorb water easily. Common bricks are used in the construction of party walls, that is, walls between attached houses, and as a filler course under masonry exterior walls of all types. Common bricks are cheaper than face bricks, but they do not have a neat, finished surface as face bricks do. Common bricks are fired at lower temperatures than face bricks, and they absorb moisture readily.

Bricks are categorized into grades as well as types. There are three grades of brick, specifically, severe weathering, moderate weathering, and non-weathering. A house located in a climate with extremely hot and cold temperatures during the year has exterior masonry made with severe weathering bricks to withstand these drastic climatic changes. Moderate weathering bricks are used in areas where temperatures remain moderate throughout the year. Non-weathering bricks are used for interior construction only because they cannot withstand weather conditions of any kind.

Houses built over the last thirty to forty years generally have been constructed with what is called a

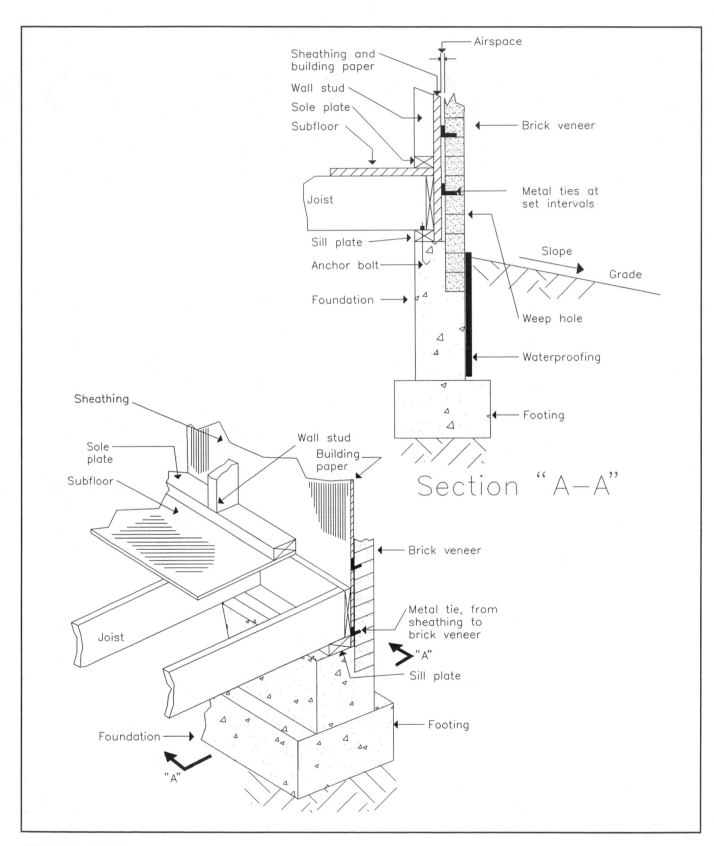

Sheathing and building paper

Wall stud

Sole plate

Subfloor

Airspace

Brick veneer

Joist

Metal ties at set intervals

Sill plate

Slope

Anchor bolt

Grade

Foundation

Weep hole

Waterproofing

Footing

Section "A-A"

Sheathing

Sole plate

Subfloor

Wall stud

Building paper

Joist

Brick veneer

Metal tie, from sheathing to brick veneer

"A"

Sill plate

Footing

Foundation

"A"

38. Detail of brick veneer

brick veneer on the exterior walls (Figure 38). This brick veneer is the thickness of only one course of bricks and the wall behind it usually is made of plywood wall sheathing. The brick veneer is tied to the sheathing with metal ties that are attached to the sheathing at preset intervals as the wall is being constructed. The metal ties project out of the sheathing for this type of construction. Usually, this type of masonry wall is fairly new, so the owners of these newer houses will need to do few repairs for a while.

The masonry on older houses may be in need of repair, other portions may need replacement, or repaired sections may need to be redone because they were made incorrectly. The repair and rehabilitation of brick work is an art requiring great skill and knowledge of the materials to do properly. Since the result of a poor job can be disastrous, let's review some of the procedures involved before a contractor is sought to do the work.

Cleaning Masonry

There are several ways to clean brick and other masonry. Sandblasting is a popular method, but it also can erode the surface of the bricks, which was hardened during manufacture to resist weathering. Once this surface is eroded, the bricks will deteriorate quickly. Chemical cleaning is another method, but it also can damage the bricks' surface. The acid in the cleaning fluids damages the bricks as they are being cleaned. This acid also damages stones, marble, and other types of masonry. Another way to clean masonry is to use a mixture of a liquid cleaner and water at high pressure. In addition to damaging the bricks, this method also can loosen the mortar in the joints between them. This is a special problem when the cleaning is being done during the winter months and there is a possibility that the water will freeze as temperatures drop later in the day. The water absorbed by the bricks freezes in them, causing the bricks to spall.

The way to clean masonry without damaging it is to use mild detergents, soft brushes, and water at a low pressure and to do the cleaning when there is no chance that freezing temperatures will develop while the cleaning is being done and before the masonry has had time to dry completely. Steam cleaning the masonry, which used to be a very popular method, also can damage it, and this method is not more effective than using water with a mild deter-

gent. The latter also is a safer method for the person who is handling the equipment, since there is less chance of being scalded while doing the cleaning.

Caring for Painted Masonry

Sandblasting is commonly used to remove paint from masonry to expose its original surface. Removing the paint in this way, however, has been known to cause the masonry to deteriorate more quickly than if it had been left with the paint on it. This is because sandblasting removes the hardened outer surface of the brick along with the paint. In fact, it is best to check the condition of the masonry under the paint before any extensive work is done to remove it. It is important to determine how badly the masonry has already deteriorated before attempting to clean it. To do this, the paint should be removed from a small test area with a paint stripper or solvent. If the masonry is sound, then the rest of the paint can be removed in the same manner. It is important to rinse the masonry thoroughly after using the stripper or solvent. Also, be certain that the stripper or solvent used will not damage the masonry. The manufacturer's label indicates how to use the product effectively and safely. Although this cleaning method is rarely used, because it is a slow, tedious, and costly one, it is the one that is the least destructive of all possible cleaning methods.

To avoid the cost and labor involved in properly removing paint from masonry, it might be a better idea to give the painted masonry a fresh coat of paint. This also is a good alternative when the masonry under the paint is badly deteriorated. Before repainting the masonry, remove any of the old paint that is peeling with a hand scraper and a natural bristle brush, being careful not to damage the masonry. A propane torch, or any other type of flame mechanism, should not be used to remove the old paint because it will damage the masonry. The masonry can be repainted with an exterior paint that the manufacturer recommends for this type of surface. (Detailed information about exterior paints and other finishes follows in Chapter 15.)

Repairing Masonry

The masonry walls in an old house, especially one that is more than 100 years old, often have loose mortar joints. The mortar is crumbling due to its age, which also causes weathering. These walls are going to have to be repointed to prevent further deterioration of the joints and masonry. The first step in repointing is to remove the loose and crumbling mortar. Then the joints can be repaired, and it is essential to repair them with the right type of mortar. When these walls were constructed, lime was probably used as the binder in the mortar mixture. Since the latter part of the 19th century, Portland cement, which is harder than lime, has been used in this type of construction. When old masonry is repaired with mortar that has a high Portland cement content, the masonry is damaged because the mortar dries too hard in the joints, causing it to crumble. Mortar with a high Portland cement content also shrinks as it dries, leaving gaps in the joints through which water can enter, causing seepage problems in the exterior wall. This type of mortar is very rigid and, as a result, it cannot bond tightly to the old masonry. This creates a special problem during extreme temperature fluctuations. All of these characteristics of mortar with a high Portland cement content are reasons it is important to use compatible materials to repair old masonry, whether the repairs are large or small, to achieve successful results. That is why it is essential to hire a contractor who is experienced with this type of work and who knows how to do it correctly. Do not hesitate to get recommendations from the contractors and to check them thoroughly as well as to inspect previously completed projects to be certain that you are hiring the best professional for the job. After the work starts, observe its progression to be assured that all of the work is being handled properly from start to finish.

Exposed Party Walls

Some old houses, especially those in urban areas, were built attached to each other on one or even both sides. When, for any reason, one of the attached houses is demolished, an exposed wall — called a party wall — is left visible. This exposed wall presents a special problem for a variety of possible reasons. As stated earlier in the descriptions of the various types of bricks, a party wall is constructed with non-weathering common bricks, which cannot withstand exposure to the weather. This party wall also may have been damaged during the demolition, further weakening its resistance to the weather. Since the wall was built as a hidden wall, it may have been constructed with mortar joints that were not

filled completely or were filled sparsely. These voids allow water as well as cold or hot air to enter the house now that the wall is exposed to the various existing weather conditions. This exposed party wall has to be recovered as quickly as possible with some type of siding or with a brick veneer, especially to prevent rainwater from entering the house where it can damage interior walls, ceilings, floors, household items, etc.

One homeowner who faced this kind of situation decided to take the time to settle his differences with the demolition contractor in court. Unfortunately, justice takes a long time to be served. During that time, the exposed party wall was subjected to rain, snow, and numerous freeze/thaw cycles. The homeowner eventually had to completely repair the inside of his house as well as the party wall because water had damaged the interior parts while adding to the existing deterioration on the outside. The repair job cost him twice as much as the court case awarded him, so he had a hollow victory. He should have had the exterior work done while awaiting the court's decision. It would have saved him substantial money as well as grief.

Identifying Problems

When speaking with contractors about the repair or replacement of masonry, it is helpful to understand what causes the different types of failures in a masonry wall. For instance, mortar joints that are crumbling, loose, or missing were probably damaged when water entered the wall. Stepcracking (Figure 39) over a window, arch, or door opening indicates that the lintel is not able to support the weight of the masonry above it. Wavy or sloping mortar joints may mean that there is a settlement problem. Cracks that get longer and wider as time progresses indicate that there is movement within the wall. When the surface of the masonry is pitting, flaking, or spalling (Figures 40 and 41), it may mean that the previous homeowner had the masonry sandblasted, or that water got into the bricks, froze, expanded, and spalled the face of the bricks. Bulging masonry may indicate that there is a settlement problem in the footing, or that the metal ties used to hold the masonry onto the block wall or plywood sheathing behind it have rusted and failed.

There are several other visible indications of problems in a masonry wall. Example: a white deposit on

39. Stepcracking of exterior brickwork

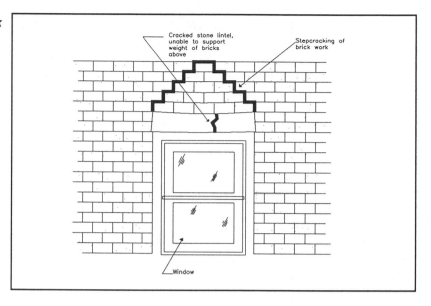

40 and 41. Spalling masonry showing how the bricks and mortar become deteriorated. Photos by the author.

the surface of the masonry, called "efflorescence," can mean that any one of several conditions exists, depending on the age of the masonry. Efflorescence on newly constructed or repointed masonry is not a problem. Usually it will disappear as the masonry weathers. On old masonry, however, this white deposit may mean that the wall is being subjected to excessive dampness.

Masonry that has been painted also can have visible indications of different problems. A painted finish that is blistering and peeling indicates that the coating of paint cannot breathe on the wall and that moisture is being trapped by it in the wall. Eventually, spalling will develop on it. A waterproof coating that has not been applied correctly also can trap moisture in the masonry, causing it to spall as well.

Parapet Walls

Houses built with flat roofs often have a masonry wall that extends a few feet above the roofline and runs along the perimeter of the roof. The extended section of masonry is referred to as a parapet wall. It is essential to keep parapet walls watertight because they can be one of the primary sources of water entry in a house. One of the worst things to do to keep a brick parapet wall watertight, however, is to coat it with roof mastic. As the mastic ages, it dries and pulls away from the wall, damaging the hardened outer surface of the bricks. In some extreme cases, the dry mastic actually pulls off part of the bricks from the wall, leaving voids in the wall for water to enter into the house. This problem is then exacerbated as the exposed pieces of brick soften and disintegrate, creating more and larger openings in the wall for water entry.

Many parapet walls are made with roof copings at the top of them. These copings are made of concrete or terra cotta tiles. When they are damaged, or when mortar between the joints of these copings loosens, water enters the wall and eventually finds its way under the roof covering and into the structure. This deterioration and water damage causes the parapet wall to lean out of plumb; that is, it no longer stands upright and level. If the parapet wall is left unrepaired, it will either fall onto the roof, where it can damage the covering, or onto the streetwalk, where it can injure passersby. For this reason and to prevent water entry into the house, it is important to repair the parapet wall before it

disintegrates. Depending on the extent of the damage, the masonry may have to be repointed, bricks may have to be replaced, or the entire wall may have to be rebuilt and new roof copings installed.

Regular or at least annual examinations of the conditions of the exterior walls and parapet wall, if you have one on your house, will ensure proper, timely maintenance to keep them in good condition and keep repair costs at a minimum. A knowledgeable, reliable masonry contractor can handle any problems you may find, enabling the masonry to last for many years while looking beautiful.

Stucco Walls

Exterior walls made of stucco are commonly found on old wood-frame houses. Nowadays stucco is used mostly on houses that have been built on block or concrete foundations. A thin layer of stucco is used to enhance the foundation wall just above grade level and up to where the siding material begins.

Stucco is a mixture of cement, sand, lime, and water. It is applied in its natural tone or with a coloring tint added to the mixture, when a particular color is desired. In its natural tone, the stucco can be painted, but only after it has been allowed to dry completely. The stucco mixture is applied over metal lath that is attached to wood sheathing. The sheathing was covered with building paper before the metal lath was attached to it. The metal lath enables the stucco mixture to adhere tightly to the wall. Three coats of the stucco mixture usually have to be applied to have an ample stucco covering with the desired textured finish. The total thickness of these three coats is approximately 1 inch.

New technology has developed a fiber mesh fabric that can be used instead of metal lath under the stucco to achieve proper adhesion. This fiber mesh fabric can be installed on an existing exterior wall or on new wall sheathing. After the fiber mesh fabric is installed, two coatings of stucco are applied using a mixture of cement and a synthetic binding material. The third finish coating is then applied using a typical stucco mixture. This type of application often is used to cover old, cracked exterior walls as well as in adobe construction. No matter what method is used for its application, stucco needs to be protected from the weather since it is not waterproof. Unless a waterproofing adhesive was added to the mixture when it was being applied, the stucco should either be painted or coated with a waterproofer such as Thoroseal.

Annual or semi-annual visual examinations of the stucco walls will make the homeowner familiar with its condition so that he can be aware when problems arise and deal with them before they become serious. These regular examinations also will reveal a variety of changes in its condition as it ages. Some of these are serious while others are not. For instance, hairline cracks will develop in the stucco walls from time to time. These are small, superficial cracks that can easily and effectively be covered with a waterproofer or a coat of good paint. Cracks that are wide and deep must be opened to clear them of any debris, repaired, and then waterproofed. If these larger cracks are left unrepaired, water will continue to enter into them and will enlarge them, causing further damage to the wall. The cost to repair the wall will grow as the number and size of the cracks increase, causing the damage to the wall to become more and more extensive.

When moisture is allowed to continue to get behind the stucco, it eventually causes the metal lath to rust and loosen from the sheathing. As more time passes, the sheathing rots and separates from the wall. Finally the stucco in this area bulges out from the rest of the wall due to the complete failure of the metal lath and the sheathing behind it. These types of problems can only be resolved with a costly, extensive repair project to rebuild the wall from the inside to the outside.

Wide cracks in a stucco wall indicate that there is a settlement problem. They may be caused because the framing behind the wall has failed, or the foundation under that section of wall has settled. A knowledgeable engineer or contractor has to be hired to tell the homeowner how to proceed. The framing members under the sheathing may be damaged because water was able to seep behind the cracked stucco for several years. The sheathing as well as the framing members may be rotted behind the wall, causing it to fail.

As a result of the visual examination, the homeowner may find that there are slight bulges in the stucco walls. These simply may have been left by the person who applied the stucco coatings while working with a trowel. The presence of these small bulges does not necessarily mean that there is a major problem. In fact, there may be no problem at all. To determine the extent of the problem, the homeowner simply needs to tap the bulge lightly, listening for what type of sound it makes. If he hears a hollow sound, the stucco probably has pulled away from the sheathing. In this case, the bulge is going to have to be repaired to prevent serious problems from developing.

Other Types of Masonry

In addition to using bricks on exterior walls, several types of stones also are used on the exterior surfaces of houses, each with its own special characteristics and possible problems. These materials include limestone, sandstone, granite, and marble. Limestone is basically a composition of calcium carbonate and calcium magnesium carbonate. This type of stone is formed from pieces of shells, coral, and marine organisms. Limestone was once a very popular exterior facing material because it is fairly easy to work with and it has excellent resistance to extreme weather conditions. Unfortunately, this type of stone is also susceptible to pollutants in the air and to acid rain, which is why it has become less popular. In addition, limestone can be destroyed by acid solutions when they are used to clean dirt and grease from the stones.

When sandstone is used on houses in cities, it is often called brownstone although its color is not always brown-toned. Sandstone is a composition of quartz and feldspar, which is held together with one of several minerals including iron oxides, silicates, liminite, calcite, and clays. The characteristics of sandstone vary depending on what mineral is in it. Sandstone containing silica is strong, decay resistant, and very hard. Sandstone that contains calcite is susceptible to acid damage, and sandstone that contains clays absorbs water and is more susceptible to deterioration than other types of sandstones. In fact, most types of sandstones tend to absorb moisture and are susceptible to damage from frost.

Granite is composed of quartz, feldspar, and mica, and it is very hard and resists wear quite well. Since most types of granite have a low porosity and permeability, they tend to resist damage and deterioration from extreme weather conditions such as frost. Marble, which is a composition mostly of calcite or dolomite, generally is used for ornamental detailing on exterior facades because it can be damaged easily by pollutants. As a matter of fact, many types of marble cannot be used on exterior surfaces because environmental conditions, especially those in urban areas, cause it to deteriorate rapidly.

ASPHALT SHINGLES

The base sheet used in the production of asphalt shingles is an organic one that looks like a felt-type covering. This organic base is composed of cellulose fibers that have been saturated with asphalt. The base sheet is coated on both sides with asphalt, then mineral granules are applied to the sides. These granules are used to shield the asphalt from the sun's ultraviolet rays. The granules also make the shingles more fire-retardant, while adding color to the shingling material.

Asphalt shingle siding is not used very much these days, so its availability has become quite limited. It was a popular siding material in some parts of the country at one time because it could be installed easily over old asphalt shingles already on a house, making this type of siding replacement fairly simple and fast. When installed initially, the shingles are nailed directly onto the wall sheathing, which has been covered with building paper. A house with asphalt shingle siding should be checked regularly so that any broken or loose pieces can be repaired or replaced immediately to prevent water entry into the house.

ASBESTOS SHINGLES

Asbestos shingles are attached to the wall sheathing with galvanized nails, after the sheathing has been covered with building paper. This type of shingling usually needs to be repainted after it has been exposed to the weather for a number of years. Asbestos shingles were available in a variety of sizes and colors; however, now that the health hazards associated with asbestos have become known, this product is no longer available for use. Fiber cement shingles with very small amounts of asbestos are being manufactured to replace the use of asbestos shingles.

Any house that still has this type of siding material on it should be examined regularly to check for broken or crumbling sections. These sections are emitting asbestos fibers into the air, creating an unhealthy environment. Asbestos shingle siding in this condition will have to be removed by a certified asbestos removal company. The local Environmental Protection Agency office will tell the homeowner what must be done to meet its code requirements, which may include the removal of all of this siding material from the house.

ALUMINUM AND VINYL SIDINGS

Aluminum siding is one of the most popular siding materials used today, most notably because it is practically maintenance-free. Other advantageous features of aluminum siding are that it can be installed directly over the existing material on a house and it can be installed either horizontally, the more common way, or vertically. Many manufacturers guarantee the siding for at least forty years, a substantial amount of time between replacement costs. The manufacturer's warranty also indicates what type of product can be used to clean the siding safely, a procedure that should be done once a year for best results. Still more advantages of aluminum siding are that it is fire-resistant and rustproof, and cannot be infested with termites.

When aluminum siding first became available, it did not have any holes in it for ventilation. New aluminum sidings installed on houses today have vent holes at the bottom of each section of siding in horizontal installations. Aluminum siding is available in a number of different colors and styles. The color will fade after many years of exposure to the sun's ultraviolet rays, but the siding can be repainted. Aluminum siding also can be dented easily. Since there is no way to remove these dents, the dented sections of siding have to be removed and replaced. It is necessary to install a ground on any house with aluminum siding to prevent lightning from striking the house during an electrical storm.

The color of vinyl siding is homogenous; that is, it has not been baked onto the surface of the siding, but is actually part of the siding material itself. As with aluminum siding, the color of vinyl siding will fade after many years of exposure to the sun's ultraviolet rays. Vinyl siding is available in fewer colors than aluminum siding and, unlike aluminum siding, it cannot be repainted when it fades. Vinyl siding does not rust, but it is not as fire-resistant as aluminum siding. Vinyl siding resists dents better than aluminum siding. In cold climates, vinyl siding can become very brittle and when it is brittle, it can crack and be damaged very easily. Vinyl siding, like aluminum siding, cannot be infested with termites, and it should be washed annually to extend its life expectancy. Again, the manufacturer's warranty should be followed to determine what type of washing solution is safe to use. Vinyl siding is only installed horizontally.

Both aluminum and vinyl sidings can be installed easily over most exterior wall surfaces; however, it is essential that these surfaces be sound. If they are not, the siding will not be installed tightly against it and, particularly in the case of aluminum siding, rattling sounds will be heard on windy days because the siding is loose in certain areas of the house. The installation of insulation boards behind the siding muffles this noise while it improves the house's energy-efficiency.

Reasons to Consider New Siding Installations

A house with stucco, asphalt shingles, or asbestos shingles on its exterior walls may be in poor condition because of its age and exposure to extreme weather conditions. The stucco may be so badly cracked that it no longer is watertight, and the shingles may be so cracked, broken, or missing that water entry is a constant problem. In either case, it is obvious to the homeowner that the exterior walls need to be recovered. An excellent alternative may be to consider the installation of aluminum or vinyl siding.

The condition of the windows on these houses also may warrant that they be changed. If the windows are old and were not maintained properly, their sashes may be rotted, putty may be missing, and the glazing may be loose or cracked. There is no doubt that these windows are not very energy-efficient. If the windows are in fairly good shape despite their age, it may still be a good idea to change them to make the house energy-efficient.

It is best to have any new windows installed before the exterior walls are recovered with the aluminum or vinyl siding. This can be done afterwards, but it means that you will have to replace old windows with the same sizes and configurations as the new siding dictates, unless, of course, you are willing to disturb the newly installed siding. On the other hand, if the jobs are done consecutively, that is, first new windows are installed, then new siding, the size and/or number of windows can be increased or decreased and configurations can be altered without disturbing the newly installed exterior siding. Changes can be made afterwards, but not as easily or as inexpensively.

One homeowner, for instance, decided to install a sliding patio door in place of an existing window a few years after aluminum siding had been installed on his house. To hide the fact that this work was done later than the siding installation, he used a contrasting color of siding rather than trying to match the already faded color that was in place. Also, he had the siding installed vertically to contrast with the horizontal siding previously installed. As a result, this homeowner's renovation did not look like an afterthought when it was completed. Although the newer siding looked as if it had been installed when the rest of the siding was done, the project did cost him more money that it would have if he had done it all at once.

How to Choose a Siding Contractor

It is important to get at least three contractors to come to your house to give you cost estimates for the work you want done. Afterward, it is necessary to compare these estimates based on the specific work the contractor is going to do as well as the types and amount of materials he will provide for the job. To determine these various factors, the homeowner should ask a number of questions about the following basic items:

1. Ask for the name of the manufacturer of the siding material. It should be a name that is well-known in that field.

2. Ask what kind of warranty or guarantee is offered by the manufacturer of the siding. This guarantee or warranty specifies how long the color on the siding will last before it begins to fade. It also indicates its durability in terms of changing weather conditions as well as various types of possible damage.

3. Ask the contractor how he is going to attach the siding to your house. Usually wood firring strips are

nailed into the walls and the siding is attached to these firring strips.

4. Ask the contractor if he is going to install insulation boards behind the siding. The use of insulation boards is a good idea to increase the house's energy-efficiency. Insulation boards are foam-like sheets that are either 1/2 inch or 1 inch thick. Be sure that your contractor's estimate includes the installation of these insulation boards. If not, the contractor will want to charge you more than his estimate at the end of the job for the installation of these boards (Figure 42).

5. Ask the contractor if he is going to install new gutters and downspouts when he installs the siding. New gutters and downspouts should be installed when the siding is installed so that they match it in terms of color scheme and style. Screens also should be installed over the gutters to prevent leaves from falling into them and eventually clogging the downspouts. As water continues to back up in the downspouts, it will eventually rot the wood fascia board supporting the gutters. If left uncorrected for an extended period of time, this will lead to water entry into the house. Tell your contractor to include the cost of new gutters and downspouts and screens for the gutters in his estimate before you let him begin work.

6. If soffits are installed on your house, they will need to be covered with aluminum or vinyl when the siding is installed. In many applications, these soffits are vented for air to be able to flow from them into the attic and out through the ridge vent at the peak of the roof. Ask the contractor to include the cost of this work in his estimate, if it needs to be done, before any work starts.

7. Ask the contractor to explain how he intends to trim the house. Some contractors choose one color for the siding and a contrasting color for the trim that covers the wood frames around windows and doors. This type of decorative application of the siding and trim makes a house look very attractive; however, it entails additional work for the contractor, which is why he is going to charge more for the same job. To finish a siding job more quickly and less expensively, some contractors do not install the trim in a different color. Instead, they extend the same siding over the wood frames, bringing it flush

against the face of the windows and doors. Although this type of siding job looks less attractive after it has been completed, it is often preferred by homeowners who must keep costs to a minimum. The homeowner can have the work done either way, as long as he knows that his contractor's estimate is based on his preferred method.

8. Ask the contractor how long he will take to complete his siding job. Some contractors finish the job in a few days, while others take weeks and even months because they work on several siding jobs simultaneously, leaving all of their clients waiting for their jobs to be completed. Most siding jobs take no more than a week or two from start to finish, depending on the size of the house.

Generally speaking, it is fair to say that the homeowner needs to know exactly what the contractor's estimate includes and what it does not. This will eliminate the possibility of surprises at the end of the job in terms of its final cost as well as its finished appearance. In fact, this is sound advice for any occasion when the homeowner is dealing with any type of contractor.

WOOD SIDINGS

There are several types of wood sidings available today, including plywood siding, hardboard siding, wood shingles, and wood board siding. Each is made from different materials and each has special characteristics. In addition, each can be used for specific applications using appropriate application techniques. Let's discuss them, one by one, to clarify these differences.

Plywood Siding

A popular type of plywood siding is called Texture 1-11 (Figure 43). It is available as a panel in sizes from 4' x 8' to 4' x 16' and it is manufactured with fully waterproof adhesives for exterior uses. Texture 1-11 is made in many grades including select, premium, and rustic, and in a variety of textures such as rough sawn and brushed, among other surfaces. The select grade has smaller and fewer knots as well as fewer repaired knots in it than other grades. The wood species used to make this paneling include Southern pine, Douglas fir, cedar, and redwood. Texture 1-11 is available with shiplapped edges and

42. Aluminum and vinyl siding installation

Firring strips nailed into exterior wall

Wood firring strips

Exterior stucco wall

Foam insulation board. 1" thick. Nailed to firring strips

Aluminum or vinyl siding nailed through insulation board into firring strips

Nail siding onto strips

43. Texture 1-11 rough-sawn plywood siding is used on architect William U. Donald's own house. Donald and Wittenberg, Delony & Davidson, Inc., of Little Rock, won a Citation of Merit in the 7th Annual Plywood Design Awards Program. Courtesy of the American Plywood Association.

parallel grooves and it is made in two thicknesses, 19/32" and 5/8". Texture 1-11 is not fireproof, and it is susceptible to termite infestation.

One of the advantages of using Texture 1-11 as an exterior siding is that it can be installed directly onto the wall studs, eliminating the need for wall sheathing. The installation of the wall sheathing behind it, however, makes the finished wall stronger than it would be without it as a backing. Usually Texture 1-11 is installed vertically on a wall, fastened to it with a good grade of galvanized nails. Aluminum and stainless steel nails also can be used because they do not rust, but they are expensive. Ordinary iron nails are not used because they will rust after many years of exposure, and the rust will stain the siding.

Although Texture 1-11 has several other advantages, such as its easy installation and its ability as a natural insulator, there also are some disadvantages associated with its use. For instance, Texture 1-11 has to be painted or stained to extend its life expectancy as well as to protect it from dampness, high humidity, and other weather conditions that will destroy it after many years of exposure. When using Texture 1-11, the siding should not be finished until the manufacturer's recommendations for doing so have been determined. In addition to its use as an exterior siding, Texture 1-11 also has become a popular paneling for surfaces inside the house.

Another popular type of plywood siding available is called lap siding. It is manufactured with square or beveled edges in widths up to 12" and in 16-foot lengths. It is available in rough sawn or smooth overlaid textures and in thicknesses of 11/32", 3/8", 1/2", 19/32", and 5/8". Lap siding is easy to install, and it also should be painted or stained to protect it from the weather. Again, the paint or stain used should be one that is recommended by the manufacturer.

Hardboard Siding

Hardboard siding is available as a panel in sizes that range from 4' x 8' to 4' x 16', and as a horizontal lap board that is 12" wide by 16' long. It is approximately 7/16" to 1/2" thick and it is available with a smooth or textured finish. Hardboard siding is manufactured with V-grooves, shiplap joints, clapboard styles, and with many other joint details. The finish, which is usually covered by a fifteen-year warranty, is baked on the siding. The result is a textured panel

with a wood-grain texture look that resists splitting, cracking, checking, and delaminating. This siding has a high impact resistance and is uniformly thick. Hardboard siding is denser than natural wood. It is easy to keep clean and it is available in many colors.

As with Texture 1-11, hardboard siding should be installed over wall sheathing to make the finished wall stronger than one that is installed directly onto wall studs. The advantages of hardboard siding include its reasonable price as well as its easy installation. Its disadvantages are similar to those of Texture 1-11, specifically, that it is susceptible to termite infestation and it must be painted or stained regularly to extend its life expectancy by protecting it from various weather conditions. Once again, it is necessary to use the paint or stain recommended by the manufacturer for best results.

Wood Shingles

Wood shingles are cut mostly from Western red cedar and redwood. They are 16", 18", and 24" long and are available in No. 1 and No. 2 grades. The No. 1 grade shingles (Figure 44) are a clear heartwood that is knot-free and 100% edge-grained. The No. 2 grade, which is less expensive than the No. 1 grade, has knots in it, causing more waste when the shingles are installed. The No. 2 grade also is more difficult to install because the knots in it cause the shingles to split frequently during installation. Wood shingles are available in a variety of precut fancy shapes and some also are available in preassembled panels (Figures 45 and 46).

Wood shingles are installed in one of two ways, depending on what material is being used as the underlayment. Either they are attached to plywood sheathing directly, or onto 1" x 4" nailing strips when a non-wood sheathing is being used as the underlayment. The nailing strips are nailed to the wall studs through the non-wood sheathing and then the shingles are nailed to the nailing strips. In this application, the non-wood sheathing may be a gypsum sheathing or a fiberboard. Space equivalent to the width of a nailing strip is left between each strip as it is nailed to the non-wood sheathing. Roofing felt is used in both methods of installation, either attached directly to the plywood sheathing, or placed between the nailing strips and the shingles. This roofing felt acts as a water-resistant membrane while allowing air to circulate behind the shingles.

Hot-dipped galvanized nails are used to nail the shingles to the nailing strips or to the plywood sheathing. Stainless steel nails also can be used, but they are much more expensive than the galvanized nails.

44. Wood shingles can be installed over old wood siding or plywood sheathing, or onto nailing strips when a non-wood sheathing is used as the underlayment. Courtesy of the Cedar Shake & Shingle Bureau.

The amount of exposure of the shingle, that is, the amount of a shingle's surface visible on a wall, varies, depending on the length of the shingles being installed. For instance, the exposure for a No. 1 grade 16" shingle is 5". An 18" shingle has an exposure of 5½", and a 24" shingle has an exposure of 7½".

Left unfinished, wood shingles weather naturally, and they can also be stained or painted. The weathering process can be expedited by applying a weathering stain to the shingles. On the other hand, the natural color of the wood can be maintained by applying a clear, water-repellent preservative on the shingles.

Wood Board Siding

Wood board siding is available in many widths, grades, and thicknesses. The most common species of wood used for this type of siding are pine, redwood, and Western red cedar, and the boards are made for both vertical and horizontal applications. Horizontal wood board siding, which is called bevel siding, is common in either redwood or Western red cedar. It is available in three sizes: ½" x 6", ¾" x 8", and ¾" x 10". Bevel siding is sold in several grades, all of which are kiln-dried, including Clear Heart, and the A, B, and C grades. The price of the siding increases as the grade goes from the C grade, the lowest, to the Clear Heart grade, the highest. Some manufacturers grade the siding as either Standard or Select grade. In this case, the Select grade is the better of the two and the more expensive. The grading of wood board siding is based on the wood's grain, knot structure, size of knots, number of knots, etc. — typical criteria for the grading of just about any wood product.

Wood board siding used for vertical applications is called Channel Rustic siding, and it also is available in several grades. The best is the Clear grade, followed in descending order by the Select and Standard grades. Tongue and groove siding also is used in vertical applications and it has a similar grading system as Channel Rustic siding (Figure 47).

All wood board sidings are nailed to the wall sheathing, and there are several ways to do this. For instance, bevel siding is face nailed to the sheathing. Channel Rustic siding can be face nailed or nailed in the groove of the siding. Tongue and groove siding is attached to the sheathing by driving the nails into the tongue at an angle and then setting the nail below the tongue with a nailset so that the groove of the next piece of siding can fit easily over the tongue of the one previously nailed.

Hot-dipped galvanized nails or stainless steel nails are used to install wood board siding. A poor grade of galvanized nails or simple iron nails should not be used because these nails will rust after exposure to the weather, and the rust will stain the siding. If the siding is not nailed to the sheathing by using the correct nailing technique, eventually the siding will split as the wood expands and contracts due to changing weather conditions during the year. Wood board siding is nailed to the sheathing after the sheathing has been covered with roofing felt or building paper. Extra layers of felt or paper are applied around window and door frames along with a bead of a good grade of caulk. These precautions help to keep moisture away from the sheathing at

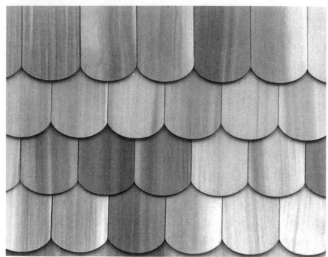

45. Five-inch exposure Fancy Cuts round panel shingles in a typical application. Courtesy of the Shakertown Corporation.

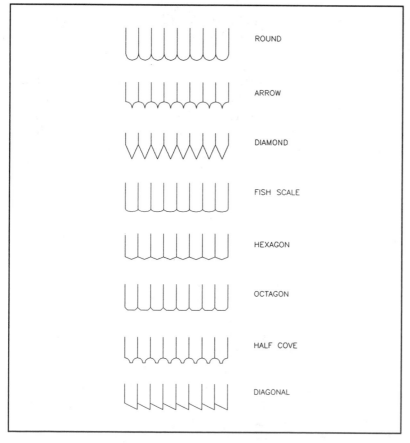

46. These decorative cedar shingles are drawn from the Shakertown Corporation's template of Fancy Cuts Decorative Cedar Shingles.

47. A vertical application of tongue and groove wood siding enhances the exterior of this house. Courtesy of Lindal Cedar Homes.

areas on the wall where seepage is a common problem.

The homeowner should examine the wood board siding regularly for pieces of siding that have split and for openings in joints and around windows and doors. If the felt, paper, or sheathing behind the split pieces of siding or the opened joints is visible, the damaged pieces of siding are going to have to be replaced to prevent water from getting behind them. Left unrepaired, the water will cause the paper and/or sheathing to deteriorate.

There are a number of advantages to using Western red cedar or redwood siding instead of siding made of pine. Cedar and redwood are very resistant to decay and insect infestation. They also can be left unstained or unpainted to weather naturally. Pine siding, on the other hand, must be painted, stained, or at least coated with a wood preservative to protect it from deterioration due to extreme temperatures, high humidity, rain, etc.

As untreated redwood siding is left exposed to the weather, at first it blackens, then it turns silver-gray. This is called the weathered look. As untreated Western red cedar weathers, it turns to a brownish color, then gradually to a light gray. The weathering process in cedar and redwood can be accelerated by applying a weathering stain, which is also called bleaching oil by some manufacturers. The weathering stain reacts with the sunlight and rain to hasten the weathering process as well as to make the weathered look more uniform in these types of sidings. This is important because various weather conditions can affect the natural weathering process, leaving the wood with some unattractive results. For instance, in drier climates, cedar siding may turn to many different shades of tan, instead of brownish and then light gray. In harsher climates where temperatures range from freezing to sweltering levels, redwood and cedar siding blacken and then either turn to an uneven gray or to a blackened gray and brown.

In addition to weathering stains, there is a variety of finishing products available. The choice of what product to use depends on the type of wood siding installed as well as the homeowner's preference. Although a detailed description of exterior and interior finishes is included in Chapter 15, let's review some of those specifically used on wood board sidings. For example, water-repellent preservatives are used on wood siding, and they are available as a clear liquid, or as semi-transparent or solid stains. These preservatives and stains protect the wood from moisture, which can cause it to decay, as well as from mildew and fungus. New wood siding should be coated on both sides before it is installed to prevent moisture from destroying the wood either on its surface or on the hidden side of the siding. Clear water-repellent preservatives are used to achieve a natural wood finish, or as a prime coat for the wood when it is going to be stained or painted. Clear water-repellent preservatives also can be used to slow down the weathering process to make the wood weather more evenly than it would if left to do so naturally. This is done by slowing down the bleaching process caused by the sun's ultraviolet rays. Semi-transparent stains are used to add color to the wood siding while allowing the texture of the grain to remain visible through it. Solid color stains are used to add lots of color to the wood siding, so they do not let the grain of the wood remain visible. The chemicals in all of these water-repellent preservatives effectively control wood-destroying fungus and mildew. These preservatives also minimize the extent of staining caused by rain and other sources of humidity.

Newly installed, unfinished redwood and cedar siding also can be painted; however, both sides of the wood should first be coated with a good grade of oil-based primer. The resins in these species of wood keep paint from adhering properly unless it is primed. Once redwood or cedar is painted or stained, it will have to be repainted or restained regularly to keep the wood in good condition throughout the duration of its use on the house. Pine siding cannot be left untreated because if it is, it will deteriorate and have to be replaced in a fairly short period of time. To protect pine siding from the weather and the damage it can cause, it must be coated with either a water-repellent preservative or an exterior paint.

There are a few procedures to follow before any wood siding is repainted or restained. First, dirt, soot, and grease must be cleaned from the siding, and any loose paint removed. This is done with a stiff bristle brush and a mixture of water with mild detergent in it. After the siding has been given sufficient time to dry thoroughly, any loose or decayed sections of siding must be repaired or replaced. Finally, a fresh coat of paint or stain can be applied to it.

In addition to stains from dirt and soot, wood siding also can be stained by mildew, or it can have what are called extractive staining and iron staining discoloring its surface. Extractive staining occurs when the extracts in the wood rise to its surface after the siding has been exposed to excessive rain or humidity. As the rain and humidity evaporate, the extracts are drawn up to the surface where they leave stains on the wood. Iron staining is the result of a chemical reaction between wood and iron. This occurs when simple iron nails are used to install the wood siding instead of galvanized or non-corrosive nails. As the nails rust due to exposure to the weather, the iron leaves blue-black stains on the wood siding. This type of staining is particularly intense on cedar and redwood. Iron staining also will occur if the water-repellent preservative used on the siding was iron-contaminated. In fact, these are only a few of the reasons stains appear on wood siding, but they are the most common ones that the homeowner will encounter.

Mildew is one of the most common causes of stains on wood siding, and it is visible as a gray or black discoloration. Initially it looks like a series of black dots in one area of the siding, and later it has a moldy appearance. Mildew stains can be removed with chemicals such as a mildewcide produced especially for this type of stain removal. Mildew stains also can be removed with a mixture of household bleach and water, or with oxalic acid. Before the homeowner uses any chemicals, it is a good idea to read the manufacturer's instructions on the container to prevent personal injury because these chemicals are quite potent. A chemical such as oxalic acid, for example, is toxic and will burn your skin if it comes into contact with it. In addition, the fumes from oxalic acid can cause respiratory irritation when they are inhaled. Prior to attempting a cleanup such as this one, the homeowner might benefit by calling the nearest Western Wood Products Association representative to get advice on how to properly and safely care for wood siding and any problems that develop in it.

7
Dealing with Windows and Doors

INSULATION AND NATURAL LIGHT

One homeowner had an old house with many windows and doors, but he still felt that his house was dark and dreary. As he renovated it, room by room, he realized that his problem was solving itself. What his house had needed, he learned, was more natural light to brighten and enliven its interior spaces. With each modernization project, he added and/or enlarged windows, put round-top or vent windows over existing and new windows and doors, and made existing doors wider and higher to make the house as bright as possible, even during winter's short, dark days. He put vertical blinds on his patio door and mini wood blinds on the windows to accommodate the sun's daily movement, and he installed drapes or curtains only on windows where privacy was paramount. When he had finished all of his renovation projects, he had a cheerful, bright old house that made him and his family, including plants and pets, happy.

This homeowner's experience illustrates the importance of having an adequate number of windows and doors in a house, and sizing them to provide as much natural light as possible. Today's window and door manufacturers are making this choice difficult because, happily, they give the homeowner so many types to choose from. Many things need to be considered to make this determination. For instance, the homeowner in a tropical climate may not need super-insulating windows, but he does need them to be fairly well insulated to keep the cool, air conditioned air inside his house. He also wants windows that are large enough to offer an expansive view and an airy feeling. Homeowners in cold climates, on the other hand, need to be concerned with keeping their houses as energy-efficient as possible, but they also want large windows to let as much natural light as possible into their homes. All homeowners want doors that add to the beauty of their houses while keeping rain, snow, and cold and hot weather outside. They may want wider doors to allow for easy access for furniture and other objects as well as to add natural light to their homes. The homeowner must consider all of these factors as well as security considerations when choosing windows and doors to be installed on the house. Fortunately, the possibilities open to the homeowner are quite broad, so you are bound to find windows and doors to suit your needs and tastes. Let's discuss some of the types of windows and doors available along with their special features to help you decide what you want to do.

WINDOWS

There are many types and styles of windows available today. There are replacement windows made of aluminum, aluminum with a thermal break, or vinyl. They are made with insulating glass and Low-E® glass, with diamond and Colonial grids, and they are even manufactured with triple glazing. There are wood windows that are made with insulating glass, storm panels, special coatings on the glass, and even a transparent polyester film installed between two panes of glass to make them more energy-efficient than they otherwise would be. These wood windows use aluminum or vinyl cladding or a special coating to cover the exterior wood members and protect them from harmful weather conditions. Windows made with cladding need little or no maintenance to keep them looking like new. Since there are so many options, which can be confusing, let's review each type of window and its features more closely, starting with replacement windows.

Replacement Windows

Vinyl replacement windows and aluminum replacement windows with a thermal break have become very popular because they can be manufactured to fit the existing window opening; that is, they can easily be custom-sized. This makes their installation fairly simple, so much so that it is often undertaken by the homeowner, and it eliminates the need for extensive repairs on interior and exterior walls. The window jambs and exterior moldings do not have to be removed to install replacement windows. Only the interior window stop and the old sashes have to be removed to install them. The old window weights also are removed and the hollow cavity that housed them is filled with insulation to reduce the amount of heat lost through it, before the replacement window is put into place.

Aluminum replacement windows with a thermal break are preferable to those without it because they retard heat loss by conduction through the frame. A non-conductive material is placed between the interior and exterior sections of the aluminum frames to separate them from each other. This prevents heat conduction from the interior section of the frame to the exterior one where it is lost. This type of heat loss is visible when condensation or ice forms on the interior side of the window frame during a cold day. The installation of storm windows on the replacement windows can diminish the problem; however, such an addition can never be as effective as using an aluminum replacement window with a thermal break. Condensation and ice form on a window that has only a single pane of glass in it. Sometimes the heated indoor air fogs a single-glazed window when it condenses on it. To minimize the amount of heat lost through the frame of a replacement window, it is best to use a vinyl replace-

ment window or an aluminum replacement window with a thermal break. A vinyl replacement window is a good choice because vinyl is an excellent insulator.

Replacement windows are available with a variety of features including sashes that tilt out to make cleaning the glass easy. They also are available in many shapes, sizes, and styles such as bow, bay, casement, and double-hung windows (Figures 48, 49, and 50). Some of these windows are equipped with cam-style locks and interlocking meeting rails. This lock and rail combination helps to prevent dust, dirt, and air from entering the house while also making it more difficult for burglars to pry the window open. Season-All, one of the well-known manufacturers of replacement windows, also makes vinyl-capped bow and bay window units with pine or oak interior finishes. These units are available in virtually any configuration, combining single-hung, double-hung, picture, and casement windows. The unit has a preassembled wood buck for an easy, fast, and inexpensive installation by a contractor or by the homeowner as a do-it-yourself project. The head and seat boards are made of 1-inch thick birch veneer plywood or oak. Season-All's windows are made with 3/4-inch to 1-inch thick insulating glass and good quality weatherstripping to prevent air infiltration as well as water penetration.

Wood Frame Windows

A window constructed with a wood frame has greater resistance to heat loss by conduction through its frame than one with an aluminum or steel frame. In fact, the wood's resistance to heat loss is approximately 1,500 times better than that of an aluminum or steel replacement window without a thermal break. The vinyl replacement window is competitive with the wood frame window in terms of its resistance to heat loss by conduction through its frame. The resistance to heat loss by conduction is better in an aluminum replacement window with a thermal break than in an aluminum replacement window without a thermal break. According to the American Society of Heating, Refrigeration, Air Conditioning Engineers (ASHRAE), the recommended heat frame transfer coefficients for 1990 are as follows: an aluminum window without a thermal break, 1.9; aluminum window with a thermal break, 1.0; wood frame window with aluminum or vinyl cladding, .4 and .3 respectively; and vinyl frame window, .3.

48, 49, 50. Some of the variety of replacement windows available. Courtesy of Season-All Industries, Inc.

48.

49.

50.

Wood frame windows are manufactured in many different styles and sizes, and when they are made with a vinyl or aluminum cladding, they are virtually maintenance-free. Wood frame windows are coated with a waterproof preservative before they are covered with the cladding to retard the wood from swelling or shrinking and to protect it from wood-decaying fungus. The manufacturers of these wood frame windows also use an excellent grade of finish to coat the exterior of an uncladded wood window so that they can guarantee the windows for a long period of time, in some cases as much as ten years.

Wood frame windows with aluminum or vinyl cladding on the exterior side of the frame do not need to be painted regularly, which is why they have become so popular with many of today's busy homeowners. The cladding is able to resist the damaging effects of harsh weather conditions while it protects the wood under it. Although most window manufacturers prefer to use aluminum as a cladding material instead of vinyl, there are a few window manufacturers that have been using vinyl for nearly thirty years on all of the standard windows. The aluminum cladding, which is approximately .055-inch thick extruded aluminum, is fitted onto the wood frame. An even thinner piece of aluminum is used on the window sashes. A finish coating is applied onto the aluminum cladding to make it more durable than it ordinarily would be in severe weather conditions. This coating is available in standard colors including white, brown, and tan as well as in custom colors. Since the cost of the custom colors sometimes can be prohibitive, most homeowners tend to choose from among the standard ones. On a vinyl-clad window, the wood frame is covered with vinyl and the sashes are covered with a good quality coating that will need to be repainted after they have been exposed to the weather for a number of years. Vinyl-clad wood frame windows are available in only two standard colors, white and brown; however, the brown cladding can be painted with latex or alkyd paint so a variety of other colors is possible. The chemical properties of the white cladding material prevent paint from adhering to its surface, which means this color should only be chosen if white is the desired color.

Most wood frame windows are made of Ponderosa, yellow, or white pine because these species of wood are evenly toned, straight-grained, easy to work with, and accept glue well. Manufacturers of these windows bring the pine by rail to their own mills where imperfections are removed from it. Longer lengths are cut as often as necessary to remove the imperfections, and these smaller, clear pieces of wood are joined together using what is called the finger-joining method. The resulting long pieces of joined lumber are used to make the frames for windows that are going to be cladded since the cladding will hide the joints in them. The cladding also protects the wood from damage due to prolonged exposure to the weather. Interestingly enough, a frame made with finger-joined lumber is as strong or even stronger than one made with a solid length of wood. Wood frame windows that are not going to be cladded, such as those that are going to be stained and covered with a coat of polyurethane, are made with solid lengths of lumber. Rails and stiles are assembled with mortise and tenon joints. Wood frame windows are equipped with flexible weatherstripping, locks, and lift handles. Custom colors are available from some manufacturers for the hardware on these windows as well as for the aluminum cladding.

Several glazing options are available for wood frame windows, including single and double glazing as well as insulating glass (Figure 51). Some double-glazed windows and windows made with insulating glass are manufactured with a coating on the interior surface of the glass, and windows made with insulating glass also are available with Argon gas in the air cavity between the panes of glass as well as with the coating. Both the gas and the coating are used because they are able to reflect the sun's ultraviolet rays, protect the colors of the fabrics in the house, and increase the thermal efficiency of the windows. The coating keeps radiant heat, such as the heat radiating from driveways and streetwalks, out of the house during the summer. During the winter the coating is able to keep the heat rays from the sun in the house rather than letting them escape to the outdoors. In fact, as much as 90% of the heat rays in the house is prevented from escaping. The coating is used by several window manufacturers that call it Low-E glass, Low-Emissivity glass, or High-Performance glass among other designations.

Still other windows are made with a transparent polyester film that is placed in the air cavity be-

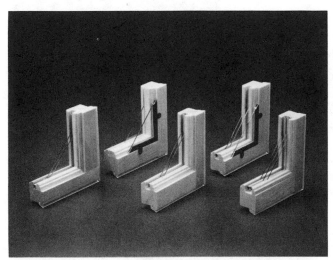

51. There are many glazing options, including single glazing with removable energy panels and insulating glass. Courtesy of Marvin Windows.

tween the panes of glass to act as an insulator, to protect rugs, drapes, and upholstery from the sun's ultraviolet rays, and to increase the thermal efficiency of the window. The Argon gas is used in the air cavity of an insulating glass window because the gas is denser and heavier than air, making it able to retard heat flow through it better than air alone would be able to do. When Argon gas, which is colorless, is used in conjunction with the Low-E coating, there is an increase in the resistance to heat transfer through the glass. In addition to the Low-E coating, other windows are made with special coatings, or even a series of coatings, to tint the glass in order to reduce solar gain.

The reason for all of these glazings, coatings, and insulating options is to increase the R value, that is, the resistance of heat flow through the window. For example, the R value of a window increases as the number of glazings in it also increases. A window with a single pane of glass, therefore, has a much lower R value than one with a double glazing. The use of Low-E glass or the transparent polyester film also increases the window's R value when used with insulating glass or a double glazing. In fact, Low-E glass is only effective when it is used in conjunction with an air space; in effect, when it is used with insulating glass or a double glazing. The Low-E coating is applied to the pane of glass that is either nearest to or farthest away from the living area, depending on the climate in the area where the house is located.

Insulating glass and double glazing have many differences, not the least of these is the method in which they are manufactured. A wood frame window with insulating glass has a hermetically sealed air space between the panes of glass (Figure 52), while double glazing is made by using two separate pieces of glass working in conjunction with each other to form a tight air cavity, or air space, between them. Various window manufacturers use one or both of these two production methods to make their products. For instance, the Rolscreen Company's Pella® windows, doors, sunrooms, and skylights use insulating glass as well as a single pane of glass with a removable glass panel, which it calls the Double Glazing Panel System, to create an air space that is 13/16" wide (Figure 53). The R value of insulating glass windows ordinarily is greater than this method of double glazing would provide; however, Pella improves its windows' thermal efficiency by adding a Low-E coating. Pella's design also accommodates the insertion of Slimshade® blinds, pleated shades, or muntins in the space between the removable glass panel and the stationary pane of glass, an option that some homeowners may prefer (Figure 54).

Wood frame windows are available in a variety of shapes and styles, including casement, sliding, double-hung, awning, bow, and bay windows (Figure 55). These can be combined to create a variety of other configurations (Figure 56). For instance, a bay window can be constructed using double-hung or casement windows. The standard sizes of these windows vary greatly, and when they are used in combination with each other, they can offer even more sizing options. Custom sizes also are available, but these windows cost a great deal more than standard size windows. To accommodate odd-sized rough openings such as those frequently found in older houses, manufacturers have alteration kits that can be used with their standard size windows that enable them to fit the space. During a renovation project, for example, vinyl or aluminum frame expanders can be used to fill gaps on the sides and top of the standard size window. These frame expanders cover the space from the jamb of the existing window opening to the new window frame.

When standard size windows do not accommodate a rough opening and frame expanders cannot adequately make up the difference, retrofit window

52. This insulating glass window has a hermetically sealed air space between the panes of glass. Courtesy of the Andersen Corporation Inc.

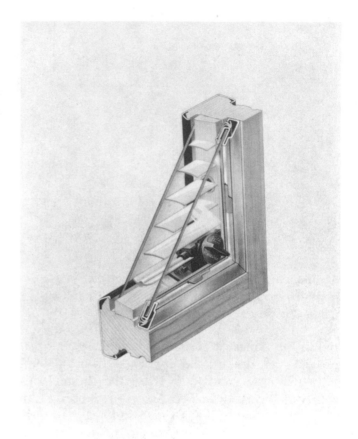

54. Pella Slimshade® blinds or Pleated Shades enable homeowners to control energy and natural light. Courtesy of the Pella/Rolscreen Company.

53. This casement window also has a double glazing panel. Courtesy of the Pella/Rolscreen Company.

55. This radial bow window with vent-size casements and windowpane dividers lends a feeling of spaciousness inside and a traditional look outside. Courtesy of the Pella/Rolscreen Company.

56. The bow window shown here has true divided lights. Courtesy of NORCO Windows, Inc.

kits, which also are offered by wood window manufacturers, can be used in the rough opening. For instance, Marvin Windows makes what it calls the E-Z TILT PAC™ (Figure 57), and NORCO Windows, Inc. offers the SASHPACK™. Basically these kits contain all of the parts of a window, except the window frame, that are needed to assemble it in a rough opening. A jamb liner is supplied with the kit so that the old wood frame does not have to be disturbed (Figure 58). In fact, the interior and exterior moldings as well as the window frame are left in place. Only the old sashes are removed to install this type of window. The new jamb liner is screwed into place and the sashes are attached to it by snapping them into the jamb liner. These retrofit kits are available in custom sizes as well as standard sizes and with a variety of glazing options, which means that their R values are quite high. The exterior side of the wood window sashes is available unfinished so that the wood can be painted, or with a cladding material on it to make it practically maintenance-free. A retrofit window is not as expensive as a wood frame window or a standard replacement window, but it only can be installed when the existing window frame is sound, plumb, and almost perfectly square, so it is not always possible to use it. This type of window can be adjusted slightly in a rough opening to level it or to adjust it to accommodate slight differences in height but, for the most part, it cannot be used successfully unless the existing window frame is in good condition and the rough opening is fairly plumb and level.

Wood window manufacturers also make what are called round top or circle head windows with insulating glass. These can be used on top of their standard size windows and doors to create beautiful designs (Figures 59 and 60). They also are available with the Low-E coating and the Argon gas filling for greater energy-efficiency. The wood frames are left unfinished for painting or staining, or they are cladded with colors that match the windows and doors being installed along with them. Full circle wood frame windows as well as quarter circle windows also are available for dramatic design accents.

It is essential to care for these wood frame windows properly to maintain their energy-efficiency and beauty. Starting with the pre-purchase, the homeowner should state that he wants the sashes and frame treated with a water-repellent preservative by the manufacturer, if it was not already done during the manufacturing process. When the windows arrive at the homeowner's house, they should be stored in a clean, dry, and well-ventilated area, not in a garage, which is usually too damp. During delivery and installation, the windows should be handled with care, not jarred or dropped, which could distort their shape. Before finishing the wood, the surfaces must be clean and dry, and it is preferable that they not be painted in damp, humid weather. It is a good idea to follow the manufacturer's instructions regarding how to properly finish the product, and it is a good policy to use high quality finishing products to do so. If the wood is going to be

57. Marvin's E-Z TILT PAC® is a good replacement alternative for numerous window openings. Courtesy of Marvin Windows.

58. Double-hung window detail

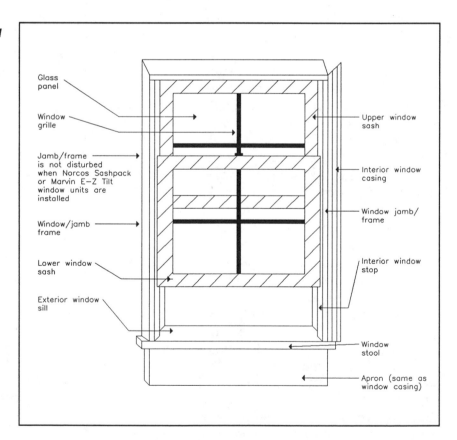

Glass panel

Window grille

Jamb/frame is not disturbed when Norcos Sashpack or Marvin E-Z Tilt window units are installed

Window/jamb frame

Lower window sash

Exterior window sill

Upper window sash

Interior window casing

Window jamb/ frame

Interior window stop

Window stool

Apron (same as window casing)

59. Andersen Circle Top windows are available with High Performance glass or High Performance Sun insulating glass. Courtesy of the Andersen Corporation Inc.

60. Roundtop windows, including full, half, and quarter rounds, and ellipticals, are available to accent almost any architectural style. Courtesy of NORCO Windows, Inc.

painted, an oil-based prime coat should be applied first, followed by two to three coats of a good quality trim paint. If a clear finish is preferred, then a sanding sealer should be used before several coats of polyurethane are applied. An excellent trick is to overlap the glazing with the finish to seal the joint between the wood and glass.

Storm windows or even storm panels often are found on older houses since they were very popular at one time. They were installed to protect the wood frame on the window from the weather and to prevent drafts from the single-glazed windows that usually were behind them. Storm windows are still available from some manufacturers; however, the introduction of double glazing, insulating glass, vinyl and aluminum cladding, etc., has made their use su-

perfluous on modern houses. Although storm windows are fairly inexpensive, money spent on them is better used to purchase aluminum replacement windows with a thermal break or wood frame windows with insulating glass or double glazing. The latter options may cost more initially, but the energy saved over the years will ultimately be cost-effective.

Today's window manufacturers such as Marvin and Andersen® make storm and screen panels to fit over some of their standard size windows for homeowners who live in particularly harsh climates and want even more protection from the weather than the windows by themselves can offer. These storm and screen panels are put into place or removed as the seasons change during the year. The panels are made with weatherstripping, and they increase the house's energy efficiency when they are in use. These storm and screen panels are given different names by manufacturers. Marvin, for example, calls it the Combination Window while Andersen refers to it as its Combination Unit. No matter what name has been given, these storm and screen panels work the same way to protect the wood frame window and increase a house's energy-efficiency.

DOORS

It is counter-productive for any homeowner to have new energy-efficient windows installed in a house while leaving drafty, worn exterior doors on it. These old doors will continue to waste energy, and they will detract from the beauty of the house. In addition, many old doors can be pried open easily by a burglar, so the installation of new exterior doors also improves a house's security. It is a good idea to replace old doors when new siding is about to be installed because doors can be made wider or larger and any changes to the exterior can be covered easily and promptly by the siding. Bear in mind that such changes in the size of the doors are going to require repair work inside the house as well.

There are many types and styles of doors available to match any architectural design. Entrance doors available include insulated steel doors, laminated wood core doors, fiberglass doors, and solid hardwood doors. Standard style doors are available, as well as French doors and sliding patio doors (Figure 61). Cutouts, sidelights, and top lights are made to be used with any of these styles of doors as well as half-round top and vent windows that can be used with them (Figure 62). Storm doors also are made for use most often in areas where weather conditions are extremely cold and harsh. Prices vary greatly, depending on the construction of the door as well as its special features such as glazing, hardware, locks, etc. Let's review some of the many options available to the homeowner to help eliminate some of the confusion.

Entrance Doors

Insulated steel doors have high energy-efficiency ratings because their polyurethane and polystyrene core acts as an effective insulating material. This type of door also is made with a thermal break to separate the exposed exterior surface of the door from its interior surface. The thermal break prevents the cold outside air from being transferred through the door into the house. This keeps condensation from building up on the interior surface of the door. Insulated steel doors are made with magnetic weatherstripping that seals the door to the magnetic door stop, working in much the same way that a refrigerator door does. The seal prevents drafts and water penetration. An insulated steel door is made as a preassembled unit with an aluminum sill that can be adjusted to seal tightly against the magnetic weatherstripping at the bottom of the door. Locksets and deadbolts are included with these doors when they are purchased. The steel surface is available prefinished, which eliminates the need for painting or staining it, and unfinished so that it can be painted to match the house's color scheme.

Laminated wood core entrance doors are made of cross-banded wood layers glued together to a prescribed thickness. Aluminum vapor barriers cover each side of this wood core, then a hardwood veneer is glued to them so that the door looks like a solid hardwood door. This type of laminated construction virtually eliminates the possibility of the door warping or cracking. These doors are made as prehung units, and they are prefinished with a wood preservative. An aluminum sill is attached to the door unit and a good grade of polymer weatherstripping is installed at the head and on the jambs. This weatherstripping stays flexible, even in cold temperatures, so it seals effectively, allowing very little air filtration through it.

Fiberglass doors are available from several door manufacturers. Pease® Industries Inc., for example, makes what it calls the Ever-Strait® Fiberglass Door System (Figure 63). This prehung door unit is made with a weatherstripped frame, an adjustable sill, and all necessary hardware. The core is made of polystyrene foam, and the door panel is constructed of molded fiberglass that has been reinforced with polyester resin. Wood stiles and rails are installed around the perimeter of the door. The wood grain pattern on the door duplicates that of red oak to give the door a solid hardwood appearance and, as with any such door, it can be painted or stained. Because these doors are made of fiberglass, they are quite weather-resistant and they cannot be damaged

61. This traditional French door has removable wood muntins. Courtesy of the Pella/Rolscreen Company.

62. Natural Wood Gentry™ Double Swing door has extra wide panel stiles and rails. Courtesy of NORCO Windows, Inc.

easily. In fact, any gouges that may occur can be repaired by filling them with fiberglass putty. Surface scratches also can be repaired by refinishing the surface, just as you would any hardwood door. Of course, some scratches do not have to be repaired at all because they are hidden by the natural woodgrain appearance of the door. The adjustable sill and flexible weatherstripping reduce air filtration as well as water penetration.

Solid hardwood doors are available in numerous styles and they can be combined with top lights, sidelights, etched glass and/or wood inserts, and many other design options. These doors usually are made of oak, teak, or mahogany because these species of wood are stable, strong, and beautiful. The finishing process for these doors involves several procedures to help protect the wood from exposure to the weather. Pease, which manufactures solid hardwood doors as well as the fiberglass doors

mentioned above, gives a five-year limited warranty for the finishes on its solid hardwood doors. Pease uses a good quality magnetic weatherstripping on these doors and offers locksets and hinges made of polished brass. The adjustable sill made of solid brass also is available. Pease's adjustable frame design makes the door's installation, as well as any future adjustments that might be necessary, as easy as possible.

Solid wood doors manufactured by the Simpson Door Company are available with arched top windows and sidelights (Figures 64 and 65) as well as with top lights and sidelights. Hand-cut glass is available and it can be beveled, leaded, or etched, depending on the homeowner's preferences. Simpson's doors are made of Douglas fir or Western hemlock, and they can be painted, stained, or coated with a clear finish such as polyurethane. Glass designs of finely carved wood inserts in the doors

63. Ever-Straite Fiberglass Door System. Courtesy of Pease Industries, Inc.

are also available (Figure 66). The glass is ½ inch thick and Low-E glass is an option.

French Doors and Sliding Patio Doors

Sliding patio doors, sliding French doors, and traditional French doors are available from many window and door manufacturers (Figures 67, 68, 69, and 70). These doors are made with unfinished exterior wood surfaces and with aluminum or vinyl cladding on the wood frame. They are made with insulating glass or with double glazing that utilizes the removable glass panel. This removable glass panel is either clear glass or glass with a Low-E coating. Argon gas-filled, Low-E insulating glass also is available in many of these doors. Pella's doors, which are made with a single pane of glass and the removable glass panel, can have a Slimshade, pleated shade, or muntins installed in the air space between them, the same option offered in their windows manufactured using this same construction method. The Slimshade is available with a Low-E, Type E Gold Tone finish that improves the window's energy-efficiency. Andersen's patio and French doors are made with High-Performance insulating glass. The frame is covered with a vinyl cladding, and the doors are treated with a long-lasting preservative. Patio and French doors made by Marvin and NORCO use Argon gas-filled insulating glass with a Low-E coating to make them more energy-efficient.

The traditional French door with true divided lights is available from several manufacturers. The individual panes of glass are made with insulating glass to increase their energy-efficiency as much as possible. Homeowners who are more concerned with security than with the traditional look, which is often why the traditional French door is not chosen, can have French doors that are made with insulating glass and removable mullions. The look is not as true as when individual, divided lights are used, but it is quite similar to it and very attractive. The removable mullions attach to the sashes and they can be snapped out easily when the glass needs to be cleaned.

An insulated steel patio door is available from at least one manufacturer. Pease's door of this type has a galvanized steel skin that resists cracking, splitting, rusting, and warping (Figure 71). A solid slab of polystyrene placed behind the steel skin improves the door's insulating abilities. The door is made with insulating glass, and its frame is made with a thermal break to reduce heat loss through it by conduction.

Choosing an Exterior Door

The homeowner who is in need of a new exterior door should take the time to research the subject since the choices are so numerous and the options so varied. Differences in the cost of similarly sized and styled doors may mean that one door is not as well-insulated as another, or that the type of glazing is very different, or that the locking mechanism is not as burglar-proof as it should be. The price may be low because the core of the door is made of wood particles instead of laminated wood layers or some other type of durable insulating material. A door with a wood veneer on it may be less expensive than another veneered door because it is not made of a hardwood veneer. Warranties and guarantees also vary significantly, so they should be compared by the homeowner very carefully so that he knows exactly what is being covered and for how long.

64 and 65. Mastermark® "Chateau Michelle" series is available with various options of sidelights and transoms. Courtesy of the Simpson Door Company.

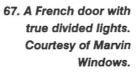

66. "Barclay" insert for the Mastermark Designer Collection series. Courtesy of the Simpson Door Company.

67. A French door with true divided lights. Courtesy of Marvin Windows.

68. *Elliptical transoms are used over this sliding patio door. Courtesy of Marvin Windows.*

69. *Sidelights and an elliptical transom are used with this Marvin terrace door. Courtesy of Marvin Windows.*

70. *A round-top transom gives this terrace door a new look. Photo courtesy of Marvin Windows.*

71. *Ever-Straite side-hinged patio door with Crystal-Etch glass inserts. Courtesy of Pease Industries, Inc.*

Finally, the homeowner has to decide if he will install the door himself or if he will have a contractor or carpenter do it for him. Many of the preassembled door units are fairly easy to install, and the homeowner can do it himself with a little time, patience, and maybe a helper who can lift it with him to set it into place. The homeowner who has practiced on a few interior doors already knows how to deal with leveling it properly and making sure that the locks work correctly. The homeowner who decides he wants a contractor to do the installation for him should compare installation prices by getting several estimates, since these costs also tend to vary significantly. References should be checked and previous work by the contractor examined to be sure that the best professional is chosen to handle the installation. After the door installation has been completed, the homeowner should check to see that the door fits snugly, that its locks operate correctly, and that caulking has been applied generously around its perimeter to prevent water entry and air infiltration. Do not pay the full cost for the job until you are satisfied that it has been done properly so that the door closes snugly and locks correctly.

8
Streetwalks and Driveways

MATERIALS AND THEIR CARE

Streetwalks generally are covered with concrete, while driveways, which may be in use to accommodate one or more families, are either covered with concrete or blacktop. No matter what material is used, it is important to keep it in satisfactory condition to prevent a variety of possible problems from occurring that could lead to costly repairs. Let's review how these materials are applied to understand how to care for them, beginning with the less complicated of the two, the blacktop-covered driveway.

BLACKTOP-COVERED DRIVEWAYS

Blacktop can be applied over the soil in the driveway or over old concrete that has not been allowed to deteriorate. Blacktop is poured while it is hot over the driveway, then it is leveled and compressed with a roller, which may be small enough to be hand-held or large enough to be driven, depending on the size of the project. This work must be done by a contractor since the homeowner is not likely to have the kind of equipment necessary to do this job. Nonetheless, it is the less expensive way to cover a driveway or streetwalk, making it the preferred choice of most homeowners, except those whose local codes require that the coating be made of concrete. A blacktop-covered driveway can be kept in excellent condition for many years by coating it with a blacktop sealer every two years in mild climates or annually in areas where temperature fluctuations

are extreme. The homeowner can apply the sealer himself fairly easily. The best time to do this is when the weather is warm and dry and night-time temperatures do not fall below 50° F. The warm temperatures help to dry the sealer thoroughly and improve the blacktop's ability to resist moisture and frost. The sealer also makes the blacktop more resistant to staining from minor oil and gasoline leaks from cars parked on it. In addition, the sealer protects the blacktop from the deteriorating effects of chemicals used for snow and ice removal during the harsh winter season.

Even if the driveway is given the best possible care, cracks will develop in the blacktop as a result of use and exposure to weather. The size and extent of the cracking will determine if the repairs can be made by the homeowner or if a contractor will have to be hired. Small cracks in the blacktop, for instance, can be filled fairly easily with a good quality blacktop sealer when the entire driveway is being recoated. Large cracks first have to be filled with a blacktop crack filler using a caulking gun, or with a blacktop patching compound using a trowel or a scraping knife. Then the entire driveway can be coated with a good quality blacktop sealer. A driveway in which the blacktop is badly cracked and deteriorated should be recovered completely by an experienced contractor. The best way to choose one is to get estimates from at least three contractors as well as lists of previous customers to check references. The homeowner should look at samples of each contractor's work to see if it was done carefully and if the homeowners are pleased with it, as well as to compare their estimates. The contractor with the most satisfied customers and the neatest work is probably the best choice. Ask the contractor how thick he is going to apply the blacktop. It should be at least 2 to 3 inches thick, and it should be sloped correctly for proper drainage.

Since the reasons for keeping a blacktop-covered driveway in good condition are the same as for a concrete-covered driveway, let's continue with the latter topic where these reasons will be reviewed in detail.

CONCRETE STREETWALKS AND DRIVEWAYS

Unless the homeowner lives in an old city where pieces of slate are used, or in rural communities where soil is left uncovered, most streetwalks and driveways are concrete-covered. For the most part, sidewalks and driveways should be covered with concrete by an experienced contractor because he has the equipment and skill needed to do this work correctly. Still, it is important for the homeowner to know how this work is done so that he can oversee this type of project. This review begins with the basics — the materials used to cover a streetwalk or driveway.

Concrete is a mixture of Portland cement; sand, which is a fine aggregate; gravel, which can be a small or large coarse aggregate; and water. The aggregates add strength to the mixture while helping to minimize shrinking and cracking during the curing process. Water is added to enable the cement to bind the aggregates together in the mixture. Portland cement is available in 94-pound bags, each containing 1 cubic foot of cement. The American Society of Testing Materials (ASTM) categorizes the types of Portland cement that are available to distinguish them for their various uses. Type I, which is used for most home construction purposes such as foundations, driveways, and streetwalks, is indicated as such on the bag in which it is packaged.

The components of a concrete mixture have to be combined in correct proportions to each other for the mixture to be strong and durable after it has cured. For example, if too much water is added to the mixture, the concrete will be weakened consid-erably. A mixture of cement and water without aggregates also is a weak one because the chemical reaction that occurs when the aggregates are mixed with the cement and water cannot take place. During this reaction, which is called hydration, some of the water actually becomes part of the bonding process.

In addition to using the correct proportions of the components, temperature and humidity levels also affect the curing process. The best conditions for pouring concrete exist when the outdoor temperature is between 70 and 80° F and the relative humidity is more than 80%. The concrete's strength increases sharply during the first several days of drying. If the humidity goes below 80%, the moisture on the surface of the concrete will evaporate more quickly than the internal moisture. This causes shrinking cracks to develop on the surface of the concrete. By the same token, if the concrete is allowed to set too slowly, as it would at outside temperatures below 50° F, hydration will be slowed and the strength of the concrete diminished. For this reason, a special additive that helps concrete to set quickly is put into the mixture when concrete is poured in temperatures below 50°. The best way to avoid this problem is to have concrete repair and replacement projects done during the late spring, summer, and early fall when temperatures and humidity levels are ideal.

There are several steps involved in paving a concrete driveway or streetwalk, and each involves the use of special equipment as well as a great deal of labor and skill. If the job is a replacement project, then the contractor will first have to break the old concrete into small pieces that can be carted away. Large chunks of concrete are broken into smaller pieces with an electric demolition hammer while smaller pieces are broken with a sledgehammer. The debris is carried in wheelbarrows, or with a mechanical arm when the project is extensive, and placed in a dumpster. Generally, a permit must be obtained from the city or town for the dumpster and a fee is required for the permit. Often the contractor also has to pay a fee to rent the dumpster since it may not be owned by the contractor's firm. After the old concrete has been removed, and also when there is no need to remove any old concrete, the soil is compressed thoroughly. Wire mesh reinforcement is installed for strengthening the concrete, and expansion

expansion joints are used to partition off sections of the concrete as it is poured as well as to prevent the concrete from cracking as it expands and contracts during seasonal temperature fluctuations.

Large contractors rarely, if ever, mix the concrete themselves whether or not the project is large or small because mixing it is tedious and time-consuming. This eliminates the need to store the materials; storage can be difficult since the Portland cement must be kept dry to prevent it from hardening. The premixed concrete is delivered to the job site in a truck. In most applications, it is taken directly from the truck to the area being covered. When a long, narrow driveway is being recovered, the concrete is poured into wheelbarrows and brought to the farthest point from it, gradually filling the space with the concrete mixture. As this is being done, other workers level the concrete and slope it so that rainwater can flow into the area drain or toward the street. All of the work must be done as quickly as possible since there is a limited amount of time to pour, level, slope, and float the concrete before the curing process starts. Speed also may be necessary because the truck driver has other deliveries to make that same day and cannot afford to waste time at one location. The concrete is floated the first time when it is poured. As the concrete sets, the water on the surface dehydrates; that is, it evaporates from the surface into the air. The concrete is floated again with a wooden trowel to give it texture, which prevents its surface from being slippery after it has dried. During the first few days, while it is still curing, the surface is kept moist to assist the concrete in reaching its greatest possible strength.

To keep the concrete in good condition for many years, the homeowner should make a habit of repairing any damage in it as quickly as possible. Small cracks can be handled easily by the homeowner. Small cracks can be filled with concrete patching mixtures available in tubes for use in typical caulking guns. Minor damage in sections of the concrete can be patched after all loose debris has been removed by using ready-mix concrete available in bags, premixed patching cement available in plastic containers, or by mixing a few bags of concrete. When cracks are large and numerous and damage involves several sections of concrete or even a total replacement, then a contractor should be hired. As with the blacktop contractor, the homeowner

should get several estimates and check the contractor's previous clients to see if his work has been done satisfactorily. Hire the contractor who is knowledgeable and reliable, not the one who is only the least expensive. There are more important things to consider than price and the next section talks about some of them.

PROBLEMS CAUSED BY DAMAGED STREETWALKS AND DRIVEWAYS

Whether they are blacktop or concrete-covered, streetwalks and driveways should be examined regularly since minor problems can lead to major costs. Because most of the damage is caused by cold temperatures and freezing conditions, it is best to look for cracking and other damage in the spring. Minor cracks in streetwalks may have widened during the winter as water got into them, froze, and enlarged them. Water also can undermine one or even several sections of concrete because it moves the soil under them or sweeps it completely away. During the winter, water that pools on these uneven sections of streetwalk freezes, creating a hazard for passersby. And as the freeze/thaw cycle repeats itself, sections of the streetwalk are lifted, creating a year-round tripping hazard for pedestrians. This type of tripping hazard also can be caused by tree roots. As the roots grow, they push up sections of the streetwalk and create another opportunity for soil erosion under them. The only way to correct this problem effectively is to remove the uneven sections of concrete and replace them with new ones.

One homeowner who had a seepage problem in his basement was surprised to discover that its origin was in the driveway. This homeowner had undertaken many fruitless efforts to resolve this problem, some quite expensive, but nothing worked. Finally a careful examination of the slope of his concrete driveway revealed the source of the water. First, the slope of the concrete had been altered so that rainwater in the driveway was draining toward his house instead of out into the street. Second, a space had opened between the wall and the concrete. Mastic had been applied to fill the space but it, too, had separated from the wall, leaving an opening for water to enter into the soil near his foundation wall. Cracks that developed in the foundation wall as it

72. Section of party driveway showing correct and incorrect driveway slope

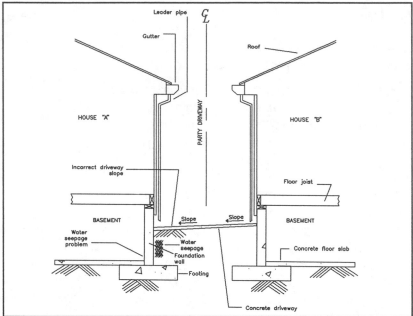

aged had allowed water to seep into his basement (Figure 72). Another homeowner who had this same problem found as much as an inch of water in his basement along 20 feet of his basement's floor.

Unfortunately for both of these homeowners, the only solution to this problem is a costly one because the concrete driveway has to be replaced. This replacement must be done as quickly as possible to prevent further damage to the structure of the house as well as to the basement. In addition, this work must be done by a professional because it may involve excavation of the soil down to the footing if the foundation wall needs to be waterproofed. In fact, any work that involves excavation around a foundation wall and footing must be done by a professional because if it is done improperly, the wall, footing, or both may be disturbed or, worse, undermined. When this type of work is going to be done in a party driveway, that is, one that is used by two or more homeowners, it should not be started until everyone who uses the driveway has been informed and given sufficient time to make alternative plans for parking. Since costs may have to be shared, all parties should be in agreement as to who will be hired to do the work and what it will cost before the work begins. If a right of easement is involved, costs also will have to be shared, so work should not begin until both homeowners have agreed to its cost and timetable.

A seemingly unrelated maintenance item — keeping the downspout and drain line clear — also can cause problems in the concrete driveway and streetwalk. One homeowner decided to remove the downspout from the drain line at the side of his house when a blockage in the drain line was causing water to back up in it. He didn't bother to clear the blockage which had developed as dead leaves and granules from the roof covering collected in it. He figured it was easier to let the water drain onto the driveway, so he extended the downspout almost to grade level and let it go at that. He got away with his scheme all summer, but when winter arrived, it backfired. The water draining from the downspout froze on the driveway and streetwalk. There was so much ice on the streetwalk that at one point passersby had to walk into the street to avoid it. The homeowner realized that he had to do something right away, so he put lots of rock salt on the ice to melt it, which it did, but it also destroyed the concrete under it. The outcome was that this homeowner not only had to clear the blockage in the drain pipe, he had to have the downspout replaced and put back into the drain line as well as have sections of the driveway and streetwalk repaired. Had he simply cleared the blockage, a process explained earlier in this section in the chapter on gutters, he could have avoided a costly repair project. The rule of thumb to remember here is to keep up with little repairs so that they do not become big and expensive ones.

PART III
Examining Interior Components of a House

9
How a House is Built

THE KNOWLEDGEABLE HOMEOWNER

As you begin reading this, you may wonder why you need to know so much about how a house is built. After all, you do not intend to build one by yourself and, as a homeowner, why should you care how the roof holds up so long as it does? But for a homeowner, ignorance, as they say, is not bliss. The footings, foundation, sill plate, main beam, roof framing, etc., are components of a house subject to lots of possible problems that only the knowledgeable homeowner can foresee and resolve. In addition, as the homeowner decides to alter his house, understanding how it is built can only make any additions or renovations effective without causing other problems to arise. A house is a very complex structure that needs proper understanding and care to make it enjoyable while providing one of the basic needs of humankind — shelter. Let's begin at the beginning, the base of the structure.

THE STRUCTURAL BASE OF A HOUSE

There are several ways to build a house, and the choice depends largely on cost as well as the climate in which the house is being built. The frame of the house either rests on foundation walls and footings or on a concrete slab. In areas where there is no problem with frost, a thickened-edge concrete slab can be constructed without independent footings or foundation walls (Figure 73). In a frost area, independent footings and foundation walls are needed before a slab can be constructed. In a frost area, the concrete slab is constructed separately from the footings and foundation walls (Figure 74). The framing of the house is built on the foundation walls. Although most of this work is not visible once the house's construction has been completed, it is a good idea for the homeowner to know something about it since problems can arise from the footings, foundation walls, and the slab as the house is subjected to constant use. The following description of all facets of home construction, therefore, also explains how and where problems may arise and how to deal with them if they do.

Construction of the Footings
The framing of the house rests on its foundation walls. These walls transmit the loading of the house down to its footings. The loading includes the weight of the structure, its furnishings, and its inhabitants as well as such factors as the wind load, snow load, etc. Local and state building codes dictate how the footing has to be designed. The size and depth of the footing are determined by the locality's frost line as well as by results from tests for soil content and water absorption levels. The soils test, or soil analysis as it is called, determines the composition of the soil, which in turn determines its allowable bearing pressure. The allowable bearing pressure of the soil tells the architect and builder how much load can be borne safely on top of the soil at the building site. When the allowable bearing

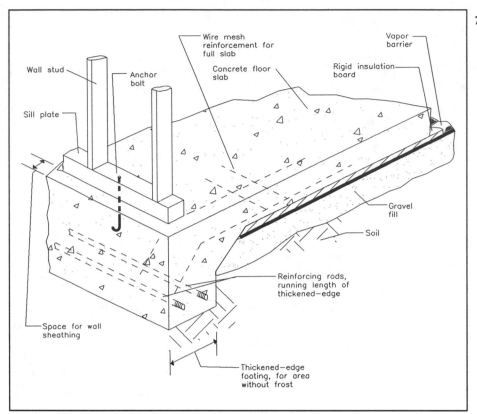

73. Thickened-edge floor slab

Wall stud

Anchor bolt

Sill plate

Wire mesh reinforcement for full slab

Concrete floor slab

Rigid insulation board

Vapor barrier

Gravel fill

Soil

Reinforcing rods, running length of thickened—edge

Space for wall sheathing

Thickened—edge footing, for area without frost

74. Concrete slab detail for frost penetration

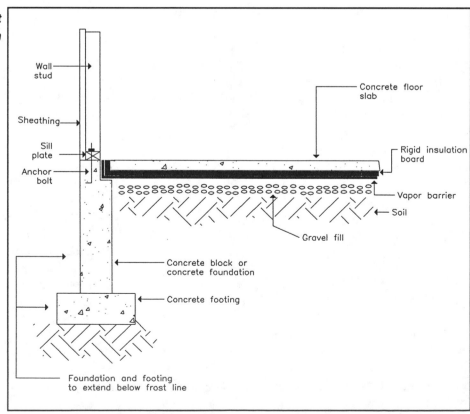

Wall stud

Sheathing

Sill plate

Anchor bolt

Concrete floor slab

Rigid insulation board

Vapor barrier

Soil

Gravel fill

Concrete block or concrete foundation

Concrete footing

Foundation and footing to extend below frost line

pressure is low, the size of the footing is increased to distribute the load of the house over a greater bearing area of the soil. Clay and sandy soils have lower allowable bearing pressures than soils that are more compacted such as those consisting of sand and gravel mixtures, all rock, or rock, shale, and limestone mixtures.

Another factor that must be considered when sizing the footing is what is called the percolation rate, which is an indication of how well the soil absorbs water. The percolation test, which is conducted to determine the percolation rate, is important because if the soil cannot absorb water fairly rapidly at the building site, then the house's footings and foundation walls will remain wet, or even worse, the water will damage them as it collects near them over an extended period of time.

Since the footing is the house's first key structural element, it must not be undersized. If it is undersized, it will not be able to support the weight of the house, and the footing will fail. The structural damage resulting from its failure will cause damage in the foundation wall and wood framing, which could lead to further damage of other structural components such as the roof, interior and exterior walls, etc. When the damage is due to the allowable bearing pressure of the soil, settlement or a partial failure of the structure can occur. Settlement also can occur when the soil below the footing was not compacted tightly before the footing was constructed on top of it. This type of settlement can continue for years, stopping only when the soil below the footing has compacted completely. Cracks caused by this condition appear in the foundation walls, and they will enlarge as time passes. Cracks caused by settlement usually are wider than 1/8", and they run vertically on the foundation walls. These types of cracks also are wider at the top of the wall. Eventually floors will slope, doors and windows will not close snugly, staircases will slope, and cracks will develop in the exterior wall coverings. If the condition is allowed to become severe, damage will occur in the framing members.

A house built in an area where the clay content in the soil is high also can have problems with settlement cracks. This type of soil expands as it becomes wet, and as it does so, it pushes the footing upward. When this happens, a licensed contractor has to be hired to correct the problem. The contractor hired should be one who is experienced in underpinning footings that have failed. The footing has to be reinforced to stop the house from settling further. Bear in mind that almost all houses settle to some degree. As a result, some minor hairline cracks will be visible in the foundation walls.

The construction of the footings and foundation walls begins with the excavation of the building site. The outline of the footing most often is set up by using forms that are braced to withstand the lateral load of the concrete as it settles in them. Sometimes the forms are not used and, instead, trenches are dug to outline the perimeter of the footing. Naturally the footings are constructed better when forms are used instead of trenches. The forms are set into place to comply with the design of the footing in terms of its depth and width. Then reinforcing steel rods are installed in the forms and the concrete is poured into them. The steel rods are used because they increase the strength of the concrete. The concrete is poured so that a slot, or key way as it is called, is created on top of the footings. This key way acts as a locking point for the foundation wall when the concrete is poured on top of the footing. The concrete footings are given sufficient time to harden, or cure, usually a couple of days, so that they can accept the weight of the foundation walls on them without being damaged by it. After the footings have hardened sufficiently, the forms are removed and work on the foundation walls can begin.

Construction of the Foundation Walls

The foundation walls, which rest on the footings, are constructed with concrete or concrete blocks. Bricks and rubble were used to build the foundation walls in old houses; today concrete and concrete blocks are preferred. A concrete foundation wall for a one- or two-family house generally is about 12 inches thick, while block foundation walls can vary up to 12 inches in thickness. Old brick foundation walls were constructed with a number of courses of bricks, while rubble foundation walls in very old buildings were built an average of 12 to 16 inches thick. Naturally, these figures vary, depending on local and state building code requirements for foundation wall construction.

Concrete foundation walls also are built with forms,

usually wood forms, which are used to outline the shape of the house. Depending on local building codes, reinforcing steel rods also are put into place in the forms to increase the concrete's strength after it has dried. Once the form work has been completed, the concrete is poured and anchor bolts are set into place at the top of the foundation walls. The sill plate is attached to the foundation wall with the use of these anchor bolts, after the foundation walls have dried. The forms are removed after the foundation walls have cured completely. Then the foundation walls are coated with a waterproofer on the exterior side to prevent seepage into the house. In areas where termite infestation is fairly common, the soil around the foundation walls and footings can be treated with a termite-repellent chemical before the soil is backfilled; that is, before it is put back up against the foundation walls. This termite treatment must be done by a certified professional. This treatment should not be done, however, if exposure to the treated soil will be harmful to the workmen at the building site. Before the backfilling is done, waterproof rigid insulation boards can be installed on the exterior side of the foundation walls to increase the house's insulating value and prevent water entry.

It is important to give the foundation walls sufficient time to cure because if this step is rushed, problems will arise later. One homeowner learned about this problem after he bought a house that had a crack in the foundation wall near the sill plate. The crack ran down from the top of the foundation wall for approximately 2 feet. Water was working its way into the basement through this opening. The seepage in the basement had alerted the homeowner to look for a problem. He was told that the crack had occurred because the foundation wall had not been given sufficient time to cure before framing began. The weight of the framing had damaged the uncured concrete foundation wall. Luckily for this homeowner, damage to the wall and basement was only minor, and he was able to have it fixed fairly easily and inexpensively. Once the water stopped seeping into the basement, it dried out completely, leaving behind no evidence of significant damage.

Horizontal cracks and bulging in the foundation walls are other indications that there is a problem that needs to be resolved. These cracks may be caused by lateral pressure from soil with a high clay content, as discussed previously in the section on footings. When the wall in the area of the cracking is not level, then there is a structural problem, specifically, the wall is not able to support the weight of the structure adequately. To determine the exact cause of these types of problems, it is best for the homeowner to hire an engineer or contractor who is knowledgeable about this type of work and can advise the homeowner on how to proceed in order to correct it.

Of course, not all cracks in the foundation walls are indications to the homeowner that he has a serious problem. One homeowner, for instance, was told by his siding contractor that there was a crack in the foundation wall and he should get an engineer to look at it before it got worse. When the engineer examined the crack, he found that it was a minor one. Indeed, the engineer speculated that it had been caused by the siding contractor himself during the installation of the siding to the exposed foundation wall. A simple repair by the contractor was all that had to be done to resolve this homeowner's problem.

Constructing Concrete Block Foundation Walls

Since a concrete block foundation wall does not need form work, blocks can be laid on top of the footing as soon as the footing has cured sufficiently. Concrete blocks are made of a mixture of Portland cement, fine aggregate, and water. They are readily available and not very expensive. Although there are many sizes available, the standard size used in foundation wall construction is about 8 inches high, 10 or 12 inches wide, and 16 inches long. The finished sizes vary during the manufacturing process, so mortar is used to make up for the differences in them as construction of the block foundation wall proceeds. Many types of mortar are available, packaged in bags. They are used in different applications because they have varying strengths. Type M has the highest allowable compressive strength, followed in descending order of strength by Types S, N, and O. Generally, Type N is used for block wall construction. When there is a loading or moisture problem, usually Type M is recommended. The Type M, S, N, or O designation is printed on the bag for easy identification.

The footing for a block foundation wall usually is

75 and 76. Application of Waterplug® is used to stop seepage in the basement around the perimeter of the concrete floor slab. Courtesy of Thoro System Products.

double the thickness of the wall. The thickness of a foundation wall for a house with a brick veneer exterior, however, is reduced near the top to provide space for, or act as a seat for, the brick veneer (see Figure 38 on page 56). Both concrete and concrete blocks have adequate compressive strength; however, the ability of walls made of concrete blocks to withstand expansive loading is less than that of walls made of solid concrete. Expansive loads are typical of those caused by soil with a high clay content that expands when it becomes wet. This expansive load acts as a lateral or sideward force against the concrete blocks.

The voids in the blocks at the top course of a block foundation wall are filled with concrete, which also is used to hold the anchor bolts in place. Again, these anchor bolts are used to attach the sill plate to the top of the foundation wall. The bolts must be set firmly into the concrete so that they cannot pull out of it when the sill plate is attached to them. The sizing, length, and spacing of the anchor bolts are determined by local and state building codes. After the foundation walls have been constructed, the exterior sides of the block walls should be coated with a waterproofer using materials specified by the architect in the plans.

A house with concrete block foundation walls is as vulnerable to dampness and seepage problems as one built with solid concrete foundation walls. These problems can be caused by a crack or other opening in the waterproof coating on the wall, or by a structural crack in the foundation wall itself. An effective way to prevent seepage and to seal out dampness is to use a waterproofing product such as Thoroseal®. Thoroseal is a cement-based, aggregate type of heavy-duty waterproofing that can be used on interior and exterior walls such as foundation walls, basement walls, and brick, block, stucco, and concrete walls. Thoro System Products also makes Thoro Waterplug® (Figures 75 and 76) to be used in combination with Thoroseal. This cement-based, quick-set hydraulic compound instantly stops running water or seepage in concrete or masonry walls and floors. Cracks, open joints, and holes can be repaired in this manner, even when there is an active water leak. If the Waterplug application does not solve the problem, then the wall will have to be excavated on the exterior side and repaired with Thoroseal Foundation Coating®. This cement-based, heavy-duty coating is designed to waterproof exterior concrete and masonry foundation walls below grade. Thoroseal also can be used in this application (Figure 77). Thoro System Products provides detailed instructions for the use of its products so that they are effective when they are applied. Thoro also makes a number of other products for various waterproofing applications as well as some that add a decorative finish to a concrete or masonry surface.

Owens/Corning also makes waterproofing products

77. Thoroseal can be applied to the foundation walls below grade. Courtesy of Thoro System Products.

for exterior concrete and concrete block foundation walls. Called the Tuff-N-Dri® waterproofing system, it consists of two components (Figures 78 and 79). The membrane, a polymer-modified asphalt, provides a highly elastomeric, monolithic waterproof covering when applied to concrete walls. Warm-N-Dri® board, a semi-rigid product made of fiberglass insulation, keeps water from building up near the foundation walls. This board also increases the insulating value to the foundation walls while it protects the membrane during construction and backfilling.

Installing Drain Tiles Around the Foundation

Drain tiles are installed around foundations in today's home construction to prevent water entry through the concrete or concrete block foundation walls. In fact, many local and state building codes currently require their installation. Drain tiles actually are perforated pipes that are placed along the perimeter of the foundation to carry water away from it. They are installed during the initial stages of construction, placed below the foundation wall and above the bottom of the footing (Figure 80). These perforated pipes collect the water and carry it away from the house.

The installation of drain tiles starts with a layer of gravel or crushed stones that is put around the perimeter of the foundation, right next to the wall. The drain tiles are then laid in this bed of gravel or stones so that the bottom of the drain tile is higher than the bottom of the footing. If it is not placed in

its proper position, the water will not drain correctly. After the tiles have been set in place, a cloth material, which allows water to filter through it, is laid over the tiles. This cloth prevents the soil from clogging the holes in the drain tiles. Another layer of gravel or crushed stones is put on top of the cloth that is covering the tiles. As the water collects in the perforated pipes, it drains into a sump pit and then is carried through piping up to grade level and into the soil or sewer system. Water from a sump pit should not be drained into a septic system because the system was not designed to handle it, and because many local building codes do not permit it.

In some houses, the drain tiles are installed inside the foundation walls, placed just below the concrete floor slab. The slab usually is 4 inches thick, and it is reinforced with wire mesh. Again, the drain tiles are placed on a layer of gravel or crushed stones. Small drain tiles are branched into the main drain tile at equal distances on center through the foundation walls at the bottom of the first course of block. Rainwater drains into these smaller drain tiles on the outside of the foundation walls, then into the main drain tile under the slab in the basement. From there, it is carried to a sump pit where it is pumped to grade level and drains into the soil or sewer system. The concrete floor slab is not poured until this drain tile system has been put into place.

Backfilling Around the Foundation Walls

Backfilling the soil around the foundation walls has to be done at the correct moment as well as in the proper way. Backfilling must be done carefully to prevent the foundation walls from cracking as a result of this procedure. Often a builder will frame the first floor level of the house before he starts to backfill the soil around its foundation walls. The weight of the framing helps to support the foundation walls and to prevent them from cracking while the backfilling is being done. The soil placed around the foundation walls also is compacted tightly to eliminate any voids that may be left in it.

Thickened-edge Concrete Slab Construction

As noted earlier in this section, houses in areas where there is no problem with frost are built on a thickened-edge concrete slab. This home building technique also is preferable when the water table in

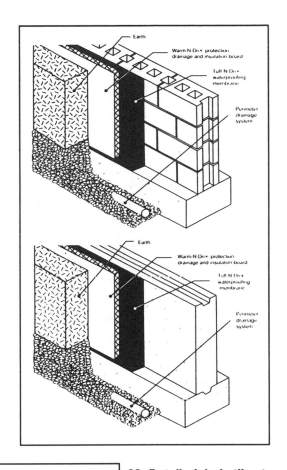

78 and 79. Tuff-N-Dri® waterproofing system is applied in two steps for best results. Courtesy of the Owens-Corning Fiberglas Corp.

80. Detail of drain tile at footing of house

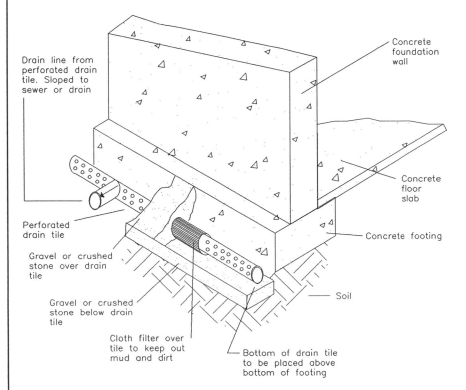

Drain line from perforated drain tile. Sloped to sewer or drain

Perforated drain tile

Gravel or crushed stone over drain tile

Gravel or crushed stone below drain tile

Cloth filter over tile to keep out mud and dirt

Bottom of drain tile to be placed above bottom of footing

Concrete foundation wall

Concrete floor slab

Concrete footing

Soil

the area is high, or when construction costs need to be lowered. The cost of construction is decreased because a full excavation of the building site is not necessary since a house of this type does not have a basement or cellar as part of its final design.

A thickened-edge concrete slab for a house is built directly on top of the soil. Since the climate in the area where the house is being built is mild, the footing for the slab is part of it and it is thicker than the slab itself to be able to support the bearing load of the house that is going to be built on top of it. The footing is approximately 12 inches to 2 feet below grade level (see Figure 73 on page 94). The concrete slab, however, is higher than the surrounding soil to prevent water from entering the house as it drains off the soil. The grade also is sloped away from the house to provide for a natural runoff away from it.

All plumbing and electrical lines have to be installed before the concrete is poured, which means that they also have to be inspected to be sure they are connected properly and are in satisfactory condition. Any damages that have to be repaired, or design changes or alterations that have to be made, must be done before the concrete is poured because any of this work will be costly after it has been poured. To alleviate this situation to some extent, the electrical and plumbing lines sometimes are installed in a form and the concrete is poured around it, leaving a hollow space around the lines. This type of installation provides better access to the plumbing and electrical lines; however, repairs to them are still not easy or simple to do.

The concrete for a thickened-edge slab cannot be poured until the soil at the building site has been prepared properly. The soil is compacted first to eliminate voids from it that could cause settlement cracking later during the building process. Trenches are dug for the footings around the perimeter of the slab. A layer of crushed stones is placed on top of the soil, and a vapor barrier is laid over the stones. This vapor barrier prevents dampness from collecting under the slab and coming up through it. At the very least, this dampness can create a musty smell in the house. At most it could cause carpeting, prefinished flooring, or vinyl tiles to loosen, if they were installed with an adhesive that is not waterproof. In some cases, waterproof rigid insulation also is installed on top of the vapor barrier. This rigid insulation prevents the coldness in the ground from being transmitted through the concrete slab. In this way, it increases the comfort level in the house. Wire mesh is installed on top of the rigid insulation to strengthen the concrete. The finished slab has to be fairly level and free of holes, bumps, or bulges.

Because concrete slabs have had a history of cracking as they are subjected to constant use, technological advances have come up with a way to enhance the slab's ability to resist cracking. Fibermesh polypropylene fibers are added to the concrete mixture before it is poured. These fibers increase the strength of the concrete, making it more resistant to cracking.

With the footings and foundation walls or concrete slab in place, cured, waterproofed, and insulated, it is time to proceed to the next step in residential construction, the framing. Again, a review of this process reveals where potential problems exist and how they can be resolved.

THE FRAMING OF A HOUSE

The framing of a house is the structure that transmits the combined loadings in and on the house to the foundation walls and footings. When the house is designed, the framing is sized so that it is able to carry specific loads. It is also sized to accommodate the length that certain wood or steel members span between the foundation walls or between any intermediate supporting members. The Certificate of Occupancy, which is issued for each house by the local buildings department, lists the type of loading its framing is designed to support; specifically, the live and dead load requirements, as they are called. The live load includes the weight of the furnishings as well as the weight of the inhabitants of the house. It also might include such factors as the weight of snow that accumulates on the roof during the winter. The dead load includes the weight of the structure such as the framing, interior partitions, ceilings, etc.

Species and Grades of Framing Lumber
The framing of a house is a combination of various sizes of lumber installed for different purposes. Wood studs used for the construction of walls vary

81 and 82. Typical applications of plywood roof sheathing and plywood wall sheathing. Courtesy of the American Plywood Association.

in sizes ranging from 2" x 3" to 2" x 6". Floor and ceiling joists, depending on the size of the house, generally vary from 2" x 8" to 2" x 12". The sill plate varies from a single 4" x 6" wood member to two 2" x 4" wood studs that are nailed to each other. Roof rafters, again depending on the size of the house, usually vary from 2" x 6" to 2" x 12" wood members. The sheathing is made of 4' x 8' sheets of plywood or strand board that are nailed to the roof, floors, and walls. The sheathing varies in thickness from 1/2" to 3/4" (Figures 81 and 82). The plywood sheets also vary in grade, and they are manufactured specifically for interior or exterior uses. Plywood sheets used for exterior applications are made with a water-resistant adhesive to protect them from rain, snow, and other wet weather conditions. The grade stamps on all lumber and plywood products indicate whether or not the wood is kiln-dry, its moisture content and, in the case of plywood, the type of allowable exposure and its thickness, among other specifications (Figure 83).

As the construction of houses continued through the years, the species and grades of wood used for framing changed. Houses that were built a century or more ago were framed with longleaf heart pine and Douglas fir (see additional information about these and other species in Chapter 17). Longleaf

heart pine is not used for framing today because it was deforested years ago. Since current climatic conditions in the United States make it impossible for longleaf heart pine to grow, it is mostly available in remilled forms that are beautiful but not inexpensive. Although Douglas fir is still used in some areas of the country, it is not preferred for framing, even though it is stronger than most species available, because it is more expensive than these other species. In some parts of the country, Douglas fir has been replaced as a framing material with such species as Southern yellow pine, hemlock, and hem fir. Years ago, the No. 1 grade of framing lumber was used for residential construction. Today, both the No. 1 and No. 2 grades are used for framing a house. The No. 1 grade is stronger than the No. 2 grade. The homeowner who can see the floor joists by viewing them from his basement will be able to take note of the grade stamp on them. The grade stamp indicates the grading number, species, whether or not the wood has been kiln-dried, and other pertinent information (Figure 84).

Wood and wood sheathing materials used for framing a house are kiln-dried to specific moisture contents to make them suitable for this type of use. After it has been kiln-dried, it can absorb moisture, especially when a building site has a higher moisture

GUIDE TO APA PERFORMANCE RATED PANELS Trademarks Shown Are Typical Facsimiles

APA RATED SHEATHING

Specially designed for subflooring, wall sheathing and roof sheathing, but also used for broad range of other construction, industrial and do-it-yourself applications. Can be manufactured as conventional plywood, as a composite, or as a nonveneer panel. SPAN RATINGS: 16/0, 20/0, 24/0, 24/16, 32/16, 40/20, 48/24. EXPOSURE DURABILITY CLASSIFICATIONS: Exterior, Exposure 1, Exposure 2. COMMON THICKNESSES: 5/16, 3/8, 7/16, 15/32, 1/2, 19/32, 5/8, 23/32, 3/4.

APA RATED STURD-I-FLOOR

Specially designed as combination subfloor-underlayment. Provides smooth surface for application of carpet and possesses high concentrated and impact load resistance. Can be manufactured as conventional plywood, as a composite, or as a nonveneer panel. Available square edge or tongue-and-groove. SPAN RATINGS: 16, 20, 24, 32, 48. EXPOSURE DURABILITY CLASSIFICATIONS: Exterior, Exposure 1, Exposure 2. COMMON THICKNESSES: 19/32, 5/8, 23/32, 3/4, 1-1/8.

APA STRUCTURAL I RATED SHEATHING

Unsanded grade for use where cross-panel strength and stiffness or shear properties are of maximum importance, such as panelized roofs, diaphragms and shear walls. Can be manufactured as conventional plywood, as a composite, or as a nonveneer panel. All plies in Structural I plywood panels are special improved grades and panels marked PS 1 are limited to Group 1 species. (Structural II plywood panels are also provided for, but rarely manufactured. Application recommendations for Structural II plywood are identical to those for APA RATED SHEATHING plywood.) SPAN RATINGS: 20/0, 24/0, 24/16, 32/16, 40/20, 48/24. EXPOSURE DURABILITY CLASSIFICATIONS: Exterior, Exposure 1. COMMON THICKNESSES: 5/16, 3/8, 7/16, 15/32, 1/2, 19/32, 5/8, 23/32, 3/4.

APA RATED SIDING

For exterior siding, fencing, etc. Can be manufactured as conventional veneered plywood, as a composite or as a nonveneer siding. Both panel and lap siding available. Special surface treatment such as V-groove, channel groove, deep groove (such as APA Texture 1-11), brushed, rough sawn and texture-embossed (MDO). Span Rating (stud spacing for siding qualified for APA Sturd-I-Wall applications) and face grade classification (for veneer-faced siding) indicated in trademark. EXPOSURE DURABILITY CLASSIFICATION: Exterior. COMMON THICK-NESSES: 11/32, 3/8, 15/32, 1/2, 19/32, 5/8.

NOTE: Specify Performance Rated Panels by thickness and Span Rating. Span Ratings are based on panel strength and stiffness. Since these properties are a function of panel composition and configuration as well as thickness, the same Span Rating may appear on panels of different thicknesses. Similarly, panels of the same thickness may be marked with different Span Ratings.

83. Grading Facsimiles. Courtesy of the American Plywood Association.

84. Facsimiles of Grade Stamps. Courtesy of the Western Wood Products Association.

a. WWPA certification mark. Certifies Association quality supervision. Ⓦ is a registered trademark.

b. Mill identification. Firm name, brand or assigned mill number. A list of mills, by number, is available from WWPA offices.

c. Grade designation. Grade name, number or abbreviation.

d. Species identification. Indicates species by individual species or species combination.

e. Condition of seasoning. Indicates condition of seasoning at time of surfacing:

S-DRY — 19% maximum moisture content
MC-15 — 15% maximum moisture content
S-GRN — over 19% moisture content (unseasoned)

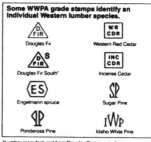

Some WWPA grade stamps identify an individual Western lumber species.

Douglas Fir	Western Red Cedar
Douglas Fir South*	Incense Cedar
Engelmann spruce	Sugar Pine
Ponderosa Pine	Idaho White Pine

*Lumber manufactured from Douglas Fir grown in Arizona, Colorado, New Mexico and Utah.

Dimension Grades

Decking

level than that of the wood. Conversely, if the moisture level at the building site is less than that of the wood, then the wood's moisture content will decrease further. All wood, whether it is used for framing or any other application, expands or contracts as it absorbs or releases moisture. It is possible to hear wood expanding or contracting as its moisture level changes, such as during the heating season when the moisture in a house decreases and during the summer when there is particularly high humidity in the air.

When a great deal of moisture is absorbed by the wood, it twists, cups, or bows. This occurs most frequently in wood flooring. Unfortunately, the only way to correct this problem is to remove the distorted wood members and replace them with new wood flooring, which is a difficult and expensive project. One homeowner encountered this situation shortly after the installation of a new hardwood floor in his newly constructed house. Only a week after the flooring had been installed, sections of it cupped badly. An investigation into how the hardwood flooring was stored revealed what had happened. Prior to its installation, the flooring had been stored in a damp exterior garage, where it was able to absorb moisture. After the flooring was installed, the heating system in the house was turned on and the excess moisture in the wood flooring dried, cupping sections of it. In this particular case, the cupping was so extensive that sections of the tongue and groove joints actually had separated. The flooring should have been stored in the house while the heating system was operating before it was installed to allow the wood to acclimate itself to the conditions in the house. That is why it is important to store all wood materials appropriately at the construction site, especially flooring and paneling products. Once the wood has had time to acclimate itself to conditions at the construction site, problems due to changes in temperature and humidity levels can be avoided.

Installing the Sill Plate

The first wood member installed to begin framing a house is called the sill plate. It is attached to the foundation wall with anchor bolts and nuts. The size of the sill plate in today's home construction is smaller than it used to be in houses built fifty or more years ago. In addition, the type of wood used for today's sill plate either is pressure-treated pine, or for more expensive houses, redwood. This is an improvement over what was used because the pressure-treated pine and redwood are more rot- and insect-resistant than other species that were used years ago, with the exception of heart pine. Improved house construction techniques also have introduced the placement of a thin layer of insulation between the bottom of the sill plate and the top of the foundation wall before the sill plate is anchored to the wall. This insulation prevents drafts from coming into the house from under the sill plate. After the sill plate has been attached to the foundation walls, the floor joists, rim header, and stud walls arc installcd, as wcll as thc floor and wall sheathing. The order in which these framing procedures are done depends on which type of house construction is being used, either balloon-frame or platform-frame construction.

House Framing Techniques

Most houses built before 1940 were constructed using the balloon-frame construction technique (Figure 85). In a balloon-frame-constructed house, long 2" x 4" wall studs are attached directly to the sill plate. These wall studs run continuously up to the highest level of the house. The floor joists are attached to the sill plate and to the side of the wall studs. Since plywood was not available at that time, 1" x 4" and 1" x 6" tongue and groove pine boards were used as wall sheathing. These boards were nailed to the wall studs after the studs had been put into place. Also, 1" x 3" and 1" x 4" slats were nailed directly to the floor joists to function as floor sheathing. Today plywood, plywood compositions, and waffle-board are used as wall and floor sheathings. Since fire codes for residential construction were not as rigid as they are today, much less fire-stopping was installed in a balloon-frame-constructed house than is put into today's houses using modern construction techniques.

Residential construction done after 1940 and to the present uses the platform-frame construction technique (Figure 86). With this method of framing, once the sill plate has been attached to the foundation wall, the floor joists are nailed to it. Then the rim joist, which is put around the perimeter of the house, is nailed to the sill plate and floor joists. After this procedure has been completed, the floor

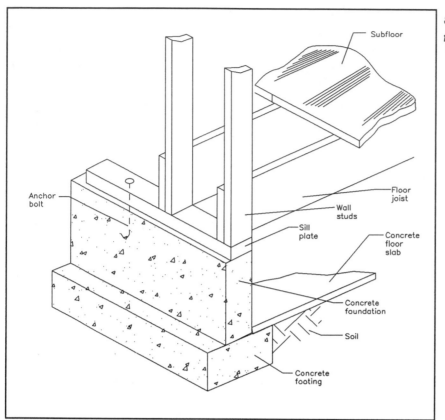

85. Balloon-frame construction, first floor framing

Subfloor

Anchor bolt

Floor joist

Wall studs

Sill plate

Concrete floor slab

Concrete foundation

Soil

Concrete footing

86. Platform framing

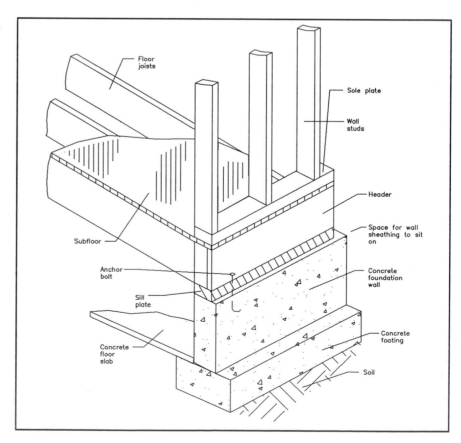

Floor joists

Sole plate

Wall studs

Header

Space for wall sheathing to sit on

Subfloor

Anchor bolt

Concrete foundation wall

Sill plate

Concrete footing

Concrete floor slab

Soil

sheathing, or subfloor as it is called, which is usually plywood or a plywood composition, is nailed to the floor joists, extending out to the rim joist. The stud walls, which already have the wall sheathing nailed to them, are then attached to the floor sheathing and joists. In some cases, the wall sheathing is attached to the stud walls after they have been attached to the floor sheathing and joists. Because of today's emphasis on energy-efficiency, fiberglass sheathing often is used on the wall studs. This sheathing, which is made of glass fibers, attains its insulating capacity by trapping air in the tiny pockets between the fibers (Figure 87). The sole plate at the bottom of the stud wall is nailed to the floor sheathing as well as to the joists below it to hold the wall firmly in place. In many of today's energy-efficient houses, the thickness of the stud wall is increased by using 2" x 6" studs instead of 2" x 4" studs to accommodate the placement of 6-inch thick fiberglass insulation in the wall cavities.

In both balloon-frame and platform-frame construction, a double top plate is nailed on top of the stud walls to hold them firmly in place and to provide support either for an upper floor or for the roof framing, whichever follows, depending on the height of the structure (Figure 88). Either the roof rafters or the ceiling joists for the upper floor rest on the double top plate. Additionally, since fire codes for residential construction have become more and more strict over the years, a great deal of fire-stopping is installed in this newer type of framing than was used in the older balloon-frame construction method.

Because some houses are very wide, the floor and ceiling joists cannot support the full span of the house. In this case, a main timber or steel beam or, if the house is very wide, even several timbers or beams, is installed perpendicular to the first floor joists in the cellar or basement to reduce the width of the span. Bearing walls also are installed from the first floor upwards, again, perpendicular to the floor and ceiling joists. The bearing walls decrease the width of the span and make the framing structurally sound. To help stiffen floor and ceiling joists laterally, intermediate bracings are installed mid-span on these joists.

It is essential that the homeowner not eliminate or move any of these bracing and strengthening fram-

ing elements to maintain the structural integrity of the house's framing. One homeowner who was not aware of this situation decided to make the living room in his house spacious by removing the wall between the living room and the enclosed porch. The room looked great, but just for a little while, until the second floor joists, which had been supported by the removed wall, began to sag, cracking the plaster ceiling on the first floor and buckling the wood floor on the second. The homeowner was told by a contractor who came to examine it that the reason the damage was so extensive was that he had removed a bearing wall. The load above the wall had no way of being supported without it. Anytime a homeowner is considering any renovation project that involves the removal of walls or other framing elements, he should first consult an architect, engineer, or contractor to be sure that he is not about to remove a part of the framing structure that is load-bearing.

Importance of the Main Beam

A homeowner can determine if the house he owns is wider than the allowable span of the floor and ceiling joists by looking at the framing in the basement or cellar to see if a main beam is located at about the middle of the house, perpendicular to the existing floor joists. If the house is very wide, there will be more than one main beam visible. In older houses, the main beam usually is a wood timber, 6" x 6" or 8" x 8", while in newer houses, it is more likely to be a steel beam. The main beam runs the full length of the house, front to back. When a wood beam is used, it is usually supported along its length with several concrete-filled steel lally columns. In addition, to increase the stability of the floor joists, joists are installed from each end of the sides of the house to the wood beam where they rest on it, overlap each other, and are nailed together. This procedure is called sistering (Figure 89). There are times when a homeowner may find a steel beam in use in an old house. This usually indicates that the old beam failed and it was replaced with the steel beam. It also can mean that the structure of the house was settling or failing, because of its age, and that a steel beam had to be installed to prevent further settlement or even damage to the structure. Happily, such a solution generally is an effective one.

One of the reasons many of the old wood main

87. Typical application of Owens-Corning Fiberglas® sheathing to exterior framing walls. Courtesy of the Owens-Corning Fiberglas Corp.

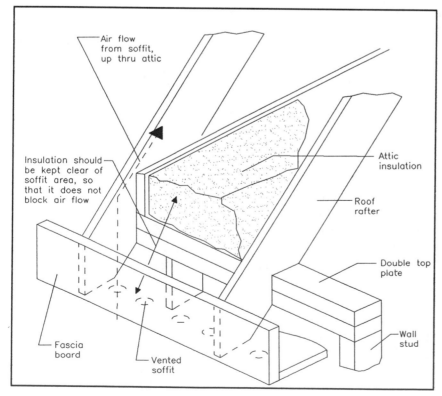

88. Insulation placement near vented soffit area

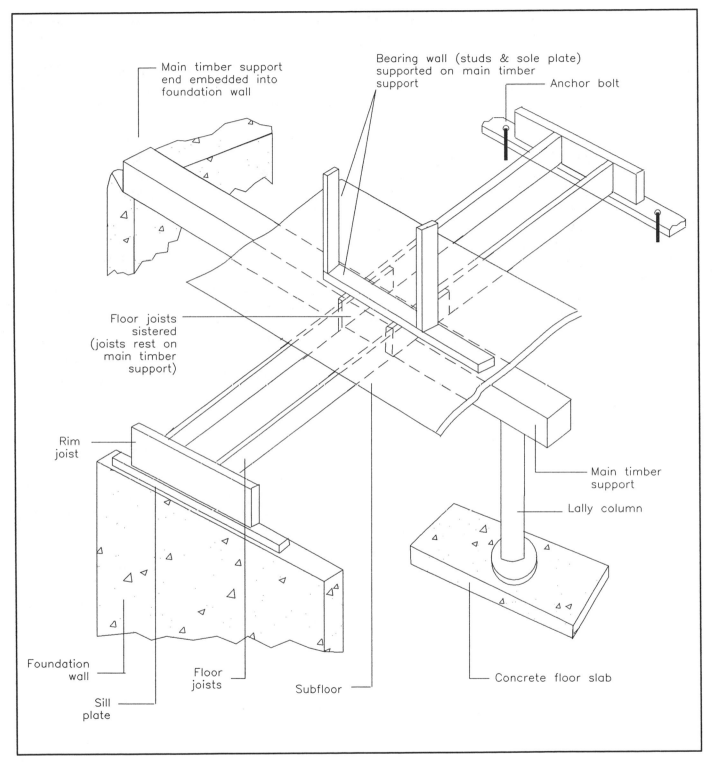

89. Detail of main timber support with sistered joists and bearing wall above

beams fail is that the ends of the beams, embedded into the foundation walls, become decayed and deteriorated, losing their ability to support the framing structure. In this situation, the wall is being used as a means of support for the main beam and for the load that rests on it. Unfortunately, the wall also provides an area for decay because it leaves the ends of the wood main beam exposed to moisture and possible insect infestation. A homeowner with a house that has a main beam supported in this way should check the ends of the wood beam regularly to be sure that its support is not being undermined by decay or insect infestation. A failure at the ends of the wood main beam and, ultimately, of the beam itself, could undermine the floor joists that are being supported by and resting on the main beam. If the homeowner sees any damage to the wood main beam, he should have an engineer, architect, or contractor examine it to determine its condition and to decide whether or not it needs to be replaced.

One homeowner encountered a different problem, though equally destructive, with the wood main beam in his house. His house was at least sixty-five years old and the wood main beam installed in it had been in place for that period as well. Over the years, it had dried out and now it was cracked structurally, so much so that long cracks were visible in the beam on both sides of it. There also were a number of cracks along the bottom of the beam in several places. The damage was so severe that the homeowner had to have a steel beam installed to replace the old wood beam. Apparently, the intense heat from the large boiler as well as poor ventilation in the basement had caused the damage to this wood main beam.

Any columns used to support the main beam, whether it is made of steel or wood, have to meet local and state building code requirements, which means that they must be fire-rated. In fact, concrete-filled steel lally columns should be used. In some old houses, wood columns or even tree trunks are being used to support the main beam. The use of these types of makeshift columns is a violation of most local building codes, for the most part because they are not fireproof. One homeowner who had steel lally columns decided to remove them because he wanted to increase the clear span in his basement. Shortly after he removed them, he noticed that the floor and floor joists as well as the main

beam were starting to sag. The homeowner quickly realized that the columns had been put in place to support the floor joists, bearing walls, and main beam in his house. To prevent further settlement, which could have led to extensive structural damage, the homeowner had to hire a contractor to install a steel main beam as well as concrete-filled steel lally columns. The house had to be jacked up very carefully to do this. Afterwards, the sagging floor joists also had to be repaired. Although the repair project was a costly one, luckily the damage was not irreparable so when the job was completed, the house was fully repaired.

In addition to the use of the main beam, the framing of a house is strengthened in several ways. Bracing or blocking is sometimes installed between the floor joists to provide extra lateral support for them. This added support will be visible in the basement if the floor joists have not been covered with a suspended ceiling, for example, when the area was made into a finished basement. Since state and local building codes do not always require the use of blocking or bracing of floor joists, it is not necessary in the framing of all houses. Some building codes require blocking or bracing when the depth of the joist being used is 2" x 12" or greater. In addition to blocking or bracing the framing for extra strength, wall and floor sheathing is run diagonally to increase the bracing strength of the framing against the wind load. This also will be visible in the basement if the floor joists have not been covered or hidden in some way. The presence of any of these strengthening techniques in a house is an indication that the house is well-designed and well-built, a credit to the architect, builder, or both.

Roof Framing Techniques

The framing procedures used in the construction of the attic and roof rafters also can be indications of how well a house was built. As mentioned earlier, the roof rafters and top floor ceiling joists rest on the double top plate, where they are nailed to it. The roof rafters for a pitched roof extend from the double top plate upward at a certain pitch or slope and are attached to the ridge board, which is located at the center of the roof. In many cases, collar beams are installed to increase the stability of the roof's framing structure. These beams are placed a few feet below the bottom of the ridge board and they run from one roof rafter on one side of the ridge board to a roof rafter on the other side of the ridge board. The collar beams will be visible in the attic if the attic is unfinished. They may only be partially visible, if at all, in a finished attic.

Obviously a house with a flat roof is framed differently at the roof than one with a pitched roof. In this case, there are two sets of framing members, the ceiling joists and the roof rafters, which form a space between the roof and the ceiling in the living area below. This space, called a cockloft, is only about 18 inches high, and it is visible from the hatchway that leads up to the roof. A ladder usually is placed in the hall, or in a closet off the hall, which is used to gain access to the hatchway. During the summer, a great deal of heat builds up in the cockloft. As a result, the living space below it becomes very uncomfortable, making the use of an air conditioner practically a necessity. It is essential to ventilate this area to assist the air conditioner. It is also practical to install insulation in the cockloft to save energy that could be lost during the heating season. A good way to handle this situation is for the homeowner to ask his local utility company to conduct an energy audit in his home. It will determine how to deal with this condition effectively to meet both summer and winter needs.

Ventilation and insulation are essential in an attic as well as in a cockloft, which is why both topics are discussed in great detail in Chapter 14. As a general rule, and to state the important points briefly here, there should be at least 6 inches of fiberglass insulation, or a similar type of insulation, in the attic. Before any insulation is put into place, a vapor barrier has to be installed, and it should be placed face down toward the living area to prevent moisture from building up in the attic. One homeowner who decided he wanted to increase the amount of insulation in his attic simply installed an additional layer of fiberglass insulation in it. This homeowner did not know about vapor barriers, how they function, or if he had one in his attic. He believed that the more insulation he had in his attic, the better. The insulation he used had a vapor barrier attached to it and the insulation he already had in the attic also had its own vapor barrier. The two vapor barriers trapped moisture in the lower layer of insulation. This moisture lowered the R value of the insulation and, eventually after prolonged exposure, it damaged the ceiling joists underneath it.

The correct way to add insulation is first to check the existing layer to see if it has a vapor barrier. If it does, then the next layer of insulation should be put into place without a vapor barrier. On the other hand, if the existing layer of insulation does not have a vapor barrier, then it will have to be removed and a vapor barrier will have to be installed before any insulation is put on top of it. This can be a difficult job, especially if the attic has only minimal ventilation. This is another occasion when it is a good idea to have your local utility company conduct an energy audit to determine what kind of insulation should be used and how much is needed. Then a contractor who specializes in this type of work can be hired to handle the installation for you.

It is also important to have sufficient ventilation in the attic. Since this topic also will be covered extensively in the next chapter, suffice it to say that an unfinished attic needs to have at least one vent window or vent louver in place. Newer houses generally have soffit vents installed along with ridge vents to provide for adequate ventilation. An attic with little or no ventilation poses a potential problem because the lack of ventilation decreases the insulating effects of the insulation in it. Additionally, any moisture that collects in the attic eventually can damage the roof framing structure.

After the roof rafters have been installed, the roof sheathing is nailed to them. In an older house, this sheathing is made up of wood strips that have been spaced to allow air to circulate between and under them. Plywood is more likely to have been used in a newer house as roof sheathing. If the attic is unfinished, the grade stamp will be visible on the sheathing to indicate what species of wood has been used, its grading number, etc. Roofing felt is laid over the sheathing and stapled to it, then the roof covering is installed. (A thorough discussion of roof coverings appears in Chapter 4.)

The stack vent pipe and the chimneys should extend up into the attic and out through the roof. When a stack vent pipe ends in the attic, it is a violation of most local and state building codes, because it creates a health hazard. The foul odor emanating from this shortened stack vent pipe is an unforgettable indication that it does not exit the attic through the roof. Some local building codes permit the use of a back flow valve in the stack vent pipe so that it can end in the attic but only when the drainage system is connected to a vented sewer. When an attic is going to be used as a living space, however, the stack vent pipe must exit the attic through the roof. (A complete discussion of this topic is in Chapter 12.) The chimney must always extend beyond the attic and exit through the roof. In an older house, it is often made of bricks and lined with tiles, while in newer houses, a metal flue pipe is used. Any damage to the chimney that is visible in the attic should be repaired immediately to prevent a health hazard, not to mention a possible fire. (Fireplaces and chimneys are reviewed in depth in Chapter 16.)

Framing Alterations Due to Concrete Slab Construction

When a house is built on a concrete slab, the framing at the grade level, or what is actually the first floor level, is done differently than it is for a balloon- or platform-frame constructed house. The sill plate either is anchored to the slab or to the independent foundation wall/footing built adjacent to the slab. As mentioned in the previous section, an independent footing is used in a frost area (see Figure 74 on page 94). In a house with a concrete slab, the slab is the floor, therefore, floor joists do not have to be installed at the first floor level. When a wood floor is going to be installed on top of the concrete slab, either prefinished flooring is installed with a waterproof adhesive, or a moisture-resistant plywood is installed to serve as a subfloor, and carpeting, linoleum, or vinyl tiles is installed over the plywood. Any of these types of installations can leave the existing floor cold during the winter. To improve its comfort level, wood sleepers, a vapor barrier, and insulation boards are installed on top of the concrete slab before wood flooring or plywood sheathing is installed (Figure 90). This helps to keep moisture and the cold in the ground below the slab away from the floor covering or flooring, making it more comfortable to walk on, especially during the winter.

INTERIOR WALL AND CEILING CONSTRUCTION

The interior walls and ceilings in a house are either plaster or drywall constructed, depending on how old the house is and/or to what extent it has been renovated. Drywall-constructed walls and ceilings generally are level throughout because the drywall is manufactured to a specific thickness, then attached to the studs or joists to form walls and ceilings. Plaster-constructed walls and ceilings, on the other hand, tend to be slightly uneven because the plastering was done by hand with a trowel, and it may have been applied more heavily on some areas of the walls and ceilings than on others.

Construction procedures for the walls and ceilings in old houses began after the stud walls and ceiling joists were put into place. Wood lath strips approximately 1 inch wide and 1/4 inch thick were nailed to the studs and joists. A roughing coat, also called the scratch coat, was applied over the wood lath strips. As soon as the roughing coat began to set — that is, to dry and harden somewhat — it was scratched to ensure a strong bonding of the second coat to the first. The second coat, which was a plaster coat, was considered to be the leveling coat. It was followed by the third and final coat, called the finish coat. This type of application sometimes was done over metal lath instead of wood lath strips; however, the procedure was the same.

Gypsum wall boards were installed in newer plastering applications to eliminate the need for a scratch coat. The gypsum wall boards had perforations made in them during the manufacturing process, which improved the bonding of the first coat of plaster to the board. The scratch coat and the second coat of plaster were combined into only one coat, and the second coat became the finish coat. Some local and state building codes require the use of gypsum wall boards with perforations when doing this kind of plastering work.

Drywall is used almost exclusively today for residential and even commercial construction. It is available in 4' x 8' and 4' x 10' sheets, and its thickness varies from 3/8 inch to 1 inch. Drywall also is available with a coating on it that makes it fire- and moisture-resistant. Fire-resistant drywall is used in areas where it is important to decrease the time a fire needs to spread, such as in the kitchen or in an attached garage. In fact, most local and state building codes require the use of fire-rated drywall in these types of applications. Drywall can be nailed or screwed onto wood studs and joists or even to metal

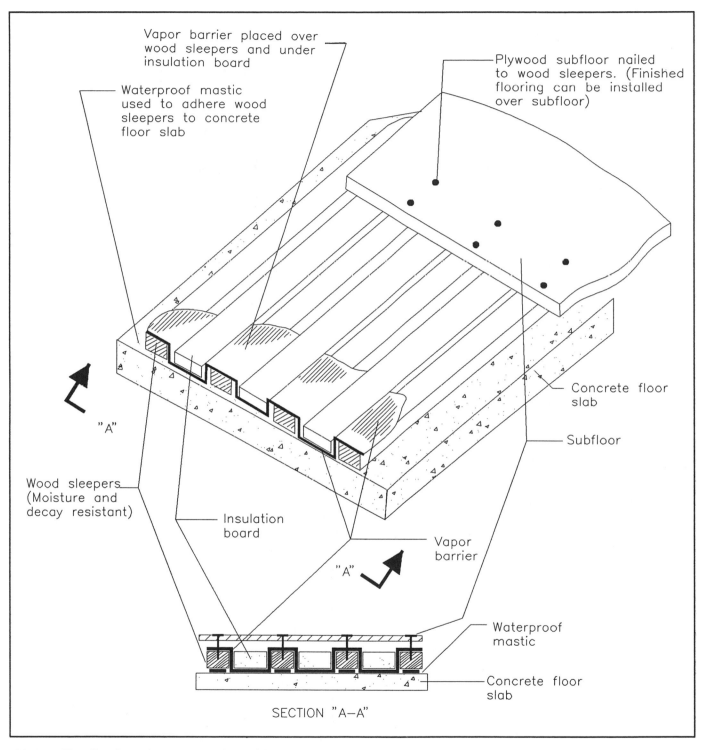

Vapor barrier placed over wood sleepers and under insulation board

Waterproof mastic used to adhere wood sleepers to concrete floor slab

Plywood subfloor nailed to wood sleepers. (Finished flooring can be installed over subfloor)

Concrete floor slab

Subfloor

"A"

Wood sleepers (Moisture and decay resistant)

Insulation board

Vapor barrier

"A"

Waterproof mastic

Concrete floor slab

SECTION "A—A"

90. Installing flooring over concrete floor slab

91, 92, and 93. Some of the application procedures for using Rustiver wall covering on old plaster walls and masonry surfaces to repair them. Courtesy of the 3G Mermet Corp.

studs using drywall screws. The seams between the sheets of drywall are covered with tape. Then joint compound is applied over the tape to hide the seams, nails, and screw heads. The joint compound is sanded after it has dried completely. At this point, the drywall can be painted or covered with any type of wall covering.

Since drywall construction is faster and less expensive to do than any other method of plaster construction, its use has just about eliminated plastering as part of house construction. Despite this fact, many homeowners still prefer the finish of a plaster wall. To accommodate them, a new product has been manufactured called blueboard. Blueboard is a drywall sheet with a textured blue paper on its surface, which gives it its name. Blueboard is installed in the same manner as drywall. Its advantage is its textured surface, which enables a thin coat of veneer plaster to bond to it when it is applied with a trowel. The veneer plaster is applied to a thickness of approximately 1/8 inch. It can be applied in either one or two coats; however, the two-coat method results in a smoother finish. This new technique for plastering looks as impressive as any traditional plaster work done on walls or ceilings, and it is just as durable. Fiberglass mesh tape is used to cover the seams between the sheets of blueboard. Metal or plastic corner bead or tape is used to hide the joints in the corners.

Repairing damaged plaster walls and ceilings has always been a problem for homeowners, especially those with old houses. One U.S. firm, 3G Mermet Corp., has brought a European product into the market. The product is called Rustiver, and it is a fiberglass wall covering that can be used to repair old walls, even those made of raw concrete blocks. The wall covering, which is available in six textures, is attached to the wall with a premixed vinyl wall covering paste (Figures 91, 92, and 93). After the paste has dried for two days, it can be painted with a roller or brush in any color or finish. The homeowner can handle this job himself, using a little time and patience to make the walls look like new.

10
Learning About Heating Systems

TYPES OF HEATING SYSTEMS

Although there are many types of heating systems available for use in a house today, three are used most frequently — the steam, hot water, and forced hot air heating systems. Because they are so popular as well as fairly complex, they are reviewed extensively in this chapter. All of the other possible choices such as radiant floor, heat pump, and solar heating systems also are discussed so that the homeowner can become familiar with any type of heating system he might have installed in his home. This section also examines the various components of a heating system as well as such topics as testing a boiler's efficiency or dealing with a converted boiler. The idea is to cover just about any situation the homeowner may encounter and to make him aware of how best to deal with any problems. First, however, let's begin with the heart of the three most popular heating systems, namely, the boiler for a steam or hot water system or the furnace for a forced hot air system.

DECODING BOILER AND FURNACE MANUFACTURERS' STANDARDS

A boiler is made of either cast iron or steel, and its construction is regulated by the American Society of Mechanical Engineers' (ASME) Boiler and Pressure Vessel Code. All state and local codes are derived from the ASME code, which states, among other specifications, the maximum allowable working pressure on the boiler or furnace. The ASME code does not, however, determine the heating capacity, which is dictated by other factors. The ASME symbol is displayed on each boiler or furnace to indicate that the manufacturer has based his production standards on ASME code specifications.

Each boiler or furnace also may have other symbols displayed on it from such organizations as the American Gas Association (AGA), the Steel Boilers Institute (SBI), and the Institute of Boiler and Radiator Manufacturers (IBRM). These organizations also set standards for boiler construction. When the homeowner decides to have a new heating system installed, he should be sure that the boiler or furnace being supplied is certified; that is, at least one of these symbols is displayed on it. The homeowner should not purchase a boiler that is not certified or hire a heating contractor who is not willing to install a certified boiler for whatever reason.

No matter how well a boiler or furnace has been constructed, the corrosive effects of substances in the water such as sediment, impurities, and sulfides will shorten its life expectancy. A cast-iron boiler has a longer life expectancy than a steel boiler because it has a greater resistance to these corrosive materials. Corrosion can be reduced by treating the boiler water chemically, but most one- and two-family houses do not have water treatment systems installed in them. These water treatment systems are used mostly for large capacity boilers such as those installed in huge apartment buildings or in commercial properties where the boiler is in use constantly.

Generally, the older a boiler or furnace is, the lower its operating efficiency. Even boilers or furnaces that are only ten to twenty years old may be operating at efficiencies as low as 50 to 60%. Older boilers and those converted from coal-firing to gas- or oil-firing operate at efficiency rates around 50%. Because of the many improvements in boiler-making technology, today's boilers and furnaces function at operating efficiencies of anywhere from 82 to 97%. Boiler and furnace manufacturers give their products what is called an AFUE rating — an Annual Fuel Utilization Efficiency rating. The higher the AFUE rating is, the greater the fuel economy of the boiler or furnace when it has been installed correctly and is being maintained properly. In other words, the installation of a new boiler, after the removal of the old one, is cost-efficient because the fuel savings over the subsequent years will pay for the cost of the new boiler and, eventually, will add up to further energy savings for the homeowner. In addition, the new boiler may be half the size of the old one, so it will save space and look more attractive than the old one did.

Old boilers and furnaces also waste energy because they are equipped with a standing pilot light that must remain lit at all times for the boiler to turn on as needed. For example, when gas is being used as the fuel, about 6,000 cubic feet per year is wasted, according to figures from the Carrier Corporation. These pilot lights also can be pretty finicky at times. One homeowner found out about this when he could not get his boiler to turn on despite the fact that the house was cold and the thermostat was in good working condition. When he called the local utility company for emergency assistance, he was told that dust had collected in the pilot light and was preventing it from lighting. Once the dust was removed, it relit immediately and the boiler turned on.

Today's boilers and furnaces are started by an electronic ignition, so the pilot light only needs to be ignited when the heating cycle is going to be started. The rest of the time the pilot light remains unlit, eliminating any wasted energy. The electronic ignition relights automatically; therefore, in case of a

power outage in the area, there is no need to call the utility or service company to have it relit. When the homeowner is away during the power outage, this automatic feature prevents a freezeout in the water piping during the winter.

Modern boilers and furnaces also are equipped with burners that can fire at variable rates. Old burners could only fire at one rate. Since the rate of the burner varies to accommodate the heating needs in the house, it also saves energy and cuts fuel costs for the homeowner.

STEAM HEATING SYSTEMS

In a steam heating system, the boiler heats the water to its boiling temperature so that the water changes to steam. This steam is distributed through a piping system to all of the radiators in the house. When the steam is distributed by natural means, the system is called a gravity system. Once the system shuts off, the steam in the piping cools, condenses, and water returns to the boiler, via the force of gravity, through a condensate return pipe. This type of system also is called a one-pipe system because the steam is distributed to and from the boiler through a single system of piping (Figures 94 and 95).

A boiler used in a steam heating system usually is equipped with an aquastat, a low-water cutoff, a pressuretrol, and a pressure safety valve (Figures 94, 96, and 97). Some of these boilers also have an automatic feed. Each of these devices has a specific function to make the boiler operate safely and effectively. It is helpful for the homeowner to understand what these devices do and how they do it to keep them in good working condition at all times.

The aquastat, which is mounted on the boiler, shuts off the burner in the boiler when the temperature of the boiler water gets too high for its safe operation. The aquastat has a sensing tube that either is immersed in the boiler water or is in contact with an immersion well that is immersed in the boiler water. A screw on the face of the aquastat can be adjusted to set the desired temperature of the boiler water, which usually is set between 180° and 200° F. The higher the temperature setting chosen, the more frequently the boiler has to operate. For this reason, manufacturers recommend the correct temperature setting to provide comfortable heating levels without wasting fuel. This temperature setting is stated in the manufacturer's maintenance booklet, and usually it is preset when the boiler is installed.

The low-water cutoff, which also is mounted on the boiler, is another important safety device. It has a float inside the boiler or in the low-water cutoff housing. When the water level falls below the proper level for the boiler to operate safely, the float mechanism sends a signal through the low-water cutoff to shut off the burner in the boiler. The proper water level is visible on the water gauge, which is attached to the side of the boiler. It is essential to clean and maintain the low-water cutoff regularly because if it fails and the water falls below the proper level for safe operation of the boiler, the internal parts of the boiler can be damaged and it will have to be repaired.

Homeowners can add water to the boiler when the water level in the water gauge is low. This is done by shutting off the boiler, allowing time for it to cool, and then opening the water inlet valve slightly so that water refills the boiler very slowly. Once the water has reached the proper level in the water gauge, the water inlet valve is closed and the boiler is put back into operation. A homeowner should not let himself be distracted when he is doing this, as one homeowner learned. While filling the boiler, his telephone rang. He went to answer it and forgot to return to the boiler to close the water inlet valve. The water filled the boiler, backed up into the steam piping all the way up to the top floor in his house, and began to pour out of the air valves connected to the radiators. Since the openings in the air valves are very small, the pressure in the piping system could not be relieved, in spite of the leaks throughout the top floor. Consequently, the pressure safety valve on the boiler blew and water came pouring out of the boiler, flooding the basement. Water damage was extensive throughout the upper and lower levels of the house and it was all because the homeowner allowed himself to be distracted.

Rather than fill the boiler manually, many homeowners prefer to have an automatic water feed installed in conjunction with the low-water cutoff on the boiler. The automatic feed adds water whenever it falls below the correct level in the boiler. This device saves numerous trips up and down basement or cellar stairs, and it is especially useful for homeown-ers who must leave their houses empty frequently because of business travel or personal commitments. An automatic feed will fail, however, if it is not cleaned and maintained properly. One homeowner who had a fairly new boiler could not get it to function. It was lucky that he couldn't, as a matter of fact. The automatic feed had broken and water in the boiler was far below the correct level. The low-water cutoff had shut off the burner because the water was not at its correct level. Had the boiler not shut off, its internal parts would have been completely burned and a new boiler would have had to be installed. Instead, all this homeowner had to do was have a new automatic feed installed to put his boiler back into operation again.

Another component of a boiler used in a steam heating system is the spring-loaded valve, which operates in conjunction with the low-water cutoff. At least once a month during the heating season, the homeowner should open this valve to flush the boiler, removing about two gallons of water, or as much as is recommended by the manufacturer in the maintenance booklet. This water is scalding hot so this job must be done carefully, using a metal pail with a wide mouth and thick, heat-resistant gloves to prevent spills and burns. Before this valve is opened, the shutoff switch on the boiler should be turned to the "Off" position. Then the boiler must be given sufficient time to cool. The water from this spring-loaded valve is dirty as well as hot because it is filled with sediment and other impurities. After the two gallons of water have drained out of the boiler, the spring-loaded valve should be closed tightly. This hot, dirty water has to be mixed with cold water to be discarded into an outdoor area drain, or it has to be given sufficient time to cool to be discarded into a slop sink in the basement. This water must not be discarded into a sink or toilet fixture because it may crack it. Additionally, it should not be drained into a garden where the impurities contained in it may affect the flowers or vegetables planted there.

While the boiler is still shut off, the water inlet valve can be opened to refill the boiler to its correct level, which also is indicated in the manufacturer's maintenance booklet. A marker or grease pencil can be used to indicate the desired water level permanently on the water gauge to make regular refills more

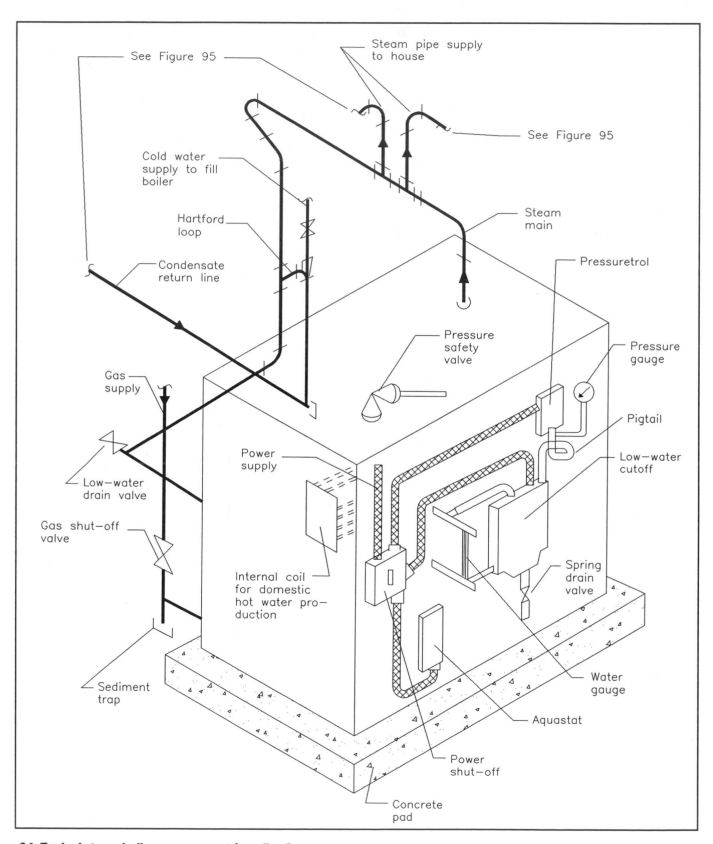

See Figure 95

Steam pipe supply to house

See Figure 95

Cold water supply to fill boiler

Hartford loop

Condensate return line

Steam main

Pressuretrol

Pressure safety valve

Pressure gauge

Gas supply

Pigtail

Low−water cutoff

Power supply

Low−water drain valve

Gas shut−off valve

Internal coil for domestic hot water production

Spring drain valve

Water gauge

Aquastat

Sediment trap

Power shut−off

Concrete pad

94. Typical steam boiler arrangement (gas-fired)

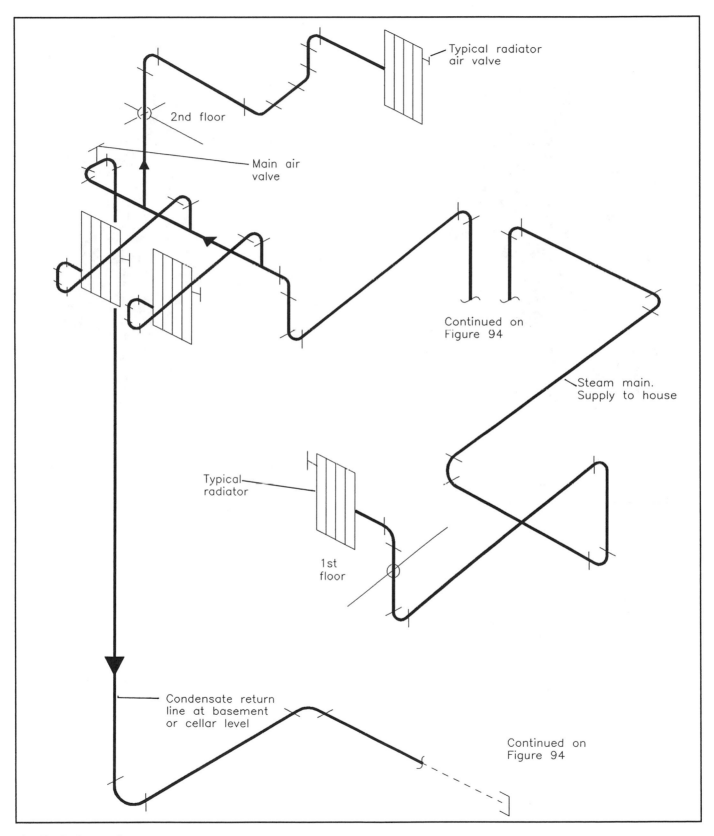

Typical radiator
air valve

2nd floor

Main air
valve

Continued on
Figure 94

Steam main.
Supply to house

Typical
radiator

1st
floor

Condensate return
line at basement
or cellar level

Continued on
Figure 94

95. Typical one-pipe steam system

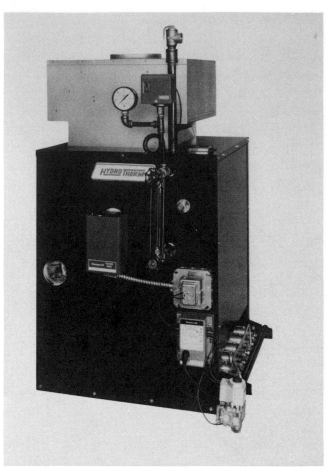

96. Gas-fired Model VS-A steam boiler. Courtesy of Hydrotherm Inc.

97. Gas-fired Galaxy 80 PLUS steam boiler. Courtesy of the Slant/Fin Corporation.

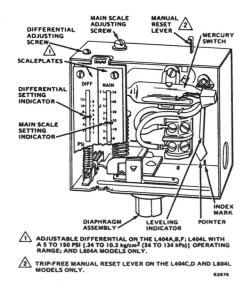

98. Pressuretrol controllers. Courtesy of Honeywell Residential and Building Controls.

efficient. The boiler has to be filled very slowly since the fresh water is cold and the boiler is hot, especially if it was recently operating. When cold water is added to the boiler too quickly, its internal parts can be damaged because of the extreme differences in temperature. The water inlet valve should be closed before the boiler is put back into operation.

Sometimes the spring-loaded valve cannot close tightly because sediment in the water has lodged itself in the valve closure. This may not be apparent immediately, so the homeowner will have to check it for leaks several times after closing it. When the homeowner sees drops of water in a dry pail left sitting under the spring-loaded valve, he knows that the valve is not closed tightly. Leaks from the valve also may become visible after the boiler has been operating for several hours. There also may be a drastic decrease visible in the water level in the water gauge. When the spring-loaded valve is leaking, the boiler must be turned off again and the valve flushed one more time to clear away any impurities at the closure. If this procedure does not correct the problem, then the valve will have to be replaced by a heating contractor.

The homeowner needs to be aware of the fact that water evaporates from a boiler at all times as a result of its use. A boiler for a steam heating system may have to be refilled daily during cold winter days, every three to four days during milder winter days, and weekly when temperatures are very mild. In this case, water is not leaking from a valve, it is being lost due to evaporation. The homeowner has to use his judgment to determine the cause of the water loss in the boiler. If he is concerned, or simply is not sure of what is causing the problem, then he will have to call a heating contractor who can check the condition of the boiler and its various components.

The blowoff valve, or mud valve as it is sometimes called, is also a drain valve. It is installed at the lowest level of the boiler and it is used to remove all of the water from the boiler when it is being cleaned, repaired, or replaced. A boiler should be cleaned once a year by a heating contractor. It is best to have this done before or early into the heating season. After the boiler has been turned off and water has been drained from the spring-loaded valve and

blowoff valve, a variety of cleaning tasks is undertaken. As much as 14 gallons of water may be drained from the boiler, depending on its size. A section of the outer casing is removed to clean away the dirt and soot that have collected in the boiler. The metal flue pipe is detached to clean the chimney thoroughly. All of the valves and safety devices are tested to be sure they operate properly. If any of them do not, they will be replaced.

After all of this maintenance work is done, the spring-loaded valve and blowoff valve are closed and water is added very slowly to the boiler to refill it. If the manufacturer's maintenance booklet states that chemicals can be added to the boiler, the heating contractor will pour a chemical cleaning solution into the fresh water. Some manufacturers do not recommend the use of chemical cleaner in their boilers because it corrodes the internal parts. When the cleaning solution is used, the boiler is put back into operation for a specific period of time, then it is drained again to remove all of the water as well as the cleaning solution in it. The heating contractor's final step is to fill the boiler once again, this time to its correct water level, and to turn it back on. At this point, it is ready for use during the coming heating season.

The pressuretrol, which is also called the high-limit switch by some manufacturers, is a pressure-activated device that is mounted on the boiler (Figure 98). The pressuretrol receives an electrical signal from the thermostat when heat is needed. An electrical current flows from the pressuretrol to the operating controls to fire the burners in the boiler so that the heating process can begin. As the pressure in the boiler rises, the pressuretrol breaks the electrical circuit and turns off the burners. In this way, the pressuretrol is able to act as a pressure safety control for the entire heating system. The pressuretrol is connected with a section of tubing to a pressure gauge that is mounted on the boiler near it. The tubing is pigtailed between them to prevent steam in the boiler from flowing through the tubing into contact with the internal parts of the pressure gauge. The pressure gauge measures the internal steam pressure in the boiler.

In addition to the pressuretrol, another important safety device for the boiler is the pressure safety valve. This valve relieves pressure that builds up in the boiler due to the increased water temperature as well as the steam collecting in it. The pressure safety valve, which is spring-activated, is designed to open at a predetermined limit of pressure. When the valve opens, the pressure in the boiler decreases until it falls below the preset limit, and the valve closes again. When the pressure safety valve is malfunctioning, it is clearly visible since the lever on top of the valve remains in the open position. A new valve has to be installed by a heating contractor since this repair job, as well as all others for a boiler, cannot be done by the homeowner. All valves and safety devices also are manufactured to ASME code specifications; however, the ASME symbol is not printed on them as it is on boilers and furnaces.

One of the problems with steam heating systems that is particularly worrisome to homeowners is the banging they sometimes hear in them. For the most part, these banging noises can be ignored. One homeowner, on the other hand, had such loud banging noises when his heating system was turned on that it was frightening his children. The heating contractor he called for assistance told him that the only way to silence the system was to have an entirely new system installed. Such a drastic step turned out not to be necessary after the homeowner discussed his problem with an engineer. It seemed the homeowner used to add water to the boiler himself, since it did not have an automatic feed on it, and he had added so much water that it had backed up into the piping where it battled with the hot steam. This was the cause of all that noise. The homeowner had not been waiting long enough for the water to return to the boiler and settle after it had turned off before he added more water to it.

This homeowner's problem was solved by turning off the boiler, draining the water to its correct level, and replacing old air valves with new ones that had larger vent openings in them. These new valves allowed air that was trapped in the radiators to escape more quickly, which enabled the steam to fill them more rapidly than it could with the old valves. When the boiler was turned back on, it was still making some noises, but they were not as loud as they had been. These noises, however, indicated that there was still too much water in the heating system, so it was turned off again and drained a second time. There were no noises to be heard at all when the boiler was turned back on. Even so, it was turned

off one more time to let the water settle to be absolutely certain that it was at its correct level and stayed there, then it was turned on one last time to give it a final test and at last, all was quiet again.

When a steam heating system is in use in a house, it is a good practice to replace old air valves on the radiators with new ones. A new air valve also should be installed on the steam main in the basement near the boiler. These air valves help the steam heating system to operate efficiently, yet their cost is minimal. Air valves are made with different vent openings to accommodate the various distances from the boiler to the radiator. Generally, the farther away the radiator is from the boiler, the larger the vent opening in the air valve should be. This allows the air to vent more quickly from the radiator and hastens the heating process in the house. The homeowner can do this replacement job himself, but only after the heating system has been turned off and the radiators have been given sufficient time to cool down completely.

HOT WATER HEATING SYSTEMS

A hot water heating system is designed to heat a house by providing hot water, which is supplied by the boiler, to the radiators or baseboard units in the various rooms of the house (Figure 99). When gravity is used to distribute the hot water throughout the piping, the system is called a gravity hot water heating system. Such a system uses a single piping system to carry the hot water to the radiators or baseboard units as well as to return the cool water to the boiler. This type of system is not the most commonly used hot water heating system.

The most frequently used hot water heating system is the forced hot water heating system in which a circulating pump is used to circulate the hot water throughout the piping system (Figures 100, 101, and 102). Basically, the circulating pump is an in-line pump; that is, it is an integral part of the piping system that forces the hot water to circulate to the radiators and/or baseboard units throughout the house. The circulating pump should be lubricated as often as is stated in the manufacturer's maintenance booklet, a task that can easily be done by necessary.

The boiler in a forced hot water heating system works in conjunction with an aquastat, which

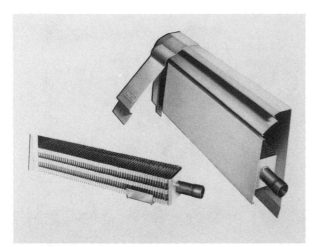

99. Baseboard heating unit. Courtesy of the Slant/Fin Corporation.

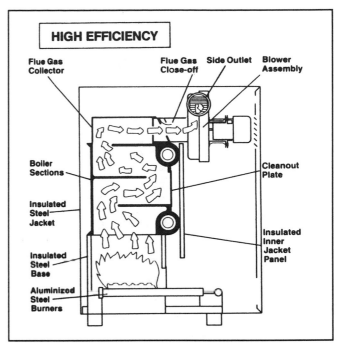

HIGH EFFICIENCY

Flue Gas Collector

Flue Gas Close-off

Side Outlet

Blower Assembly

Boiler Sections

Insulated Steel Jacket

Insulated Steel Base

Aluminized Steel Burners

Cleanout Plate

Insulated Inner Jacket Panel

100. The operation of a high efficiency, gas-fired hot water boiler. Courtesy of Weil-McLain, a division of The Marley Company.

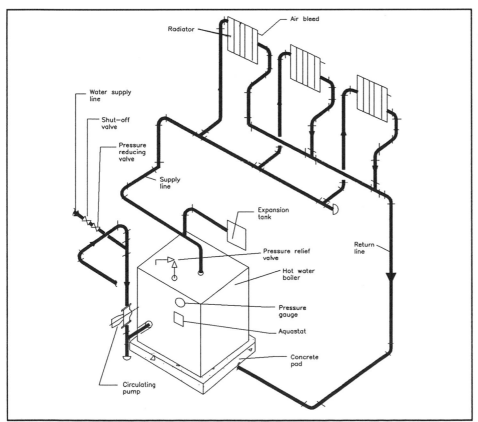

Air bleed

Radiator

Water supply line

Shut—off valve

Pressure reducing valve

Supply line

Expansion tank

Pressure relief valve

Hot water boiler

Return line

Pressure gauge

Aquastat

Concrete pad

Circulating pump

101. Forced hot water system — two-pipe

102. Galaxy 80 PLUS water boiler. Courtesy of the Slant/Fin Corporation.

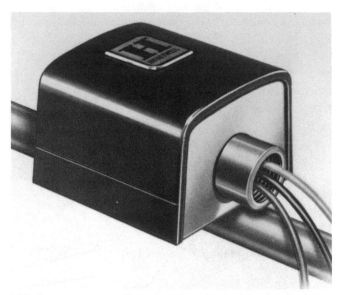

103. Aquastat controllers for electric thermostats in hydronic heating/cooling systems. Courtesy of Honeywell Residential and Building Controls.

controls the temperature of the boiler water or operates the circulating pump. An aquastat is a switching device (Figure 103). It has a sensing element in it, which is either liquid-filled or made of metal, that detects any increase or decrease in the temperature of the boiler water. The aquastat is either mounted on the boiler so that its sensing element can be immersed in the boiler well or it is mounted onto the hot water supply line. Aquastats that are the non-immersion type also are available, and they are used as safety control devices in hot water heating systems. When the temperature of the boiler water decreases, the sensing element signals the aquastat to close. The aquastat receives a signal to open when the temperature of the boiler water increases. When the aquastat is not being used to control the temperature of the boiler water, but instead to operate the circulating pump, it closes when the temperature of the boiler water increases. An adjustable scale with a pointer is attached to the aquastat and the temperatures on it usually range from 150° to 200° F.

One of the most important parts of a hot water heating system is the pressure-reducing valve. This valve feeds water into the boiler whenever the pressure in the system drops, then it closes automatically when pressure returns to its proper level. The pressure-reducing valve also is called the boiler-feed

water valve and the water pressure regulator by several manufacturers. No matter what it is called, it always handles the same function in hot water heating systems.

One homeowner experienced the most common problem associated with hot water heating systems when several sections of his radiators could not become heated, even though the system was operating. A few sections of the radiators were hot to the touch, but many remained cold. Generally, there are only two possible reasons for this problem. The most frequent is that air has become trapped in the radiators and is blocking the flow of hot water throughout the radiators. The solution is simply to "bleed" each radiator — to release the trapped air by opening the bleed valve installed on each radiator for this purpose. Once the air has been released, the hot water can flow freely into all sections of the radiator. The second possible cause of this type of problem is that the pressure-reducing valve is malfunctioning. An adjustment may be all that is needed to correct this problem. If it does not correct it, then the pressure-reducing valve will have to be replaced. The pressure-reducing valve must be replaced by a heating contractor. As with the circulating pump, these types of replacements cannot be done by the homeowner.

An expansion tank is a necessity for any type of hot

water heating system because it provides storage space for the water after it has been heated. The volume of the water increases as its temperature increases and the expansion tank stores this extra volume as it flows from the boiler. Hot water heating systems have either an open or closed expansion tank. A closed expansion tank is used for high pressure systems, and an open tank is used for low pressure systems. An expansion tank can be elevated such as when it is placed in an attic. When it is elevated, the boiling point of the boiler water is higher than it normally would be, enabling the boiler water to be heated to a higher temperature without producing steam. As a result of this higher water temperature, the radiators and/or baseboard units radiate a greater amount of heat into the rooms than they would if the water had been heated to a lower temperature.

With the development of new high-efficiency, gas-fired hot water boilers, venting of the exhaust gases can now be accomplished by venting directly through the exterior wall (Figure 104). For older boilers, the venting had to be done into a masonry chimney because the temperature of the exhaust gases was much higher. The new boilers also can be vented through a chimney or metal flue pipe through the roof when such an installation is easier or necessary due to construction techniques.

High-efficiency boilers have come into great demand as energy costs continue to increase, and many manufacturers are responding to their popularity. One new gas-fired, high-efficiency boiler, made by Hydrotherm Inc., is called the Hydro-Pulse® (Figures 105 and 106). This boiler is 90% seasonally efficient, which means that when it is compared to a currently installed modern boiler, it provides a fuel cost savings of up to 35%. Naturally, when this boiler is installed to replace an old oil or electrically fired boiler, the savings can increase dramatically in a short time.

Air and gas are mixed in the combustion chamber at the top of the Hydro-Pulse boiler. Since it has been designed without a pilot light, the air and gas mixture in this boiler is ignited by a spark plug in the initial combustion cycle only, thereby eliminating the need for additional electrical power for combustion. Each mixture or burn cycle thereafter is ignited by heat from the previous cycle. Burners

also are not needed in this type of boiler because the pulse combustion principle utilized in it eliminates the need for them. The pressure resulting from the combustion process forces the hot gases down through the heat exchanger tubes inside the boiler and closes the gas and air inlets. The heat is transferred to the boiler water surrounding the heat exchanger tubes, and the hot water is circulated throughout the house's heating system. As the hot gases are forced into the heat exchanger, the pressure drops and more air and gas are drawn into the combustion chamber. This air and gas mixture is ignited and the pulse cycle repeats itself again. The pulsing rate is in excess of 60 cycles/second. More than 90% of the heat from the hot gases is transferred to the boiler water.

The efficiency of the heat exchanger reduces the exhaust temperature to a low range of from 110° to 130° F when the boiler is operating in the condensing mode. This low exhaust temperature is easily vented outdoors through a pipe with a small diameter, eliminating large heat losses up the chimney such as those usually associated with conventional systems.

In addition to its small size, which wastes less floor space, the Hydro-Pulse has several other features. For instance, the air needed for combustion comes into the system through a small plastic pipe, instead of being taken from air inside the house as is done by conventional boilers. This eliminates the typical drafts and cold air spilling in and around doors and windows. Also, when the boiler is turned off, there is no standby heat loss. The Hydro-Pulse boiler also can be used to supply domestic hot water in the house. In addition, it can be combined with a hot water heat exchanger coil in a forced air ducted system to provide a highly efficient hydronic/warm air heating system.

FORCED HOT AIR HEATING SYSTEMS

In a forced hot air heating system, air is heated in the furnace and then circulated throughout the house to each register. As with steam and hot water heating systems, gas, oil, or electricity is commonly used to fuel forced hot air heating systems. Since gas-fired systems are most frequently used, this

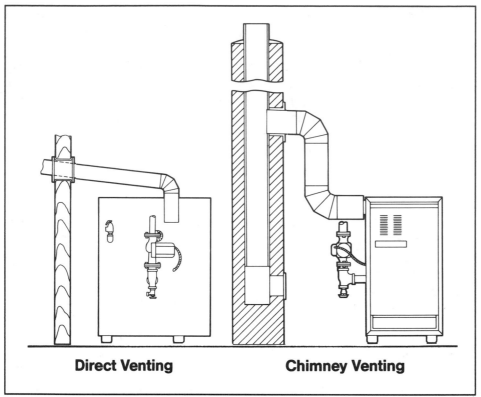

Direct Venting   **Chimney Venting**

104. Two venting options for high efficiency, gas-fired boilers. Courtesy of Weil-McLain, a division of The Marley Company.

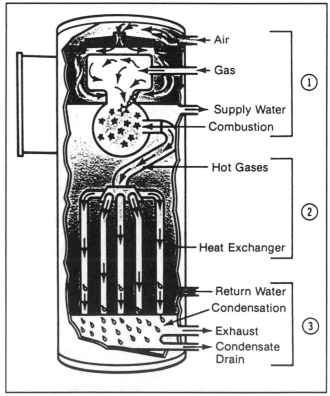

106. How the Hydro-Pulse operates to save energy costs. Courtesy of Hydrotherm Inc.

105. Hydro-Pulse® pulse combination boilers for gas-fired hydronic heating systems. Courtesy of Hydrotherm Inc.

discussion focuses on the gas-fired type (Figure 107). All oil and electrically fired heating systems will be reviewed later in this section.

A gas-fired furnace used for a forced hot air heating system is equipped with gas burners, a heat exchanger, a blower, and a filter. The blower circulates the hot air around the ducting system installed throughout the house. This blower is driven in one of two ways, depending on the age of the furnace. In newer furnaces, the blower apparatus consists of a squirrel cage motor encased in a blower housing. The blower in older furnaces is driven with a belt and pulley arrangement.

Gas and air are mixed in the burner section of the furnace where combustion also takes place. A gas control valve located near the burners regulates the flow of incoming gas. When the thermostat signals the furnace to start heating the air, the gas control valve opens and gas and air start to mix together. A pilot light, which is located in the burner section, ignites the air and gas mixture. The exhaust, heated by the combustion of gas and air, passes through the heat exchanger. Exhaust gases that result from the combustion process are vented outdoors through a vent pipe in an exterior wall or chimney.

When the heat exchanger reaches the proper temperature, a fan switch turns on the blower. The blower sends air across the metal surface of the heat exchanger where heat is transferred from the hot metal surface to the cooler air. This hot air is then sent through the ducting system to the various registers in the house to warm the rooms. The combustion process continues in the burner section until the thermostat signals the gas control valve to close. This in turn turns off the burners and the pilot light. The blower continues to operate until the heat exchanger has cooled, which only takes a short time. Once the heat exchanger has cooled, the fan switch turns off the blower.

The incoming cool air from the return in a forced hot air heating system is cleaned with a filter that is installed in the furnace. This filter removes a minimal amount of particles from the air such as dust, bacteria, and pollen. An electronic air filter installed in conjunction with this type of heating system usually is used to remove the rest of the impurities from the air (Figures 108 and 109). This type of filter is very efficient. It can remove up to 95% of

all particles from the air. Electronic air cleaners improve the air quality in a house because they are so effective, and they eliminate many of the particles that cause allergies. For the most part, they have become standard equipment for the forced air heating system in new houses. They also can be installed fairly easily in older forced air heating and cooling systems. The wires in the electronic air filter are charged electrically so that they can charge particles in the air as it passes over them. These charged particles become attached to a number of electrically charged plates in the filter and, in this way, they are removed from the air. The filters in an electronic air cleaner can be used over and over again when they are removed and cleaned regularly.

The efficiency of modern furnaces has been greatly improved over those that were manufactured even a few decades ago. Carrier's Weathermaker® SXi Infinity®, for instance, has an AFUE (Annual Fuel Utilization Efficiency) rating of nearly 94%, while older furnaces had ratings lower than 60% (Figures 110 and 111). In addition, the blower motor in this furnace is a variable speed motor that is able to maintain the temperature in the furnace without having to turn off and on constantly. It also operates quietly. A variable speed motor is a significant improvement over single-speed motors because it adjusts automatically, allowing the blower to operate only as fast as necessary to reach the desired comfort level. The blower motor also circulates the hot air throughout the ducting system in the house. A variable speed motor adjusts the combustion, temperature, and airflow so well that it saves the homeowner money on fuel bills. The Weathermaker SXi Infinity uses sophisticated microprocessor controls to monitor the house's heating needs constantly and to adjust automatically to accommodate them. When heat is needed quickly, the furnace switches to a high-output mode, but when conditions return to normal, it switches back to the low-output mode, which is where it stays about 90% of the time.

Another new gas furnace, the G14 from Lennox Industries Inc. (Figure 112), operates on the principle of pulse combustion. The process begins when small amounts of gas and air are induced into the combustion chamber through the flapper valves (Figure 113). Then, following the drawing: (1) A spark ignites the mixture, causing the first pulse. (2)

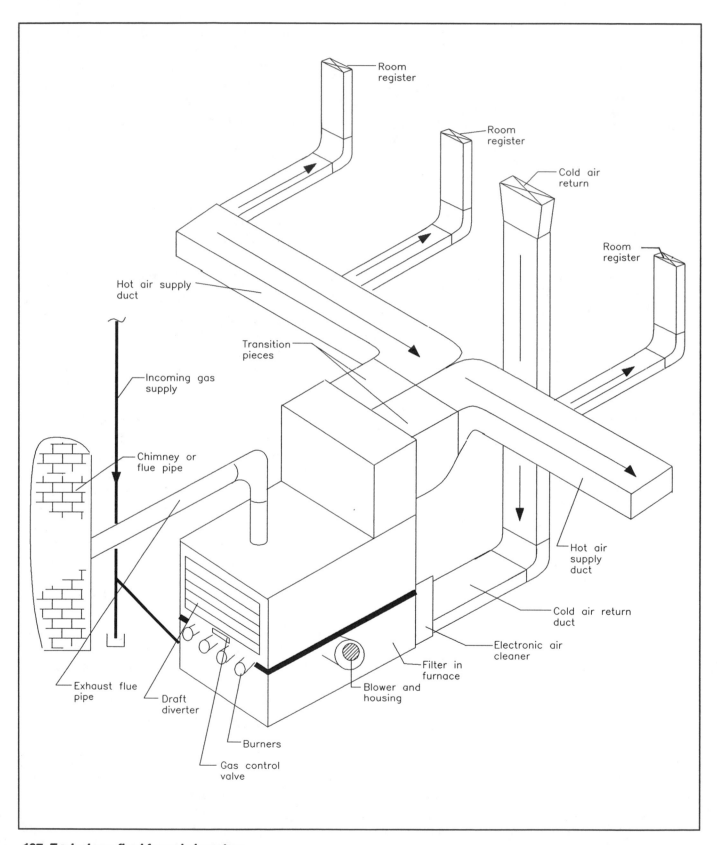

107. Typical gas-fired forced air system

108 and 109. Electronic air cleaner and its internal parts. Courtesy of Honeywell Residential and Building Controls.

110 and 111. Weathermaker® Infinity® SXi gas-fired furnace with cutaway showing its internal parts. Courtesy of the Carrier Corporation.

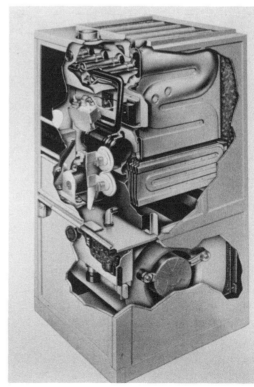

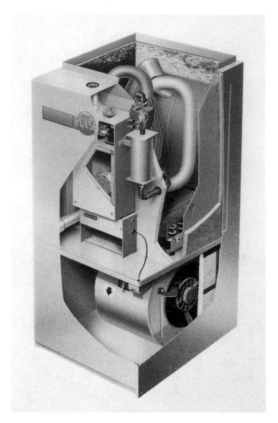

112. Cutaway of G14 Pulse furnace. Courtesy of Lennox Industries Inc.

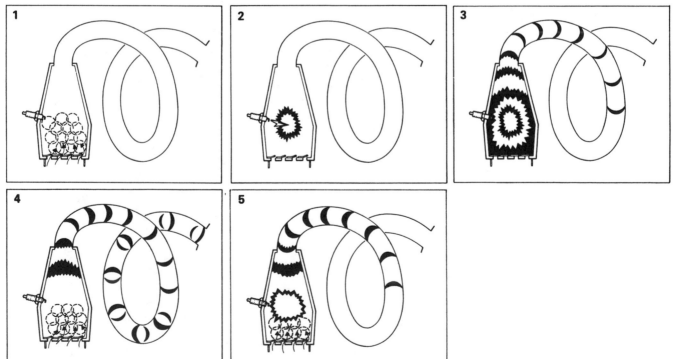

113. How the Lennox pulse combination furnace operates. Courtesy of Lennox Industries Inc.

Each pulse produces ¼ to ½ of a Btu of heat. The first pulse closes the flapper valves and forces the products of combustion down the tailpipe. (3) As the shockwave of the pulse reaches the end of the tailpipe, it is reflected back to the combustion chamber. Meanwhile, negative pressure created in the chamber has allowed the flapper valves to open again, admitting more gas and air. (4) When the reflected wave re-enters the chamber, there is sufficient flame to ignite the new mixture, causing the second pulse, and the process starts all over again. (5) Once combustion is started, it becomes self-perpetuating, allowing the combustion blower and spark igniter to be turned off. This happens sixty-eight times a second.

When a new furnace for a forced hot air heating system is going to be installed, it is important to have it sized properly, since a larger unit than necessary will not operate efficiently. The installation of a heat pump and a humidifier also should be considered at this time. The heat pump, which is reviewed fully later in this section, can provide for cooling during the summer while also serving as an alternate heating system during the winter. The humidifier, working in conjunction with both heating and air conditioning systems, can maintain the humidity level in the house to the desired level of between 30 and 35%. When humidity stays at this level in the house, it can be kept comfortable while maintaining a lower temperature than ordinarily would be adequate. This results in fuel savings. A zoned temperature control system also should be considered since the combination of electric thermostats and volume dampers can keep every room at a comfortable level while saving energy.

Another way to cut fuel costs is to have vent dampers installed in the vent pipe attached to the gas-fired furnace. Vent dampers prevent heat from being lost through the vent pipe while the furnace is not operating. Vent dampers that are electrically operated use a motor to activate a disc that blocks the flue pipe when the burners are off while bimetal vent dampers have heat-activated parts that open the damper when the furnace is operating. Both types use safety controls to prevent the burners from turning on when the flue pipe is blocked, an important safety feature.

The best way to prevent the loss of hot air from the house is to get the air needed for combustion from outdoors using ducts or vents. This method also prevents exhaust gases from backing up into the house, a condition called backdrafting. Today's houses are so tightly sealed that they sometimes cannot supply a sufficient amount of air for combustion, air that used to be readily available from drafts around windows and doors, for example. Since gas-fired furnaces, as well as stoves and fireplaces, need substantial amounts of air for combustion, it is essential to use vents or ducts to bring in an adequate supply of air for efficient combustion.

Careful maintenance of the furnace for a forced hot air heating system can keep it operating efficiently and safely. This includes procedures that should be done on a monthly basis as well as those that should be done annually by the heating contractor or servicing company. The manufacturer's maintenance booklet indicates when various procedures should be done such as when the blower motor has to be lubricated. The filter, which is at the bottom of the furnace near the cold air inlet, should be cleaned monthly. If it is in poor condition, it will have to replaced before a new heating season begins. If the blower is belt-driven, the tension on the belt will have to be checked annually. If the furnace is equipped with a squirrel cage motor, it will have to be cleaned at least once a year. The cost for the annual maintenance by the heating contractor or servicing company is relatively small; however, its effect can be significant. An efficient furnace uses less fuel and lasts for many years more than one that has not been cared for properly. Additionally, the energy savings can be substantial as they accumulate over the passing years.

OTHER FUELS FOR HEATING

Steam, hot water, and forced hot air heating systems can operate as oil- or electrically-fired heating systems as well as gas-fired systems. Depending on what type of fuel is used, there are some differences in the way the system has to be installed as well as in the type of boiler or furnace used. A careful review of these differences can help the homeowner to deal knowledgeably with any type that he might encounter.

Oil-Fired Heating Systems

Special burners are installed in a furnace for a forced hot air heating system, which enable the oil to burn efficiently. These burners increase the pressure of the oil dramatically to aerate it as it passes through the nozzle. This aerated oil or mist is then mixed with air again by a blower. Instead of using a pilot light to ignite it as is done in a gas-fired system, the oil-fired system uses electrodes to create a spark to ignite the oil and air mixture. The draft that is exerted on the burner system, which comes from the vent or flue system, also has to be controlled very carefully to enable the oil-fired forced hot air heating system to function properly.

A set of burners and a pilot light are used to start the combustion process when gas is firing a steam or forced hot water heating system. On the other hand, an oil burner gun is used to start combustion for heating as well as for domestic hot water (Figure 114) when these types of systems are oil-fired (Figures 115, 116, 117, and 118). The oil burner gun is controlled by a thermostat. When the room temperature falls below the desired temperature setting, or when the thermostat indicator is raised to a setting above the temperature in the room, a switch in the thermostat closes and approximately 24 volts of electrical current signal the primary control unit to turn on the oil burner gun. This puts several parts of the gun into operation, including the motor, fuel pump, ignition transformer, and safety timing circuit. The fuel pump, which is controlled by the motor, sends oil to the oil burner nozzle. The internal check valve in the fuel pump opens at a preset pressure of approximately 100 psi. Once this valve has opened, the oil is able to enter the burner nozzle. There the oil is atomized, that is, it is changed into a fine spray and then mixed with air, which is sent into the nozzle by the fan. The atomized oil is ignited by the ignition transformer, which raises the voltage so that the electrode in the burner nozzle creates a spark. This spark is fanned by the rush of air in the nozzle and ignites the oil.

The safety timing circuit, which is in the oil burner gun's primary control unit, acts as a safety mechanism for the gun with the use of a cad cell housed in it. When, for any reason, the burner does not function properly, the safety timing circuit turns off the oil burner. The safety timing circuit monitors the flame in the oil burner nozzle with the use of the cad cell, which is light-sensitive. When there is no flame in the nozzle, the cad cell sends a signal to the oil burner gun to shut off. To be certain that all of the various parts of any oil-fired system operate properly, the system should be installed so that it meets all of the codes and standards set by federal, state, and local building codes as well as by the National Fire Protection Association.

Whether a heating system is gas- or oil-fired, the products of combustion — the exhaust gases — must be vented out of the house through either a flue pipe or a masonry chimney. This also is necessary when gas or oil is being used to fire a domestic hot water heater. The products of combustion include deadly gases, which must be removed from the house completely.

Heating Your House with Electricity

Naturally, the homeowner's choice of fuel depends largely on the cost and availability of gas, oil, or electricity in the area. Some homeowners live in areas where gas and oil are difficult, if not impossible, to get for use by their heating systems. Therefore, electrical power becomes the only viable choice. As with other types of fuels, electricity has its advantages and its disadvantages. Electrical power is quieter, cleaner, and safer than some other fuels. Electrically fired heating systems do not need a chimney or flue pipe because there are no exhaust gases or other products of combustion emitted that need to be vented out of the house. Therefore, there is no loss of heat, making this type of system very, very efficient. Electrically fired heating systems also do not remove oxygen from the air, and they need less maintenance than some of the other types of heating systems. Heat from an electrically fired heating system is produced as soon as the thermostat calls for it.

The only disadvantage, which can be a major one, is that in some areas electricity is quite costly. This high fuel cost can be reduced, however, by insulating the house very well and by keeping it that way at all times. Electrically fired heating systems need at least 220 to 240 volts to operate, much more than gas- or oil-fired heating systems where electricity is not being used as the main fuel supply. To function safely and efficiently, electrically fired heating systems must comply with the National Electrical Code®, with state and local electrical codes, and

114. Cutaway of No. 68 high efficiency, oil-fired boiler-burner unit. Courtesy of Weil-McLain, a division of The Marley Company.

115. Oil-fired steam boiler with a Beckett oil burner. Courtesy of Hydrotherm Inc.

116. Liberty® oil-fired boiler. Courtesy of the Slant/Fin Corporation.

117. Cutaway showing internal parts of Liberty boiler. Courtesy of the Slant/Fin Corporation.

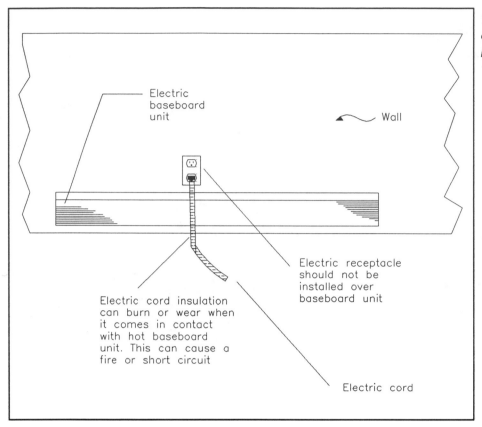

118. Detail of improper location of electrical receptacle with electric baseboard

Electric baseboard unit

Wall

Electric receptacle should not be installed over baseboard unit

Electric cord insulation can burn or wear when it comes in contact with hot baseboard unit. This can cause a fire or short circuit

Electric cord

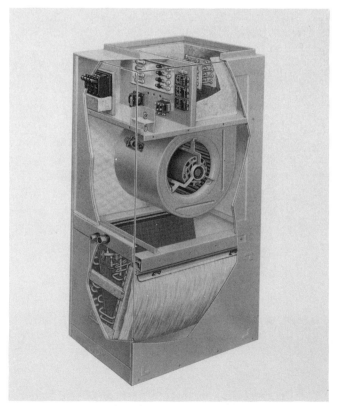

119. Cutaway of E-16 electric furnace. Courtesy of Lennox Industries Inc.

120. Tankless domestic water heater for water or steam boilers. Courtesy of Weil-McLain, a division of The Marley Company.

with the standards set by the National Fire Protection Association. Components of such heating systems should be approved by the Underwriters Laboratories for Construction and Safety in Operation.

When electricity is being used to fire a furnace (Figure 119), usually the furnace is installed in conjunction with a ducting system similar to the type used for a conventional hot air heating system. In this type of system, high voltage electrical resistance coils, specifically 220 volts, are used to produce heat. These coils are heated gradually, and they are timed to be put into operation at specific intervals. The time-delay control unit, which is built into the fan circuit, allows the coils to be heated before the fan starts to operate. In this way, the fan does not circulate air into the living areas while it is still cold. Once the desired temperature has been reached, the coils are shut off on a timed sequence again.

In addition to using electricity to fire a boiler or furnace, it can be used to power various electric heating units. Each unit has to be connected to a 240-volt circuit to function efficiently and effectively. Electric heating units can be hidden easily behind furniture. They are especially fuel-efficient because each unit can be controlled individually by its own thermostat. Since the only moving parts in the unit are in the thermostat, very little maintenance is needed. A single thermostat can be connected so that it controls the temperature in only one room or in several rooms. Of course, heating systems fired with other types of fuels also can accommodate any of these arrangements; however, additional piping or ducting would have to be installed throughout the house to establish the various individual heating zones. This type of work is expensive and requires extensive damage throughout the house.

Electric heating units are available in baseboard, wall-mounted, and floor-mounted styles and, as with any electrical installation, they must be installed to comply with national, state, and local electrical code requirements. Electric baseboard heating units, for example, according to the National Electrical Code, must not be installed below receptacle outlets in the walls (Figure 120). This is necessary to prevent the electric cord, which is plugged into the receptacle, from touching the hot baseboard as well as to prevent abrasions on the cord. If the wire in the cord becomes exposed, it could cause an electric shock or a fire from an electrical spark. The National Electrical Code also states that when a receptacle outlet is incorporated into the baseboard unit, its circuitry must be installed independently of the heating unit's circuitry. These units should be installed by a licensed electrician who knows how to install them properly to ensure that they are used safely and that they remain fuel-efficient.

PROBLEMS ASSOCIATED WITH BOILER CONVERSIONS

An older house may be heated with a boiler that originally was fueled with coal but has since been converted to oil or gas. This type of conversion can lead to several problems because of the age of the boiler. This converted boiler may be the original one in the house or it may be a replacement that was installed many years ago. In any case, it is quite old and, as it ages, problems can develop. This converted boiler also is not as efficient as today's modern boilers. It is probably a good idea to have its efficiency determined by a heating contractor, the local utility company, or a servicing company. These efficiency tests, which are described later in this section, can help the homeowner decide if the boiler needs to be replaced.

If the boiler is functioning well enough that it does not have to be replaced, then it should at least be cleaned and serviced annually to maintain it as well as possible. If the gas or oil gun in the boiler is old, it will have to be replaced because a new gun will increase or at least maintain the current efficiency of the boiler. In fact, every effort should be made to keep this old boiler operating at maximum efficiency. Another way to do this is to examine the condition of the fire box and the fire bricks in the box. They can be examined when the shutoff switch is in the "Off" position and the boiler has been given sufficient time to cool completely. Then the door to the fire box chamber can be opened and the fire bricks examined, looking for bricks that have crumbled or have fallen down onto the floor of the fire box. This examination should not be done by hand. It can be done safely and fairly easily by using a long stick or a metal rod. If the fire bricks are loose or crumbling, the fire box will have to be rehabilitated.

The fire bricks in the fire box are called the refractory walls, and it is important that they be intact to withstand the high temperatures they are subjected to when the boiler is operating. As the oil or gas gun fires, flames are sent across the fire box. The heat from these flames is reflected back into other flames coming from the gun by these refractory walls. This effect increases the temperature of the flames as well as the rate of combustion. As the rate of combustion increases, the fuel burns more efficiently. The refractory walls are set high enough above the flames to prevent them from coming into contact with the walls of the boiler, which would damage them (Figure 121). While the gun is firing, the temperature in the fire box is at least 2,000° F. To be able to withstand this intense heat, the fire combustion chamber is made of high quality insulating fire bricks that have been installed with the cement material recommended by the manufacturer for this type of application.

If the boiler has to be replaced, the homeowner should be aware of materials used in its construction that may be hazardous. These hazardous materials are not always apparent. For example, the fire bricks normally are reinforced with a second layer or wall of insulating material. This material may be dry sand or common bricks, neither of which is harmful. On the other hand, this material may be made with asbestos, which was frequently used in the manufacture of boilers before it became known as a health hazard. In addition, if the fire box is at the floor level, asbestos insulation boards may have been used as an underlayment for the fire box chamber. Additionally, the old boiler or furnace may have been covered with asbestos cement to insulate it. Any material found to contain asbestos, or even suspected to contain asbestos, should be removed by an asbestos abatement company that is certified to test for it and to remove it. (A complete review of asbestos and how to handle it when it is found in a house appears in Chapter 24.)

Another possible problem that the homeowner should be aware of, one that is not only limited to a converted boiler, is the location and condition of the flue pipe that connects the combustion outlet on the boiler or furnace to the chimney. This flue pipe should not project beyond the inner liner of the chimney, and it should not be used if it is damaged or corroded. It should be replaced if it is in bad

condition because deadly carbon monoxide can enter the living area from it. In addition, a flue pipe should never be connected to the flue being used for a fireplace, again because carbon monoxide can enter the living area from the fireplace. A flue pipe that is installed correctly rises toward the opening of the chimney and is sealed with the appropriate chimney cement at the point where the pipe enters this opening.

TESTING YOUR FURNACE OR BOILER'S EFFICIENCY

It is not an easy or inexpensive decision to have an old boiler or furnace replaced with a new energy-efficient one. Therefore, before going ahead with the replacement, it may be wise to have the existing boiler or furnace tested to determine its efficiency. These tests also can help the homeowner determine how many years it will take for the energy savings to pay back the cost of the new furnace or boiler. The homeowner's servicing or utility company conducts these tests by cutting a 1/4-inch hole in the flue pipe and inserting several measuring devices into it to acquire an accurate picture of the furnace or boiler's condition. Five tests, in all, are conducted to get a complete and thorough determination of its condition.

The draft is tested by inserting a draft gauge into the 1/4-inch hole. The intensity of the draft is of paramount importance for efficient combustion because it influences the flow rate of the combustion gases through the furnace or boiler. The draft also determines the amount of air being supplied to the furnace or boiler for combustion. If the draft is too high, the stack temperature will increase.

An intense draft, however, is necessary to reduce the presence of carbon dioxide in the combustion gases. The carbon dioxide value in the combustion gases is determined by inserting a carbon dioxide indicator into the same hole. Carbon dioxide readings usually are good when they are about 9 to 10%.

A thermometer is inserted into the same hole to determine the stack temperature. Service companies that conduct these tests generally agree that a stack temperature between 400° and 500° F is about normal. A higher stack temperature can indicate several possible conditions such as that the draft is

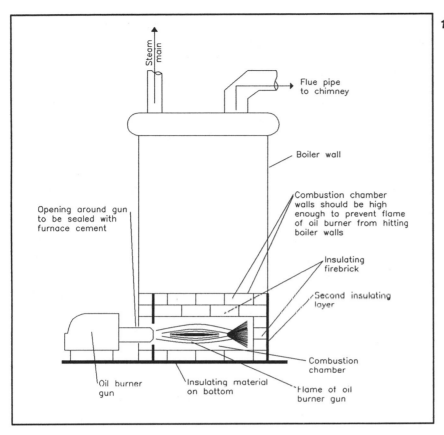

121. Oil burner conversion of old boiler

Steam main

Flue pipe to chimney

Boiler wall

Combustion chamber walls should be high enough to prevent flame of oil burner from hitting boiler walls

Insulating firebrick

Second insulating layer

Opening around gun to be sealed with furnace cement

Combustion chamber

Oil burner gun

Insulating material on bottom

Flame of oil burner gun

122. Radiant floor heating under concrete floor slab

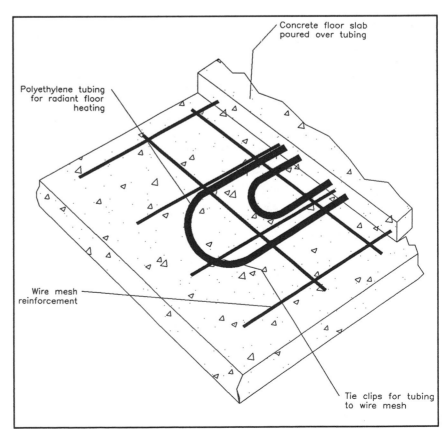

Concrete floor slab poured over tubing

Polyethylene tubing for radiant floor heating

Wire mesh reinforcement

Tie clips for tubing to wire mesh

too high, the furnace or boiler is over-firing, a great deal of soot has collected in the furnace or boiler, or even that the furnace or boiler is undersized. If the furnace or boiler is very old, it may be difficult to determine what the stack temperature normally should be. In this case, it is best to rely on the servicing company's recommendation.

Another test conducted as part of this series determines the oil pressure in the oil burner's fuel pump. This is done by inserting a pressure gauge into the connection of the fuel pump. The fuel pump operates at between 90 and 100 psi when it is operating properly.

The smoke test measures and analyzes the contents of the smoke in the flue pipe. A piece of filter paper is exposed to the smoke through the hole in the flue pipe. The tone of the stain on the filter paper is then compared with a smoke comparison scale. The various tones in the scale indicate when there is a poor draft, when the fuel/air mixture is not in proper proportion, when the combustion chamber is defective, and when there is a very serious problem in the furnace or boiler, which the servicing company will explain fully to the homeowner.

The results of these tests are presented to the homeowner along with the servicing company's recommendations as to how to follow up on them. Armed with the knowledge of the present condition of the furnace or boiler, the homeowner can more readily decide whether or not its efficiency can be improved, or if it is more economical in the long run to install a new boiler or furnace. The final decision, of course, is left to the homeowner.

RADIANT FLOOR HEATING SYSTEMS

In addition to its frequent use in new house construction, a radiant floor heating system often is installed in an older house to heat a room addition built on a concrete slab, or to heat a room where a conventional heating system would be difficult to install. Radiant floor heating is accomplished by sending hot water through one or a series of tubing systems. The tubing system may be encased in a concrete floor slab (Figure 122), or attached to a subfloor and covered with a lightweight mixture of concrete or with hardwood flooring. The heat from

the hot water in the tubing radiates upward through the flooring into the room to bring the living area to the desired comfort level.

When radiant floor heating systems were first introduced some twenty-five years ago, there were several problems associated with them. For instance, the material used for the tubing was either made of steel or copper, and connections made in the tubing were soldered or braised. The temperature of the water generally ranged from 120° to 140° F and to as high as 180° F in some systems. Leaks developed in the tubing within twenty-five years after installation for two reasons. First, the dissimilar metals at the joints corroded the tubing and, second, the lime and moisture in the concrete, which was in contact with the tubing, was highly corrosive. Leaks also developed in the tubing when cracks developed in the slab. In addition, some of the earliest radiant floor heating systems to be installed had great difficulty with temperature control. For example, a thermostat set at 70° F would not shut off the heating system until the room temperature rose to as high as 78°. This discrepancy wasted a great deal of heat energy while it made the room uncomfortably warm.

With the advent of many technological advances, most of these early problems have been eliminated in today's radiant floor heating systems. For example, polyethylene is used instead of metal to manufacture the tubing. This new tubing, which is guaranteed for at least twenty years, is very flexible, which makes it easier to install than the old metal tubing. It also is less expensive than copper and it resists abrasions and punctures very well. The polyethylene tubing can be placed in a tighter looping pattern around the floor than the metal tubing, which enables a greater amount of heat to radiate into the room from it. Although the new tubing is rated for as high as 180° F at 100 psi, the operating temperature of the water in the tubing actually ranges from 80° to 140° F. These temperatures are much lower than they used to be in the old tubing installations.

Because the polyethylene tubing is available in 400- and 800-foot rolls, it can be laid without any joints in it in a fairly large room or in several smaller rooms. When joints are needed, the tubing can be joined with special compression fittings. Since there are fewer joints in these types of installations, there are also fewer leaks at joints in these newer radiant floor heating systems. The use of polyethylene tubing also eliminates the problems of corrosion caused by dissimilar metals being in contact with each other and by metal tubing being in contact with concrete. In modern installations with the polyethylene tubing, the tubing is placed very close to the surface of the concrete slab, usually only 1½ inches below it, and mortar or a lightweight mixture of concrete is poured over it. In old installations, on the other hand, the tubing often was placed very deeply into the concrete. This depth prevented some of the heat in the tubing from radiating into the living area, a problem that has been resolved in modern installations.

There are several ways to install a radiant floor heating system. The choice depends on what surface is already in place. For instance, when the installation is being done on grade, wire ties are used to attach the tubing to the wire mesh reinforcement that is placed on grade. The tubing is tied at 2-foot intervals on straight runs and at 1-foot intervals on curves and turns. Then the concrete is poured over it. When the installation is being done on wood subflooring, the tubing is installed by fastening it to the subfloor with staples, again using the same intervals for spacing the staples that were used for wire ties. The concrete is poured over the wood subfloor and tubing to a thickness of about 1½ inches, and the tubing used is approximately ¾ inch in diameter. When the installation is being done under hardwood flooring, wood sleepers are installed first. The sleepers are 2" x 2" or 2" x 4" wood studs that are laid at intervals of 1 or 2 feet on center so that the hardwood flooring can be nailed to them. Before the flooring is installed, the tubing is placed between the sleepers and a mortar mixture of sand, cement, and water is poured to cover the tubing between the sleepers. This is done carefully so that the tubing is not damaged during the pour. Then the hardwood flooring is installed carefully to prevent the nails from puncturing the tubing during its installation.

Today's radiant floor heating systems, which are installed in every room in the house, are engineered to create an even distribution of heat throughout the house. The controls also are designed to provide for adequate temperature anticipation for each zone in the house. In these systems, a single zone can accommodate one room or several rooms, or several zones can accommodate all of the levels in a house. More zones can be added later as additions are made onto the house. While the heating system is in operation, the thermostat and zone valves work in conjunction with each other to heat the living areas. The anticipator in the thermostat, working with the zone valves, prevents each zone in the system from being overheated. The zone valves, which are actually connected to the thermostat, measure the outside air temperature, the temperature of the water in the tubing, and the room temperature simultaneously. By using a timed sequence, the zone valves open and close to control room temperatures, which are preset on the thermostat.

The water in a radiant floor heating system can be heated in a variety of ways. For instance, solar energy can be used as long as it can produce an adequate amount of hot water. The most common method is to heat the water by using the same boiler or furnace that is supplying the domestic hot water in the house. A four-way mixing valve mixes a specific amount of hot water taken from the boiler or furnace with some of the cool water in the tubing. A pump sends this water to the supply manifold where it circulates the water through its various loops to raise the temperature of the water. This hot water then flows to the return manifold where it mixes with the rest of the water from the boiler. The hot water is finally pumped back into the tubing to be circulated throughout the house.

HEAT PUMP HEATING AND COOLING SYSTEMS

A heat pump system can be used to heat or cool a house. It functions by extracting heat from one source and delivering it to another, based on the principle that heat flows from warm to cold. A household refrigerator operates by using this same principle. When heating a house, the heat pump system uses outdoor air as the heat source. When cooling it, heat is discharged from the house to the air outside. Some heat pump systems extract heat from the ground or from a water supply to provide heating, and discharge heat into the ground or into a water supply to provide cooling. Air-to-air heat pump systems, however, are the most common and practical for use in most localities.

When exterior air is being used as the heat source during a heating cycle, the air is brought into contact with a cold evaporator coil, which is located outdoors. Heat is transferred from the outside air to the refrigerant in the evaporator coil. Freon® or a similar type of liquid refrigerant is used in the heat transfer process. The temperature of the refrigerant rises as the heat from the air is transferred to it. The Freon changes from a liquid to a gaseous state as its temperature rises to between 20° and 40° F. Once it is in a gaseous state, the Freon flows into a compressor, where it is compressed. As it is compressed, the temperature of the Freon gas increases significantly. This very hot Freon gas is then sent to a condenser, which is a heat exchanger, where another heat transfer process takes place. The heat is transferred from the Freon gas to a cooling medium, either air or water, in the condenser. As a result of this heat transfer process, the Freon changes back to a liquid state from a gaseous state. The liquid Freon flows into an expansion device where it is depressurized. As the pressure drops, the temperature of the Freon falls to nearly its original level, which is usually between -20° and -30° F. The Freon returns to the evaporator coil so the heating cycle can begin all over again (Figure 123).

Meanwhile, the cooling medium in the condenser, which was heated by the hot Freon gas, is being distributed throughout the house, either as hot air through a ducting system, or as heated water through a piping system, depending on whether air or water is being used as the medium. A fan at the condenser blows the hot air through the ducting system, or a pumping system disperses the hot water through the piping system.

When the heat pump system is being used as a cooling system, it functions in the opposite way; that is, the flow of the refrigerant is reversed. Heat is removed from the air in the house and discharged to the air outdoors, while cool air is brought into the house. The heat pump system's heating and cooling cycles can be switched by installing valving to accommodate both of these functions. The valving reverses the direction of the refrigerant's flow in the evaporator coil, condenser, and heat exchangers so that, while the system is in the cooling cycle, it can perform functions exactly opposite of those it would perform if it were in the heating cycle.

As with any conventional heating system, a heat pump heating and cooling system is controlled by a thermostat. This type of heating system can heat and cool an entire house with the use of a ducting system installed throughout the house. A heat pump heating system can be installed as a single, self-contained unit or as a split system. In a self-contained system, all of the components, including the evaporator coil, condenser, etc., are housed in one unit. With this type of installation, the outdoor air is brought into the system through an opening in the foundation wall. The opening, which is covered with a screen to prevent blockages, supplies air to the system, starting with the evaporator coil. A split system, on the other hand, includes two units: an interior unit that includes the fan, condenser, compressor, and electric controls; and an exterior unit that includes the evaporator coil, another fan, and electric controls (Figures 124 and 125). Refrigerant and electrical lines connect the interior and exterior units to each other, enabling them to operate simultaneously when heating or cooling is needed in the house.

A heat pump system can be used to supply domestic hot water as well as heat and cool a house. This is done by installing an additional heat exchanger in the system to send a small portion of the heat from the refrigerant to the water supply where it heats it. This additional cycle in the heat pump system takes place before the heat transfer process occurs in the condenser. During the summer when the cooling cycle is in use, some of the heat extracted from the air in the house is sent to this additional heat exchanger to heat the domestic hot water supply. Most of the heat, however, is still exhausted outdoors.

When heat pump heating systems are installed in houses located in cold climates, they usually are used in conjunction with a conventional heating system because the heating cycle cannot always be totally effective. When outdoor temperatures get as low as -20° F or lower, for instance, air-to-air heat pump heating systems cannot transfer an adequate supply of heat to the cold liquid Freon to heat it properly, and this inadequacy interferes with the heat pump's heating cycle.

Although heat pump systems that utilize heat from the ground or from a water supply operate more efficiently than conventional air-to-air systems, their

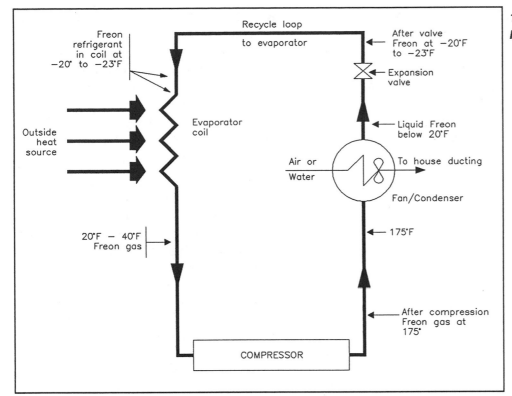

123. Schematic drawing of heat pump cycle for heating

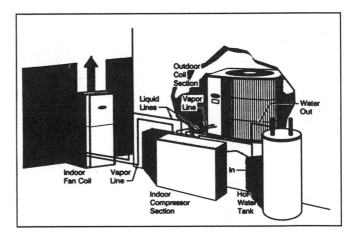

124 and 125. HydroTech® 2000 heat pump and how it is used. Courtesy of the Carrier Corporation.

high cost and feasibility problems limit their use in many locations. For example, to extract an adequate amount of heat from a water supply, it is necessary to have a well with a specific flow rate. This is not always possible, especially in a city, or even in a suburb of a city. Extracting heat from the ground also can be difficult because such a heat pump system requires extensive lengths of piping or tubing, buried at least 4 feet deep, to operate properly. A glycol solution is used in the piping or tubing to extract heat from the ground and transfer it to the Freon. Such an extensive amount of piping or tubing needs a great deal of acreage to accommodate it, which is why this type of heat pump system is impossible in most cities and suburbs of cities.

SOLAR ENERGY AT WORK IN YOUR HOME

More and more homeowners across the country are using energy from the sun to heat their homes as well as to supply domestic hot water. This is done by installing solar collectors on the roof of the house. Fuel costs can be reduced, sometimes dramatically, with the use of solar energy and, in some applications, air conditioning costs also can be cut in this way.

In a solar system, the solar collectors absorb solar radiation, which is then stored in a medium such as air or water until it is needed. Most solar heating systems use some type of auxiliary system to serve as a backup when the solar system cannot adequately provide the necessary heat and hot water in the house. Sometimes this backup system is as simple as a wood-burning stove, while in other applications it is as complex as a fully-installed heating system. The complexity or simplicity of the backup system depends largely on the climatic conditions of the area where the house is located.

Flat, plate-like solar collectors are used in a solar system to collect heat from the sun. The collectors are placed so that they face a southerly exposure to collect maximum solar radiation from the sun at all times. The collectors are made of metal such as steel, copper, or aluminum. Each solar collector has a cover plate to trap the heat in it. The heat is transferred from the collector to the medium as the air or water passes through or near the collector plate.

The heated medium is then either sent to the storage tank to be used when it is needed or directly to the place where it is needed. Generally, water is used as the medium in solar heating systems. Since solar systems rely on the sun to function, most of the thermal energy is collected on sunny days and then stored to be used on cloudy days and during evening hours when the collection of thermal energy is limited or impossible.

A variety of technical instruments is needed to enable solar systems to function properly. These devices measure the water temperature, activate the pumps to transfer the heated medium to the storage tank or to the outlet points in the house, and sense any temperature fluctuations in the system to turn it on and off as needed. Some solar systems are equipped with an alternate source of energy to operate the pumps and other necessary devices for its operation, while others use solar energy exclusively. The choice is made case by case, with the installer and homeowner deciding what is best to do since an alternate energy source is not always necessary. If it is needed, it will add to the total installation cost. The heating of the domestic water supply also may be done using only a solar system, or by using one in conjunction with a conventional domestic hot water heater. Again, this decision must be done case by case because variables have to be considered, such as how much water is needed and how much hot water the particular solar system can supply.

Several factors, in addition to positioning, affect the amount of heat the solar collectors can collect. For instance, the orientation and tilt of these collectors is important because the solar collectors absorb heat reflected from the ground and from adjacent building surfaces as well as from the sun. The solar collectors have to be positioned so that they are not shaded by adjacent buildings or by objects protruding from roofs, such as chimneys or dormers. Any of these obstructions can reduce the ability of the collectors to absorb the sun's thermal energy. To prevent these types of obstruction, it is a good idea to observe the location of the sun as it rises and sets on the roof so that the correct orientation and tilt of the solar collectors can be determined before they are installed. The solar collectors work best when they are placed in a position to gather maximum thermal energy from the sun during daylight hours.

Basically, a solar system can only function as efficiently as the climate in which it is located allows. Therefore, a solar system that is installed in an area with mild winters and lots of sunny days performs more efficiently than one in an area with very cold winters and many cloudy days. Generally, it is wise to have a conventional heating system installed to serve as a backup system for the solar system.

The homeowner who is considering the installation of a solar system in his house should become familiar with some of its components and their costs before making any final decisions. For instance, he should read carefully and understand clearly what parts, labor, etc., are covered by the manufacturer's warranty or guarantee. He should determine the life expectancy of the solar system and know exactly how many of those years are actually covered by the warranty or guarantee. He should know how long the parts are covered by the warranty or guarantee and whether they are readily available from local service centers. If the parts are going to have to be ordered, he should be aware of the length of the waiting period.

It is also important to know what type of metal has been used in the construction of the solar collectors and how that particular metal can be affected by the medium. When water is used as the medium, corrosion problems can develop in the solar system. Inhibitors may have to be added to the water to prevent this corrosion. This is especially important when the solar collectors are made of metal and when the domestic hot water supply is supplied by the solar system. Since this corrosion can create a health hazard in the water supply, it has to be considered very carefully. Problems with corrosion also can arise from joints in the tubing made with dissimilar metals. The homeowner should ask how the joints are being made and with what metals. He also should make sure that his contractor understands that he wants the installation done with as few joints as possible to lessen the risk of leaks at the joints.

All of the mechanical equipment such as the pump, motor, and other internal parts should be covered by the warranty or guarantee for many years to ensure a maximum life expectancy for the entire solar system. The system should be installed so that there is very little, if any, vibration in the mechanical equipment. This vibration can cause the system to be very noisy and parts of it to deteriorate prematurely. The newly installed system should be tested to be sure that is operates satisfactorily. This testing should include checking all of the instrumentation as well as the mechanical equipment. After heat has been transferred from the collectors to the medium, the water temperature should be measured to be sure that it has reached the correct temperature setting.

ALL ABOUT THE THERMOSTAT

The thermostat, or as is the case in some houses, several thermostats, is installed in the house to control the heating and cooling cycles of the heating and air conditioning systems. The thermostat operates on a 24-volt electrical circuit coming from the furnace or boiler. In some cases, this electrical current also operates a clock on the thermostat; however, the clock may be battery-operated. A thermostat houses many components enabling it to perform its complicated tasks. For instance, it houses a temperature sensing device that activates an electrical switch, which signals the furnace, boiler, or air conditioning unit to turn on or off. The anticipator in the thermostat controls the temperature — that is, the firing time for the heating system (Figure 126) and the cooling time for the air conditioning unit, which prevents the house from being overheated or undercooled. For example, when the thermostat is preset to heat the house to 68° F, the anticipator signals the thermostat to turn off the furnace or boiler at 67° F. The heat produced before the boiler or furnace was shut off is sufficient to bring the temperature in the house up to 68° F. During the summer, the anticipator functions in the opposite way. For instance, when the house is to be cooled to 76° F, the anticipator signals the air conditioning unit to start operating to allow for sufficient time for it to produce cool air (Figures 127 and 128).

Some thermostats called set-back thermostats can put the heating or cooling system into operation at a specific time so that the house can reach the desired comfort level before it is occupied (Figure 129). Set-back thermostats have become very popular in homes today because they save energy, yet they are easily programmed to achieve personal heating and cooling comfort levels. The U.S. Department of

Energy has estimated that these types of thermostats can save anywhere from 25 to 35% on home heating bills. Actual savings vary depending on where the house is located as well as what temperatures are chosen. Set-back thermostats also can accommodate several settings at different times of the day whether or not anyone is at home (Figure 130). For instance, a lower temperature setting can be used during the day when the house is empty. Later in the day, a higher setting can be achieved by programming the set-back thermostat to turn the boiler or furnace on for a specific period of time prior to the first person's arrival. By the time one family member comes home, the house has already reached the higher temperature, making it quite comfortable. The thermostat can be programmed to return to the lower setting at night when the family is asleep. Before the first family member rises in the morning, the thermostat can be set to turn the boiler or furnace on so that the house has once again returned to the comfortable, higher temperature setting. This same thermostat can be programmed to cool the house to different comfort levels at specific times of the day, again based on the family members' activities and schedules. Depending on the degree of sophistication and the cost of the thermostat, temperature settings can range from 5° to 10° for heating and from 4° to 6° for cooling.

As with any piece of equipment, sooner or later, a thermostat can fail to operate. One homeowner was surprised to learn about this type of failure when he least expected it. His heating system turned on during a hot summer day. Although outdoor temperatures hovered in the high 80s, his thermostat had put his boiler into operation. Since the boiler also was being used to supply domestic hot water in his house, it had been left on during the summer. After some puzzlement, he realized that the thermostat had malfunctioned, preventing the boiler from turning off.

The homeowner decided to replace the thermostat himself so he removed the old one and brought it to a store to purchase its replacement. This was a good idea because it is essential to install a thermostat that is compatible with the heating system, especially if it is a steam or hot water heating system. If it is not compatible, the thermostat will not function properly, if at all.

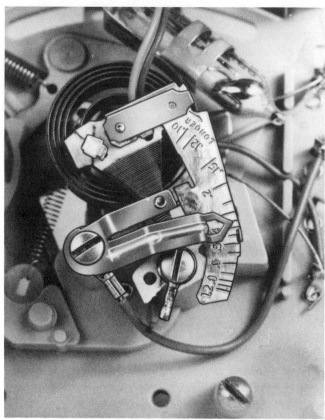

126. Honeywell's anticipator controller. Courtesy of Honeywell Residential and Building Controls.

The anticipator rating on the old thermostat also must match the rating on the new one. Again, if it does not, the thermostat will not function properly. Sometimes the thermostat is so old that the anticipator rating is not visible. In this case, it may be necessary to hire a heating contractor who can determine the correct rating, or to call the manufacturer of the thermostat to get the recommended rating for that particular model. If all else fails, sometimes the boiler manufacturer can provide the correct anticipator rating. When the anticipator rating is not set correctly, the house is overheated, underheated, overcooled, or undercooled. Additionally, an incorrect anticipator setting can burn out the anticipator and, in so doing, destroy the thermostat. Some old steam heating systems appear to interfere with the anticipator's operation, causing the house to become overheated frequently. Such a problem cannot be resolved very easily, in fact, it may require the services of a heating contractor.

Our intrepid homeowner was able to replace his old thermostat fairly easily. It is not a very complicated

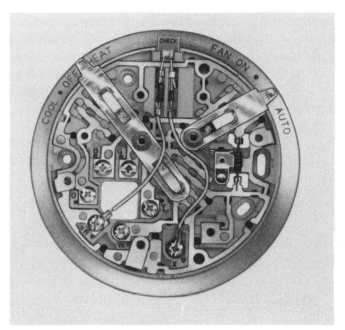

127 and 128. Heating and cooling thermostat with cutaway showing its internal parts. Courtesy of Honeywell Residential and Building Controls.

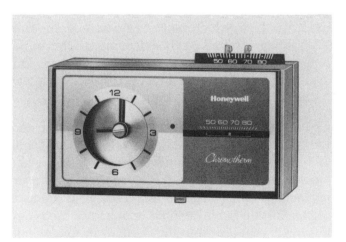

129. Set-back thermostat. Courtesy of Honeywell Residential and Building Controls.

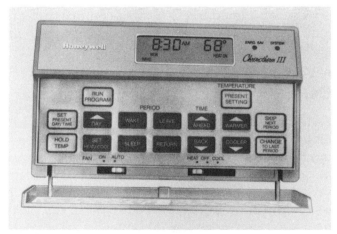

130. Chronotherm III set-back thermostat. Courtesy of Honeywell Residential and Building Controls.

 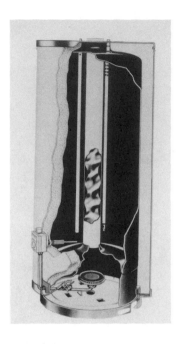

131 and 132. Conservationist® residential gas-fired heater and cutaway showing its internal parts. Courtesy of the A.O. Smith Water Products Company.

job. All he had to do was to match the colors of the wires with the letters marked on the wall plate indicating what color should be connected to each terminal. He also followed the manufacturer's instructions to set the anticipator rating and to program the thermostat to accommodate his specific needs.

The homeowner who does not think he can do this on his own should hire a heating contractor or the local utility company to have the thermostat installed correctly.

DOMESTIC HOT WATER HEATERS

As the prices of fuels increase, it becomes more and more costly to use a coil in the boiler to supply domestic hot water for household needs. This task can be accomplished with greater efficiency and energy savings by installing a domestic hot water heater, which means the boiler does not have to fire every time hot water is needed. It also minimizes wear on the boiler, and it is especially economical during the summer when the boiler can be turned off completely because it does not have to heat the house or the hot water supply. Fuel consumption is greatly reduced because only the domestic hot water heater has to be fired. This is particularly significant in a house with a large family or one with several families living in it and using a great deal of hot water. In some of these cases, the coil in the boiler cannot produce an adequate supply of hot water for

all of the family's needs. Generally, the initial cost for the installation of the domestic hot water heater can be offset by the savings accrued during its many years of use.

Domestic hot water heaters can be fired with gas, oil, or electricity. They are available in a variety of sizes to meet specific residential needs. The capacity of the tank, which ranges anywhere from 30 to 120 gallons, is stated on the information label at the bottom of the heater near the burner controls. This label also lists the heater's recovery rate, its wattage requirements, and its Btu input per hour rating.

The capacity of gas-fired domestic hot water heaters ranges from 30 to 100 gallons (Figures 131 and 132). The tank is insulated internally and is glass-lined to resist corrosion during its use. Its life expectancy is approximately ten years. The products of combustion from gas-fired heaters are exhausted through a vent pipe into the chimney or flue pipe to the outdoors. This vent pipe has to be secured tightly to the chimney or flue pipe. When the vent pipe becomes damaged or corroded, it must be replaced immediately, and any blockage in it must be cleared so that the products of combustion can exhaust from it completely. A temperature and pressure relief safety valve is installed on the hot water heater to prevent pressure from building up in it. The heater ranges from 18 to 27 inches in diameter and it stands from 56 to 70 inches high. Its thermostat has a fuel savings temperature setting indicator, which helps it conserve energy. The cold water inlet and hot water supply are located on top of the tank. A shutoff valve and vacuum valve are installed at the cold water inlet. The vacuum valve relieves the hot water tank as it expands and contracts. A gas shutoff valve and a sediment trap are installed near the burner controls. The sediment trap prevents sediment from damaging the burner controls (Figure 133). To increase the life expectancy of a gas-fired domestic hot water heater, the heater should be drained and flushed regularly. When corrosion becomes visible on the heater, it is an indication that it is near the end of its life expectancy and that it will have to be replaced shortly.

Electrically fired domestic hot water heaters range in capacity from 30 to 120 gallons (Figure 134). The diameter ranges from 18 to 30 inches and the height from 45 to 62 inches. The voltage requirement is 240 volts and the wattage ranges from 4,500 to 6,000 watts. The number of heating elements inserted into the tank is determined by its size. The life expectancy of this type of heater is ten years. This tank also is glass-lined to resist corrosion, as is the gas-fired type, and it has foam insulation installed internally. A thermostat is used to control the temperature of the water. The cold water inlet and hot water supply also are on top of the tank. Electrically fired domestic hot water heaters do not emit products of combustion as gas-fired heaters do;

however, they are subject to the problems associated with sediment that also are present in gas-fired heaters. Iron and lime particles, which are produced in the water in an electrically-fired heater, adhere to the heating elements in the tank. As the sediment collects there, the life expectancy of the heating elements is reduced. Corrosion can be seen at the cold water inlet and hot water supply as well as on the tank itself. A pressure safety valve installed on the tank prevents pressure from building up in it.

Oil-fired domestic hot water heaters, as well as all other types of hot water heaters, must be installed in accordance with state and local safety codes and with codes specified by the National Fire Protection Association. Once again, the cold water inlet and hot water supply are installed on top of the tank. A pressure safety valve also is installed on an oil-fired domestic hot water heater, and an adequate draft is needed for proper combustion to take place. Since the products of combustion in oil-fired heaters must be vented as they are in gas-fired heaters, a vent pipe is installed, which is attached to the chimney or to a flue pipe. This vent pipe should be examined regularly for any signs of damage or corrosion. It also should be checked for any blockage that might develop in it. Necessary repairs or replacement must be done as quickly as possible to prevent the products of combustion from collecting in the house, since they are harmful or even deadly.

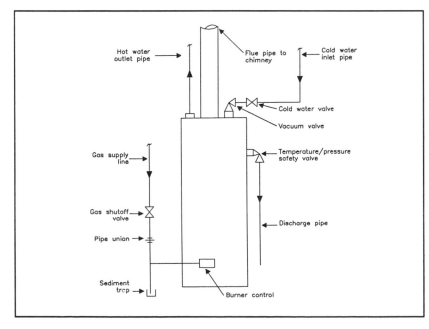

133. Typical gas-fired domestic hot water heater arrangement

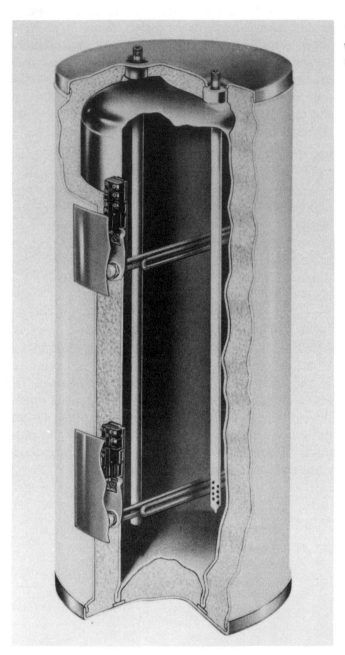

134. Cutaway of Conservationist® electric water heater. Courtesy of the A.O. Smith Water Products Company.

11
Examining the Electrical Service

COMPONENTS OF AN ELECTRICAL SYSTEM

Another important system in a house is the electrical system. A house that was built only twenty or thirty years ago probably has an electrical system installed in it that is able to provide adequate power to meet the demands of today's modern appliances and equipment. It probably has a circuit breaker panel box with 110/220 volts and at least 100 ampere service, and the wiring throughout the house is relatively new and in good condition. Switches and receptacles also are fairly new, are grounded for safety, and have been installed in sufficient numbers to be more than adequate for today's lifestyles. A house that is much older, perhaps one that was built forty or more years ago, on the other hand, probably has an old 110 volt system with a mere 30 to 60 ampere service. Its wiring, switches, and receptacles also are old and, most likely, there are not enough of them for modern use. No matter which kind of electrical system the homeowner has, new or old, adequate or inadequate, he ought to be aware of how it functions and what components are used to do so in order to be certain that his electrical system is plentiful and safe.

Adequate electrical service depends on several factors, such as the number of rooms in a house and how many people are using them; what types of appliances and electrical equipment are used by family members; and if the house has special features such as central air conditioning, a home workshop, an outdoor pool, etc., that increase the family's demand for electricity. The more electricity the homeowner and his family need, the greater the electrical service in the house must be.

Electricity is brought into a house either from an overhead or underground power line and the line runs through a meter located inside or outside the house (Figure 135). The electric meter is installed by the local utility company to measure the amount of electricity used so it can bill the homeowner for it. The electric line carrying the electrical current travels from the meter to the main circuit breaker or fuse box, which usually is located in the basement, cellar, or an interior garage (Figure 136). The electrical current runs through a main shutoff breaker or a main fuse in the main box, depending on which type of system is installed, then travels to individual circuit breakers or fuses in the box. The electricity runs from these individual circuit breakers or fuses, which have smaller capacities than the main circuit breaker or main fuse, to the various switches and receptacles installed throughout the house.

Fuses

Fuses are available in several styles, such as the round screw-in type that screws into a socket in the fuse box, or the cartridge type that can be the Ferrule or knife-edge style. Generally, the cartridge type fuse is used as a main fuse. When a knife-edge

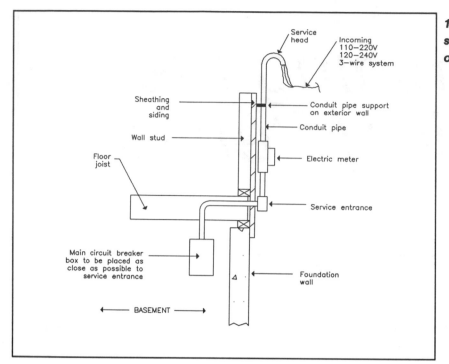

135. Elevation of overhead main service entrance (electric meter outside)

Service head

Incoming
110–220V
120–240V
3–wire system

Sheathing and siding

Conduit pipe support on exterior wall

Conduit pipe

Wall stud

Electric meter

Floor joist

Service entrance

Main circuit breaker box to be placed as close as possible to service entrance

Foundation wall

BASEMENT

136. Section of main circuit breaker box

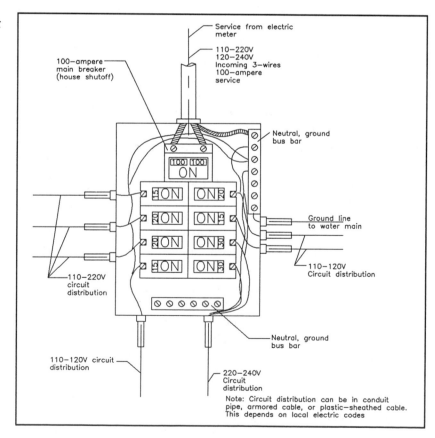

Service from electric meter

100-ampere main breaker (house shutoff)

110–220V
120–240V
Incoming 3–wires
100–ampere service

Neutral, ground bus bar

Ground line to water main

110–120V Circuit distribution

110–220V circuit distribution

110–120V circuit distribution

Neutral, ground bus bar

220–240V Circuit distribution

Note: Circuit distribution can be in conduit pipe, armored cable, or plastic–sheathed cable. This depends on local electric codes

fuse is used, it is important to keep it corrosion-free to enable it to operate efficiently. A round fuse has a glass-enclosed metal strip in it. When the circuit is overloaded, the metal strip blows or melts, leaving a gap in the circuit that stops the flow of electricity in it. A fuse blows when too much current is flowing through it because of a short circuit or because too many appliances are plugged into it. The glass at the top of the fuse blackens when a round fuse blows. When the glass is clear but the metal strip is broken or melted, it is an indication that the circuit was overloaded. The damage to a cartridge fuse when it blows is not visible, although the causes for its blowing are the same.

A circuit breaker trips, that is, it moves from the "On" to the "Off" position, to stop the flow of electricity to the receptacle or switch that it is connected to, and it can be reset easily by flipping it back to the "On" position. When a fuse blows, however, it must be removed and replaced with a new one. When a circuit breaker continues to flip to the "Off" position, or a fuse keeps blowing, it is an indication that there is a problem with the circuit. Since there could be a fire hazard associated with the problem, an electrician should be called immediately to determine the cause of the problem and to correct it. Frequently the cause of the problem is that the circuit is overloaded and the breaker or fuse is tripping or blowing as a safety measure to prevent the wiring from becoming overheated. This is an important safety feature; however, some homeowners have been known to try to bypass it by replacing the smaller-sized fuse with one with a larger ampere rating. This is easy to do because any size fuse can be screwed into any socket in the fuse box, but it is *not* a smart thing to do. The wiring in this circuit can overload and cause an electrical fire in the house. Other homeowners have another trick to circumvent this safety feature. They put a copper penny behind a blown fuse to make it operate again. This is dangerous because it also can cause an electrical fire. The smart homeowner never takes any chances with electricity, so he never attempts these kinds of tricks to save the few cents a new fuse costs.

Circuit Breakers

In modern electrical systems installed in new houses and in old houses that have been completely reno-

vated, circuit breakers are used instead of fuses. They are available in a variety of amperages such as 15, 20, 30, 50, etc., and they are installed in the main circuit breaker box. When the electrical demand on the wiring is too great, the switch on the breaker flips from the "On" to the "Off" position to stop the flow of electricity in that circuit. The switch cannot be flipped back into the "On" position until the electrical demand on the circuit has been reduced. It is easy to see which breaker is off since it is the one in the "Off" position in the circuit breaker box. In addition to the ease with which a circuit breaker can be put back into operation, it has another advantageous feature. A circuit breaker can carry a small overload in an electrical circuit for about 20 to 30 seconds before it flips, or trips as it also is called, and turns off. A circuit breaker can carry a large overload as well, but only for a few seconds before it trips. This can be helpful when a great deal of current is needed all at once such as when the motor on a table saw first starts. Such a delay enables the saw to start operating without turning the breaker off. Once the saw is operating, the overloading stops and the electrical flow in that circuit returns to a normal, safe level.

Proper Grounding

Every electrical system in a house has to be grounded. This is done by connecting the ground wire either to the water main in the cellar or basement, or to a ground rod, which is located outside of the house. The ground wire, which has no voltage, protects the system in several ways. For instance, it prevents the electrical system from becoming overheated and possibly causing a fire. It also protects members of the household by directing electricity into the soil where it is harmless, instead of into a person's body where it could cause a fatal electrical shock. The homeowner who does not see the ground wire connected to the water main or ground rod should call an electrician to determine whether his electrical system has been grounded. Sometimes a new water main is installed and the ground wire is not attached to the new water main afterward. In addition to looking for the placement of the ground wire, the electrician also should be sure that the ground rod has not corroded. The corrosion could make the connection incomplete or totally ineffective. It is also a good idea to examine the grounding clamp to see that it is secured tightly to the water

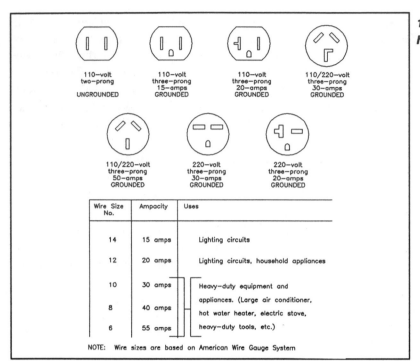

137. Various household receptacles and household wire sizes

110–volt two–prong UNGROUNDED	110–volt three–prong 15–amps GROUNDED	110–volt three–prong 20–amps GROUNDED	110/220–volt three–prong 30–amps GROUNDED

110/220–volt three–prong 50–amps GROUNDED	220–volt three–prong 30–amps GROUNDED	220–volt three–prong 20–amps GROUNDED

Wire Size No.	Ampacity	Uses
14	15 amps	Lighting circuits
12	20 amps	Lighting circuits, household appliances
10	30 amps	Heavy–duty equipment and appliances. (Large air conditioner, hot water heater, electric stove, heavy–duty tools, etc.)
8	40 amps	
6	55 amps	

NOTE: Wire sizes are based on American Wire Gauge System

138. Grounded and ungrounded receptacles

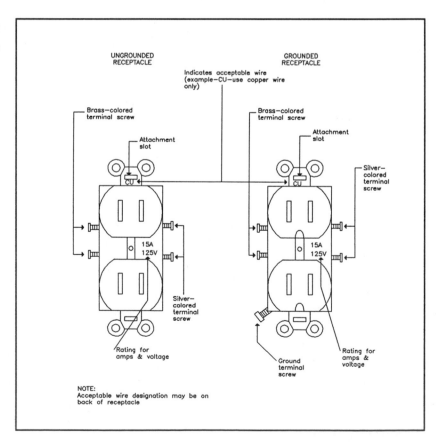

main or ground rod and that it also is in good condition. These are simple but essential maintenance procedures that can cause unnecessary harm or damage if left undone.

Switches and Receptacles

Switches and receptacles are the parts of the electrical system that enable the homeowner and the family to use the electricity in the house for their various needs. Switches are available in many styles, including the standard flip type, the push button, and the rocker type. The newest style is called the dimmer switch, and it enables lighting in a room or other living space to be adjusted from a bright to a subdued effect by controlling the amount of electricity flowing through it. In fact, all switches function by connecting or breaking the flow of electricity in the electrical circuit. When a switch malfunctions, it may produce a spark as it is turned on, or even an odor of something burning as well as a little smoke. If this happens, an electrician should be called immediately to have a new switch installed. Until he arrives, it is a good idea to shut off the circuit breaker that is connected to that switch to prevent an electrical fire from starting in it.

A receptacle is different from a switch in that it cannot be turned on and off. In fact, a receptacle always has electricity in it coming from the circuit breaker that is connected to it. A polarity tester, which is available at most home centers and hardware stores, can determine if a receptacle is wired correctly and whether or not it is grounded. When a receptacle becomes damaged or even burned, an electrician should be called immediately. Since either the receptacle is malfunctioning or the wiring connected to it is deteriorating, a new receptacle is going to have to be installed and, perhaps, new wiring to it installed as well.

It is important to have additional receptacles installed in an older house that has few receptacles already in place. The added receptacles can improve the electrical distribution around the house while eliminating the need for extension cords, which can be tripping hazards. Extension cords with multiple sockets can cause a fire by overloading the electrical circuit on the receptacle. In some localities, in fact, it is a violation of the electrical code to use extension cords as permanently placed receptacles. This is because the wiring is unarmored; that is, it is

not protected by metal tubing or cable, and because the sockets of the extension cord are not installed in a metal box. Both conditions are more susceptible to electrical fires starting in them.

Many types of receptacles are available, each manufactured to accommodate specific electrical requirements (Figure 137). Receptacles with only two openings in them usually are the older types. Newer receptacles have three openings to accommodate the grounding prong as well as the other two prongs on an electrical plug (Figure 138). Replacement of a two-hole receptacle with one with three openings does not automatically mean that the receptacle has been grounded. The installation of a pigtail adapter, which enables a two-hole receptacle to accept a three-prong plug, also does not mean that the receptacle has been converted into a grounded receptacle. Again, in some localities it is a violation of the electrical code to install a three-hole receptacle where a two-hole receptacle used to be unless it has been grounded. A polarity tester can be used to be certain that all of the receptacles in the house are grounded. Those that are not should be replaced by an electrician.

When receptacles and switches are installed in the wall cavities, they are enclosed in either metal or plastic boxes, depending on which material local and state electrical codes permit. In many cases several switches and receptacles are connected to a single breaker. This type of connection is acceptable as long as it does not exceed the electrical capacity of the breaker. The connections for the switches and receptacles also are made in a metal or plastic box, called a junction box, taking the circuit from the circuit breaker box. The junction box also is hidden behind a wall or ceiling surface. Light fixtures for walls and ceilings also are connected to junction boxes using a circuit from the circuit breaker box. When these connections are not done correctly (in junction boxes), they are dangerous because they can cause a fire. Loose wires may cause a short circuit, which could create a spark to start an electrical fire. That is why junction boxes are essential components of any electrical system and why they should always be used to make these types of connections.

Light Bulbs

The light bulbs used in lighting fixtures should

never exceed the wattage recommended by the fixture manufacturer because the wiring in the fixture has been sized to carry that specific amount of electrical current in it. If a higher wattage is used, it could cause the wiring to overheat, resulting in a fire. The correct light bulb size usually appears on a tag attached to the light fixture when it is purchased. Since the proper light bulb size is not always apparent on old fixtures, it may be necessary to replace them with new ones, or to call an electrician who can recommend the size for safe use of the fixture.

When a light bulb continues to burn out prematurely in a fixture, it is usually an indication that there is some kind of problem. There may be a short in the wiring in the fixture, or the wiring may be exposed, or there may even be a problem in the receptacle. Again, since the potential for a fire exists, an electrician should be called to determine the exact cause of the problem. An electrician also should be hired to fix loose or frayed wiring on electrical cords on light fixtures as well as to fix any switches or receptacles that are loose or not functioning properly. Receptacles that are so old that they can no longer hold a plug in place, and those that cannot make contact with the prongs on a plug, also should be replaced to prevent an electrical fire. These repairs and replacements are relatively inexpensive when compared with the loss of life and property that could result if they are not done.

MATERIALS USED FOR ELECTRICAL WIRING

Older electrical systems used to be wired with copper and later, in some areas, with aluminum wiring; however, copper wiring is preferred in today's modern houses. Although aluminum wiring is less expensive than copper, it has serious drawbacks that have affected its use. For example, aluminum wiring has a greater resistance to an electrical current flowing through it than copper wiring. This characteristic causes aluminum wiring to heat and expand more than copper wiring. Aluminum wiring is attached to switches and receptacles with brass or silver screws. As the aluminum wiring heats and cools — expands and contracts — it eventually loosens from the screws. This causes a short in the electrical circuit, creating a fire hazard. This problem with

aluminum wiring as well as several others associated with it have made it a very unpopular material in most electrical codes. In fact, many state and local electrical codes have already banned its use. Copper-clad aluminum wiring remains an acceptable alternative.

To be on the safe side of this conflict, all electrical circuits with aluminum wiring or copper-clad aluminum wiring should be replaced with copper wiring because copper wiring has many advantages. For instance, copper wiring can carry a higher ampere rating than aluminum wiring when matching each specific size to one another. The National Electrical Code uses the term "ampacity" to explain this characteristic of wiring. The Code defines ampacity as "the current in amperes a conductor can carry continuously under the conditions of use without exceeding its temperature rating." This simply means that a 20 ampere circuit, for instance, needs only a No. 12 copper wire to carry the electrical power safely, while this same circuit would need a No. 10 aluminum wire to function equally well. Even more simply stated, this states that a thicker, heavier wire is needed when aluminum wire is being used instead of copper in the same size circuit.

A partial list of wire sizes and their ampacity is presented in Figure 137. The sizes are based on the use of copper wiring for the corresponding amperage given. The table was prepared by the National Electrical Code to state clearly and specifically what types and wire sizes can be used safely for the various wiring projects listed. The wire sizes are dictated by the American Wire Gauge System. The types and sizes are printed on the insulating coating on the copper wiring. As a simple rule of thumb, the homeowner can just remember that as the numbered size of the wire increases, its ampacity decreases or, the higher the numbered wire size, the lower the amount of current it can carry.

Electrical wiring is color-coded to help make connections correctly, although the color-coding cannot be fully trusted. Black or red coverings, for example, usually indicate the "hot" wires — the wires that are carrying the electricity from the circuit breaker or fuse box to the switch or receptacle. Wiring with a white covering usually is attached to the "neutral" position, and wiring with a green insulating covering or a bare copper wire is attached to the "ground" position on the switch or receptacle. Sometimes, during manufacturing, the colors of the coverings are reversed on the wires, so they are not always 100% accurate. When the wires are not attached to their correct positions, the switch or receptacle cannot function. Such an incorrect connection also may cause a short in the electrical circuit. The hot wire should be connected to the switch or receptacle with the brass terminal screw and the neutral wire should be connected with the silver screw. To determine which wire is hot, etc., it may be necessary for the homeowner to hire an electrician.

In addition to the types and sizes of the electrical wiring, the amperages and voltage ratings also are printed on the wiring, switches, and receptacles so that they can be installed to accommodate appropriate electrical uses. For instance, many types of switches and receptacles are available to serve a variety of purposes, such as heavy-duty electrical receptacles for large air conditioning units or for electric stoves. They are made so that they can carry large amounts of electrical current through them without overheating (see Figure 137). Old switches and receptacles as well as old wiring may not have any of these markings on them because electrical codes in effect at the time may not have required them when the receptacles and switches were manufactured and installed. Ungrounded receptacles and switches are still in use in many older houses. Generally, most unmarked switches and receptacles that are installed in an older house were made for 15 to 20 ampere service, and they were intended for use with copper wiring.

Prior to the early 1970s, switches and receptacles that could be used with aluminum or copper wiring were marked with the letters "CU-AL" to denote this usage. After that time, when changes were made in the National Electrical Code, switches and receptacles that could be used with either aluminum or copper wiring were marked with the letters "CO/ALR" to indicate this new usage. "CU" is the chemical abbreviation for copper and "AL", the chemical abbreviation for aluminum. When the code was changed, the Underwriters Laboratories, Inc. decided to denote copper with the letters "CO" and aluminum with the letters "ALR" so that the code changes could be identified easily. Under the new code requirements, therefore, aluminum wiring can be used when the letters "CO/ALR" appear on the switch or receptacle, but it cannot be used when it is marked with the letters "CU-AL."

The newest type of switch and receptacle is called the push-in type because the wiring is held in place by pushing it into slots at the back of the switch or receptacle. This is a much easier way than connecting them with screws as is done on the older types. Aluminum wiring should never be used with push-in receptacles or switches, and the wiring materials should never be mixed when connecting a single type of switch or receptacle. Only copper or copper-clad aluminum wiring can be used safely with push-in type switches or receptacles.

WHERE TO USE GFCI RECEPTACLES

Most local and state electrical codes require the use of ground fault circuit interrupter receptacles (GFCIs) in the kitchen, the basement, and the bathroom, for whirlpool baths and spas and hot tubs, and outdoors such as in the garage, near the swimming pool, or on the patio. It is essential to have ground fault circuit interrupter receptacles in these areas to use electricity safely. The GFCI receptacle uses a two-wire installation and a ground to prevent electrical shock. The black wire, which is the hot wire, carries the current to the receptacle, while the white wire, which is the neutral wire, returns it to its source. The amount of electrical current in these wires is equal when the receptacle is functioning properly. When there is a short circuit and the current is redirected through an individual's body, the current becomes unequal. Acting as a monitoring device, the ground fault circuit interrupter measures the current in both wires and when it notes that there is a drop in the current in the white wire, it shuts off the circuit, taking only about 1/40th of second to do so. Since the current is shut off so quickly, electric shock to the individual is minimal, so it will not harm a person who is in good health.

Ground fault circuit interrupters are available in many useful forms. They can be installed in a wall, or as a circuit breaker in a panel box, or even into an existing three-slot receptacle for temporary use. During any kitchen or bathroom modernization, replace ungrounded receptacles with GFCI receptacles. The cost is minimal for a life-saving result.

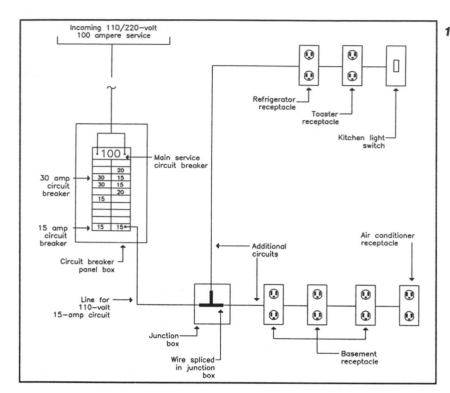

139. Overloaded 15-ampere circuit

140. Schematic of distribution of electrical service

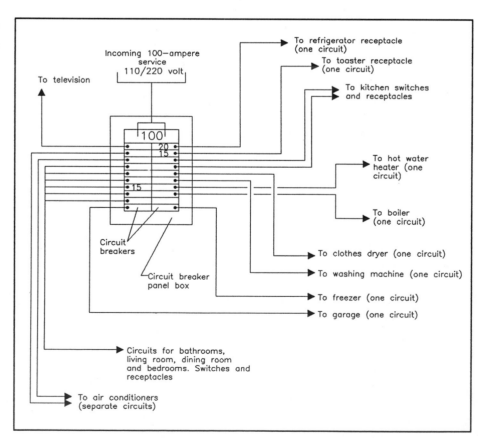

UPGRADING THE ELECTRICAL SYSTEM

The best way to modernize an old electrical system is to have an adequate supply of electricity brought into the house. A minimum of at least 110/220 volts with 100 ampere service should be brought into the house from the city or county service line outside. An old electrical system usually has an old fuse box in use. It should be removed and a main circuit breaker panel box should be installed to accommodate the new electrical service. The new main circuit breaker box should be large enough to accommodate additional circuit breakers as the need for them arises. One homeowner upgraded his electrical service to 100 ampere service, but he allowed his electrician to install a small circuit breaker box with little, if any, space for additional circuit breakers. As his family grew and his electrical needs increased, he found that he could not simply add circuit breakers to the existing box. Instead, he had to hire another electrician to install a larger box that could accommodate his additional electrical needs. As a result he had to pay twice for work that should have been done initially. Neither he nor his electrician had anticipated future electrical demands. That is why it is best to start big so that the main circuit breaker box can meet all future electrical needs as well as current demands.

As part of any modernization project, it is a good idea to eliminate all electrical circuits that you know are overloaded or that your electrician determines are overloaded. Electrical service in a house should be distributed evenly among the circuit breakers installed in the main box. This even distribution is especially important for electrical appliances that use lots of electricity, such as the refrigerator and toaster, for instance. One homeowner who experienced this problem had to make regular trips to the basement every time the toaster was used. The circuit kept blowing because he had too many circuits on a single breaker. He had the kitchen lights, basement receptacles, and the refrigerator on the same breaker as the receptacle used for the toaster (Figure 139). Plugging in the toaster on this single breaker was simply the last straw, electrically speaking, because it needed so much electricity to operate that it overloaded an already fully loaded breaker. The homeowner had to hire an electrician who installed

additional breakers to serve all of the individual circuits.

The best way to handle distribution of the electrical service is to use a single breaker for each major appliance as well as for each air conditioning unit. Lights and receptacles can be combined into a single breaker, but only as many as can be safely accommodated. The washer, dryer, refrigerator, and electric range should be connected to individual circuit breakers as well as the domestic hot water heater or the boiler ignition for the pilot light, when these are in use (Figure 140). The electrician's recommendations for these installations should always be part of the plans made for a renovation or modernization project so that the work is done correctly and the electrical service is distributed evenly.

A great deal of work is needed in a very old house with an electrical system that was never updated. Any pull-chain fixtures that are in use have to be replaced with new switches, and additional receptacles and switches have to be installed throughout the house to meet current electrical standards. This is especially important in the kitchen where food processors and microwave ovens are going to be used because these electrical appliances demand plenty of electrical power. Additional switches and receptacles also are going to be needed in bathrooms to accommodate blow dryers and electric shavers used today by both men and women. These types of electrical devices had not even been invented when the house originally was equipped for electrical service. Of course, it is best to do this work while renovations and modernizations are underway, not only to save on the cost of their installation, but also to be able to customize the rooms for their updated electrical needs.

Another important part of any electrical system's updating in a very old house is to have new electrical wiring installed throughout the house since the existing wiring may be as old as the house itself. In some cases, a mixture of old and new wiring can be made workable, but for the most part, this is not the case, especially when heavy electrical usage is anticipated. The old wiring may be loose at various connections, or brittle, or it may be in a general state of disrepair. This is a dangerous situation that should be corrected early in the renovation process. Since walls and ceilings have to be broken to install the

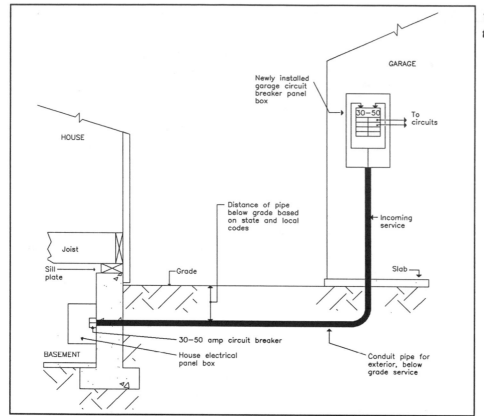

141. Supplying additional power to garage

GARAGE

Newly installed garage circuit breaker panel box

30-50

To circuits

HOUSE

Distance of pipe below grade based on state and local codes

Incoming service

Joist

Sill plate

Grade

Slab

BASEMENT

30-50 amp circuit breaker

House electrical panel box

Conduit pipe for exterior, below grade service

new wiring, this work also should be planned simultaneously with major renovation projects, especially for those that involve the removal and/or replacement of walls and ceilings. The homeowner who does not know the condition of his wiring, or who is concerned that it may be old and brittle, should hire an electrician to determine its age and whether or not it needs to be replaced.

During the upgrading of the electrical system, it is good time to add or upgrade electrical service to the garage to provide lighting for auto repairs and electrical power for cleaning or polishing the car. If the homeowner intends to use the garage as a workshop, it also may be a good time to install a separate 110/220 volt system with a secondary circuit breaker box in the garage. This would provide sufficient electrical power for all tools and lighting while freeing all of the other breakers in the main box for

electrical demands in the house. If the line happens to get overloaded, or if it has a short circuit, the breaker in the secondary box in the garage can be flipped back to the "On" position without the homeowner having to go into the house and down into the cellar or basement to do so (Figure 141). Electrical work can be dangerous work if it is done improperly. A connection that is made incorrectly can cause a fire or give an individual an electrical shock that could be fatal. It is for these very important reasons that most electrical codes require that a licensed electrician do all of the electrical work in a house. Licensed electricians are familiar with national, state, and local electrical codes so that the installation is done as safely as it can be done. The do-it-yourself homeowner can find plenty of other projects to undertake that are a lot less dangerous to do and that, if done improperly, will lead to less severe problems.

12
Probing the Plumbing System

FUNCTIONS OF THE PLUMBING SYSTEM

The plumbing system in a house serves two functions (Figure 142). First, it supplies domestic hot and cold water throughout the house, and second, it removes soil and waste discharge through a piping system that drains into the city or town's sewer system or into a septic tank. Each household receives its water supply either from the municipality's water system or from well water. The water supply enters the house through a water main that is located in the basement or cellar, or in the first floor level when there is no cellar or basement in the house. From this main, the water is carried through the plumbing system to the kitchen, bathrooms, laundry area, etc., and to the heating system or domestic hot water heater, depending on which is being used to supply domestic hot water in the house (Figure 143). Common household piping fittings are used to connect the various components of the plumbing system (Figure 144). Let's review the various components and materials of the plumbing system to understand how it functions and to foresee what problems may arise because of age and use over the years, starting with the water main.

THE WATER MAIN AND ITS VALVES

The water main that brings water into the house generally is made of copper when installed in a new house or in an old house when the old main was replaced. One homeowner who had an old house did not know that the water main in it also was old until it failed and his basement was flooded with water — many, many gallons of water. The old water main was made of lead and it was the one that had been installed originally when the house was built. After many years of use, the lead water main failed, destroying the boiler and many of the personal belongings that had been stored in the basement. That is why it is a good idea to have an old lead water main replaced. There are several other reasons to do this replacement that are of equal importance.

For example, the valves on an old lead water main may not function properly as a result of their age. The water shutoff valve, to cite one example, may not be able to stop the flow of incoming water even though the handle on the valve turns as if to do so. The valve cannot function because the disc inside it cannot advance to block the flow of the water. The drain valve on the old lead water main also may not be able to function properly. This valve is used to flush the plumbing system of all of its water. Due to its age, the drain valve may not be able to open to release the water left in the plumbing system. This drain valve is opened to drain the plumbing system after the incoming water valve has been closed, all of the faucets on the sink have been opened, and all of the water closets have been flushed.

Although age alone is a good reason to replace an

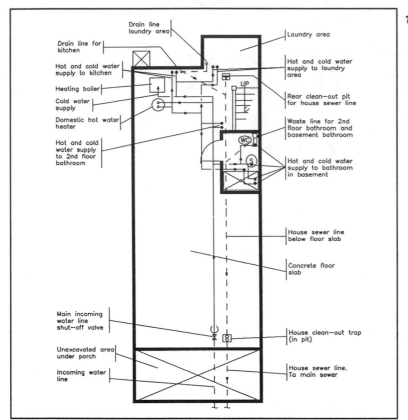

142. Basement plan — plumbing and drainage

Drain line laundry area
Drain line for kitchen
Hot and cold water supply to kitchen
Heating boiler
Cold water supply
Domestic hot water heater
Hot and cold water supply to 2nd floor bathroom
Main incoming water line shut-off valve
Unexcavated area under porch
Incoming water line

Laundry area
Hot and cold water supply to laundry area
Rear clean-out pit for house sewer line
Waste line for 2nd floor bathroom and basement bathroom
Hot and cold water supply to bathroom in basement
House sewer line below floor slab
Concrete floor slab
House clean-out trap (in pit)
House sewer line. To main sewer

UP
WC
S

143. Typical house water supply system

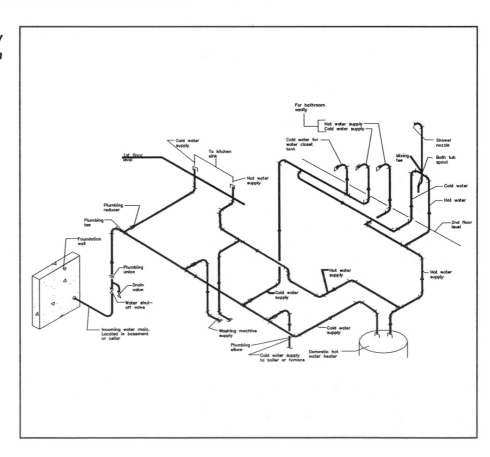

For bathroom vanity
Hot water supply
Cold water supply
Cold water for water closet tank
Shower nozzle
Mixing tee
Bath tub spout
Cold water
Hot water
2nd floor level
Cold water supply
To kitchen sink
Hot water supply
1st floor level
Plumbing reducer
Plumbing tee
Foundation wall
Plumbing union
Drain valve
Water shut-off valve
Incoming water main. Located in basement or cellar
Washing machine supply
Plumbing elbow
Cold water supply to boiler or furnace
Cold water supply
Domestic hot water heater
Hot water supply
Cold water supply
Hot water supply

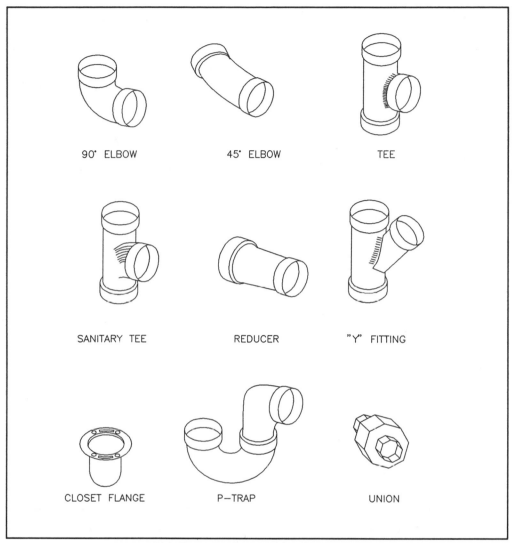

90° ELBOW   45° ELBOW   TEE

SANITARY TEE   REDUCER   "Y" FITTING

CLOSET FLANGE   P—TRAP   UNION

144. Common household pipe fittings

old lead water main and its valves, another even more important reason exists. After conducting many extensive studies, the U.S. Environmental Protection Agency (EPA) has concluded that drinking water from a lead water main has a high enough lead content to be harmful to a person's health, especially to the health of children (see the section on lead in paint in Chapter 24 for more details). This conclusion is not one that a homeowner can ignore. Therefore, a copper water main and new shutoff and drain valves should be installed if they are not already in place, to protect the health of the family as well as their possessions. If the electrical ground was attached to the old lead water main, it will have to be reattached to the new copper main after installation has been completed.

WATER SUPPLY SYSTEM

Over the years, water supply piping has been made of a variety of materials. In the first half of this century, galvanized piping was used extensively. This type of piping is made of iron, and it is coated with zinc to minimize the corrosive effects of water when it is in contact with iron. Galvanized piping was first replaced with yellow brass piping, later with red brass piping and, most recently, with copper tubing. Yellow brass has higher zinc and lead contents than red brass. Yellow brass is inferior to red brass because it can crack and corrode more easily than red brass. The presence of yellow or red brass is easy to determine by their colors. Yellow brass is either yellow or gold in color, while red brass is reddish-brown in color. Yellow brass piping is no longer used in plumbing systems. In fact, copper tubing has just about replaced the use of red brass piping because it is easier to install and less expensive than red brass.

For the most part, the age of a water supply piping system can be determined by the types of material used in it. An old house, or one with some renovations already made in it, probably has galvanized piping in use to supply water to the kitchen sink and bathroom fixtures. It also may have a mixture of galvanized piping, brass piping, and copper tubing. This mixture of piping materials usually indicates that repairs have been made on an as-needed basis, or that renovation projects have not been extensive enough to include the complete replacement of old plumbing materials with new ones. Corrosion and rust may already be visible on the surface of the galvanized fittings that connect the various piping materials throughout the house. Small drops of water also may be leaking from some of these weakened connections. The presence of galvanized piping may be causing rusty water to flow from the faucets when they are turned on, or it may be causing the water pressure to be quite low. The water pressure continues to decrease as the internal section of the piping corrodes. These conditions are indications that the galvanized piping throughout the house is going to have to be replaced shortly with red brass piping or copper tubing. As it ages, yellow brass piping also may cause leaks in the water supply system. This type of piping becomes pitted as time goes by and, after a while, it has to be replaced before it deteriorates further and causes significant damage.

The best time to repair the plumbing system in an old house is during a kitchen or bathroom modernization. A skilled do-it-yourselfer may be able to do some of this work. The homeowner who is not skilled should hire a licensed plumber who has the knowledge, skill, and tools to do the job correctly. No matter who is going to do the work, it is easier to replace the old water supply piping with copper tubing than with brass piping. There are several reasons for this. Copper tubing can be cut and assembled with much less effort than brass piping. In addition, special equipment is needed to cut brass piping that is not needed for copper tubing. Brass piping has to be cut with pipe cutters and then threaded with a threading machine, tools the home-

owner must either own or rent to use. On the other hand, copper tubing can be cut easily with a tubing cutter and the connections can be soldered, which requires minimal experience to do properly. In addition, it is more difficult to position brass piping in a wall cavity than copper tubing because copper tubing is flexible while brass piping is rigid. Besides all of these advantages, copper tubing works as well if not better than brass piping in a water supply system since it lasts as long and needs fewer repairs.

In installations where some galvanized piping must be left intact it is essential to be aware of some of the characteristics associated with connections that are made with dissimilar materials. For example, at the point where the dissimilar metals contact each other — that is, where the galvanized piping and copper tubing meet — the weaker of the two materials will eventually corrode. This corrosion can be prevented by using one of two types of fittings — the dielectric union or the brass union. The dielectric union has an internal gasket, which is made of neoprene, to separate the dissimilar metals so that they cannot come into contact with each other. The brass side of the dielectric union is connected to the copper tubing and the steel side to the galvanized piping and both sides are separated from each other by the neoprene gasket to prevent corrosion. A brass union and a nipple also can be used to connect copper tubing and galvanized piping because the brass will not corrode even if it is placed in contact with either of the two metals. Galvanized strapping should not be used to support the copper tubing because it also can cause corrosion. The best way to avoid corrosion problems as well as any other problems is to have an entirely new water supply system installed to replace an old plumbing system or one in which repairs were done improperly.

In modern water supply systems, flexible connectors made of stainless steel piping or vinyl tubing are used to connect the copper tubing and brass piping. The flexible connectors are attached to shutoff valves under sinks by screwing them into position and then tightening them with a pair of pliers. Shut-off valves always should be installed under every sink in the house so that the water can be turned off when leaks need to be repaired or new fixtures installed. Copper tubing also is used widely in modern plumbing installations for the water supply system because it is reasonably priced and easy to install.

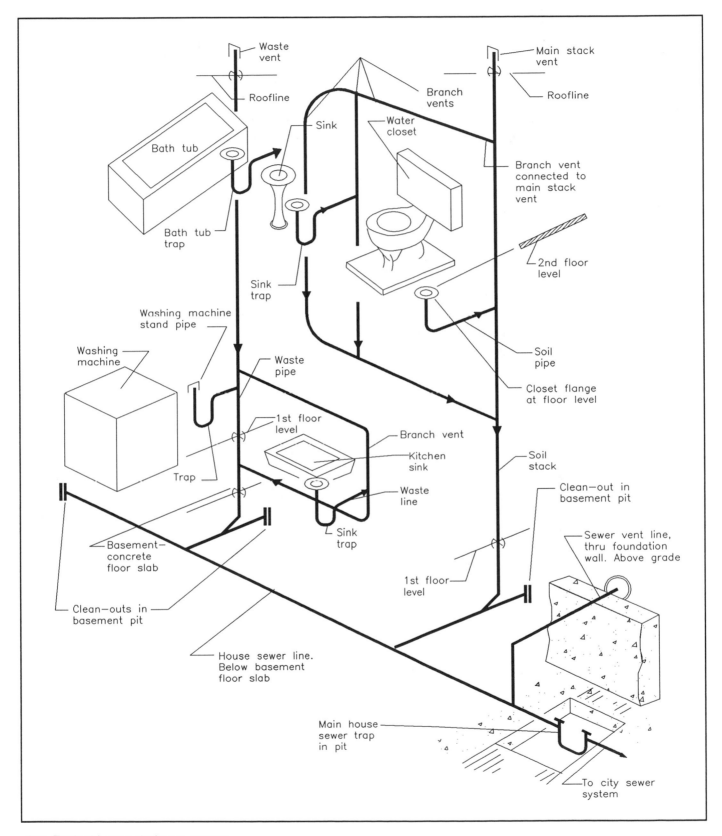

145. Typical house drainage system

DRAINAGE SYSTEM

Soil and waste discharge is removed from a house through its drainage system. Soil discharge includes water from any toilets, bidets, and urinals installed in the house, while waste discharge includes water that is free of feces. Piping that is being used to carry soil discharges from toilets, etc., also can carry water from other fixtures such as from the bathtub or the vanity sink; however, the reverse is not allowed in a drainage system. Drainage system piping is made of several materials including cast-iron, galvanized, PVC (polyvinyl chloride), which is off-white, and ABS plastic (acrylo-nitrile-butadiene-styrene), which is black. Prefabricated connectors such as elbows and traps usually are made of polypropylene plastic. The newest material used for modern drainage systems is called no-hub cast-iron piping, and it has a neoprene sleeve and stainless steel collars. The age of a drainage system as well as how much work has been done in it usually can be determined by the types of materials present in that system. Most often older systems have more cast-iron and galvanized piping in them, while newer ones have more PVC, ABS, or no-hub cast-iron piping.

The drainage system carries the soil and waste discharge through the house's sewer line into the house trap, and then out into the city or town's sewer system or into the septic tank, depending on which of these is in use (Figure 145). The house's sewer line is positioned to be the lowest drain line in the house. For the most part, the house's sewer line is placed under the concrete floor slab in the basement or cellar. In houses that are seventy-five years old or older, the house's sewer line is located above the floor slab, or at a specific elevation above grade in the cellar so that it can drain properly into the town or city's sewer system or into the septic tank. Besides draining the soil and waste discharge from the house, the house's sewer line also may carry rainwater from the gutters and downspouts to the sewer system. Thus, the gutters and downspouts also are connected to the house's sewer line as well.

All fixtures such as toilets (also called water closets), sinks, bidets, etc., either have a trap built into them or have a trap installed as part of their piping arrangement. The trap is a pipe bent into the shape of the letter "U", which makes it easily visible to the homeowner. The trap is an essential component of any fixture because it acts as a seal for it each time the fixture is flushed. When the fixture is flushed, the trap fills with water and seals the fixture to prevent sewer gases from entering into the house.

As with all piping materials, toilets have been significantly affected by today's technological advances. The prices of toilets vary greatly, and the differences in them are due to the varied durability and performance of each fixture. Toilets that have been molded in two pieces are less expensive than those of one-piece construction. Inexpensive toilets usually have parts made mostly of plastic, while more expensive models have brass parts in them. Expensive toilets also are made of high-quality china that has been fired in a kiln for a longer period of time than the less expensive models. The expensive models also are subjected to higher firing temperatures to make the glazing on them stronger and less susceptible to cracking and chipping than glazing fired at a lower temperature. The built-in trap in expensive toilets has a larger diameter to make the flushing action more effective than it would be with a smaller diameter. In short, style is not the only thing that affects the cost of a toilet.

Water conservation also has become a very important factor in the price and performance of toilets. Because many areas of the country have been suffering through water shortages, numerous states and localities are enacting legislation to require the installation of low-water consumption toilets in all new house construction.

In fact, the U.S. Congress is considering national water conservation effort in the form of the Water Conservation Act, which, if enacted, would limit all types of water consumption. This action seems to be imminent despite a trend from the 1950s to the 1980s that shows a decrease from 7.0 to 3.5 gallons per flush. If the new legislation is passed, it will require that toilets in new houses and new installations in older houses use only 1.6 gallons per flush, showerheads and kitchen faucets use only 2.5 gallons per minute, and bathroom faucets use as little as 2.0 gallons per minute. For those homeowners whose water consumption is already metered or is about to be metered, these limits will represent savings on their water and heating bills.

STACK VENT FOR THE DRAINAGE SYSTEM

In addition to carrying the soil and waste discharge out of the home, the drainage system also exhausts sewer gases and odors from the house through the stack vent. The stack vent extends upward through the house and exits through the roof. In some localities, building codes dictate the specific distance that the stack vent must extend above the roofline. Generally, two stack vents are installed in a house; however, the exact number depends on how many bathrooms and kitchens are in the house as well as where they are located. A single stack vent may serve both the kitchen sink and washing machine while another may serve only the bathrooms, for instance. The homeowner can determine how many stack vents have been installed in his house by counting those that can be seen exiting the house through the roof.

When the plumbing system in a house is being designed, the various bathroom fixtures such as the vanity, bathtub, shower, and toilet are positioned so that they can be tied directly into the stack vent. Individual branch vents for each fixture are connected to the main stack vent at a specific point beyond each fixture's trap. Usually these branch vents are manifolded together into a single connection, which is then connected into the main stack vent. The Uniform Plumbing Code as well as local building codes specify what type of venting system is needed for each specific application along with what sizes the vent lines need to be and at what height above each fixture the branch vents need to be connected to the main stack vent. The plumbing system cannot be vented properly if these specifications are not followed.

Besides venting sewer gases and odors, the stack vent has another important function. It provides a positive pressure on the drainage piping to prevent waste water from being sucked out of one trap in a fixture while another one is in use. This is done by connecting branch vents from the various sink and toilet fixtures to the main stack vent. This piping arrangement minimizes the number of stack vents needed in a house and, in so doing, reduces the number of holes that must be made in the roof to accommodate them (Figure 145).

Stack vents and branch vents are made of a variety of materials including cast iron, galvanized, PVC, and ABS plastic. The type of material selected depends largely on state and local building code requirements. In old houses, a cast-iron pipe that is 4 inches in diameter is installed to function simultaneously as the drainage pipe and stack vent, while galvanized piping is used for the branch vents. Plastic piping is used in modern installations to function as both the stack vents and branch vents, and its sizes vary from 1½ to 4 inches in diameter, depending on how much service is needed.

A large vent pipe is tapped off of the house's sewer line near the house trap. It runs through the foundation wall above grade and its exposed end is covered with a perforated face plate. This face plate prevents small animals from crawling into it and debris from collecting in it. The face plate should never be obstructed by landscaping, exterior components of air conditioning systems, outdoor furniture, etc., which would prevent the sewer gases and odors from being vented from the vent pipe.

Cleanout connections are made in the main sewer line to clear obstructions from it. Local and state building codes require these cleanout connections, which usually are installed in the basement or cellar. When an obstruction blocks the main sewer line, it has to be removed immediately to prevent soil and waste discharge from backing up into the house.

As with most home projects, plumbing repairs and replacements require a great deal of knowledge, skill, and the proper tools to do the job correctly. Whether the homeowner chooses to do this work himself or have it done by a licensed plumber, there are a few facts that he needs to know. For example, of all of the piping materials available, plastic piping is the easiest to install and it is much less expensive than cast iron or copper. Plastic piping can be handled easily because it weighs very little, and it can be cut to the desired sizes simply with a saw blade. Joints on plastic piping are made effortlessly using special adhesives manufactured for this purpose.

Despite all of these advantages, plastic piping does have some disadvantages. For instance, water running through plastic piping can be readily heard. Plastic piping also needs to be supported more than metal piping materials because it is lightweight and cannot support the heavier weight of water as it flows through it. Cast-iron piping, on the other hand, needs less support than plastic piping and it is able to mute the sound of the running water because of its density. Joints made in cast-iron piping, however, have to be packed thoroughly to avoid leaks. Copper piping is very expensive piping material for use as drain lines, and the joints in it have to be soldered. This is why copper piping is not preferred by homeowners or plumbers.

As with the electrical system, the plumbing system should be repaired or replaced by a professional unless the homeowner is very skilled and knowledgeable as a do-it-yourselfer. Mistakes in a plumbing installation can lead to costly repairs because leaks may damage other parts of the house as well as personal property stored in it. Repairs to the plumbing system should not be delayed because further damage could result from it. Again, as with the electrical system, it is best to have plumbing repairs and replacements done immediately by a professional.

SEPTIC TANKS

When a municipal sewer system is not available in an area, a septic tank is used to dispose of soil and waste discharge from the house. Solid wastes are collected in the septic tank and bacteria in the tank are used to disintegrate them. While a septic tank does not need a great deal of maintenance, some care is necessary to keep it functioning properly. For instance, the tanks should be checked at least once a year by the installer to be certain that it is operating properly. In addition, the solids have to be pumped out of the septic tank on an annual basis to keep it from getting clogged and to prevent the solids from backing up into the house. This type of backup is a health hazard and it can damage the tank. This damage could result in the need for the tank to be replaced.

Chemicals, oils, grease, fats, and any kind of thick paper products can ruin a septic tank by causing it to become clogged. This also could result in a backup into the house. The chemicals, oils, grease, and fats also destroy the bacteria in the tank, and this prevents the solid wastes from being disintegrated. A proper balance of solids, liquid, and scum is needed on the bottom of the tank to enable it to

function effectively. Since bacterial action is slower during the winter, it is best to have the sludge and some of the scum pumped out of the tank at the start of the spring season. In fact, the homeowner should have the septic tank cleaned as often as the installer and/or manufacturer recommends to keep it trouble-free. It is essential to prevent all of these possible problems since the only resolution of them is to have a new septic tank installed and this is a costly solution.

WATER SOFTENING AND WATER FILTRATION SYSTEMS

Most problems associated with water can be resolved with the use of water softeners or filters. These easily installed systems remove impurities from the water at minimal cost to make the water safe for consumption and household use. Water softeners, for instance, treat the mineral deposits that are found in hard water. Calcium, magnesium, and iron deposits cause water to be hard. A water softener substitutes sodium for these other minerals and, in so doing, softens the water. The mineral deposits in hard water pose potential problems for domestic hot water heaters as well as for other water-using appliances such as coffeemakers and washing machines. Hard water also can clog the plumbing system. The mineral deposits collect in the pipes where they restrict the flow of water in them.

The presence of hard water is evident when a rust-colored ring forms around the bathtub after it has been used. The mineral deposits in the hard water combine with soap to form soap scum. This soap scum leaves spots on glassware washed in the dishwasher as well as by hand and it discolors the laundry after several washings. The removal of the calcium and magnesium results in water with a better taste. Soaps and shampoos also are able to clean better than they can when hard water is in use. Clothes are cleaner after each washing, and the life expectancy of the domestic hot water heater is increased. The homeowner or other family member who must limit or reduce his or her intake of salt should have the water softener system connected to the hot water piping so that only the water used for bathing and washing is treated. With this connection, the drinking water is not altered, making it safe for consumption by everyone in the house.

Water filtration systems also remove chemicals from the water (Figure 146). Tap water may contain numerous contaminants such as rust from a broken water main or from a corroded water supply piping system. It also may contain such chemicals as chlorine, sulfur, and lead, which can be hazardous to an individual's health. These chemicals also can damage the piping or water-using appliances. A variety of water filtration systems is available to deal with just about any possible problem. The type of filtering system chosen depends on what the homeowner needs to handle his specific problem. Some contaminants are not clearly visible in the water and, in these cases, laboratory tests are necessary to find and identify them. The best procedure for any homeowner who has problems with his water or who thinks he might have a problem with it is to call several companies and have each of them conduct tests to determine the types and amounts of contaminants as well as the costs involved in their removal. Then the homeowner can choose the company offering the best price and service to meet his particular needs.

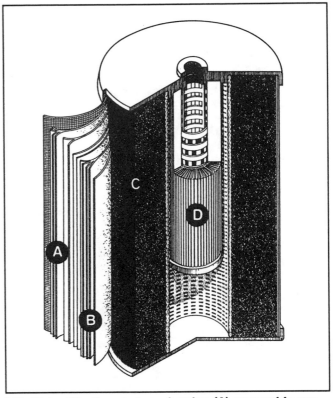

146. Water filtration system showing (A) removable pre-filter, (B) bonded pre-filter, (C) activated carbon block, and (D) patented Nylon 66 final filter. Courtesy of the Bionaire Corporation.

13
Focusing on Flooring and Floor Coverings

CHOOSING THE BEST SUBFLOOR AND FLOORING MATERIALS

Floors take an awful beating in a house, so it is important to have a durable flooring material installed over a sturdy, level subfloor. The flooring material can be hardwood boards that do not need to be covered, or plywood sheathing installed in anticipation of it being covered with carpeting, area rugs, tiles, or vinyl or linoleum floor covering. The following review of how a subfloor and floor are laid reveals some of the problems that can arise, depending on which type of flooring or floor covering is chosen. Since carpeting and area rugs are personal choices made for decorating a home, they are not included in this discussion. An extensive review of hardwood flooring and tile installations as well as some general information about vinyl and linoleum floor coverings should prove helpful to the homeowner.

SUBFLOORING AND HARDWOOD FLOORS

The subflooring in today's modern houses usually is made of plywood sheathing. Before plywood sheathing was used, 1" x 4" wood strips were nailed onto the floor joists to serve as the subfloor. After the strips were installed, building paper was laid over the subfloor and then finish wood flooring was attached to the strip subfloor. The finish wood floor-

ing was made of a hardwood species that had to be finished after it was installed. These floors, which are called parquet floors, were not installed in 12" x 12" prefinished sections as they are today. Instead, each individual piece of wood had to be nailed into place, and several of them formed a pattern or design in the floor. The pieces of wood flooring were face-nailed onto the subflooring material with small brads and then several coats of varnish were applied to finish them.

Over the years, several problems developed in these parquet floors. For instance, the applications of numerous coats of varnish on wood flooring discolored and darkened it, while the flooring itself was scratched and damaged as a result of its constant use. To restore the parquet floors, the wood flooring was sanded several times and, eventually, these sandings loosened the flooring from the subflooring. The nail heads on the brads that held the flooring in place actually were sanded or even sheared off. When this happens in an old house, the best thing to do is to finish sanding the floor, then renail the wood flooring strips onto the subfloor with new brads. The parquet floor can then be stained, varnished, or coated with polyurethane, whichever the homeowner prefers.

In some cases, the parquet floor in a newer house has been installed onto the plywood subfloor with an adhesive instead of with nails or brads. In this type of installation, the parquet floor is installed in

12" x 12" sections that are either unfinished or pre-finished. These sections are approximately 3/8 inch thick, and they can only loosen when the adhesive under them loosens. Loose sections can easily be reinstalled with new adhesive unless they have been damaged, in which case they will have to be replaced.

Some homeowners prefer full thickness, tongue and groove hardwood or heart pine floorings to the thinner parquet type. These range in thickness from 3/4 inch to a full inch, while parquet strips or sections are only 3/8 inch thick. Although full thickness flooring is a good choice, there are several things to do to prepare a floor for its installation unless, of course, the installation is being done while the house is being constructed. For example, an old parquet floor has to be removed before a new full thickness floor can be installed. In very old houses, the sub-flooring material also has to be removed and replaced with plywood sheathing. Strip subflooring generally was installed in these old houses with a space left between each strip, and this type of sub-floor cannot serve as a sturdy support for the new full thickness flooring. The strip subflooring also may be cracked or broken or even missing in some spots. For that matter, the parquet floor also may be cracked or gouged as a result of many years of use, and sections of it may be loose. Any of these conditions would create problems for a new full thickness flooring installation, and they could cause it to loosen or wear prematurely. The removal of the parquet floor and old subfloor and installation of new plywood sheathing will create a subfloor that is a firm, strong base for the new hardwood or heart pine flooring.

Newer plywood subfloors also can cause problems for a hardwood or heart pine flooring installation. Plywood sheathing that is delaminated, cracked, or damaged has to be replaced with new subflooring material before the full thickness flooring is installed. When an adhesive was used to install 12" x 12" parquet floor sections and these sections are removed, the adhesive left sticking to the subfloor also can make the surface uneven. Such a condition would make installation of full thickness flooring almost impossible. In this case, it is necessary to remove the subfloor as well as the parquet floor and to install new plywood sheathing. This new sheathing then serves as the base for the full thickness

flooring, making the installation fairly easy.

Some homeowners try to avoid doing this much work, or having it done by the contractor, because it is difficult and it can add to the cost of an installation. This shortcut, however, can lead to even more problems. One homeowner, for instance, told his contractor to install a thinner plywood sheathing over the old, thicker one that was covered with adhesive. The homeowner felt that the adhesive that was stuck on the subfloor was not thick enough to be a problem. He was right. The new hardwood flooring was installed on top of the new plywood sheathing without any really serious problems. What the homeowner had not considered was that the additional weight of both the hardwood flooring and the extra layer of plywood sheathing could not be supported by the existing floor joists. The installation was too heavy for the floor joists, which had not been designed to carry that much weight. Eventually, the floor joists sagged and, in doing so, they damaged the new floor along with everything under it. Although this type of problem does not arise very often, it does illustrate clearly how just about any problem can arise when a full thickness hardwood floor is not installed properly. This homeowner had to install new floor joists as well as a new subfloor and hardwood floor to correct his mistake. This is why it is always important to install a floor correctly in the first place.

Finishing a hardwood or heart pine floor properly is about as important as installing it correctly and, if it is finished correctly, it will last for many years. Although this work is not appropriate to be done by most homeowners because it involves a great deal of skill and knowledge, it is a good idea to know what is involved in finishing a floor of this type. Working on a floor also can be very tiring for the back, legs, and knees because it requires more physical strength than it seems, which is another reason a professional may be the better choice for this job. After the flooring has been installed, it is sanded to a very smooth finish. The sanding also removes any splinters or smudges made during its installation. Dust caused by the sanding is thoroughly removed from the wood with a vacuum and a dust cloth, then a coat of wood sealer is applied. A wood filler is used before the coat of sealer when the hardwood species installed has an open grain such as oak.

After the filler and sealer have dried completely, the floor is sanded and dusted again. Then two to three coats of high quality polyurethane are applied to finish the wood and protect it from use and moisture. Tung oil, which is a penetrating oil, can be used instead of polyurethane, but several additional coats of the oil are needed for a strong, durable finish when the job is done. Naturally, the wood can be stained before polyurethane or tung oil is applied. The stain should be applied after the filler and sealer have been used. Whether or not the wood is stained depends more on the homeowner's decorative needs than on any need to protect it. (Complete information on wood finishes appears in Chapter 15.)

TILE FLOORS

There are numerous types of tiles available for use as flooring. The choice depends on how much the homeowner wants to spend and what designs and colors he prefers. There are ceramic, quarry, stone, terrazzo, terra cotta, mosaic, slate, and flagstone tiles in a variety of colors, designs, styles, and textures. The choice is almost endless, and it involves matching the decorative style and colors the homeowner prefers. Tiles are durable and attractive; however, some individuals find that they are uncomfortable to stand on for long periods of time. Unless the homeowner is a skilled do-it-yourselfer, it is best to leave the installation of tiles to a professional. This work requires a great deal of patience and skill and some installations can be back-breaking, so not all homeowners are up to the task. In addition, some special equipment is needed to cut the tiles to fit, which also requires some skill. Each type of tile has unique characteristics, therefore, a review can prove helpful.

Glazed ceramic and terra cotta tiles resist stains well because their surfaces are not porous; however, they can crack as they age. Typical floor tiles are available in 12" x 12" and larger sizes, and they vary in thickness from ⅜ inch to 1 inch. Their resistance to cracking varies, depending on the firing temperature reached during the manufacturing process. Tiles that can be installed on walls as well as on floors also are available in 12" x 12" sheets, and they are called mosaic tiles. The sheets are made with a mesh backing that holds the tiles together on it.

Each tile is only about 1-inch square. Mosaic tiles usually are installed in bathrooms and in toilet facilities or half-bathrooms. The sheets are installed with an adhesive and, after the adhesive has dried thoroughly, the tiles are grouted, as are most but not all types of tiles.

Unglazed tiles such as quarry, slate, and flagstone tiles are porous unless they have been treated with a special sealant that protects the surface from staining. These tiles are available in a variety of shades of red, buff, brown, and black. Quarry tiles are made in 6-inch and 8-inch squares as well as in hexagonal and rectangular shapes. Because quarry tiles are very thick, they also are very durable. To prevent them from staining easily, they should be coated with a sealant after they are installed. Color is added to unglazed tiles before they are fired, and minerals are sprayed on them during the firing process to seal the tiles. In this way, the minerals are fused onto the surface of the tiles to create a hard surface that is strong and stain-resistant.

A terrazzo floor is made with marble chips that are mixed with Portland cement mortar. After the floor is poured, it has to be ground and polished to achieve a smooth, durable surface. As a result of this type of installation, a terrazzo floor is very moisture-resistant as well as quite strong.

As with most floor installations, the secret to a good tile floor installation is the construction of a level, sturdy subfloor, no matter what kind of tile is installed on it. The subfloor and joists have to be strong enough to support the weight of the tiles without allowing for any deflection. The subfloor must not be flexible at all because, it if is, the tiles on it will crack. The subfloor has to be free of any bumps, gouges, cracks, or other types of damage because the presence of any of these can cause the tiles to crack. Some tile manufacturers specify what type of subflooring material to use with their products and, if it is not used, they will not warranty their products. That gives the homeowner some idea of how important the choice and proper installation of the subflooring material is for a tile floor.

The presence of cracks in a tile floor can be the result of several possible problems. For example, the house may have settled and this settlement caused the tiles to crack. A weak subfloor with some deflection in it also may have caused the tiles to crack.

If the homeowner suspects that settlement has caused the problem, he will have to hire an engineer or architect to examine the house's foundation and framing to determine if settlement is the cause. If the cracks are the result of a flexible subfloor, the homeowner will have to have the tiles and subfloor removed so that a new subfloor can be installed. If wood strips were used as the subflooring material, they will have to be removed and plywood sheathing installed that is thick enough to prevent any deflection in the floor after the tiles are installed.

In some cases, an underlayment called a tile backer board is installed over the plywood subfloor, which eliminates flexibility in the subfloor. Tile backer board is made by sandwiching a layer of concrete between two layers of fiberglass. The tile backer board is coated with thin-set mortar and then the tiles are set into place in the mortar. When the tiles are being installed onto a thick plywood sheathing without the tile backer board, either thin-set mortar or an adhesive can be used to install them. In other installations, a mud bed or mortar bed, which is a dry mixture of concrete, is poured onto the subfloor and the tiles are set into place on top of it.

The final step in most tile installations is the grouting. Grout, which is a mixture of fine mortar and water, is available in several colors to match or contrast with the colors of the tiles. It is pushed into the joints between each of the tiles, usually with a float. Sometimes a latex additive is mixed into the grout mixture to make it stronger and less likely to crack after it dries.

VINYL FLOOR COVERINGS

A vinyl floor covering is a very resilient flooring material that can be used in any room in the house where lots of activities take place, such as in the kitchen, dining room, family room, etc. This flooring material is available in a variety of colors and patterns. Its price varies greatly, ranging from as little as $6 a square yard to as much as $40 a square yard. The manufacturer's warranty for the life expectancy of the covering is longest for the most expensive type and shortens as the price decreases. Some of these warranties also may be voided if the floor covering is not installed by a professional installer and if a certain type of subflooring material or un-

derlayment is not used as part of the installation. The homeowner should be aware of the specific requirements of the warranty before deciding who should install it and how it should be done.

Vinyl floor coverings are available in 6', 9', 12', and 15' widths that are cut from a roll, hence, they are called sheet goods. Vinyl floor tiles, which are 1-foot square, also are available and they are preferred by many do-it-yourselfers because they are easier to handle than long, large pieces of sheet goods. The main ingredient in the manufacture of vinyl floor coverings, whether they are sheet goods or tiles, is polyvinyl chloride. Resin binders, pigments, and plasticizers also are used in their manufacture. These coverings also are made of pure vinyl or vinyl compositions by some manufacturers. Depending on the size of the room, there may be a seam or two when sheet goods are used; however, the seams are barely visible when the installation is done correctly. This is another excellent reason to have the installation done by a professional.

For installations with sheet goods or tiles, the subfloor or underlayment has to be level, clean, and free of any bumps, gouges, cracks, or other defects. If it is not, they will be visible after the vinyl floor covering has been installed. These defects also can cause the covering to wear out prematurely. A damaged subfloor should be covered with plywood sheathing or particle board with the finished side facing up. The subfloor also has to be nailed tightly to the floor joists to prevent any movement in it that may crack the floor covering. For best results from this type of installation, the sheathing or particle board should be nailed with ring shanks so that the nails cannot pop up after the installation of the vinyl floor covering has been completed. When the vinyl floor covering is being installed in houses in areas with extreme temperature fluctuations, expansion gaps have to be left next to the walls and between the sheets of plywood or particle board. The plywood or particle board has to be clean so that the adhesive can cover it evenly and thoroughly for proper adhesion. The adhesive is applied to the plywood or particle board with a notched trowel, and the vinyl floor covering is installed over it. The vinyl floor covering has to be installed without any bumps or gaps left in it, again, for proper adhesion, and if there is a pattern in it, the pattern must match exactly at the seams.

Some homeowners may try to simplify an installation by putting a new subflooring material on top of the old one without moving all of the appliances or furniture out of the room. This makes the floor uneven and it can be the cause of problems later. A year after one homeowner did this, he discovered what one of these problems could be. He tried to remove his dishwasher to replace it with a new one and found that he could not get it out from under the counter top. The extra layer of plywood sheathing had raised the height of the floor in the rest of the kitchen, but not under the dishwasher, which the homeowner had left in place when he installed the vinyl floor covering. He had to remove the vinyl floor covering and the second subfloor to replace the dishwasher. He would have had the same problem with his refrigerator, which was placed under kitchen cabinets as well, had he not moved it when he installed the extra subfloor and the vinyl floor covering. As this homeowner learned, it is always best to install the new subfloor and vinyl floor covering, or whatever flooring for that matter, correctly in the first place.

LINOLEUM FLOOR COVERINGS

Linoleum floor coverings have been used for many years in rooms where there is a great deal of activity, such as in the kitchen, living room, family room, etc. This floor covering material predates vinyl floor coverings, and it also is available in many colors and patterns. It is cut from a roll, as is vinyl floor covering, and it is available in a variety of widths.

Linoleum floor covering is made of linseed oil, pigments, fillers, binders, and other materials. It is bonded to an asphalt-saturated felt, which serves as its backing. Some types of linoleum floor coverings are made with hard, durable surfaces that are fairly wear-resistant. Linoleum floor coverings can be cleaned easily; however, they also can be damaged by cleaning products that contain alkali solutions, so these should not be used.

As with any flooring installation, the subfloor or underlayment has to be clean, smooth, and free of any defects or damages before the linoleum floor covering can be laid over it. Again, the subfloor should be made of a high quality plywood sheathing or particle board and, depending on the climatic conditions in the area, expansion gaps may need to be left next to the walls and between the sheets of sheathing or particle board. When the subfloor is being installed over a crawl space or other area that will be exposed to a great deal of moisture, an exterior grade of plywood sheathing should be used as well as an adhesive made for exterior use. As usual, the plywood or particle board has to be attached tightly to the floor joists with ring shank nails to prevent any movement or flexibility in it. Since the manufacturer's warranty also may become void if the installation is not done by a professional installer and if a specific type of underlayment is not used, it is probably a good idea to read the warranty carefully before the homeowner decides who will do the installation and what materials will be used for its installation.

PART IV
Examining Additional Components of a House

14
Investigating Insulation and Ventilation

DISPELLING ENERGY MYTHS

Today's homeowners are making their houses as energy-efficient as possible to reduce their heating and air conditioning bills. The use of insulation throughout the house along with the installation of energy-efficient windows and doors and high-efficiency boilers can effectively cut fuel costs. That is why an in-depth review of insulation is appropriate. Before this discussion can begin, however, it is important to correct false impressions homeowners have about how to make a house energy-efficient by preventing heat loss.

Homeowners are frequently told that heat rises, and if they make sure that the attic is well-insulated they will prevent heat loss. Although this information is indeed correct, the installation of a great deal of insulation in an attic is not the only solution to a homeowner's energy problems. There is much more involved in it than that single statement explains. For instance, heat can be lost anywhere in a house because heat travels from any area with a higher temperature to any other area with a lower temperature. In effect, this means that heat does not only have to rise to be lost. It also can be lost in a cold crawl space, for instance, or in a cold basement under the heated living area.

In an old house, a great deal of heat can be lost through cracks around windows and doors, through window and door stops and trims that have not been caulked, through air spaces around loosely fitted windows, and even through large openings under doors near the threshold. Drafts around windows and doors can account for between 15 and 25% of all heat lost from a house. Drafts also can be found at openings around the base moldings on floors as well as around the base of the house at the sill plate or under the siding. These openings let heated indoor air escape to the outside while cold exterior air enters the house. Heated indoor air also can be lost from the attic, escaping through the roof and through openings around chimneys, stack vents, skylights, etc., that protrude through the roof.

Naturally, the amount of heat lost from an attic decreases as soon as insulation is installed in the attic. An attic that already has insulation installed in it, however, may not be as insulated as it should or could be, which is why it is a good idea for the homeowner to determine what is happening there. One homeowner who went up into his attic was surprised to discover that the insulation in it was not doing its job. He saw that the insulation had a vapor barrier on it and that the vapor barrier was facing down toward the living area as it should be. Unfortunately, he also found black spots on the back of the insulation that was installed at the location where the roof framing meets the top plate. These dark spots are evidence of heat being lost in the attic; that is, heat was rising up though the wall cavities into the attic. This homeowner also found dark stains on the framing members in the attic such as on the roof rafters in the vicinity of the top plate.

These stains were evidence of condensation taking place in his attic as a result of heat loss. The homeowner had to increase the amount of insulation he had in his attic to prevent this waste of energy.

TYPES AND CHARACTERISTICS OF INSULATION

When installing or adding insulation in a house, it is helpful to know about the types of products available, the special characteristics of each type, and what rating system is used to determine the insulating values of these products. The "R" value of a specific type of insulation is the measure of its resistance to heat flow. As the R value increases, the resistance to heat flow becomes greater. The R value of an insulating material can vary as existing conditions change. It also can vary depending on how and where it is installed. For instance, when fiberglass insulation becomes wet, its R value decreases dramatically. When voids are left in insulation that is pumped into wall cavities, this insulating material has a lower R value than it ordinarily would if it had been installed without voids. The voids allow for air infiltration, which decreases the R value of the insulation. Foamboard insulation, also called closed cell insulation, reaches its maximum R value when it is manufactured. This type of insulation is called closed cell insulation because the cells trap air and gas bubbles in it. As moisture and air infiltrate these cells as the foamboard ages, its R value decreases from its original rating. In fact, it still has not been determined to what degree the R value of this type of insulation will decrease after years of use in a roofing system.

Although there are many types of insulation available, the homeowner probably only needs to know about three or four of them, since he is not likely to be using all of the insulation materials in his house. The exception would be the homeowner who is involved with the construction of a new home in which many types of insulation are used. The average homeowner needs to be familiar with fiberglass, rock wool, and cellulose insulation as well as with the polystyrene and polyisocyanurate types, so let's review them one by one.

Fiberglass Insulation

Among all of the types of insulation available, fiberglass insulation is the one most commonly used in a house. It is manufactured from a blend of soda ash, ground sand, and boron, and it is available as batt insulation with a vapor barrier, or blanket insulation, which is unfaced so that a separate vapor barrier can be installed only when it is needed. The R value of fiberglass insulation varies greatly. It can be as high as R38. The vapor barrier on it is made either of Kraft paper or foil-covered paper. Batt insulation is made with flanges on it, which are used to staple the insulation to the framing members in a house. Blanket insulation is available in 4-foot and 8-foot lengths, and both the batt and blanket types are available in 16-inch and 24-inch widths. Typically, 3½-inch batt insulation with an R11 or R13 rating is used to insulate in wall cavities and 6-inch insulation with an R19 rating is used in ceilings and attics. The U.S. Department of Energy recommends the use of 12 inches of insulation in an attic. The melting point, or fire-resistance, of fiberglass insulation is lower than that of other types. Its R value also decreases significantly when it gets wet, so it should be installed in areas that are dry. Those areas must be kept dry at all times or the fiberglass insulation will not remain effective as an insulating material. Chopped fiberglass insulation also is available for use in houses. It is blown into wall and ceiling cavities as well as into attics and cocklofts.

The thickness of the fiberglass insulation used in a house depends on where it is going to be installed in that house. For instance, when the walls are built with 2" x 4" wall studs, the thickness of the batt insulation is limited to 3½ inches, the thickest size that can be accommodated in that space. It is not a good idea to install insulation thicker than 3½ inches in this wall cavity because the insulation becomes compressed in it and this lowers the R value of the insulation. In many houses being built today, the size of the wall studs has been increased to 2" x 6" to accommodate 6-inch thick batt insulation, which has a higher R value and therefore is more effective.

Rock Wool Insulation

Rock wool insulation also is frequently used in a house as an insulating material. It is made from slag, a byproduct in the manufacture of steel. Its melting point is almost double that of fiberglass, which means that it is very fire-resistant. Rock wool also is very dense, and this characteristic makes it more sound-retardant than fiberglass insulation. Rock wool insulation is an appropriate choice in sound-deadening applications. Rock wool is blown into wall cavities and attics as is fiberglass or cellulose insulation; however, the holes needed to do so are much smaller than those needed to blow in fiberglass or cellulose insulation.

Cellulose Insulation

Cellulose insulation is produced from recycled paper and it is used as an insulating material in wall and ceiling cavities. Before it is used, however, it is treated chemically to make it fire- and insect-resistant. Cellulose insulation has excellent sound-proofing qualities, as does rock wool, and its R value decreases significantly after it gets wet, as with fiberglass insulation. After it has dried, the texture of cellulose insulation is similar to tissue paper and, in this state, it is ineffective as an insulating material. Additionally, since the chemicals have been washed out of it, its flammability increases and it becomes more susceptible to insect infestation.

Other Insulation Materials

Extruded polystyrene and polyisocyanurate insulation materials are used in exterior and interior applications, and they are applied as panels to the surfaces. Extruded polystyrene is used to insulate foundation walls below grade. It also is installed under a concrete slab before the concrete is poured to prevent the cold air from the ground from entering the house through the slab. Extruded polystyrene is manufactured with benzine and ethylene as well as with Freon gas. Polyisocyanurate insulation is manufactured with a foil face so that it can be used as a sheathing material. It is very strong and has a very high R value. Because it is not fireproof, polyisocyanurate insulation must be installed with a fire-retardant sheeting material on the interior side of the polyisocyanurate insulation panels.

VAPOR BARRIERS

A vapor barrier cannot function properly when it is not installed correctly. In fact, it can cause more harm than good when placed incorrectly in an insulated space. A vapor barrier slows down the heat transfer process from a warm space to a cold one and, in so doing, it limits the amount of condensation that can take place. For example, during the heating season, the moist, heated air in the house penetrates the wall cavities, where its moisture condenses. While a vapor barrier installed in the wall cavities cannot eliminate this process altogether, it can slow the process down, limiting the amount of moisture that collects in the wall cavities. This is significant because if a a lot of moisture is allowed to collect there, it could lower the R value of the insulation in the wall cavities. Also, if moisture is allowed to collect in the wall cavities for an extended period of time, it could damage the wood framing.

In most cases, the vapor barrier should face the interior or warm surface of the walls, ceilings, and floors when the insulation is installed. In a house that is located in an area where temperatures remain warm all year, however, the vapor barrier should not face the interior or warm surfaces of the walls, ceilings, etc. The air inside these houses usually is being cooled by a central air conditioning system. Under these circumstances, the hot air outside travels into the house instead of a reverse flow as is common in houses located in areas where there are four seasonal temperature changes. When the vapor barrier is placed toward the living area in a house in a warm climate, the hot exterior air can condense in the wall cavities, where it could damage the wood framing and the insulation. In addition to the build-up of moisture in these walls, the incorrect placement of the vapor barrier could lead to the growth of mildew and fungus in the walls as well as to peeling and blistering paint on the interior surfaces.

When insulation without a vapor barrier is to be installed, a polyethylene film has to be installed over the studs and insulation to serve as a vapor barrier. A vapor barrier cannot always be installed when insulation is being pumped into wall cavities from the exterior side of the house. In this case, a coat of vapor barrier paint can be applied to the interior walls in the house to help retard moisture from seeping through the walls. When a concrete slab is being constructed, a vapor barrier such as polyethylene, heavy asphalt paper, or rolled roofing felt is installed before the concrete is poured to prevent moisture from seeping through the slab into the living area. In a crawl space, polyethylene or rolled roofing felt is laid on the soil to act as a vapor barrier to prevent moisture from condensing on the floor joists above the crawl space (Figure 147).

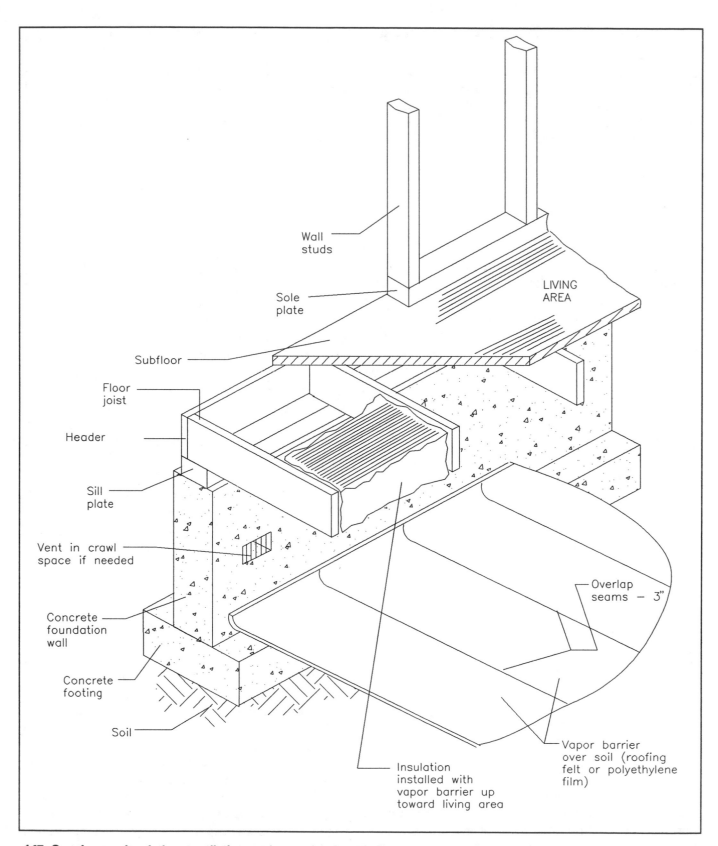

Wall studs

Sole plate

LIVING AREA

Subfloor

Floor joist

Header

Sill plate

Vent in crawl space if needed

Concrete foundation wall

Concrete footing

Soil

Overlap seams — 3"

Insulation installed with vapor barrier up toward living area

Vapor barrier over soil (roofing felt or polyethylene film)

147. Crawl space insulation, ventilation, and vapor barrier detail

USING INSULATION TO MAKE THE HOUSE ENERGY-EFFICIENT

There are many things a homeowner can do to make his house energy-efficient. Some were reviewed earlier in the book, such as installing energy-efficient windows and doors and a high-efficiency boiler or furnace. Others include installing insulation throughout the house, caulking openings around windows and doors to seal them completely, and having the local utility company conduct an energy audit to obtain recommendations for other energy-saving options. Unfortunately, some of these projects can be very expensive to undertake, so the homeowner has to decide what he can afford to do and when he can afford to do it. For the moment, let's deal with the subject of insulation.

Whether the insulation is installed by a contractor or the homeowner, there are several basic principles that have to be followed to insulate the house correctly and effectively. For instance, insulation should be installed so that no gaps or voids are left in it because these gaps and voids would allow heated indoor air to be lost from the house and cold exterior air to infiltrate into it. Unless the manufacturer's tag states otherwise, insulation should be kept at least 3 inches away from any electrical fixture to prevent fires and electrical shorts. It should be kept at least 3 inches away from any receptacles and switches for the same reasons. Unless a fire-rated insulation made specifically for flue pipes is being installed, insulation should be kept 3 inches away from a metal flue pipe. It is essential to put insulation between any hot and cold areas in the house such as in a wall that is adjacent to a cold garage and in the floor of a living area that is located on top of an interior garage, an unfinished attic, or a crawl space (Figure 148).

The correct placement of insulation in an attic depends on how it is being used. When the attic is being used as a living space, the insulation should be installed between the finished walls and ceilings and the roof sheathing. In an unfinished attic, the insulation should be placed between the exposed ceiling joists. When it is necessary to increase the amount of insulation in an unfinished attic that already has insulation with a vapor barrier in place, the new insulation installed should not have a vapor barrier. If

insulation with a vapor barrier has to be installed, such as batt insulation; the vapor barrier should be cut extensively to make it ineffective as a vapor barrier. If the vapor barrier on the batt insulation is not cut, moisture will be trapped between the two vapor barriers in this type of installation. This moisture will reduce the R value of the insulation, and eventually it can destroy the roof framing members.

In a house with a flat roof, the insulation should be installed on the ceiling joists in the cockloft and on the back of the hatch that opens for entry to the cockloft and roof. When a house is built on a concrete slab, rigid foamboard insulation should be installed around the perimeter and on the bottom of the slab before the concrete is poured (see Figures 73 and 74 on page 94). The living area above a crawl space is insulated by placing insulation under the floor (Figure 147). A basement is insulated by placing insulation on the walls below grade before they are backfilled. Insulation also should be placed between the floor joists in the basement and around the perimeter of the structure at the location of the rim joist and sill plate (Figure 149).

Fiberglass batt insulation generally is used to insulate attics, basements, crawl spaces, and even wall cavities when it can be installed from the inside of the house. Before this insulation is installed, however, these areas must be cleared of any moisture collecting in them. A wet or even damp basement, crawl space, or attic can reduce the R value of this insulation so dramatically that it will be totally useless as an insulating material. These areas need to be vented or dehumidified to keep the insulation in them dry at all times. (For more information on venting crawl spaces, see the end of the attic ventilation discussion later in this chapter.)

The insulation in the walls in the kitchens and bathrooms has to be kept dry, so these rooms need natural ventilation. Moisture is a particular problem in the bathroom and kitchen because these rooms are more prone to it than other rooms in the house. As moisture collects from the heating system as well as from the use of these rooms, it can reduce the R value of the insulation in the wall cavities and eventually damage the wood framing. Anti-sweat insulation should be installed on the cold water piping in the basement or cellar to prevent condensation

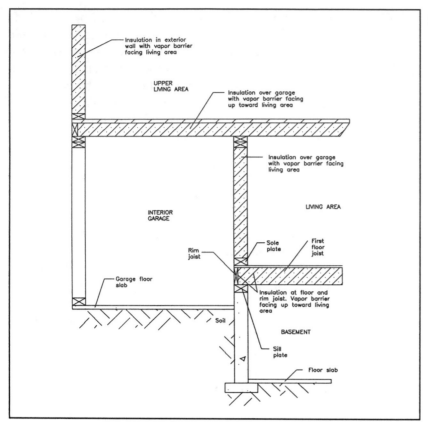

148. Placement of insulation

149. Placement of insulation around house

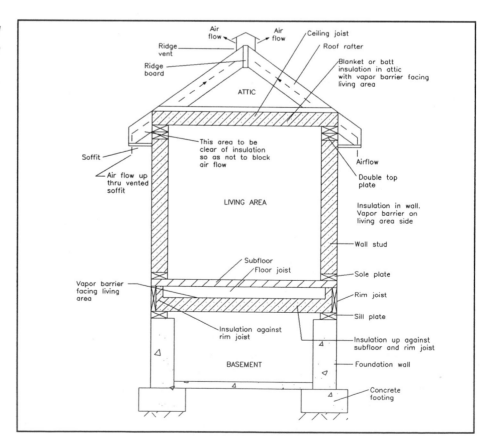

as a result of exposure to the heated air inside the house. A great deal of humidity in the basement or cellar can cause the pipes to "sweat"; that is, water to condense on them. This sweating can be corrected easily with the installation of anti-sweat insulation on the pipes.

Of course, it is easier to install insulation in a house while it is being built than after it has been constructed. There are ways to install insulation in difficult places in a house, however, so the homeowner does not have to feel that he has to live with a house that is poorly insulated. For example, insulation can be blown into wall cavities behind exterior masonry walls by making holes in the masonry at specified distances from each other along the entire wall. It also can be blown into wall cavities behind exterior walls that have been covered with wood siding. This is done by carefully removing the siding and making holes in the wall sheathing. The holes are repaired, if necessary, or just covered with the siding when it is reinstalled. A knowledgeable insulation contractor can handle this type of work fairly easily. When renovations are being made inside the house, insulation can be placed in the wall cavities while they are exposed. When old wood windows are being replaced, insulation can be placed in the hollow casings that housed the window weights to prevent drafts after the new windows have been installed. Openings around doors also can be filled with insulation before new energy-efficient doors are installed to prevent drafts from these openings.

Much of this work can be done by the homeowner with a little time, patience, and proper protection. He should wear a face mask, eye goggles, gloves, and old clothes that can be discarded after he has finished the work. The clothing should cover his body as much as possible to prevent skin irritation. Some individuals are quite sensitive to fiberglass particles, which cause them to cough and feel itchy. A good face mask and proper clothing should prevent most problems that could occur. These items are especially important when the homeowner is working in areas with little ventilation such as in attics, cellars, basements, and crawl spaces. If he does this work himself, however, the homeowner can save quite a bit of money that he would have to pay an insulation contractor.

The last recommendation about insulation actually refers to the next topic in this chapter — ventilation. After all that has just been said about insulation, it is important to add that it is better to have a house with some drafts than one so super-insulated and tightly sealed that air cannot circulate in and out of it naturally. Today's heavily insulated, super-tight houses are too dry because air cannot infiltrate the exterior frame. The amount of air exchanged into and out of a house per hour decreases greatly as a house is sealed more and more tightly. This traps household gases and irritants caused by everyday living that would ordinarily escape through thin cracks and small openings. As these gases and irritants accumulate, they reduce the quality of the air in the house. That is why, when the homeowner is thinking about insulation, he should consider the old saying, "Everything in moderation." A house that is fairly well insulated but still has a few small openings to enable fresh air to enter it and stale air to escape from it is preferable to one that is so tight that ventilation must be added.

HEAT RECOVERY EXCHANGERS CLEAR THE AIR

One effective way to deal with a tightly sealed house is to install a heat recovery exchanger. This has become a popular solution to a problem that is becoming more and more frequent in today's energy-efficient homes. A heat recovery exchanger exhausts stale air from the house while it simultaneously draws fresh air into it from outside. Because this incoming air is cold during the winter months, it is warmed with the use of a heat transfer process that takes place in the heat recovery exchanger. Working in conjunction with the necessary ducting system, the heat recovery exchanger provides warm, clean air to all parts of the house (Figure 150).

One homeowner with a tightly sealed house, who was advised to have a heat recovery exchanger installed in his house, felt that its installation was a waste of time and money. He decided it was just as efficient and a lot less costly to simply open his windows whenever he wanted to refresh the air in his house. During the winter, however, the opened windows cooled the air in his house, which in turn made his thermostat turn on the heating system frequently to heat the house. This homeowner might as well have been throwing money out of his open

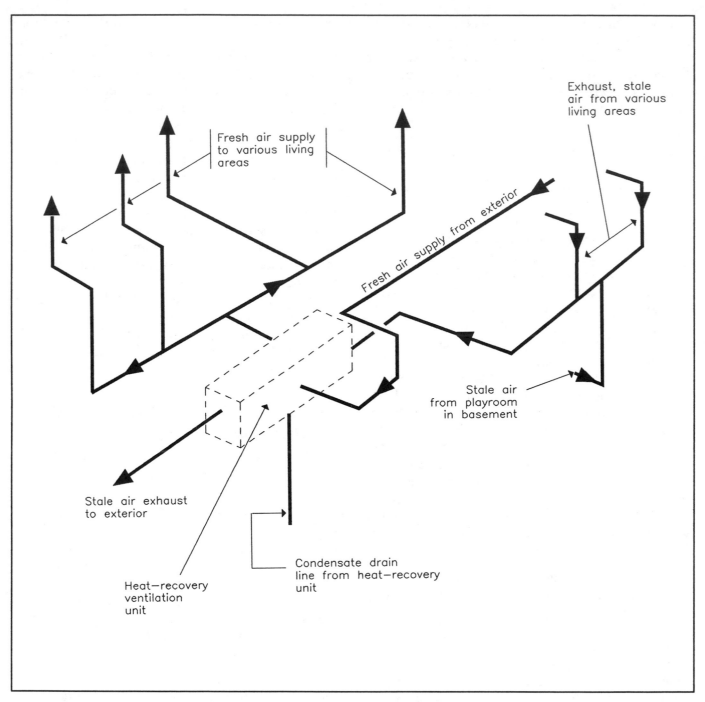

Fresh air supply
to various living
areas

Exhaust, stale
air from various
living areas

Fresh air supply from exterior

Stale air
from playroom
in basement

Stale air exhaust
to exterior

Condensate drain
line from heat—recovery
unit

Heat—recovery
ventilation
unit

150. Schematic layout for heat recovery ventilation unit

windows. He quickly learned that one advantage of a heat recovery exchanger is that it heats the cold exterior air before it gets into the living area. In this way, it reduces the need to heat the house as often as ordinarily would be necessary. Eventually, he also realized that the fuel savings from the heat recovery exchanger would reimburse him for the cost of its installation. Another advantage of a heat recovery exchanger is that it is able to control the atmosphere in a house. This is especially important in a house with an individual suffering from asthma or a severe allergic condition. The clean air in the house helps these individuals breathe more easily than they would otherwise.

The ideal way to install a heat recovery exchanger is to have fresh air inlets and stale air outlets installed in every room of the house. Generally, this is not possible because the location of these inlets and outlets has to be determined by the layout of the house. For instance, a post and beam constructed house needs fewer inlets and outlets than one built in the more traditional way in which rooms are enclosed and spaces are partitioned. The single constant factor in the installation of a heat recovery exchanger is that it must be placed centrally in the house to minimize the lengths of the ducting and to reduce the number of pressure drops in the ducting system. In this way, a heat recovery exchanger with a smaller capacity can be used effectively in a space where a larger one might have been needed. Most heat recovery exchangers should not be placed in a garage or attic since they are not designed to operate in an unheated space. They also should not be placed near any piece of equipment that exhausts fumes because the fumes may be carried throughout the house accidentally by the heat recovery exchanger.

All heat recovery exchangers use the same heat transfer principles as any heat exchanger does, such as one used in a furnace or boiler. The two most commonly used types of heat recovery exchangers are the counterflow and the cross-flow types. In the counterflow heat recovery exchanger, the stale indoor air and the fresh outdoor air flow parallel and counter to each other for the heat transfer process to take place. In a cross-flow heat recovery exchanger, the incoming and outgoing air transfer heat while crossing each other at right angles (Figures 151, 152, and 153).

The heat recovery exchanger collects the stale indoor air from the different spaces in the house and exhausts it through ducting that is connected to an outlet opening located in an exterior wall. In the meantime, fresh air enters the house through an inlet opening also located in an exterior wall. The fresh and stale air pass each other in the part of the heat recovery exchanger called the plenum. The fresh and stale air cannot mix together in the plenum, but a heat transfer process can take place between them: the fresh air becomes heated. During this heat transfer process, moisture in the warm air condenses and flows into the drain connection in the heat recovery exchanger, where it is collected. In extremely cold climates, this water can freeze in the heat recovery exchanger. That is why several manufacturers have installed an electric heater in their heat recovery exchangers at the location where the heat transfer process takes place. The electric heater prevents the condensed moisture from freezing there.

The controls for the heat recovery exchanger can be installed on it, or they can be located in a different area of the house. These controls include an on/off switch and timers. Some heat recovery exchangers also have controls that enable the homeowner to vary the speed of the fan as well as the rate of air exchanged in it. Still other types available include dehumidifiers as a component of the controlling mechanism. A heating contractor can assist the homeowner in choosing the appropriate size and type of unit that best meets his requirements and needs.

VENTING THE ATTIC ADEQUATELY

It is as important to ventilate the attic as it is to insulate it. Proper ventilation can prevent a variety of possible problems caused by the collection of warm moist air in the attic during mild summer months as well as during the heating season. For instance, during the winter, the heated indoor air rises into an attic that has not been vented. The moisture in the air condenses in the attic and water collects on the roof sheathing, roof rafters, and ceiling joists. When a house is located in a particularly cold climate, this water can freeze on these various framing members. Later, as the weather turns mild, it defrosts and damages the sheathing, rafters, and joists.

151 and 152. Air-to-air heat exchanger. Courtesy of Bossaire, Inc.

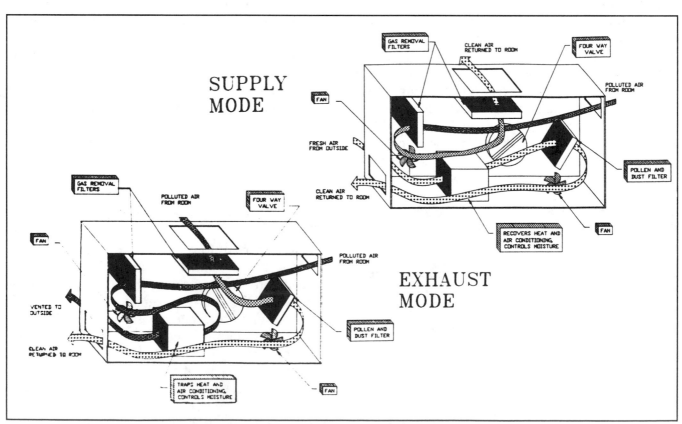

153. AQ Plus+ air-to-air heat exchanger with its recirculation filtration system. Courtesy of Berner Air Products Incorporated.

An unvented attic in a house that has eaves over-hanging its exterior walls also can be the cause of ice damming. Again, during the winter, as the heated indoor air rises into the attic, it melts the snow collecting on the roof. This melting snow freezes at the edge of the roof near the soffit because this area is colder than the rest of the roof. As the snow continues to melt, it backs up under the roof shingles (see Figure 27 on page 41). This condition eventually will damage the shingles, roof sheathing, and the roof framing members, if it is allowed to collect there for an extended period of time.

Mold and mildew also can grow in an attic when it is not vented properly. The warm, moist air collecting in the attic creates the perfect climate for this type of growth. In extreme circumstances, inadequate ventilation in an attic has been known to cause paint to peel from ceilings and walls, and condensation to build up on the outer surface of these ceilings and walls.

As the energy-efficiency of houses has been improved over the years, adequate ventilation of the attic has become even more critical. Although old houses did not make any provision for ventilation when they were built, they were able to avoid problems associated with it because the structure usually was not sealed tightly. The use of wood shingles on top of open-spaced 1" x 4" wood slats, for instance, allowed for more than enough ventilation in the attics in these houses. These old houses also did not have insulation in the attic, and energy-efficient windows and doors certainly were not installed in them. In addition, openings around door and window wood trims and near the sill plate allowed for more than adequate ventilation. In fact, heat and moisture could not be trapped in these old houses, even when it was important to do so such as during the winter.

Today's modern houses have been designed for maximum energy-efficiency. As a result, moisture cannot escape from them, and ventilation of the attic is now of prime importance. The standards for adequate ventilation are set by Federal Housing guidelines as well as by state and local building codes. These standards are based on the ventilating area needed per cross-sectional area of ceiling space. For example, the minimum standard ventilat-ing area for an attic in a house with a pitched roof is $\frac{1}{300}$th of the ceiling area below the roof, provided that a vapor barrier is installed at the ceiling level. When there is not a vapor barrier at the ceiling level, $\frac{1}{150}$th of the ceiling area is required for minimum standard ventilation of this same attic. Ventilation of the attic cannot be adequate unless at least the minimum amount of space is used for it.

There are a number of ways to ventilate an attic, and the method chosen depends largely on what type of roof has been constructed on the house. Ventilators are used on houses with flat or pitched roofs. Louvered vents are installed at opposite end walls on a house with a gabled roof that does not have eaves overhanging its exterior walls (Figure 154-A). Louvered vents at opposite end walls and soffit vents are installed on a house with a gabled roof that does have eaves overhanging its exterior walls (Figure 154-B). Louvered vents at opposite end walls, soffit vents, and a dormer vent are installed on a house with a gabled roof that has a dormer constructed at the roof level (Figure 155). Soffit vents and an outlet ventilator near the ridge of the roof are installed on a house with a hip roof (Figure 156).

A popular venting arrangement on a house with a pitched roof is to install soffit vents and a ridge vent. A ridge vent is a continuous vent that is installed along the ridge line of the roof. Ridge vents are made with filters in them to keep insects from entering the attic as well as to resist rain and snow infiltration. This type of arrangement also is commonly seen when the attic is being used as a living space because it provides for ventilation between the roof and the living area. A continuous ridge vent and soffit vent arrangement also is used on a house with a cathedral ceiling.

Special care is needed when ventilating and insulating an attic that is being converted for use as a living space. For example, before the drywall is nailed into place, insulation has to be installed in the wall cavities so that at least a 2-inch space is left between the roof sheathing and the insulation. The space from the soffit vents to the ridge vent should be left unobstructed for air to circulate freely through it. If it is not left unobstructed, it will create a dead air space; that is, a space in which air cannot circulate and where moisture can build up during the heating

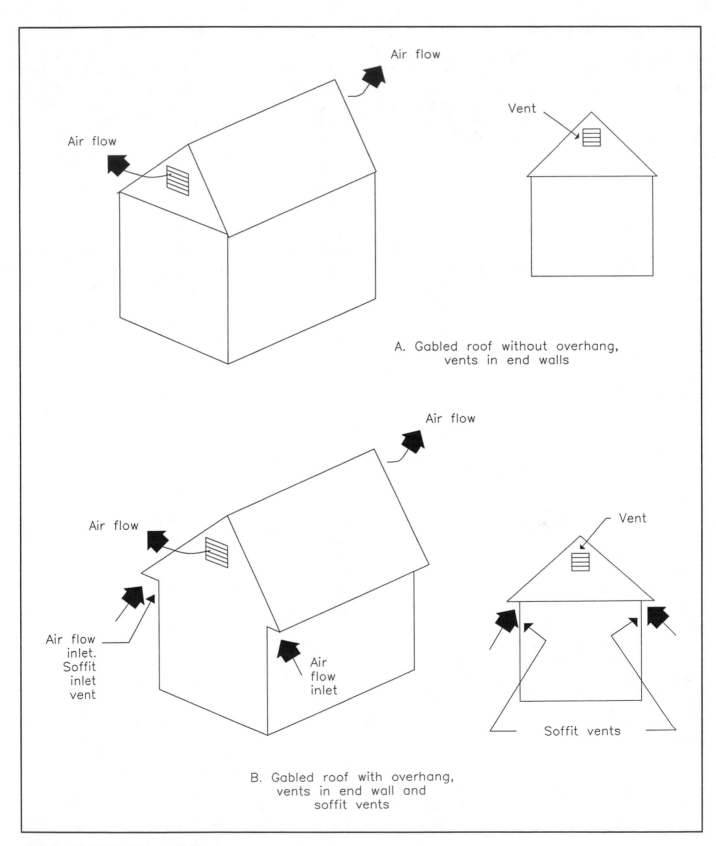

Air flow

Air flow

Vent

A. Gabled roof without overhang,
vents in end walls

Air flow

Air flow

Vent

Air flow
inlet.
Soffit
inlet
vent

Air
flow
inlet

Soffit vents

B. Gabled roof with overhang,
vents in end wall and
soffit vents

154-A and 154-B. Attic ventilation

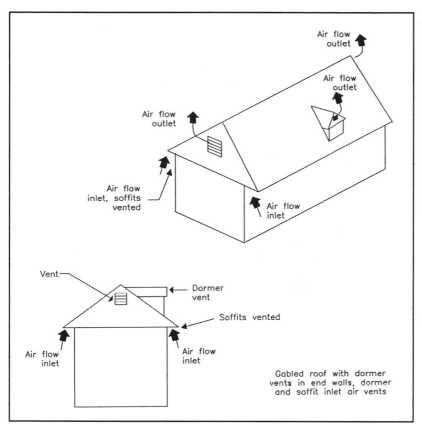

155. Attic ventilation

Air flow outlet

Air flow outlet

Air flow outlet

Air flow inlet, soffits vented

Air flow inlet

Vent

Dormer vent

Soffits vented

Air flow inlet

Air flow inlet

Gabled roof with dormer vents in end walls, dormer and soffit inlet air vents

156. Ventilation for hip roof

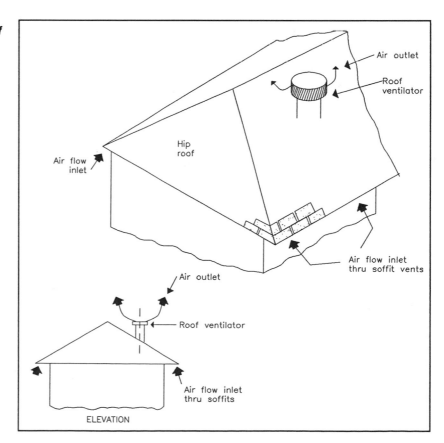

Air outlet

Roof ventilator

Hip roof

Air flow inlet

Air flow inlet thru soffit vents

Air outlet

Roof ventilator

Air flow inlet thru soffits

ELEVATION

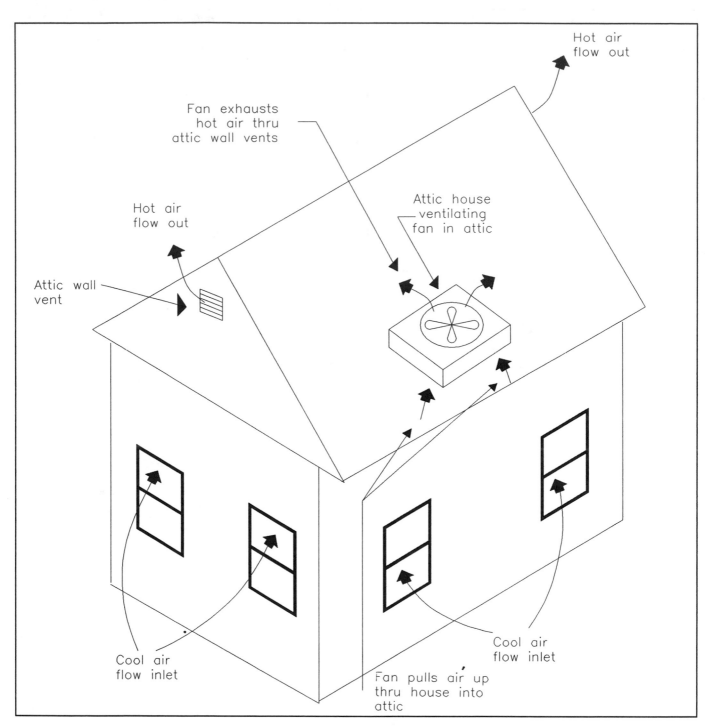

Hot air
flow out

Fan exhausts
hot air thru
attic wall vents

Attic house
ventilating
fan in attic

Hot air
flow out

Attic wall
vent

Cool air
flow inlet

Cool air
flow inlet

Fan pulls air up
thru house into
attic

157. Attic ventilating fan

and cooling seasons. The insulation placed near the double top plate and the soffit also must not interfere with the air coming from the soffit vents. It should be placed away from the top plate and soffit to allow air to flow freely from the soffit vent to the ridge vent (Figure 148 on page 180 and Figure 88 on page 106).

The homeowner who lives in an area where snowfalls are fairly frequent can determine whether his attic is insulated properly by observing how long it takes for the snow accumulation on the roof to melt off it. An accumulation of snow that stays on a roof for a long period of time probably is being kept cold by an attic that is very well-insulated and properly ventilated. Otherwise, the snow would melt rapidly as heated indoor air entered the attic, warmed the roof, and melted the snow on it. The homeowner has to use his judgment when attempting to assess this condition. He must consider many factors, such as the fact that the snow melts more quickly on a sunny winter day than on a cloudy one. The homeowner might find it helpful to compare what is happening, or is not happening, to the snow on his roof with what is occurring on a neighbor's roof. If he knows that his neighbor has a well-insulated and properly ventilated attic, then he can easily compare the snow on that roof with the accumulation on his own to assess how well his attic is insulated and ventilated.

The correct amount of insulation in an attic can reduce air conditioning costs as well as heating bills. The insulation does this by reducing the flow of hot air from the attic to the living area below it. In a house with a flat roof where the living area under it can be quite warm in the summer, insulation in the cockloft reduces the flow of hot air from it to the living area below during the summer. Another way to reduce the amount of heat that collects in a living area below an attic during the summer is to install a ventilating fan in the attic. The ventilating fan draws air into the house from outside and exhausts the warm air in the attic to the outdoors through roof vents. When a ventilating fan is placed in an attic, an opening must be made in the ceiling of the upper level living area, usually in a hallway, to provide for maximum ventilation and air flow (Figure 157).

Adequate ventilation and insulation in a crawl space is as important as in an attic. Generally, the typical

way to do this is to vent the crawl space as well as to place insulation under the floor and between the floor joists above the crawl space. Usually a vapor barrier also is installed to cover the exposed soil in the crawl space. This practice has been criticized lately since some experts feel that the ventilation and insulation together can cause problems. These experts say that during the summer when the air in the crawl space is cooler and less humid than the air outdoors, letting the warm, humid air into it can cause condensation. This condensation in the crawl space can ruin the insulation by making it wet, and it can damage the floor joists there as well. These experts believe that the crawl space should not be vented and, if a vent is already in place, that this vent should be sealed. Sealing the crawl space, however, may cause other problems. For instance, if radon gas is seeping from the soil in the crawl space, preventing it from venting will cause the gas to build up to a dangerous level. The experts suggest that a radon test be conducted before a vent in a crawl space is sealed, and they urge homeowners to consult with a heating, ventilating engineer or contractor before making any change that might prove drastic in the long run.

Since ventilation and insulation in an attic or crawl space can be very confusing, it might be a good idea for the homeowner to consult an insulation contractor or a heating, ventilating engineer to get some recommendations on how to proceed. An energy audit by the local utility company also may prove helpful and, in the case of the attic, a roofing contractor also might have some good ideas for the homeowner.

INSULATING THE BASEMENT FOR USE AS A LIVING SPACE

As mentioned earlier in this section, there are many reasons for a basement or cellar to be damp or for moisture to collect on the walls. One simple reason is that the air in the basement or cellar may be cooler than it is in the rest of the house because the basement or cellar is not heated or is heated insufficiently. Another reason is that the house may be located in an area with high humidity. Adding heat in the first instance or installing a dehumidifier in the second example can immediately alleviate these problems. After doing so, the homeowner can restore the condition of the foundation walls by removing debris and loose cement from them with a wire brush and applying one or two coats of a waterproofer such as Thoroseal. When the homeowner wants to use the basement as a living space, these procedures are just the beginning of what he must do to complete the conversion.

After the foundation walls are coated with a waterproofer, a wood partition has to be built around the perimeter of the basement to define its new shape and later to serve as the framing for the moisture-resistant drywall and/or wood paneling that is going to be installed. Before the drywall or paneling is installed, fiberglass batt insulation should be placed in the wall cavities. The insulation can be nailed to the wall studs of the new partitions with the use of the flanges already on it. The vapor barrier on the insulation should face toward the living area. The bottom plate of the new partition has to be made either of pressure-treated lumber or redwood to prevent it from rotting due to dampness or seepage that may come through the concrete floor slab or from the perimeter of the slab where it is not sealed tightly. New outlets and switches have to be installed, as well as water supply and drainage piping, prior to the installation of the drywall or paneling. The heating system's piping also has to be installed before access to these wall cavities becomes limited, if not impossible.

If the existing concrete floor slab is not perfectly level throughout the living area in the basement, then it will have to be leveled. This can be done by applying one or several coats of any leveling cement made to correct this problem. Once it is level, floor tiles, carpeting, or vinyl floor covering can be laid on top of it. If the homeowner wants to insulate the concrete floor slab to keep his finished basement warmer during the winter, he can do so; however, it will raise the height of the floor. This is because space is needed to install the wood sleepers, vapor barrier, and insulation that are going to have to be put in place (see Figure 90 on page 111). This decreases the height from floor to ceiling, so it should be considered carefully before it is done. Either the ceiling can be drywall-constructed or a suspended ceiling can be installed using either 2' x 2' or 2' x 4' ceiling tiles and runners. These ceiling tiles are available with fiberglass insulation as backing on them to improve the basement's energy-efficiency.

15
Learning About Exterior and Interior Finishes

HOW FINISHES ARE MADE AND WHAT THEY DO

The finishing and refinishing of exterior and interior surfaces is a costly project, whether the homeowner does the work himself or has a professional do it. When finishing work is not done correctly, it is just as costly to have it redone. That is why it is important to know about the various types of finishing products available as well as how they should be used. The type of material being finished and whether or not it has been finished in the past affects what kind of finishing product can be used and how it must be applied. In addition, some surfaces need to be prepared before they can be finished; others may need to be repaired or replaced before any finishing product can be used. All of this information is reviewed here along with related topics such as paint removers, caulking compounds, and glazings to understand what to do and how to do it to finish any household surface. Let's begin with a review of the many types of finishing products available, starting with what finishes are made of and what jobs they are meant to do.

Finishing products available include oil-based and latex paints, clear silicone solutions, varnishes, polyurethanes, water-repellent preservatives, bleaching oils, semi-transparent stains, and solid-color stains, among others. What the product is made of and how it should be used is printed on the container's label, and each manufacturer provides instructions and precautions for the careful and proper use of each of its products. These should be read and followed specifically for best results as well as for safe use.

A variety of liquid and solid materials is used to make the many finishing products available to the homeowner, so this review obviously is a simplified version of these complex mixtures. Nonetheless, this discussion can assist the homeowner who wants to do some of this work himself, or who wants to buy the materials for someone else to apply.

Paints

Paint is made with a combination of binders, which are either dissolved in a solvent or emulsified in water, and an opaque or color pigment. Mixtures containing only binders and solvents are used to make varnish, polyurethane, lacquer, and other products that the homeowner is probably already familiar with by now. A coating of a varnish, polyurethane, or clear silicone dries through the process of oxidation, while a coating of lacquer dries by way of evaporation of the solvent in it. The amount of gloss in the mixture, which is designated usually as high gloss, semi-gloss, or flat, is achieved by varying the pigment concentration in the mixture. Rust- and corrosion-resistant paints made for use on exterior surfaces such as metal railings contain red lead or zinc chromate pigments. Aluminum paint used on radiators is made by adding metallic pigments to varnish.

There are several types of binders, and the type used in a finishing product determines how long it will last on the surface. Oil paints are made with either an alkyd or a linseed oil binder. Alkyd binders are used to make flat, semi-gloss, and high gloss paints, which are available in many colors for interior and exterior applications. Although these paints can be applied effectively onto most surfaces, they are not recommended for use on fresh (alkaline) concrete, masonry, or plaster surfaces.

Linseed oil is used as the binder in most exterior house paints, and it is one of the oldest types of binder available. The amount of linseed oil binder used in the paint is stated by the manufacturer on each label. Linseed oil-based exterior paints are used on wood siding and shingles as well as on metal siding. These paints are not recommended for use on interior surfaces or masonry walls because their high alkaline content makes them dry too slowly. Under normal conditions, linseed oil-based paints are quite durable; however, the finish is not a hard one and it can be scratched or chipped easily. Some manufacturers mix linseed oil with alkyds to make an oil-alkyd paint with a reduced drying time as well as improved hardness and gloss retention. Oil-alkyd paints are easy to apply and to level on a surface, and they resist fading. Oil-alkyd paints are recommended only for exterior use and most often for exterior wood trim around windows and doors.

Latex paints are made with a mixture of polymers, resins, and pigments in a water solution, and they are as durable as any of the oil-based paints when used under normal conditions. Polymers such as polyvinyl acetate and polyacrylic along with vinyl acrylic resin or another type of resin are mixed with water and a silica pigment to make latex paints. Unlike most oil-based paints, latex paints are virtually odorless and nonflammable. They are applied easily, they dry quickly and, when the job is done, clean-up is painless. The brush can be cleaned easily with water.

Latex paints, which are available in many colors and in flat, semi-gloss, and high gloss, are used on exterior siding as well as on brick, stucco, and other masonry surfaces. Because latex dries so quickly, many surfaces can be recoated with latex paint on the same day without causing any problems. The manufacturer's label states how long it takes for the product to dry between coats as well as the specific contents and their percentages used in making the product. For proper adhesion, the surface has to be clean and dry and, when it is being applied over a glossy finish, the surface has to be sanded to a dull finish before it can be coated with the latex paint. Before most latex acrylic paints can be applied onto wood siding, especially on redwood or Western red cedar, an oil-based primer should be applied.

Silicone

A clear silicone solution, which is used on porous masonry to resist water absorption, is a mixture of silicone binders in a water-repellent solution. The manufacturer's label on the container usually is marked with the words "5% solution," which means that 5% of the contents in the gallon is made up of silicone resin solids. A clear silicone solution, which is transparent, also is used on concrete driveways and streetwalks to help water bead on these surfaces. The beading enables the water to drain quickly from the concrete surface. This coating also helps keep the surfaces from spalling or cracking.

Varnish

Varnish is a mixture of an alkyd, oil-modified resins, solvents, and driers. The driers help the varnish dry thoroughly through the process of oxidation. Varnish, which is transparent, is used after a sealer such as shellac has been applied to raw wood. A varnish coating is not as hard as a polyurethane coating. Varnish adheres best to a clean, dry surface that has been wiped clear of any dirt or grease. Spar varnish is an improved version of varnish. It is used on exterior surfaces that are subjected to a great deal of moisture during use, such as boats and other marine equipment.

Polyurethane

Polyurethane is a mixture of alkyd resins, driers, mineral spirits, and inert ingredients. The manufacturer's label on the container states its correct usage, such as when it can be used on surfaces that have already been coated with shellac or lacquer, or over a sanding sealer that contains stearates or silicones. Polyurethane is transparent and its use results in a strong, durable surface that is resistant to both water and alcohol. It should be applied to a clean, dry surface that is free of dirt or grease to achieve best results.

Water-based Wood Finishes

In response to consumers' concern for the environment, some manufacturers are making water-based wood finishes. Traditional finishes such as polyurethane, varnish, and lacquer contain volatile organic compounds (VOCs) that react with nitrous oxides to form ozone, which is one of the main components of smog. Several states have already enacted laws limiting the use and amount of volatile organic compounds in finishing compounds. This legislation may be followed shortly by equally restrictive federal laws. These actions have spurred the development of these new water-based products. In addition to lower volatile organic compounds, water-based finishes have other advantages over the traditional wood finishing products. For example, water-based finishes are not as toxic as other wood finishes, and they dry more quickly and are much less flammable than the traditional finishes. Care still needs to be taken, however, to provide for adequate ventilation when using water-based wood finishes. For spraying applications, a good respirator is necessary when using water-based finishes, as it would be when any type of finishing product is being used. When applying water-based or traditional wood finishes, finish sandings are needed between each application of the finish to achieve a smooth surface after the finishing process has been completed. Although water-based wood finishing products are still very new, they are sure to be developed and distributed extensively as homeowners and professionals become more familiar with them and start to prefer them over other finishing products available.

Water-repellent Preservatives

Water-repellent preservatives with mildewcide are used to give wood a natural-looking finish while protecting it from cracking, checking, and splitting. The mildewcide resists fungus attacks on the wood as well as mildew and, as a result, it protects the wood from discoloration. Most of these types of preservatives contain pentachlorophenol along with resin and a water-repellent additive such as wax. The water-repellent quality of these preservatives enables water to drain quickly from the wood siding, a characteristic that helps to reduce the warping, shrinking, and swelling in the wood caused by water absorption. Some water-repellent preservatives can be stained or painted after they have been applied to the raw wood and given sufficient time to dry thoroughly.

Weathering Stain

Weathering stain, which is also called bleaching oil by some manufacturers, also contains mildewcide to resist fungus attacks as well as mildew. In this way, the mildewcide also prevents discoloration caused by mildew and fungus. Weathering stains usually are used on redwood or cedar to speed up the weathering process that occurs as a result of the wood's exposure to rain and to the sun's ultraviolet rays. The weathering stain eliminates the initial darkening stage that usually would occur during the weathering process and, in so doing, it enables the wood to weather more evenly as well as more quickly than it would if left uncoated.

Semi-transparent Stains

Semi-transparent stains are used to accent and beautify the wood grain by tinting it without hiding it. These stains are available in many different tones and shades, and many contain mildewcides and water-repellent additives. The water-repellent additive helps water bead on the wood so that it can roll off the siding quickly. This rapid drainage of the water from the siding prevents the wood from warping, cracking, or splitting. The mildewcide prevents the wood from discoloring as a result of attacks by fungus or mildew. The light-fast pigments in semi-transparent stains screen out the sun's ultraviolet rays to help prevent the wood from fading or graying. Semi-transparent stains are used on unprimed wood surfaces and on wood surfaces that already have been stained with a similar or lighter semi-transparent, oil-based stain. These stains are used frequently on wood siding, decks, fences, and outdoor furniture. A single coat of semi-transparent stain on a smooth surface can last approximately two to three years, and a second coat can double its longevity. Two coats of a semi-transparent stain on a rough-sawn surface can last as long as ten years.

Solid Color Stain

Solid color stain resembles paint in that it also hides the wood grain, but it differs from it in that it accents the texture of the wood instead of hiding it as paint does. Oil-based solid color stain is used on unprimed wood and on wood previously coated with an oil-based stain. An acrylic latex solid color stain can be used on wood previously coated with an oil-based primer only when the manufacturer says that it is compatible with it. The homeowner should check the manufacturer's recommendations on the container to determine the appropriate applications.

Solid color stains are water-repellent, which enables water to drain off the wood quickly. The mildewcide and light-fast pigments in these stains enable the wood to resist mildew, fungus, discoloration, and the fading effects of the weathering process. Solid color stains hide any imperfections in the wood such as blotches or uneven coloring, which can be found in wood siding and exterior wood trim. Solid color stain frequently is used on rough-sawn wood siding and cedar shakes. Some of these stains are recommended only for use on smooth-surfaced siding so, again, it is important to read the manufacturer's recommendations for use on the container before the homeowner chooses a product to do a specific job.

WHY EXTERIOR FINISHES FAIL

Exterior finishes may fail for a variety of reasons. That is why it is so important for the homeowner to select the right finish for the appropriate surface. Some generalities, however, can be kept in mind. For instance, oil-based and latex paints as well as stains and preservatives are preferable for use on exterior wood siding materials. Oil-based trim paints are used around windows and doors and on soffits, gutters, and downspouts. Paints manufactured specifically for use on metal surfaces also can be used on gutters and downspouts. Exterior masonry walls such as stucco or concrete block-constructed walls usually are coated with latex paints. Porch and deck enamels are preferred on wood porches, decks, steps, etc. Even when these general rules are followed, problems can occur, so let's review some of them as well as how to deal appropriately with them.

An exterior stain recommended for use on a rough-sawn surface will fail, for example, if it is applied to a smooth wood surface because it cannot adhere to that type of surface. Some manufacturers of this type of stain recommend that the smooth wood surface be primed first to help the stain adhere to it. It

is best to use the correct stain for its appropriate surface. Sometimes the finish on an exterior wall fails because a vapor barrier has not been placed on the inside of the wall, or because the vapor barrier has become so damaged that it is virtually useless. When a vapor barrier is not being used, or is badly deteriorated, moisture seeps through the walls, damages the surface, and destroys the finish on the surface. The application of a coat of vapor barrier paint on the inside of the wall can help prevent moisture from seeping through it.

Generally, paints and stains fail after many years of exposure to the sun, wind, rain, and snow as well as to extreme temperature fluctuations. That is why exterior finishes should be examined regularly. When a deteriorated exterior finish is found, it should be refinished promptly to prevent further deterioration of the exterior surface as well as water entry into the structure. Conversely, while extended neglect of an exterior surface is not recommended, it also is not a good practice to refinish a house too often. Not only is this practice uneconomical, but it can accelerate the finish's deterioration because of the heavy buildup of finishes on the surface. Since most homeowners tend to neglect an exterior surface rather than take care of it too much, the latter problem is not a common cause of failure of exterior finishes.

WHY PAINTS FAIL ON EXTERIOR SURFACES

Paint on an exterior surface initially shows signs of deterioration when its color starts to fade. This fading color, which is caused by constant exposure to the sun's ultraviolet rays, does not affect the paint's ability to protect the surface under it. As it ages, paint also loses its gloss due to exposure to air pollution, dirt, salt, and droppings from trees, shrubs, birds, etc. Again, the surface at this point is still being protected by the aging paint. It is when the paint starts to flake, blister, and become chalky that it has lost its ability to protect the surface under it (Figure 158). If the surface is not refinished within a relatively short period of time, the paint will become so deteriorated that the prime coat or raw wood will deteriorate under the paint. If the homeowner does not refinish the exterior surface at this point, extensive damage to the surface is inevitable.

158. Paint that has blistered and flaked on exterior wood trim. Photo by the author.

The homeowner can determine the cause of the paint's failure by the type of damage present in it. Often, several causes are involved simultaneously. For instance, chalking indicates that the paint has weathered so much that it is being destroyed by the weathering process. Chalking is visible when a powdery residue appears on a glove or a person's hand after it is rubbed on the surface. Chalking is caused by exposure to excessive amounts of sun and rain, which make the paint weather too quickly. Cracking in the paint is an indication that the paint has become brittle and, as a result of its brittleness, it no longer can expand and contract as easily as it did when it was first applied. Both the paint and the surface below it expand and contract as temperatures fluctuate. The brittle paint, however, loses its ability to expand and contract and, as temperatures change, it cracks on the exterior surface. Initially, small cracks become visible in the paint, a condition that is called checking. Then the cracks widen as the condition worsens. Checking and cracking occur more often on exterior surfaces where several layers of paint have been applied than on those with only one coat of paint on them. If the paint is left in this deteriorated condition, moisture will get behind the paint and the paint will start to peel and flake, which will damage the finish further.

Other common terms used to describe paint failures include lifting, alligatoring, crawling, sagging, blistering, and wrinkling. All of these terms are indications of one common problem: specifically, that the coat of paint did not adhere to the surface below it, whether the surface was prefinished, primed, or raw. There are numerous reasons for improper adhesion and they can be avoided by following the manufacturer's instructions for use as well as by preparing the surface correctly. For example, exterior paint will fail if it is applied when the outside temperature is below that recommended by the manufacturer on the label. Paint will flake and peel prematurely if it is applied to a surface that is not clean because the paint cannot adhere to it. In fact, any coat of paint applied over this coat also will fail for the same reason. Exterior paint will fail if it is applied over a prime coat that is not compatible with it. This information is stated on the manufacturer's label on the container. Again, any additional layers of paint over this one also will fail prematurely due to poor adhesion.

A wood preservative applied prior to the coat of paint will cause the paint to fail if it is not compatible. In some cases, the preservative will "bleed" through the paint; that is, it will become visible on the surface of the paint. Paint that is applied to a painted surface also will fail if it is not compatible with the paint already on the surface because it will not be able to adhere to it. Paint will fail if the holes and cracks in the surface were not repaired before it was applied to the surface. The holes and cracks allow moisture to seep behind the paint, causing it to blister. Blistering also will occur if a second coat of paint is applied over the first coat before the first one has had sufficient time to dry thoroughly. In this case, the second coat of paint pulls away from the first damp coat. Paint wrinkles when the second coat dries too quickly such as on a very hot day. Paint also wrinkles when it is applied on a very cold day and it cannot dry quickly enough for proper adhesion.

When very thin or very thick paint is applied, it also fails prematurely. If it is too heavy when it is applied, the paint will sag. It also will sag if too many coats are applied to the same surface within a short period of time. This occurs because the previous layers were not given sufficient time to dry thoroughly before the next coat was applied. Thin paint fails prematurely because it cannot adhere to the surface properly. Its durability and gloss also are adversely affected, especially when the paint is applied to a porous surface. As a result, thin paint chalks faster than the same type of paint would if it had not been made thin before it was applied to the exterior surface. The homeowner can avoid these problems by following the manufacturer's instructions carefully. Most paints need no preparation other than a good stirring to mix any ingredients that may have settled on the bottom of the container.

Since moisture is a common cause of many of the problems associated with painted finishes, it is essential to keep these surfaces dry not only when the paint is being applied but also long after its application. Loose windows and rotten sills should be repaired quickly, and trims around windows and doors should be caulked thoroughly to prevent water entry. Gutters and downspouts should be installed on a house that does not already have them, and they should be repaired as soon as they become damaged to prevent water from getting behind the exterior surfaces where it can damage the walls and finishes on them. Adequate ventilation should be provided for in the attic, crawl space, and basement to prevent moisture from condensing on the walls where it can damage the coat of paint. Vapor barriers should be installed or a vapor barrier paint should be applied to walls to prevent water vapor from seeping through the walls and damaging the exterior paint finish. Loose or rusted nails on siding and loose sections of siding should be repaired or replaced to keep water from getting behind the siding where it can damage both the siding and the paint on it. All exterior finishes, including paints, will last for many years if they are protected as best as they can be from the weather. Usually this can be accomplished through diligent maintenance. Since refinishing a house is an expensive project, it is worthwhile for the homeowner to maintain the exterior finishes on his house.

INTERIOR FINISHES AVAILABLE

It is as important to use the right kind of finish on interior surfaces as it is to do so on exterior surfaces. Since there are so many to choose from, the homeowner's preference can easily be accommodated. Interior finishes available include oil-based and latex paints, stains, polyurethanes, and varnishes as well as sealers, penetrating oils, teak oils, and much more. There are some generalities that can be made about these products to make the home-

owner's selection a simpler one. For instance, oil-based and latex flat paints are used on walls and ceilings. The EPA prohibited the use of interior latex paints containing mercury in 1990. Interior moldings and trims are coated with high or semi-gloss enamel paints, oil-based or latex, or with any of the various penetrating oils or stains. When penetrating oils or stains are used on moldings and trims, they also are coated with polyurethane or varnish. High gloss enamel paint often is preferred on bathroom and kitchen surfaces. New plaster and drywall installations are coated with a primer before paint is applied.

There also are some general rules that can be followed when finishing wood floors. Most raw wood floors are coated with a sealer before several coats of stain and/or polyurethane are applied. An oak or other open-grained wood floor also is coated with a paste wood filler after the sealer has been applied to fill the open pores in the wood before the stain and/or polyurethane is used. The paste wood filler gives the wood a very smooth surface because it does not shrink after it has dried and because it fills the pores in the wood. The paste wood filler is manufactured specifically for this purpose; it is not the other type of wood filler that the homeowner may already be familiar with, which is made to fill nail holes in wood. As with all wood products, the paste wood filler must be compatible with the sealer and with the finish that is going to be applied over it. Wood cabinets and paneling also are coated with varnish, polyurethane, or penetrating oil. The choice usually depends on what type of wood has been used in their construction as well as what type of finish is preferred. All wood surfaces, whether they are floors, cabinets, or paneling, must be clean, dry, and free of dust, dirt, and grease before the finishes are applied to have successful results.

Since oil-based and latex paints, stains, polyurethanes, and varnishes were discussed in the previous section on exterior finishes, there is no need to repeat them here. There are, however, several other interior finishes that need some further explanation, including sealers, penetrating oils, and teak oils.

Sealers
A sealer is a varnish that has been thinned with a solvent. It is used on raw wood to seal the surface of

the wood and to serve as a prime coat before stain, varnish, or polyurethane is used. Neither varnish nor polyurethane can penetrate into the structure of the wood; these substances only cover the surface. Sealers are used to fill the pores in open-grained hardwoods as well as in porous plywoods. They prevent the grains from rising, which would make the grain uneven, and they prevent uneven stain penetration. Sealers also can be used as a prime coat on interior wood walls.

Penetrating Oil

Penetrating oil, which is a mixture of oil and resin, is used on raw wood. It also can be used on prefinished wood such as on cabinets and paneling; however, the old finish must be removed completely for satisfactory results. Because penetrating oil penetrates deeply into the pores of the wood, usually several coats are needed to achieve a satisfactory finish. Penetrating oil is preferred by many woodworkers because it has the ability to give wood a hand-rubbed appearance after several coats have been applied. It is available as a clear liquid as well as in a variety of wood tones. Although it can be used on all wood species, it is important to choose the tone carefully because it can give uneven results on various species of wood. For best results, the homeowner should strictly adhere to the manufacturer's recommendations on the label.

Teak Oil

Teak oil is similar to penetrating oil in that it seals the pores in the wood. It also is used on raw wood and on wood surfaces that have been completely stripped of any previous finishing coats. Teak oil protects both interior and exterior surfaces from moisture and weathering. It can be used quite successfully on any interior wood surface, such as paneling and molding, as well as on exterior surfaces such as hardwood doors. Since teak oil products are not interchangeable in terms of interior or exterior use, the homeowner should be sure to purchase the one that is appropriate for the project he is about to do.

PAINT REMOVERS

No discussion about finishing products can be complete without mentioning some facts about paint removers. A paint remover is a mixture of methanol, methyl chloride, and toluol. Paint removers are used to remove paint from wood, metal, and plaster. They are very flammable, so they should be kept away from any heat or flame source inside or outside of the house. In fact, most finishing products should be stored carefully since they are flammable. Although latex and water-based finishing products are not fire hazards for the most part, they should be stored where they cannot freeze during the winter, so appropriate storage areas are also important for them. All finishing products should be kept out of the reach of children since accidental swallowing of any of these products can be fatal. Some paint removers act as skin irritants, so it is best to wash any spills off the skin immediately. Sufficient ventilation also is needed when using paint removers as well as many finishing products. Some paint removers and finishing products can cause dizziness and nausea when they are used without proper ventilation. The homeowner should read the manufacturer's instructions for use to determine how much ventilation is necessary.

PREPARATION OF INTERIOR SURFACES

As with exterior applications, it is essential to prepare interior surfaces properly to achieve satisfactory results and to prevent premature failure of the finish. For example, before old interior walls constructed of drywall or plaster are finished, any holes or cracks in them should first be patched with spackle, patching plaster, or drywall compound, depending on the extent of the damage on the surface. Spackle and drywall compound are available in two forms: premixed and as a powder to be mixed easily with water. These products are used to repair small cracks in interior walls and ceilings. Patching plaster, which is only available as a powder, is used to repair large cracks and holes in interior surfaces. Because patching plaster hardens shortly after it has been mixed with water, repairs made with it must be done quickly. Drywall compound is used to cover the tape on drywall joints.

Other types of surfaces such as tile and wood surfaces also should be repaired before they are finished. For instance, open joints around a bathtub should be refilled with a grout filler. This is done while the tub is filled with water. The weight of the water deflects the bathtub downward, enlarges the openings around it, and enables them to be refilled thoroughly. After the water is drained from the tub, the grout filler seals the bathtub tightly to the wall tiles. Gouges and holes in wood trims around windows and doors should be filled with plastic wood filler. Wood filler is available premixed in a number of wood tones chosen to match the kind of wood being repaired. Plastic wood filler also is available as a colorless powder so that it can be mixed with wood stain to closely match the stain's tone on the wood. After the plastic wood filler has dried thoroughly, it should be sanded to achieve a smooth finish before it is coated with stain and/or polyurethane or varnish.

CAULKING, SEALANTS, AND GLAZING COMPOUNDS

Caulking compounds and sealants prevent drafts and leaks, while glazing compounds seal the perimeter of glass to prevent drafts and leaks. They are essential materials, yet the homeowner can use them fairly easily for do-it-yourself repairs. Caulking compounds are available in several types, including acrylic latex, butyl rubber, and styrene-butadiene rubber. These products are used to seal small cracks in wood, metal, masonry, and concrete, among other materials. Their use prevents drafts and water entry from around windows and doors as well as along streetwalks or driveways that are flush against the exterior wall of a house. A clean, dry surface is necessary for the caulking compound to adhere tightly. The homeowner should follow the manufacturer's suggestions for use, printed on the tube, to use the correct product for the appropriate surface. These instructions also tell the homeowner how deep and wide the opening can be for effective use of the product as well as the appropriate temperature and humidity conditions for proper adhesion. Some caulking compounds can be coated with paint after they have been given sufficient time to dry thoroughly. Other caulking compounds can be used successfully in applications where the opening to be filled is quite deep. In this case, the opening usually

first has to be filled with oakum, rubber, fiberglass insulation, or polyurethane rods that are manufactured specifically for this purpose. Caulking compounds are available in several colors as well as clear.

Sealants are improved versions of caulking compounds. They last longer than caulking compounds because they are more flexible in a moving joint than a caulking compound would be. They are especially effective in such moving joints as a control joint on a brick wall. Sealants also can be used in precast masonry, around window and door frames, and even in the assembly unit around air conditioning ducting. Better grades of sealants are available, including acrylic latex, butyl, and solvent base acrylics. The most expensive grades are available in polysulfides, silicones, polyurethanes, and ethylene copolymer compounds. As with caulking compounds, sealants are available in several colors as well as clear. They are sold in tubes for application with a caulking gun and in bulk quantity containers as large as 55 gallons. For proper adhesion, the surface should be sound, clean, and dry, and the temperature and humidity levels should be appropriate for the type of sealant being used. Again, the manufacturer's instructions for use, which are printed on the tube or container, should be followed carefully for an effective application.

Glazing compounds are used to seal glazings in wood and metal window sashes on both interior and exterior surfaces. These compounds also act as a "bedding" to cushion the glass as it is sealed against the window or door frame. Face glazings seal the gap between the glass and the frame to prevent water entry as well as drafts. Glazing materials dry to a firm but not hard state to remain somewhat flexible. In fact, glazing compounds are more flexible than putty. Glazing compounds, which are available premixed, can be painted to extend their life expectancy. Since glazing compounds are only sold in one color, often it is a good idea to paint them to match the house's color scheme. Glazing compounds are fairly easy to use; however, care must be taken when using them not to break the glazing material, especially if it is glass, which is fragile.

16
Figuring Out Fireplaces and Chimneys

THE PROS AND CONS OF FIREPLACES

The fireplace still holds great appeal as a cozy or even romantic setting in a home. Many houses, both old and new, have fireplaces installed in them, even when heating is done by means of a central heating system. Fireplaces are made of masonry and are built into the structure of a house, or they are factory-built, prefabricated units that have been added or built into the house. Some prefabricated units, called zero clearance fireplaces, also are in use, and they function as well as built-in masonry fireplaces. The chimneys in a house are made of masonry or metal, and they serve the fireplace and the heating system. When there are several fireplaces, a heating system, and a domestic hot water heater to exhaust in a house, several chimneys are in use to serve all of these units and systems.

Despite their friendly appearance, fireplaces can be the cause of disaster in a house. According to the National Chimney Sweep Guild, in 1987 alone, 72,100 residential fires in this country started in fireplaces, chimneys, wood stoves, and connector pipes, killing 150 people, injuring 333 others, and causing $186 million in property damage. And, the Guild notes, although potential problems are numerous, almost all can be prevented with a little knowledge and regular maintenance. That is why it is important for the homeowner to know how a fireplace is built, how it functions in conjunction with a chimney, and how to take care of it so that it operates safely.

COMPONENTS OF A MASONRY FIREPLACE AND CHIMNEY

The Uniform Building Code as well as state and local codes have established guidelines for the safe and proper construction of chimneys used to exhaust gases and other products of combustion from fireplaces and heating systems. These guidelines include a variety of requirements for such items as the height of the chimney above the roofline, the size of the flue, and the method of support, among other specifications. Each component of the chimney and the fireplace must be built correctly so that they can operate safely.

The chimney in an old house usually is made of bricks, while in most modern houses, it is made of a prefabricated metal flue pipe. The air space in the chimney is called the flue. Usually, in older houses, the flue is lined with vitrified clay flue liners. The liner in a brick-constructed chimney helps protect the bricks and mortar behind it from exposure to the extreme and rapid temperature fluctuations that occur in it. The liner also helps to protect the masonry from the corrosive effects of the combustion gases.

Vitrified clay flue liners are available in round and rectangular-shaped profiles made in several prefabricated lengths. Each piece of the liner is set in refractory cement mortar, and the joints on the inside of the liner are smooth. The liner either rests on a concrete slab at the base of the chimney or it is supported by courses of bricks (Figure 159). The first layer of the liner begins above the brick-constructed smoke chamber, which is opposite the damper. The brickwork that is placed above the damper is built so that it forms a gradual arch to support the weight of the chimney above.

The flue should be constructed as vertically as possible to function efficiently and safely. When its direction has to be changed, that change must be made gradually because sharp directional changes in the flue can adversely affect the flow of the smoke and combustion gases in it. An air space is left between the liner and the masonry chimney surrounding it. The size of this air space is determined by the Uniform Building Code as well as by state and local building codes. The air space enables the flue liner to expand without being damaged as it becomes heated.

The damper, a hinged, cast-iron lid that covers the fire box, regulates the draft (the air flow in the flue) by adjusting the throat opening. The throat is opened wide when there is a very hot fire and it is partially closed when there is a slow-burning fire. Naturally, the smaller the throat opening is, the less heat is lost through the flue. When the damper is shut, the flue is completely closed. When the damper is shut during the summer, it prevents cooled indoor air from escaping through the flue. This helps to keep air conditioning costs at a minimum. The closed damper also helps to prevent squirrels, raccoons, and other small animals from entering the house through the flue. These rascals can cause a great deal of damage in a house, especially when they cannot find their way back out of it.

The smoke shelf, which is located in the smoke chamber behind the damper, projects out from the rear chimney wall. It prevents a downdraft by deflecting cold air upward into the smoke chamber where it exhausts out of the flue along with smoke and combustion gases. In this way, the cold outdoor air is prevented from entering the house through the flue.

A cap is installed at the top of the chimney. It is made of concrete, precast concrete, or stone (Figure 160). The concrete is poured over the top

courses of brick on the chimney when a precast concrete or stone cap is not being used. The cap slopes away from the chimney so that water can easily drain off it. This prevents water from getting into the air space between the liner and the chimney walls. The cap also helps to prevent animal entry, bird nesting, and the entry of leaves and other debris that could block the chimney. Spark arresters are installed at the top of the chimney in areas where local and state building codes require their installation. Spark arresters are needed when the fuel being burned emits sparks during the combustion process.

Flashing is placed between the roof covering and the masonry chimney to prevent water entry into the roof. Flashing is made of copper, aluminum, or galvanized metal. A chimney on a sloped roof has a saddle, which is also called a cricket, installed to prevent water entry. This cricket, which is made of built-up metal flashing, directs water away from the chimney (Figure 160). Stepflashing also is installed between the chimney and the roof covering.

A cleanout door, which is usually made of cast iron, is installed at the base of the chimney or below the fireplace hearth. Ash accumulates behind it in the ash dump or ash pit, as it also is called. Depending on what type of construction was used for the chimney, the cleanout door is either accessible in the basement or on an exterior wall behind the chimney. Ash should be removed from the ash dump before each heating season begins.

PROBLEMS ASSOCIATED WITH CHIMNEYS AND FIREPLACES

In some old houses, a cleanout door has not been installed. The only way to clear debris from the base of the chimney is to remove the vent pipe that fits into the chimney. This vent pipe is located near the boiler. Most homeowners are not even aware of this maintenance task, let alone its importance. One homeowner had been told by his heating contractor that the ash had been removed from the chimney when his heating system was installed. For several years, he remained unconcerned. In fact, he never even bothered to look at his chimney. Then one winter's day, his wife told him that the walls near the boiler were "sweating" and that there was an

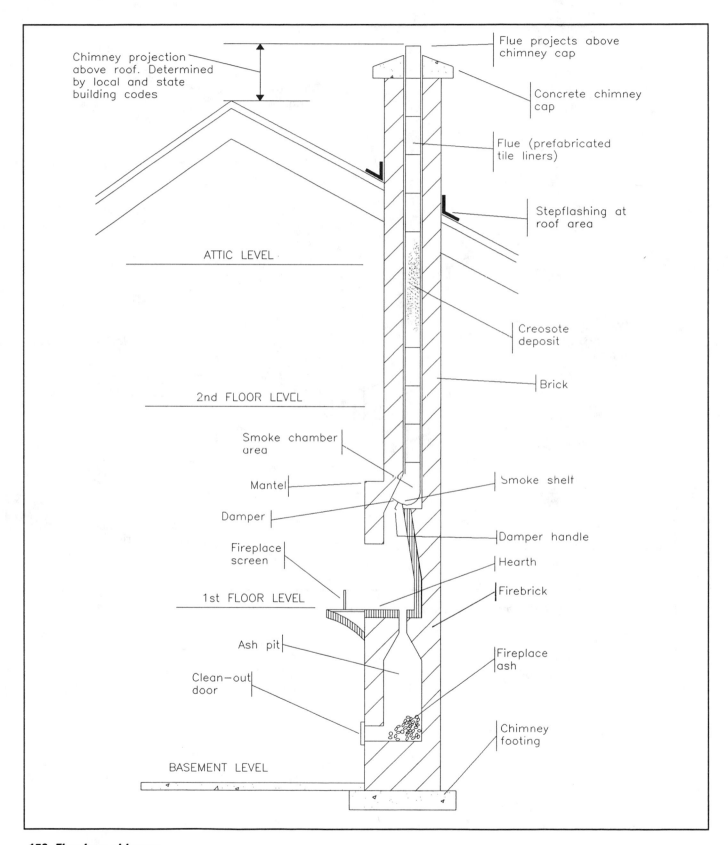

159. Fireplace chimney

Chimney projection above roof. Determined by local and state building codes

ATTIC LEVEL

2nd FLOOR LEVEL

Smoke chamber area

Mantel

Damper

Fireplace screen

1st FLOOR LEVEL

Ash pit

Clean-out door

BASEMENT LEVEL

Flue projects above chimney cap

Concrete chimney cap

Flue (prefabricated tile liners)

Stepflashing at roof area

Creosote deposit

Brick

Smoke shelf

Damper handle

Hearth

Firebrick

Fireplace ash

Chimney footing

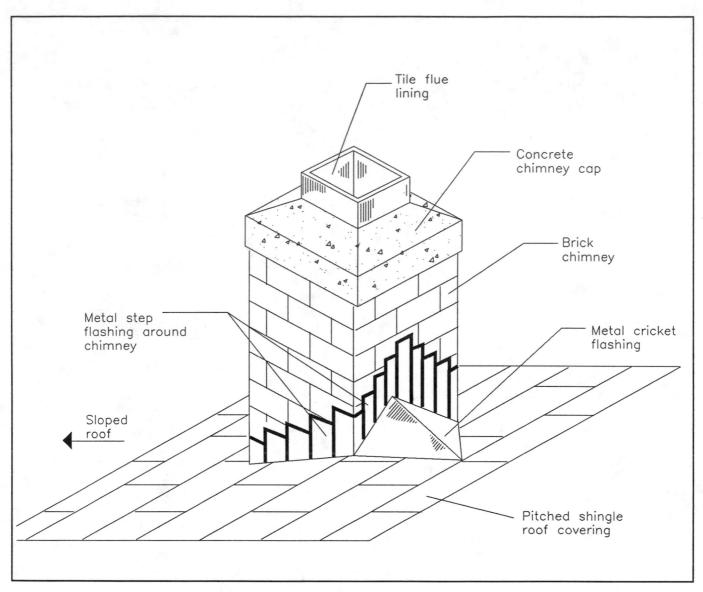

Tile flue lining

Concrete chimney cap

Brick chimney

Metal step flashing around chimney

Metal cricket flashing

Sloped roof

Pitched shingle roof covering

160. Detail of chimney cap and metal flashing around chimney

excessive amount of heat in and near the boiler room in the basement. The homeowner immediately turned off the boiler and called for emergency assistance. When the utility company representative came to investigate and removed the vent pipe, he told the homeowner that the chimney was blocked with soot, ash, leaves, and other debris. The homeowner also was told that his chimney probably had *not* been cleaned when the new heating system was installed and, as a result, combustion gases including toxic carbon monoxide were backing up into his house. The moist, heated indoor air was condensing on the cooler exterior walls, causing them to "sweat." A thorough cleaning of the chimney and annual cleaning ever since have eliminated this homeowner's problem.

In addition to blockages in the chimney, problems are caused as the chimney ages. In houses that are more than 100 years old, fireplaces can be found in several rooms on every floor because they were used for heating. Once central heating systems were installed, the fireplaces were concealed and the chimneys were sealed. If a homeowner decides that he would like to put these fireplaces back into operation, he will have to be aware of the fact that the safe use of the chimneys is questionable, if not impossible. It is more than likely that, after so many years of wood-burning, these chimneys are in a state of decay. This is especially true in chimneys that are not lined, such as those built with a single-wall chimney flue, which is often found in old houses. The combustion gases and extreme temperature fluctuations that occurred in the flue while it was in use caused the masonry to crack. Water entry also has caused further deterioration. The damage in some of these old chimneys is so severe that the bricks and mortar have literally disintegrated. These old fireplaces and chimneys cannot be used until they have been completely rebuilt and lined. In some cases, the old chimney can be lined by pumping a refractory mix into it. This mix hardens in it and acts as a liner in the chimney.

Sometimes the different types of fuels used for the heating system cause problems in a chimney. One homeowner who bought a house that was about fifty years old learned about this problem when he heard a rumbling sound in his house. Upon investigation, he found that the chimney had collapsed into itself. His heating contractor explained that the collapse was due to the change from an oil-fired to a gas-fired heating system. The soot, which had collected on the bricks and mortar in the chimney, had a high sulfur content due to the oil that had been burned by the old heating system. Then the condensation of the combustion gases from the newer boiler had a high acidity level due to the gas that was being burned as fuel for the boiler. The result was the presence of sulfuric acid in the soot, which ate away at the bricks and mortar in the chimney, causing them to spall and deteriorate. As the deterioration continued over an extended period of time, the chimney became so deteriorated that it collapsed into itself. This homeowner had to have his chimney completely rebuilt, a costly solution to a problem that could have been prevented by having the chimney cleaned regularly.

CREOSOTE DEPOSITS AND THEIR HAZARDS

Creosote is a highly combustible byproduct of wood-burning and, when it collects in a chimney, it creates a fire hazard. In fact, creosote is the major cause of chimney fires. These types of fires often reach temperatures as high as 2,000° F. This intense heat cracks and even disintegrates the liner, bricks, and mortar in a chimney. If the creosote is not removed from a chimney regularly by a professional chimney sweep, it will continue to collect in it as the fireplace is used for wood-burning. This is especially true in an unlined, single-wall chimney flue because creosote builds up more quickly in unlined chimneys than in lined chimneys.

Creosote deposits begin as a liquid, specifically as the condensation of combustion gases. This liquid cools as it comes into contact with the cold outdoor air and collects on the interior walls or liner in the chimney. Creosote appears in three forms or stages, as they are called by chimney sweeps. The major difference between them is their moisture content. Soot is different from creosote in that it is soft and black or brown in color. Soot is formed as a result of unburned carbon particles. Soot deposits often are mixed with fly ash; that is, ashes that are carried up from the heating appliance by the draft. Even though it is not a form of creosote, soot is a fire hazard, and it should be removed to prevent flue blockages as well as fires.

The method of removal of creosote deposits depends on its form or stage in the chimney. "Loose Fluffy" or "Popcorn" creosote looks as its descriptive names suggest. It is generally formed from wood fires in open fireplaces where the supply and flow of air into the fire box and up the chimney is unrestricted. Stage One creosote, as this form of creosote is called, is easily removed with wire or polypropylene chimney brushes. Stage Two creosote is the "Tarry Gummy" form, and it has the same characteristics as freshly applied road tar. It is found in a fireplace where the flow of air is significantly restricted, such as in one with a close-fitting glass door enclosure, as well as in wood stoves. The application of a chemical catalyst and heat to change its structure to Stage One is needed to remove this type of creosote. The third form of creosote, called "Hard Glazed," is a baked-on version of Stage Two. It has the consistency of marble. The use of powered rotary cleaning devices, or several chemical applications followed by brushings, is needed to remove Stage Three creosote deposits. Naturally, the best thing for the homeowner to do is to have the chimney cleaned regularly by a professional chimney sweep to minimize the amount of creosote that collects as a result of wood-burning.

ZERO CLEARANCE FIREPLACES

Prefabricated fireplace units called zero clearance fireplaces are advantageous for the homeowner who wants to add a fireplace to his house, but who does not want to go through the expense and disruption that the construction of a masonry fireplace and chimney would entail. Zero clearance fireplaces are well-insulated; therefore, they can be installed against interior or exterior walls or diagonally in a corner. Since they also are lightweight, there is no need to install extra supporting members in the floor under them. These units are available as kits. Each kit includes a hearth, chimney, screen, glass doors, gas log lighters, and other necessary parts and accessories. When they are installed, it is essential that zero clearance fireplaces meet building and fire codes because they are placed close to walls. The flue pipe and fire box should be sealed with fire-rated insulation, and fire-stopping should be installed. As with any chimney, the installation must strictly adhere to local and state specifications concerning the chimney's height above the roofline. These codes also specify how much space has to be left between the zero clearance fireplace and any combustible materials on walls or floors near it.

Manufacturers of zero clearance fireplaces usually recommend that this type of fireplace be installed in conjunction with a combustion kit. The combustion kit works simultaneously with the glass doors to force the fireplace to use outside air instead of inside air for combustion. The use of the indoor air would be counterproductive since it already has been heated. A variety of materials can be installed in the fire box such as ceramic tiles, marble, slate, bricks, etc. In many cases, this same material also can be installed in the hearth. The hearth should extend a specific distance in front of the fireplace as well as the full width of the mantelpiece. When an underlayment is needed under the hearth, it should meet local and state building and fire code specifications as well as those stated by the manufacturer for the safe use of the fireplace.

17
Working with Wood and Wood Products

CHOOSING THE RIGHT WOOD PRODUCT

Although many wood products already have been discussed in this book, there are still some facts about wood and several wood products that need to be reviewed so that the homeowner can choose wood products wisely and even use them creatively in the home. For instance, knowledge of what criteria are used by the various wood product associations to grade their many wood products, as well as what their grading symbols mean, can be helpful to the homeowner. With this knowledge, he can pick the best wood product for each specific wood project in his house. A review of the characteristics of various hardwood species used for flooring, paneling, furniture making, etc., also can assist the homeowner as he undertakes numerous renovation and repair projects (Figure 161). Wood staircases merit a separate discussion so the homeowner can keep those in his house safe and beautiful. Whether the homeowner does his own woodworking projects or has a professional do them for him, these facts about wood enable him to get more for his money in terms of materials as well as beauty. Let's begin the discussion with the grading of wood.

DECIPHERING GRADE STAMPS

The grade of a piece of wood, which is determined by its species, grain, and color as well as by the number and size of defects in it, determines its value. The higher the wood's grade is, the more the homeowner or contractor is going to have to pay for it. Each tree yields its inherent quantity of select and common boards. The select boards are taken from the outer layers of the tree where the wood is clear and knot-free. The center of the tree, where there are defects including knots that may be loose, yields the lowest grades of lumber.

One of the numerous associations that grades and supplies lumber is the Western Wood Products Association (WWPA). Its grading service divides the quantity of lumber from a single tree into different categories. These categories include dimension lumber, shop-grade lumber, common lumber, and select lumber as well as beams, posts, and timbers. Each is appropriate for specific uses (see Figure 84 on page 102).

Dimension Lumber
Dimension lumber is used as framing lumber in residential construction. This grade of lumber cannot be used for furniture making or for any other appearance detailing (decorative detailing) because it has many knots in it. The grade stamp on dimension lumber indicates its strength as well as other important information. A few of the many species of wood used for framing in residential construction throughout the United States include Douglas fir, hem-fir, Southern yellow pine, hemlock, and Ponderosa pine. Longleaf heart pine often can be found

161. Western red cedar, which has been milled as fine furniture would be, is used in this house. Courtesy of Lindal Cedar Homes.

in houses that are 150 years old or older. At that time it was the principal type of wood used for house framing. It also was used for heavy construction such as for railroad trestles and bridges. Since it is no longer possible to grow these trees in the United States, any longleaf heart pine being used in today's house construction has been reclaimed from old structures or from riverbeds. It is milled or remilled for use as paneling and flooring as well for appearance grade timbers in residential construction.

Dimension lumber suitable for light framing is indicated as such with the Construction, Standard, or Utility grade stamp on it. The strongest of these is the Construction grade, which is used for studs, sill plates, blocking, etc. Framing lumber suitable for joists and rafters is indicated with the STK (select tight knot), No. 1, No. 2, or No. 3 grade stamp printed on it. The STK grade is stronger than the No. 1, 2, and 3 grades, and the No. 1 grade is stronger than the No. 2 and 3 grades. The weakest grade is the No. 3 grade.

Shop-grade Lumber

Shop-grade lumber is milled from the wood between the select and common grades of lumber in a tree. Shop-grade lumber has fewer knots in it than common lumber. In fact, most shop-grade lumber is clear since the few knots that are in it appear only sporadically. Shop-grade lumber, which is available in several widths and thicknesses, is used in many manufactured products, especially wood windows and doors. This wood is sent to the manufacturers' own mills where the knots are cut out of the lumber. The resulting clear pieces of wood are joined together for use in the construction of window frames. Shop-grade lumber also is used to make moldings. The clear pieces are finger-jointed for use as casings, window stops, etc. As long as they are painted after they have been installed, these joints are not going to be visible, and the trim will look as if it was cut from a single length of wood.

Common Lumber

Common lumber is used for non-decorative purposes other than framing, such as shelving, siding, etc. It also is used for paneling and is cut in a variety of profiles for this purpose (Figure 162). The grades of common lumber are indicated by the No. 2 Com-

mon and No. 3 Common grade stamps. No. 2 Common, which is the better of the two grades, has fewer and smaller knots in it than the No. 3 Common grade. A section of the surface on a No. 3 Common board may be rough or unfinished because the planing machine missed it as it was being milled. Frequently there also are loose and split knots in No. 3 Common lumber that may fall out of the board as it is being installed.

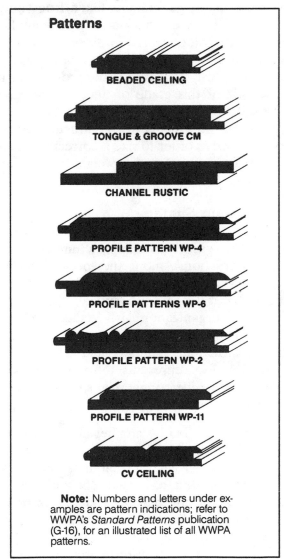

Patterns

BEADED CEILING

TONGUE & GROOVE CM

CHANNEL RUSTIC

PROFILE PATTERN WP-4

PROFILE PATTERNS WP-6

PROFILE PATTERN WP-2

PROFILE PATTERN WP-11

CV CEILING

Note: Numbers and letters under examples are pattern indications; refer to WWPA's *Standard Patterns* publication (G-16), for an illustrated list of all WWPA patterns.

162. Standard patterns. Courtesy of the Western Wood Products Association.

Select Lumber

Select lumber, or finish lumber as it also is called, is used for furniture making, moldings, cabinet making, custom flooring, etc. It also is used in a variety of profiles for paneling; however, it is more expensive than common paneling. Finish lumber is indicated with the Select and F.A.S. (first and seconds) grade stamps. It is clear and straight-grained with few if any knots in it. The few knots that may be present in select lumber usually are very small and quite tight.

Beams, Posts, and Timbers

Lumber used to support heavy loads, such as beams, posts, and timbers, generally is taken from around the center of the tree. This lumber also is available in appearance grade for use in decorative applications such as in a beam ceiling. The bearing strength of the beam, post, or timber is the most important characteristic of this grade of lumber. The length and thickness of the beam, post, or timber has to be determined by an architect or contractor before it can be installed in order to size it correctly so that it can adequately support the weight that will be bearing on it.

Other Grading Systems

The Western Spruce, Pine and Fir Association (WSPFA) also grades and supplies lumber for residential construction. Among the species graded by the WSPFA are white spruce, Lodgepole pine, Alpine fir, and Engelmann spruce. As with the WWPA, this organization also grades lumber by number and appearance, and it uses such categories as the Construction, Standard, and Utility grades. The WSPFA also represents the Canadian forest reserves that provide commercial softwoods to the United States.

In addition to grading by number and appearance, wood can be graded by the manner in which it is dressed; that is, to what extent it is sanded and planed in preparation for its sale. The moisture content of the wood also can be a major factor in a grading system. To choose the correct grade of wood for its appropriate use, the homeowner has to be familiar with the specific criteria used to grade the lumber he is about to buy. Any wood project cannot be accomplished satisfactorily when the correct grade of wood is not used.

FLOORING MATERIALS

One wood product that often is of particular interest to the homeowner is custom wood flooring, which is made from the Select and F.A.S. grades. Wood flooring milled from lower grades of wood also is available. These types of wood flooring materials are economical; however, the wood grain is not as clear as it is in those made from the Select and F.A.S. grades. Generally, the homeowner should avoid flooring with a grade stamp lower than No. 1 grade, unless he is prohibited economically from doing so. Wood flooring is available prefinished and unfinished, and it is made with tongue and groove or shiplapped joints. The flooring made with shiplapped joints also is known as plank flooring. The tongue and groove flooring varies in width from 3 to 8 inches. Shiplapped flooring is available in 8-inch widths and wider, depending on the manufacturer.

The most popular wood flooring materials used today are made from hardwoods such as oak, maple, ash, cherry, and walnut. White pine and yellow pine also are very popular flooring materials, but they are not hardwoods. One of the most beautiful wood flooring materials available is the old growth, reclaimed or recycled heart pine flooring. This wood is as hard as red or white oak, harder than walnut, but not as hard as maple. It resists rot and insect infestation very well. As noted earlier, this wood is salvaged from old buildings and reclaimed from riverbeds and milled or remilled for use. All wood flooring is kiln-dried to a moisture content of between 7 and 10%, a moisture level that is quite suitable for this purpose because the wood remains stable.

Each of the various hardwood species used for custom flooring has different physical properties and characteristics that make it appropriate for specific uses. The following list is meant to make the homeowner familiar with some of them.

Northern Red Oak: This is a strong hardwood with an average weight of 3.6 lbs./bd. ft. (pounds per board foot). Its color is reddish-brown. It has a beautifully grained texture and is used for paneling and furniture making as well as flooring.

White Oak: This hardwood is very strong, hard, and heavy. It has fine structural capabilities for use as support timbers and beams. The grain of white oak has the same characteristics as those of red oak. The white oak has an ash-gray tint. Its average weight is approximately 3.9 to 4.1 lbs./bd. ft. It is used for flooring and furniture making as well as for support beams and timbers.

Hard Maple: This hardwood is highly wear-resistant. It is strong and very hard with a yellow color, and its grain is beautifully textured, especially the grain in bird's eye maple. Its average weight is approximately 3.7 lbs./bd. ft. It is used for furniture making, cutting boards, bowling pins and alleys, custom flooring, and even gym flooring.

White Ash: This hardwood's grain pattern resembles that of red oak. As it ages, white ash turns to a rich honey color. Its average weight is approximately 3.5 lbs./bd. ft. Its excellent shock resistance makes it ideal for baseball bats, hockey sticks, and tool handles, but it is also used for paneling, furniture making, and flooring.

Black Cherry: As it ages, this hardwood changes color from a light to a dark reddish-brown. Its average weight is approximately 3.2 lbs./bd. ft. It is used extensively for furniture making, but it also is ideal for flooring and paneling.

Walnut: This is probably the most popular hardwood in use today. Like white ash, it has excellent shock resistance. Its average weight is approximately 3.5 lbs./bd. ft. The color range is quite broad, varying from a white sapwood to a dark chocolate-brown, heartwood tone. It is used for flooring, furniture making, and paneling.

STAIRCASES

A staircase can be purely utilitarian such as those often found leading down to a basement or cellar, or it can be dramatic and beautiful such as those found in living rooms and dining rooms in old, elegant houses and in new, modern ones (Figures 163 and 164). The parts of a staircase include the stair treads, risers, handrails, spindles, and newel post. These parts can be made of a less expensive wood such as pine, or they can be made of an expensive hardwood such as oak or poplar. Usually when a staircase is covered with carpeting, it is made of pine. Custom-designed staircases generally are made of a hardwood or heart pine and they are very expensive.

The finish on a wood staircase is very important because it is going to have to be able to take a beating.

Hardwood staircases often are finished with several coats of a high-quality polyurethane. An oak or other open-grained staircase is prepared before it is finished. The raw wood first is coated with a sealer, then with a paste wood filler to fill the pores of the wood. In this way, a smooth, glass-like finish is achieved that will last a long time. After the sealer and filler are applied, the staircase is sanded and then wiped clean. At this point, the staircase can be stained and coated with polyurethane, or it can be coated with a polyurethane that is compatible with the sealer, whichever is preferred by the homeowner. When the staircase is installed and as it is being used, it is important to be sure that the handrail is secured tightly to the wall and/or newel post. In addition, spindles should be spaced closely so that a small child cannot fall from between them.

The condition of a staircase can tell a homeowner a great deal about the condition of the house in which it is located. One homeowner had a house in which the staircase was sloping away from the wall at an alarming distance. It was sloped so dramatically that he could feel himself bounce on the stair treads as he walked up and down on it. He had been assured that there was nothing wrong with the house or the staircase when he bought it. After all, he was told, the house has been standing for fifty years without any problems, so why worry about it now? After some urging by family members, this homeowner finally hired an engineer to examine the staircase and the house. He told the homeowner that the staircase was so deteriorated that it could fail at any time, and he recommended against carrying any heavy equipment or appliances up or down the staircase until it was rebuilt. The staircase had failed after many years of use, and it had to be replaced before anyone was hurt as a result of its failure.

A staircase should be checked regularly for sloping and softness since these can indicate problems in the structure of the house, not just in the staircase. Any noticeable softness or sloping in a staircase can be an indication that there is a settlement problem in the house. That is why the homeowner should hire a professional engineer or carpenter to check the condition of a sloping or soft staircase to determine the cause of the problem. The staircase itself may be structurally sound, but the wall that supports it may have been weakened. An opening between the skirtboard and the wall also is an indication that

163. Wood moldings enhance this staircase and its surrounding walls. Courtesy of the Wood Moulding & Millwork Producers Association.

164. The wood staircase adds to the modern, spacious look of this house. Courtesy of Lindal Cedar Homes.

there is a problem. The support for the staircase may be failing or the wall may be settling. Either of these conditions can cause the staircase to separate from the wall. The homeowner should determine the cause of any of these problems to prevent injury to himself or a family member as a result of a failure by the staircase.

WOOD-DESTROYING INSECTS AND FUNGUS

Although termite infestations are familiar to most homeowners, there are many other insects, as well as wood-destroying fungus, that can effectively destroy the wood framing members in a house. The National Pest Control Association publishes a manual about wood-destroying insects that includes more than two dozen species. Among these are three fairly well-known insects, namely, the powder post beetle, the carpenter ant, and the carpenter

bee. All insect infestations have to be eliminated as soon as they are discovered to limit the extent of their damage to the house's framing structure. Additionally, in most states, it is illegal for a homeowner to sell his house when he knows it has termite infestations that could lead to structural damage. Wood-decaying fungus also can severely damage the wood framing members in a house, so the homeowner also should deal with this problem as quickly as possible. Let's review some facts about these wood-destroying insects and fungus so that the homeowner can recognize visual evidence of any infestations and know how to deal with them appropriately and effectively.

Termites

There are many types of termites in the United States. The two that do the most damage in houses are the subterranean and non-subterranean termites. Subterranean termites need to have access to the soil or to another source of water, while non-

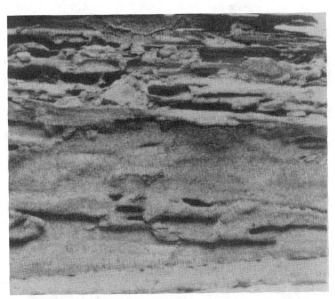

165. *Subterranean termite nests in wood. Courtesy of the National Pest Control Association.*

subterranean termites do not need moisture or contact with the soil since they can live in only damp or even dry wood. Subterranean termites, which cause most of the damage in houses, used to be found only in the southern half of the country; however, they have become more and more prevalent in the northern states. Non-subterranean termites are common in Hawaii and along the Gulf Coast from southern California to Florida and into southern Virginia. Generally, houses located in states where the climate is colder have fewer problems with termites than those in warmer parts of the country. States in which infestations are most frequent are located in the southern part of the United States, from Texas in the west to South Carolina in the east. Houses in the northern regions such as New England have fewer incidences of damage due to termite infestation than those in climates where temperatures remain mild throughout the year.

Termites swarm near a house during the spring and fall seasons. These are the best times to look for evidence of infestations. Both subterranean and non-subterranean termites exist in two forms, winged and unwinged. Termites are different from flying ants in several ways. For instance, flying ants have a narrow waist while termites do not. Also, termites have longer wings than ants and their wings are similar in shape and size and have many small veins in them, while the wings on a flying ant differ in both size and shape and have few veins in them. Male and

female termites, which are referred to as kings and queens, fly in swarms to establish new colonies. They shed their wings after flight, and each pair excavates a nest in or near wood that is in contact with the soil (Figure 165). Piles of wings on wood are sure signs of termite infestation in or near a house.

Non-subterranean termites cut across the grain of the wood, while subterranean termites follow the grain of the wood. One of the early signs of non-subterranean termites is a collection of sandy excretory pellets on or near the wood, while an early sign of subterranean termites is the formation of mud tunnels or shelter tubes on foundation walls. These tunnels or tubes, which are constructed by the subterranean termites, ascend up the wall and enter the structure at the sill plate. Shelter tubes cannot always be seen in foundation walls that have been built with concrete blocks because the termites ascend up the foundation wall through the core of the blocks where they are not visible.

Both subterranean and non-subterranean termites can do a great deal of structural damage to a house. One homeowner who wanted to remodel his basement to use it as a family room learned firsthand about this type of damage. His contractor told him he had to replace the main wood beam before he proceeded with the rest of the renovation because the beam had rotted at both ends. The main wood timber was embedded in the foundation walls, and termites had gotten into it at each end. When the main wood beam was removed to replace it with a steel beam, the homeowner could see that it was practically hollow along most of its length. In fact, the termites had done so much damage that the main wood beam was virtually useless as a support timber. This homeowner was lucky that the framing structure in his house had not failed altogether as a result of this extensive damage. He now makes a habit of checking regularly for termite infestations to prevent this situation from recurring. All homeowners should look for termite infestations in common areas such as the ends of floor joists where the joists rest on the sill plate in the basement. They should examine basement window and door frames to look for any indications of the presence of termites. In addition to inspecting the house visually, the homeowner should use a screwdriver to test wood to see if it is solid, since an insect-free wood surface can be hiding an insect-infested piece of wood.

Subterranean termites need warmth as well as moisture to survive. They cannot exist above the soil during freezing temperatures. This is another reason to look for them during the spring and fall when temperatures are quite mild and the termites are not hiding from colder outdoor temperatures. Termites also nest in any wood or cellulose product that is located near the house as well as in it. For example, they can nest in a dead tree near the house, or in posts that are being used to support a deck, especially when these posts have not been treated against termite infestations. A warm, moist area such as under a deck or open porch or a crawl space is the perfect environment for termites to nest in. These areas are favorites for termites because their high humidity levels are conducive to their growth. Termites also nest around the base of a chimney that extends down to grade. They nest inside and outside of it because they are drawn by the heat in the flue, which is helpful for breeding. Termites even nest under debris in gardens and around shrubbery near the house's foundation walls and at the bottom of the wood frame on the garage door. Shelter tubes are not always in evidence in these areas because the tubes may be hidden, or they may even be unnecessary since the wood is able to come into direct contact with the soil.

There are a number of steps the homeowner can take to prevent termite infestations in his home. One of the most important things to do is to keep wood away from the soil at all times. He can do this by keeping the grade level lower than the top of the foundation walls on his house and by making sure the grade slopes away from the walls. In fact, the soil should be at least 18 inches lower than the sill plate and wood siding installed on a house. This prevents moisture from collecting near any wood framing members or wood siding, which would create an area for termite infestation. The space between the soil and floor joists in a crawl space also has to be at least 18 inches high. The crawl space also should be kept dry to prevent humidity from building up in it and, once again, creating a perfect environment for infestation. Any plumbing that may be located in the crawl space should be maintained diligently to prevent leaks. The moisture coming

from any leaks would attract termites to nest in this area. The installation of termite shields around the perimeter of a house is helpful because the shields force the termites to tunnel around them, making their detection easier.

The homeowner who is having a new house built can take other preventive measures not available to the homeowner of a house already constructed to prevent termite infestations. This homeowner should make sure that the contractor removes all of the forming lumber used to construct the footings and foundation walls after they have been set firmly in place. If not, termites will nest in this lumber as well as in any lumber used during the construction process that is buried on or near the site of the new house. Even paper cups and other paper products should be removed from the soil before the foundation is backfilled to prevent termite infestation in them. The homeowner should visually inspect the waterproofing mastic that is placed on the foundation walls to be certain that there are no cracks or voids in it. Termites can use these cracks and voids for entry into the house. He also should be sure that there are no cracks in the foundation walls to allow termite entry.

When a new house is being built, the homeowner should tell the contractor that he wants the sill plates in it made of redwood or pressure-treated lumber to guard against termite infestation. When a house is being built in an area where the incidences of termite infestation are frequent, the homeowner should tell his contractor to have a termite exterminating company treat the soil before the footings and foundation walls are constructed. In this way, the chemicals can be applied so that they are more effective than they would be if they were applied after the house's construction was completed. The termite treatment also is less costly at this point than after the house has been constructed. If this chemical treatment is done, however, the homeowner should never plant vegetables in this soil. These chemicals are toxic and they would infiltrate the vegetables growing there. Additionally, because the workmen are going to come into contact with the chemicals in the treated soil around the house, the homeowner should ask the termite exterminating company if the chemicals pose a health hazard. If they do, treatment should not be done at this time.

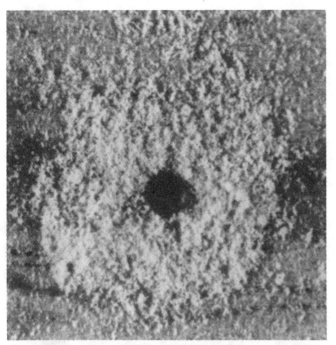

166. Evidence of wood damage by powder post beetles includes fine sawdust near the hole opening. Courtesy of the National Pest Control Association.

Once termites have gotten into a house, a termite exterminating company has to be called to treat it. The exterminator does this by drilling holes, spaced about 18 inches apart, along the outside of the house's foundation walls. If the chemical he is using can be used indoors, he also drills holes into the concrete floor slab in the basement or cellar. After the chemical has been poured, the holes have to be sealed tightly to prevent odor and vapors from seeping into the house. The treatment has to be done correctly to prevent contamination in the house and in well water or in the local water supply. Chlordane was used extensively as a termite treatment chemical until 1988 when it was found to be a health hazard. It had been popular with homeowners because it was quite effective and it lasted more than twenty-five years. The chemicals used today for this purpose are not as effective as chlordane was when it was used. Some of these chemicals do not kill the termites, they merely repel them, which is why a treatment with them is only effective for about one year. That is why the duration of most warranties given by termite exterminating companies also is only one year.

The homeowner who needs to have his house treated for termite infestation should hire an expe-

rienced exterminating company that is licensed to handle the chemicals used for the treatment. The treatment has to be done carefully to prevent the vapors from entering the living area since they can be quite toxic when trapped in a house. A careless injection of the chemicals can cause vapors to enter the living areas of a house from a variety of possible sources. For instance, they can come from the air ducts installed under the concrete floor slab in the basement when the forced hot air heating system is turned on. Vapors also can travel up from a crawl space that has been treated incorrectly. These chemicals should not be used indoors unless the manufacturer specifically says it is safe to do so. In fact, some local codes make it illegal to do any surface spraying because the vapors from the sprayed chemicals are so toxic. A knowledgeable exterminating company with experience in doing these chemical treatments can do the job correctly so that it is safe and effective. The homeowner should not attempt to do this job himself.

Powder Post Beetles

There are fewer types of powder post beetles than there are termites, but they can be just as destructive. These beetles are very small, ranging from 3/32 inch to approximately 1/4 inch in length. They are reddish-brown to black in color. They nest in hardwoods, preferring porous species such as oak, walnut, ash, and mahogany. In some western states, however, they also attack softwoods. These beetles live off the sapwood in the hardwood. The sapwood is where the high-starch content of the wood is stored. As hardwood ages and its starch content diminishes, it becomes less susceptible to infestation. Powder post beetles nest in any hardwood installed in a house, such as hardwood flooring and support beams. They also can be detected in wood window sills and often are found in barns.

Powder post beetles make tiny holes in wood that are about 1/16 inch to 1/8 inch in diameter. Wood that has been infested by these beetles appears to have been struck with bird shot. A fine, flour-like sawdust can be seen near the openings of these holes when they invade the wood (Figure 166). Tunnels near the surface of the wood also are filled with this fine sawdust (Figure 167). These tiny holes and this sawdust are evidence of powder post beetle infestations, and they often are found on window sills and near sill plates as well as in other wood framing members inside and outside of the house. A professional exterminating company has to be called when the homeowner finds a powder post beetle infestation in or near his house. Methyl bromide is one of the chemicals commonly used to treat this type of infestation. Again, the homeowner should not try to handle this treatment application himself.

167. Powder post beetles make tunnels near the surface of the wood they damage. Courtesy of the National Pest Control Association.

Carpenter Ants

Although carpenter ants are found in all parts of the United States, they are most active in the northern half of the country where infestations by them are frequently encountered. In fact, they are so common in the northeast that they often are seen on streetwalks and driveways and on trees in urban neighborhoods. Carpenter ants are black and gray-black in color. The majority of carpenter ants are called workers. The workers are approximately 1/2 inch long, while the queens are almost 1 inch long. They have narrow waists and their wings are equal in length. Carpenter ants nest in trees, in the soil, and even in piles of stored firewood. In a house, these ants nest in areas with high humidity levels such as in basements and crawl spaces that are damp. They also nest in wood framing members, wood siding, and wood trim that has become rotted or damaged as a result of water entry inside the house or constant exposure to water on the outside.

Carpenter ants leave a coarse sawdust on infested wood such as on window sills, floor joists, sill plates, and door and window trims. Once the colony is at least three years old, carpenter ants grow wings to leave the original nest and establish new ones.

When winged carpenter ants are seen swarming around a house, garage, or tree, they are about to establish new nests. Unlike termites that live in dirty tunnels, carpenter ants clear their tunnels completely of any debris when they infest the wood (Figure 168). As a result, they leave a pile of coarse sawdust outside the tunnels. This is one way to determine that there is a carpenter ant infestation. The condition of the tunnels in the wood is a way to distinguish a carpenter ant infestation from a termite infestation.

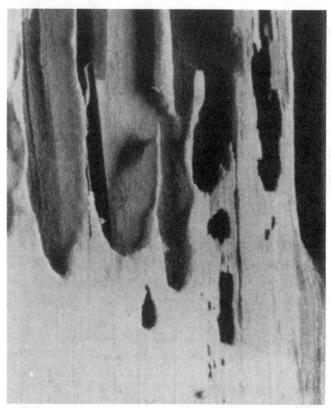

168. Carpenter ant nests in damaged wood. Courtesy of the National Pest Control Association.

As with any type of ant, carpenter ants are attracted to sweets such as candies, soda, sweet juices, and fruits. They also feed on scraps of food such as those left around garbage cans and near barbecues. For this reason, it is a good idea to keep patios, decks, porches, barbecues, and garbage cans clean. Various chemical sprays available can be used outdoors to kill carpenter ants; however, inside the house, the nest has to be found and destroyed to end the infestation. A house with a large infestation has to be treated by an exterminating company to be certain that the job is done effectively and safely. This is not a do-it-yourself job.

Carpenter Bees

There are at least twelve species of carpenter bees. Carpenter bees look like large bumblebees. They can grow as large as 1 inch long. The males range from buff to yellow, while the females of the Western species range from metallic blue-black to green and purple. Carpenter bees are found along the east coast from Maine to Florida and as far west as Nebraska and Texas. During these states' harsh winters, carpenter bees die because they cannot withstand extremely cold temperatures. Carpenter bees prefer to nest in softwoods such as pine, cedar, fir, and redwood. They also nest in hardwoods that have decayed, which softens the wood, or that have not been painted. The original bark on softwoods protects them from infestation by carpenter bees; however, once it has fallen off, they are more vulnerable. To enter the wood, carpenter bees make a hole that is about 1/2 inch in diameter. As with all wood-decaying insect infestations, carpenter bee infestations should be treated by a professional exterminating company that knows how to handle the chemicals correctly and safely. The homeowner who does this job himself not only may do it incorrectly, he may get stung by the bees as well.

Wood-decaying Fungus

Wood-decaying fungus can be as destructive to wood as any of the insects previously discussed. It grows rapidly and lavishly on wood installed in a house in areas where there is high humidity as well as on wood that is constantly wet or damp. It also grows on wood installed in areas around the house where there is poor or no drainage. The fungus softens the wood, making it almost spongy to the touch. In its early stages of decay, the wood discolors and eventually it turns brownish. As the fungus continues to destroy the wood, the wood cracks and disintegrates. Painted wood also can be destroyed by wood-decaying fungus. As the wood under the paint decays, it discolors the paint. When left in this condition for an extended period of time, the wood also cracks and disintegrates.

Wood-decaying fungus is commonly found in crawl spaces where humidity and moisture have been allowed to build up. Rim joists and sill plates also are vulnerable. As temperatures rise and fall during climatic fluctuations, the rim joists and sill plates absorb a great deal of water. The fungus thrives on this moist, warm wood. To prevent moisture in the soil in a crawl space from condensing on the wood framing members, it is best to place a vapor barrier over the soil.

In addition to crawl spaces, wood-decaying fungus also grows in the forming lumber that was used during the construction of the house and was buried in the soil under it. This fungus also grows in attics when they are not adequately vented and in walls in a house without gutters and downspouts installed for proper drainage.

The only way to get rid of wood-decaying fungus is to remove it. This is done by removing the infested pieces of wood and replacing them with new wood framing members. This may mean that an interior wall or ceiling will have to be removed and replaced. When this is done, it is also essential to minimize humidity and moisture buildup in these areas to prevent a recurrence of this fungus in the new wood framing members. When the fungus is in a painted exterior wall such as in wood siding, the siding has to be removed to get rid of the wood-decaying fungus. New wood siding has to be installed and then, most likely, the entire exterior facade will have to be repainted since matching the new paint color with the old is practically impossible. If only the new pieces of siding are painted, the exterior wall will look patched — an unpleasant alternative.

PART V
Examining the Amenities of a House

18
Adding Air Conditioning in Your Home

AIR CONDITIONING: LUXURY OR NECESSITY?

Many people feel that using air conditioning during the summer is equivalent to using a heating system during the winter. For still other individuals such as those with asthma and other respiratory diseases, air conditioning is a must to help them breathe more easily, an activity that is especially difficult when humidity as well as temperature levels are high. Air conditioning performs a number of functions simultaneously to make the house, or a room in it, comfortable on a hot summer's day. Air conditioners remove moisture from the air as they cool it. The filter at the front of the unit removes dust particles from the air. The fan in the unit circulates the cooled air around the room while it takes the heat out of the air and discharges it outdoors. In fact, the air conditioner functions in the same way that a heat pump operates.

The principles for cooling are the same for both the central air conditioning system and wall and window air conditioners. The technology for air conditioning is fairly simple and has been used in refrigeration units for many years. The compressor inside the air conditioner compresses the refrigerant gas, usually Freon, to increase its temperature. The hot gas flows into a pipe coil at the rear of the unit where a fan blows outside air onto the surface of the pipe coil. Since the outside air is much cooler than the compressed refrigerant gas, a heat transfer process takes place from the hot gas inside the pipe coil to the air outside. As the refrigerant gas loses heat, it is changed from a gaseous state to a liquid state. This liquid refrigerant is then sent to the front of the unit where it passes through an expansion device, which increases its volume. As its volume increases, the temperature of the liquid refrigerant drops dramatically to approximately 45° F. This chilled refrigerant flows into the cooling coils at the front of the unit where another fan blows the room air across the coils. This cools the temperature of the room air, which is then circulated around the room. When the refrigerant's temperature increases as a result of heat transfer from the room air, it changes back to a gaseous state, returns to the compressor, and the cycle starts all over again.

Every air conditioning unit has a built-in thermostat that enables an individual to choose the temperature setting that is most comfortable for him or her. Once the room has been cooled to the desired temperature setting, the thermostat stops the cooling cycle. When the temperature in the room increases, the thermostat turns the unit on again and the cooling cycle is repeated. Many of today's newer air conditioning units also are equipped with an energy-saving device. This device allows the fan to operate while the thermostat is off. The fan circulates the air in the room; however, no cooling of the room air is taking place at this time.

There are several types of air conditioning units available to accommodate any size house or room to make it comfortable during the summer. There are wall and window air conditioning units to cool individual rooms and central air conditioning systems to cool the entire house. Portable room air conditioners are becoming popular for single-room cooling as well as ductless systems that can handle cooling in up to three rooms at a time. They each have advantages and specific purposes, so it is a good idea for the homeowner to be familiar with all of them. Let's begin this review with the most frequently used air conditioning unit, the window or wall unit.

WINDOW AND WALL AIR CONDITIONING UNITS

An air conditioner for a single room is either installed through the wall or mounted in the window. Window models are available for installation in double-hung and casement windows. Wall models are installed by cutting an opening in the wall, installing a metal sleeve into the opening, and placing the air conditioning unit into this sleeve. When window units are not being used, such as during the winter, they are either taken out of the window or left in place and covered to prevent drafts and heat loss. Wall units, on the other hand, are always left in the sleeve. When they are not being used, they also are covered and sealed against the cold weather. Wall and window units range in size from approximately 5,000 to as much as 30,000 Btus. Smaller units operate on a 110-volt electric circuit while larger units need a 220-volt circuit. For safety's sake, it is a good idea to run separate electrical circuits from the panel box to each of the air conditioning units installed in the house.

As the cost of electrical power has risen, manufacturers have given their units what is called an Energy-Efficiency Rating or EER. An air conditioning unit with an Energy-Efficiency Rating of 9.5 or better is recommended by most utility companies because the energy savings accrued over its years of use make it a better investment, even through the initial cost for this unit is higher than for a unit with a lower EER. Wall and window air conditioning units also have to be maintained regularly for them to work efficiently and safely. The coolant has to be recharged at intervals stated by the unit's manufacturer, and the filter at the front of the unit has to be washed regularly. If it cannot be washed, then it will have to be replaced, again following the manufacturer's instructions for the unit's proper care.

Sometimes water drips out of the rear of an air conditioner. This is not an alarming condition. As the air cools, moisture in it is lost. This moisture collects on the coils and then falls into a pan at the bottom of the unit. The pan is pitched so that the water can flow to an outside pan where it drips out of the unit through a drain hole at the rear. This is the dripping water that the homeowner sees coming from his air conditioning unit. If the drain hole becomes clogged with dirt, it will have to be cleaned because it is preventing the water from draining out of the unit. In fact, the drain hole should be cleared regularly for this reason.

OTHER AIR CONDITIONING OPTIONS

Portable Units

In addition to wall and window units, portable air conditioning units also are available. These units can be rolled easily from one room to the next because no installation is required. Portable units such as one made by the Bionaire® Corporation need no special wiring and are very lightweight, which means that they have many possible uses (Figure 169). They can be used in a vacation home, mobile home, or trailer, or they can work well in an office building such as on weekends when the building's central air conditioning system has been turned off. Portable units also can follow children around the house, or they can add comfort to a room where an elderly person is staying temporarily such as for a visit or because of an illness.

Because these portable units are so compact and energy-efficient, they operate off the normal household electrical current, drawing only about seven amperes of current. Besides cooling the room, they also dehumidify it. In fact, the dehumidifying capacity of a unit of this type is approximately 30 pints of liquid. An indicator light turns on when the tank is full. The system has to be turned off and the tank emptied before the unit can be used again. Each

169. "Cold Front" portable air conditioner/dehumidifier. Courtesy of the Bionaire Corporation.

portable unit is equipped with a timer to control the cooling of a room at various intervals during the day and night. Each unit also is built with a variable speed cooling mode, numerous speed/ventilation modes, and other special features that allow them to be very efficient and to provide the most comfort no matter where they are used.

Ductless Split System

Another air conditioning option is called the ductless split system, a fairly new but already popular alternative because of its easy installation. This type of air conditioning system needs only a small hole in an exterior wall for its installation and, once it has been connected, a single unit can accommodate up to three rooms at once (Figure 170). With the ductless split system, the compressor/condenser unit is placed outside of the house, either at grade or on a deck or patio. A hole that is approximately 3 inches in diameter is made in the exterior wall and the coolant line is run through it to connect the compressor/condenser unit outside with the cooling unit mounted on a wall inside the house. The installation of this type of system does not need access to a window or to a large opening in an exterior wall. After

the coolant line has been placed through the 3-inch hole, any open space around it can be easily sealed. Several cooling units can be connected to a single compressor/condenser unit simply by making small holes in the exterior wall to connect additional coolant lines to it.

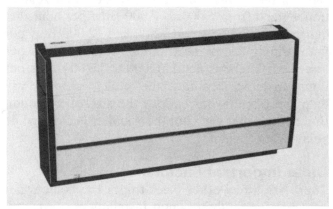

170. Detail and photo of ductless split system air conditioner. Courtesy of the Slant/Fin Corporation.

A ductless split system also is equipped with a timer, a night setback, and an energy saving device. Microcomputer remote controls enable it to be turned on and off from anywhere in the room. In addition, because the compressor/condenser unit is outside, the operation of this type of air conditioning system is especially useful in a room without windows, or in a living area where wall space is at a minimum, because it can be suspended from the ceiling as well as mounted anywhere on a wall.

Considering Size and Cooling Capacity

No matter which type of air conditioner is going to be used to cool a room, the physical size of the unit as well as its cooling capacity have to be considered for effective yet inexpensive cooling. The measurements for the width and height of an open window are needed to purchase a unit that fits appropriately in that opening. The cooling capacity of the air conditioner chosen depends not only on the dimensions of the room but on a variety of other factors, such as how many individuals use the room simultaneously, what functions are performed regularly in the room, and what kind of climate the unit is going to have to deal with, including high temperatures, high humidity, or both. An undersized air conditioner cannot cool a room effectively, while an oversized unit will keep the room too cool, making its occupants feel uncomfortable. Oversized air conditioning units also do not dehumidify the room efficiently. As a result, the room feels damp most of the time, which also is uncomfortable. There are some generalities that can be made about the cooling capacity of an air conditioner. For example, small or medium-sized bedrooms need an air conditioner sized from 5,000 to 7,000 Btus per hour; living rooms need between 7,500 and 12,000 Btus per hour; dining rooms need 8,000 to 16,000 Btus per hour; and kitchens need 10,000 to 20,000 Btus per hour. In most localities, the utility company will help the homeowner choose the size of air conditioning unit that can cool the room effectively while being cost-efficient.

Other Important Factors

There are a few other basic things the homeowner needs to know about when installing an air conditioning unit. For instance, the air flow around the outside and inside of a window air conditioner should not be blocked either by large shrubs on the outside or by chairs or other furniture on the inside. Large window air conditioners usually are available with a mounting kit. This kit should be used for its installation because the unit is fairly heavy and will need this extra support. Without it, the large air conditioner could fall out of the window, damaging property and injuring passersby. Side panels, usually the expandable type, also are available with window air conditioning units. These side panels are either attached to the unit or supplied separately. They should be installed so that the unit fits snugly in the window opening. After a window air conditioner has been installed, the top and bottom window sashes should be secured so that a burglar cannot lift them up or pull them down for easy entry. Additionally, the air conditioning unit itself should be bolted or screwed to the window sashes and window sill to prevent a burglar from pushing it into or out of the window opening for easy access into the house.

In addition to its size and placement, the supply of electrical current to an air conditioning unit also can affect how efficiently and safely it operates. Generally, it is a good idea to have each air conditioner connected to a separate electrical circuit such as a 115, 208, or 230 volt line, depending on its size and electrical requirements. An air conditioning unit that is being used in a small room, such as a 7,500

Btu per hour capacity unit, probably can function off an existing household circuit, since units of this size generally need only 7.5 amperes of electrical current. Larger units such as those that operate off heavy-duty circuits such as 208 and 230 volt circuits need separate electrical lines installed for each of them. Even small air conditioning units can be a strain on an existing household circuit when three or four receptacles also are connected to this circuit. When several electrical appliances are used simultaneously with the small air conditioning unit, a blowout can occur in the single circuit due to an overload.

To install an electrical circuit for any air conditioning unit or system correctly, it is a good idea to hire an electrician to do the installation for you. It also may be beneficial to have the electrician examine air conditioning units already installed in the house to be sure that they were installed properly. Every air conditioner has a safety seal of approval that is printed either on the unit or on a tag attached to the unit. The safety seal, such as one from the Underwriters Laboratories, Inc., lists the unit's amperage requirements, its wattage requirements, its Btus per hour capacity, and its EER. The electrician should install the electrical circuit so that it conforms strictly to the requirements listed on the safety seal. The manufacturer's guarantee or warranty, which also is supplied with the unit, explains what is covered specifically by it and for how long, as well as what it does not cover and where to obtain service for repairs and maintenance procedures suggested by the manufacturer.

CENTRAL AIR CONDITIONING SYSTEMS

The central system is the ideal way to air condition a house completely. This type of system includes a compressor/condenser unit, an evaporator coil, a thermostat, and precharged tubing. The evaporator coil is installed in the ductwork above the forced air furnace. This ductwork also is used for the heating system. The compressor/condenser unit is placed outdoors at grade level on a concrete pad. In rare instances, this unit is placed on a flat roof. When it is, the roof may have to be reinforced in the area of the compressor/condenser unit to support its weight. Although the warranty for the compressor/ condenser unit ranges only from five to seven years, the life expectancy of the unit can be extended by maintaining it properly and by covering it during the winter when it is not in use. Freon is used as the refrigerant in this type of system, as it is in most air conditioning systems. The refrigerant piping is connected from the evaporator coil to the compressor/condenser unit. A nameplate attached to this unit indicates its capacity and electrical requirements. To meet requirements set by the National Electrical Code, the electrical box with the disconnect switch has to be installed so that it is in sight of the compressor/condenser unit and the electrical requirements have to conform with those stated on the nameplate (Figure 171). For example, when the nameplate on the compressor/condenser unit states that a 40-ampere fused box is required, then the box at the disconnect switch also has to be a 40-ampere fused box. When the installation is not done this way, it is a violation of the National Electrical Code, and must be corrected to meet code requirements.

A house with a forced hot air heating system often has a ducting system installed that can be adapted to a new central air conditioning system. Blowers and motors in the heating system usually have already been sized to accommodate the addition of a central air conditioning system sometime in the future (Figure 172). In effect, this means that a central system can be added to the house relatively easily and inexpensively.

When a forced hot air heating system is not being used in a house, the installation of a central air conditioning system becomes more difficult and expensive. Ducting has to be installed throughout such a house to add a central system, and its installation involves a great deal of effort and expense. Again, the compressor/condenser unit is placed outside of the house at grade. In some rare instances, it may be put on the roof, but this is not done frequently. With the compressor/condenser unit at grade, the coolant line is brought up into the attic. Then ducting is installed, beginning in the attic and running down through the house to each of its rooms (Figure 173). Frequently, built-in closet space is utilized for the installation of the ducting. Otherwise, the walls have to be opened to install the ducting in the wall cavities and through the

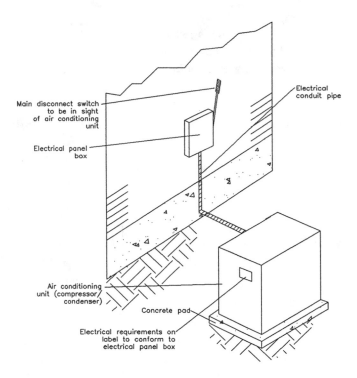

171. Exterior air conditioning unit with panel box

ceilings. This type of installation involves extensive damage to the walls, closets, ceilings, etc. That is why it is best to install a central air conditioning system when the house is being renovated completely or when the house is first being built. While the ducting is being installed, it is important to insulate it in areas of the house that are not going to be air conditioned, such as in the crawl space.

No matter which type of air conditioning system is being used, there are several reasons the house or a room in the house is not being cooled sufficiently. Some of these reasons include the possibility that the unit is undersized or that it needs to be cleaned. More serious problems may be that the electrical controls, fan motor, or compressor/condenser unit failed. Unfortunately, if the compressor/condenser unit has failed, its repair will be costly. It could cost as much as it would to purchase a new air conditioning system. All air conditioning systems need to be cleaned and serviced regularly to keep them working efficiently and safely. The manufacturer's instructions for use and care of their units should be adhered to strictly to extend the life expectancy of the unit as well as to have it operating effectively.

**172. Typical arrangement of
forced air heating system used
for central air conditioning**

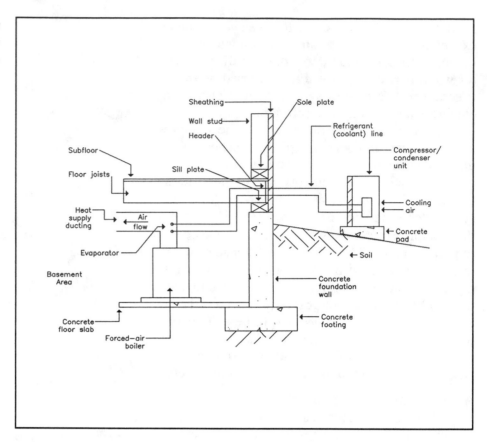

**173. Central air conditioning unit
installed independent of forced air
heating system**

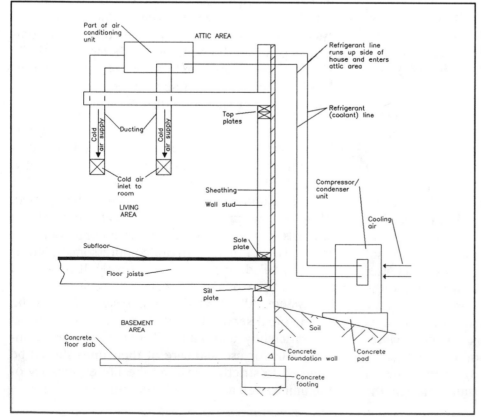

19
Looking at
the Landscaping

LANDSCAPING CAN AFFECT YOUR HOUSE

There is more to landscaping than just taking care of the plants in your garden. Although everyone knows that plants need to be watered, fed, and protected from insects to grow hearty and healthy, not every homeowner realizes that trees, shrubs, and other landscaping can be harmful to a house. What you choose to plant and where you decide to plant it can affect the condition of your house. Its condition also can be affected by where and how topsoil is added to the garden and where retaining walls are built. Some of the damage caused by landscaping is more serious than the homeowner might expect it to be, so let's review the possible problems, starting with those caused by trees and shrubs.

TREES AND SHRUBS

Never underestimate the power of a tree to cause a great deal of damage as it grows. One homeowner learned this the hard way. He had a garage at the rear of his property. It was separated from his neighbor's garage by a space about 2 feet wide. A tree had grown in this small space and the diameter of its trunk was approximately 18 inches. The tree had grown higher than the roof of the garage, and its branches had pushed the rear concrete block-constructed wall of the garage inward as they spread out in this small space. In fact, the tree had dam-

aged the block wall so badly that the wall had become structurally unsound. The branches also had damaged the roof covering and some of the roof rafters in the garage. The damage was so extensive that the garage had to be completely rebuilt because it had become unsafe for use. The job totaled about $25,000 by the time it was done, and the cost was caused solely by a tree.

The branches on a tree may be great for shading a garden or patio during the hot summer, but they can be very destructive when they are allowed to grow too close to the house or garage. That is why branches should be cut back and kept away from any structure. Tree branches have been known to grow under a roof covering such as shingles. In so doing, they damage the shingles and allow water to enter the house through the roof. Branches that hang over a chimney can be ignited by a spark coming from it. Tree branches also can damage gutters when they are left untrimmed and allowed to grow under them. Additionally, squirrels can gain access to the attic from branches that hang over the roof.

Even when branches do not actually touch the roof or gutters, they can damage the roof by keeping its shaded areas damp for long periods of time after rainfall has stopped. This delayed drying on the roof can cause portions of it to become stained or even to rot. Leaves falling onto the roof, especially during the fall, can clog the downspouts, which prevents rainwater from draining off the roof quickly.

This delay can cause water to enter the house through the roof. This is a particularly severe problem on a house with a flat roof where water can pond on it. As it ponds on the roof, the water has time to seep into the roofing structure where it can damage the roof rafters. Because the water is quite heavy, it could cause the roofing structure to fail, especially if it has already been weakened by dry rot or insect infestation. The way to avoid these problems is to keep tree branches off roofs and gutters and to clean gutters and downspouts regularly so that leaves and other debris cannot collect in them and cause a blockage.

Although a tree-lined street is beautiful, it can pose problems when overhead electrical service lines are installed near or under the trees. A severe thunderstorm or blizzard can cause a tree to fall, taking the electrical power lines with it. This creates a dangerous situation as well as disruption of electrical service to the house. For this reason, it is important to trim back branches that hang over power lines; however, this should not be done by the homeowner. The local utility company or municipality should be called to trim these branches because of the potential danger with the electrical power lines as well as with the height of the tree. In fact, most tree-trimming projects are best done by professionals who know how to cut the tree without interfering with its future growth and who have the equipment needed to do the job safely.

Tree roots can be as harmful to a house as tree branches because the roots also can damage it as they grow. For instance, roots from a tree at the front of the house often grow into sewer lines that are located there. These roots clog the sewer lines so completely that they cause water to back up into the house's basement (see drainage system section in Chapter 12 for complete details). The roots from a tree growing close to a house have been known to damage the foundation walls of that house. In so doing, they can establish a path for water to drain through the wall into the basement. When this type of damage is left unrepaired, it could undermine the foundation wall's footing.

Tree roots also can crack a concrete streetwalk or driveway. When they are allowed to grow large enough, the roots actually can lift up sections of the concrete, creating a tripping hazard and making areas for water to pond on the streetwalk. During the winter, this water freezes in these areas, creating a slippery hazard for passersby.

Even a tree that is dead or dying can cause problems, especially when the tree is near other healthy trees, or when it is very close to a foundation wall. Termites or carpenter ants that may still be living in the dead or dying tree can attack other healthy trees nearby, or they can be the source of termite or carpenter ant infestations in the house as they work through the sill plate on the foundation wall.

174. Potentially damaging vines growing on a brick wall. Photo by the author.

Vine-covered walls may look attractive on college buildings in their recruitment brochures and on landmark buildings in old, urban neighborhoods, but they can be very destructive on any exterior wall. These vines can cause the walls to deteriorate after many years of growth on them (Figure 174) and should be removed from exterior walls and from gutters. Trees and shrubs also should not be allowed to grow in areas near the house where they can block the air flow to a window air conditioner or the air venting from the perforated face plate on the plumbing's drainage line. The homeowner should make a habit of trimming all of his landscaping regularly to prevent these problems, since some of them could lead to costly repairs or replacements.

A sprinkler system that is being used to maintain the beauty of the landscaping also needs some attention from the homeowner. During the winter when it is not going to be used, the sprinkler system should be winterized against freezing temperatures.

If it is not completely winterized, water left in the piping system will freeze as it expands, and it will crack the piping. The only way to undo this damage is to have the piping replaced.

The appearance of damp spots on a lawn or in the backyard or garden is an indication of any one of several possible problems. These damp spots may mean that there is a low point, or depression, in the soil or that the main water supply line into the house has broken. They also may mean that the piping for the sprinkler system has ruptured or, if a septic tank is in use, that a problem in it has caused it to back up in that area of the lawn or garden. In some instances, these damp spots are indications that there is a high water table in the area where the house is located. The only way to determine which of these conditions is causing the damp spots to develop is to review the various possibilities and eliminate them one by one until the cause of the problem is found. After the problem has been determined, in most cases, the lawn or garden can be replanted and restored.

Even the simplest change in the garden can cause a problem in the house. For example, the addition of topsoil has been known to cause problems. One homeowner decided to fill his backyard with new topsoil because he wanted to plant a vegetable garden there and he did not think that the soil in place would be nutritious enough for proper growth. He never realized that when he added the topsoil he had sloped it toward the house instead of away from it, as he should have done. During the first heavy rainfall, he saw that water was entering his basement, but he could not imagine why. A contractor who came to examine his house told the homeowner about his mistake. He told the homeowner to put additional topsoil in the backyard to slope it away from the house. After the homeowner did this, rainwater drained away from his house and his basement remained dry.

RETAINING WALLS

Retaining walls hold back the soil in the same way that dams hold back water and, when they fail, the destruction they cause can be as devastating as rushing water from a broken dam. One homeowner who had a very long retaining wall at the rear of his property learned about this rather dramatically one day. The soil at the rear of his property sloped steeply down to a recreation area in his backyard. This area included a pool, a swing, and other toys for children to enjoy. The retaining wall was an old one. It had been constructed of stone and concrete and had deteriorated as it aged. The homeowner was reluctant to replace it, however, because it was going to cost at least $20,000 — a sum he did not want to spend. After several days of heavy rainfall one spring, the wall collapsed. Debris from the wall along with the soil, which had a great deal of clay in it, came crashing down into the homeowner's backyard. It destroyed the pool, the swing, etc., but, thankfully, it did not injure anyone because there were no children playing there at the time. In the end, the homeowner not only had to replace the retaining wall, he also had to rebuild the pool and the swing and replace the other damaged toys.

Retaining walls are made of wood, stone, blocks, or bricks. Small retaining walls that are more decorative than they are functional generally are made by simply laying railroad or landscaping ties on top of or next to each other. When a retaining wall is going to be made of wood, it is a good idea to use pressure-treated lumber to protect the wood from damage due to moisture and insects. This type of wood lasts for many years in this application; however, it should not be used in gardens where vegetables, herbs, or fruits are grown. A retaining wall made with masonry has to have weep holes either built or bored into it at the bottom of it. These holes allow water to drain from the soil behind the retaining wall. When water is able to collect behind the masonry retaining wall, pressure builds up on one side of the wall. This pressure eventually can cause the wall to crack or to fail. Tremendous pressure is exerted on a retaining wall when the soil has a high clay content because this soil expands greatly as it gets wet. When a retaining wall becomes bowed or leans out of plumb, it should be repaired to prevent further damage, which could cause it to fail. When the damage in the wall is extensive, it should be repaired or replaced immediately. It is best to repair any cracks in a retaining wall as they become visible because these cracks are indications that the wall is beginning to fail. When the cracks are repaired quickly, an expensive replacement of the wall can be averted.

20
Indoor and Outdoor Amenity Areas

GREENHOUSES AND SUNROOMS

Greenhouses were first introduced to enable home-owners to grow plants and flowers all year long, no matter what the temperature outdoors might be. As they became sought-after additions, homeowners soon realized that the greenhouse was a pleasant, comfortable environment for themselves as well as for their plants. That is when greenhouses became sunrooms and sunrooms became even more popular than greenhouses had ever been. Sunrooms enable homeowners to expand the living space in their homes while enhancing their lifestyles. This bright, airy addition with a view of the outdoors adds spaciousness to any room while increasing the resale value of the whole house.

Sunrooms are used for a variety of purposes, depending on their location in a house. For example, sunrooms are frequently added to kitchens to convert a drab, dark room into a cheerful, bright workspace (Figures 175 and 176). They also are used as a dining room, den, recreation room, or family room addition (Figures 177 and 178). Recently sunrooms have become part of bathroom renovations, placed near a whirlpool bath or spa, to create a feeling of outdoors while maintaining privacy. Plants thrive in these sunrooms so they serve a dual purpose. Of course, they also are excellent ways to enclose a pool or deck. Whether the homeowner wants open space or just more space, the sunroom is the perfect solution. Frequently, it becomes the focal point of the house.

Manufacturers of sunrooms and greenhouses have responded well to their popularity by making practically any size or configuration possible. They also can accommodate any climatic condition, so the homeowner in the northeast can have the same flexibility as the one in the southwest. These additions can be planned and executed so well that, when they have been completed, they look as if they were part of the house's original design. The materials used for framing and glazings also can deal effectively with all climatic conditions, including areas where temperature fluctuations are extreme. Since installation costs have become fairly reasonable, the addition of sunrooms or greenhouses is no longer an option reserved only for affluent homeowners.

The materials used for the construction of sunrooms and greenhouses include straight and curved wood and aluminum sections and a variety of glazings, which also are available curved to accommodate special shapes. Aluminum framing members are made with a thermal break to minimize heat loss through them (Figures 179 and 180). Frames made with straight and curved wood materials are connected with mortise and tenon joints. The wood species used for sunroom and greenhouse construction include Western red cedar, redwood, and pine. The pine is available covered with plastic laminate to

175. Kitchen layout before. Courtesy of the Four Seasons Design & Remodeling Centers.

176. Kitchen layout after, with System 6 sunroom. Courtesy of the Four Seasons Design & Remodeling Centers.

177. Living room layout before. Courtesy of the Four Seasons Design & Remodeling Centers.

178. Living room with addition of System 4 sunroom. Courtesy of the Four Seasons Design & Remodeling Centers.

179. A dining area enlarged with a System 6 sunroom. Courtesy of the Four Seasons Design & Remodeling Centers.

180. An exterior view of a "Series 300" patio room. Courtesy of the Four Seasons Design & Remodeling Centers.

181. System 8 sunroom used to enhance a living/dining area. Courtesy of the Four Seasons Design & Remodeling Centers.

182. System 8 sunroom enhances a dining room. Courtesy of the Four Seasons Design & Remodeling Centers.

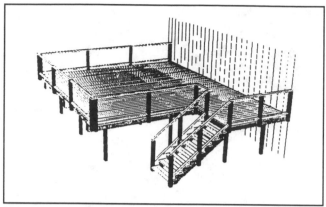

183. *Innovis' computer design system shows the homeowner how his proposed deck will look and how much it will cost before he buys the materials. Courtesy of Innovis Interactive Technologies.*

eliminate the need for regular maintenance of the wood (Figures 181 and 182).

Glazing materials used include fiberglass, acrylics, and glass. The type of glazing material chosen depends on whether direct or diffused light is needed. Diffused light is preferred for privacy; however, many plants need direct light for hearty growth. It is best to discuss how the space is going to be used with the contractor before the homeowner decides what glazing material he wants to use. Insulating glass as well as Low-E glass is available for these installations to reflect the sun's ultraviolet rays during the summer and to keep the radiant heat in the sunroom during the winter.

There are many design options for the homeowner to choose from, including a sunroom with sliding patio doors and double-hung, awning, or casement windows. Installation of a ventilating fan in the sunroom is helpful to circulate the air in it. When the purpose of the addition is to grow plants, plumbing, electrical service, and a heating system have to be installed, but the latter only if the house is located in a cold climate. In addition, an area drain is needed in the floor.

State and local building codes dictate how the sunroom or greenhouse is constructed; that is, whether it is built on a concrete slab on grade or on a concrete slab built on concrete or concrete block foundation walls. All codes also should be followed for the electrical, plumbing, and heating installations to make the addition comfortable and safe.

DECKS

Decks and patios add space for living and entertaining to any house with relatively little expense. Construction of a deck or patio is fairly simple, which means it can be done quickly and without disturbing the enclosed areas of the house. The addition of a deck or patio also adds to the house's resale value and it requires little maintenance to keep it looking attractive. A variety of materials is available to enhance any architectural style or to create attractive patterns. A deck or patio also is another way to bring the outdoors closer to the family while enhancing their lifestyle.

One homeowner who was an avid woodworker wanted desperately to build a deck at the back of his house using Western red cedar. His wife, however, insisted that she had no interest in or need for a deck, so she resisted its construction for many years. The homeowner was delighted when she finally agreed to it. The deck was constructed in just a few weeks and now his wife, not the woodworker, enjoys it more than he does. She uses it for relaxation, for entertaining, and for potting her plants. Since it was built directly off the kitchen, she enjoys growing her fresh herbs in its built-in planters where they are in easy reach as they are needed for cooking, pickling, etc. This homeowner only regrets that he had not convinced his wife sooner to make this simple addition to the house.

A deck can be made of redwood, Western red cedar, or pressure-treated lumber. Since redwood is the most expensive of the three materials used, Western red cedar more often is the one chosen. Western red cedar is as resistant to decay and insect infestation as redwood, even though it is the less expensive of the two wood species. Pressure-treated lumber also is a very popular choice for deck construction because it is the least expensive of the three possible choices. In some cases, it is used in combination with redwood or Western red cedar to reduce the total cost of construction. To assist homeowners in the design and construction of a deck, some home improvement centers and lumberyards have purchased the DesignCenter™ home improvement system created by Innovis Interactive Technologies (Figure 183). This system allows homeowners without computer knowledge to design their own decks on the spot. When the design has been finalized, the system provides a color picture of the deck, along with a complete materials list, construction plans, and the costs of the materials. It is a fast way to design a deck that is affordable.

Cedar and redwood decks last longer and look more attractive when they are treated with a wood preservative that also makes the wood water-repellent. The manufacturers of pressure-treated lumber also recommend that it be treated with a water-repellent wood preservative, but only after the wood has been given sufficient time to dry thoroughly. Generally, the manufacturers of these wood preservatives recommend that the deck be treated annually for best results. If the wood has already begun to discolor, it can be coated with products that will brighten it and enhance its natural beauty. Some of the manufacturers of these products caution that their wood restorers are not as effective on certain species of wood. Therefore, it is important to read the product label carefully to determine its application recommendations.

Pressure-treated lumber has some characteristics that are unique to it as a result of its manufacture. This lumber is treated with a preservative called chromate copper arsenate (CCA). It is driven into the wood while it is under pressure after the wood has been kiln-dried. This preservative seals itself to the cellulose in the wood to prevent it from leaching out of it afterwards. As a result of this process, pressure-treated lumber is damp and quite heavy when it is purchased. It has a very high moisture content — usually about 70%. The wood can be kiln-dried again after this treatment has been completed; however, it is not usually dried a second time unless it is specifically ordered that way. To prevent this moist lumber from twisting or warping as it dries, it is necessary to stack and bind it while it is being stored. In fact, it is best not to have to store it at all. The homeowner should plan to purchase it when it is going to be used rather than ahead of time, to avoid any problems with it.

The manufacturers of pressure-treated lumber attach labels to their products to instruct homeowners on their proper usage. For instance, this type of lumber should not be used indoors and it should not be burned in a fireplace because the chemicals used in the treatment process can be toxic under certain circumstances. In addition, the sawdust from cutting pressure-treated lumber can irritate an individual's skin upon contact with it. It is also a good idea to wear a face mask when working with it to prevent inhalation of the sawdust.

As wood posts are being treated with CCA, the preservative is not always able to penetrate the post all the way into its core. As a result, when these posts are cut, the ends should be treated with an insect-repellent and a water-repellent preservative to protect them from decay. Without this treatment, the end grain is quite vulnerable to decay because it sucks moisture into the post just as a sponge would. By applying the preservative, these ends are protected very effectively.

PATIOS

A good location for enjoying the outdoors is on a patio, perhaps near a pool, or covering a patch of grass that would not grow. Whether it is large or small, a patio can add to the homeowner's enjoyment of a garden or backyard while enhancing its beauty. It can be installed fairly easily with a little time and imagination, so it is an ideal do-it-yourself project.

Patios are made with pavers, which may be made of concrete or specially produced bricks. These pavers are available in a number of colors, textures, shapes, and sizes, and they can be installed in a variety of patterns. Brick pavers are harder than bricks made for other construction purposes. These brick pavers are available in several thicknesses to accommodate any specific need. For instance, a thicker paver generally is used in a driveway while a thinner one is used in a garden. When they are going to be installed in areas where temperatures drop below freezing, the pavers should be rated and marked with the letters "S.W.", for Severe Weathering, so that they will be able to withstand the cold temperatures.

The construction of a patio begins with the placement of wooden forms around the perimeter of the area that is going to be paved. When these wooden forms are going to be left in place to serve as a border for the patio, they should be made of redwood, cedar, or pressure-treated lumber to prevent their decay from continued exposure to the weather. Fine gravel or stone dust is placed in these forms and it is compacted to make the patio area as level as possible in preparation for the pavers. A treated plastic film is laid over the gravel or dust to prevent weeds from growing up through the joints between the pavers. The film has very small holes made in it during its manufacture. These holes enable water to drain through it while preventing the growth of weeds and other forms of vegetation. Sand is put on top of the film and it also is compacted. The pavers are then laid into place according to the desired pattern. Each one is leveled so that water can drain off it quickly and the surface can be walked on easily. The leveling is done so that the patio slopes toward the nearest area drain for proper drainage. After all of the pavers have been put into place, sand is brushed into the joints between them, usually with a broom, to fill any voids left between the pavers. This may have to be repeated several times during the next few weeks to fill any voids that may appear as the pavers settle into place as they are walked on.

21
Pools, Saunas, and Spas

FOR RELAXATION AND ENJOYMENT

There is nothing better to rejuvenate an individual after a long day at the office or with the kids or both than to swim in a pool or relax in a sauna or whirlpool spa. Because most homeowners are well aware of this fact, pools, saunas, whirlpool baths and spas, and steambaths have become sought-after additions to a home, whether placed inside or outside the house. To accommodate this new trend, manufacturers of these once-luxury items have altered their manufacturing techniques and materials to supply less costly, yet durable alternatives for homeowners. Both permanently constructed and portable types of these products enhance the homeowner's lifestyle while adding comfort and value to a house.

SWIMMING POOLS

Swimming pools are made of a variety of materials, including reinforced concrete, which is either precast or poured at the site, Gunite, steel, or concrete blocks. Pools are constructed in numerous sizes and shapes. Most of the time, tiles are used to finish the pools because they are durable, waterproof, and easy to keep clean. In areas where frost is a concern, the tiles chosen have to be able to withstand freezing temperatures to prevent them from cracking or coming loose.

A swimming pool has to be equipped with water purification and water filtration systems to keep the water in it clear, clean, and safe for constant use. These systems should be enclosed in a shelter when they are installed in areas where very cold temperatures are possible. The purification and filtration systems handle a variety of tasks using several devices to do so. For example, a chlorinator sterilizes the water, while a hair catcher removes hair, lint, and other particles from the water that could become entangled in the systems and its piping. A makeup tank is installed to replace water that is lost from the pool due to evaporation and backwashing. A recirculating pump, or several such pumps when more than one is needed, is used to drive water through the filters and back into the pool. Chemical additives have to be dissolved in the pool water regularly to restore its alkalinity.

In most localities, pool installations have to meet local and state building code requirements for both in-ground and above-ground types. The piping for the filters and pumps also has to meet these code requirements. If the installation does not meet these requirements, or if the pool is built without a permit, it will be in violation of the building code. Such a situation may mean that the pool will have to be removed and a new one built that meets code requirements. There is only one reason for such strict requirements and it is pool safety. These codes emphasize extra care in terms of the pool's construction as well as its maintenance to make each installation as safe for use as possible.

There are many specifications to follow for proper pool construction. For example, overhead power lines have to be installed so that they do not pass over the pool, or even near it, for that matter. Ground fault circuit interrupter receptacles are required when any receptacle is installed near a pool. The pool has to be enclosed with a fence to keep it from being used by uninvited guests, particularly when no one is present to see that it is being used safely. Signs listing the depth, or depths when there are several of them, of the water in the pool have to be posted near it and walkways have to be installed around its perimeter. The pool area has to be well-lit and, according to the National Electrical Code, this lighting has to be grounded. In fact, any electrical equipment installed within 5 feet of the inside wall of the pool has to be grounded, including the junction boxes and the recirculating equipment. These are just a sampling of the requirements noted in the National Electrical Code. There are many more of them in the National Electrical Code as well as in the state and local codes, and they all have to be strictly adhered to while the pool is being designed and constructed. The best way to be sure to do this is to hire a contractor familiar with pool construction standards and techniques.

In-ground pools, which are constructed of such materials as tile, concrete, and Gunite, vary in size and depth depending on what local building codes dictate. It is absolutely essential to meet all code requirements not only for the safe use of the in-ground pool, but also to protect the homeowner from the extensive liability associated with pool ownership. If code requirements are not met when the pool is being constructed, the homeowner's liability will be even more serious than it already is. That is why it is best to hire a reliable contractor who can do the installation correctly in the first place. Then the homeowner and his family can enjoy the pool knowing that it was built properly.

SAUNAS

As more and more individuals joined health clubs during the last decade and learned how wonderful they could feel after being in a sauna, saunas have become very popular. The word "sauna" refers to the dry-heat bath as well as to the room in which the bath is taken. Saunas are being installed more frequently today in homes than they ever used to be, making the trip to the health club unnecessary for these lucky homeowners.

For ease of installation, the sauna should be placed near a shower. It can be made of any one of a variety of woods; however, the wood chosen has to be able to resist staining from moisture and heat. The wood should have a low density and it should be light in tone. Redwood and Western red cedar are the popular choices for this type of construction, and Alaskan yellow cedar, hemlock, birch, and pine also can be used satisfactorily. The wood used for a sauna should be a clear heart or select grade and kiln-dried.

A sauna does not have to large to work effectively. One that is only 6' x 6', for example, can accommodate three people comfortably at one time. The height of the ceiling in the sauna should not exceed 7 feet to help conserve energy during its use. The floor can be constructed of concrete, masonry, or ceramic tiles. The use of wood flooring or carpeting in a sauna is not a good idea because these materials can be destroyed easily from continued exposure to water and heat in the sauna. The door and its handle should be made of wood and a window should be installed either in the door or in one of the walls enclosing the sauna. Lighting in the sauna is usually kept subdued to enhance the user's relaxation while in it.

WHIRLPOOL BATHS AND SPAS AND HOT TUBS

Although whirlpool bathing was originally intended for therapeutic purposes, it has quickly become popular as a source of relaxation, probably as a result of the increased interest in health and fitness. Whirlpool baths and spas and hot tubs massage the body with water, a treatment that is both restful and healthful. There are some differences between each of these relaxing choices that the homeowner needs to know to select the one that is best for him.

A whirlpool bath, for instance, contains an integrated pump, motor, and jet system. It must be drained after each use. A whirlpool spa, on the other hand, does not have to be drained after each use because of the additional equipment installed with it. A whirlpool spa, which is a vessel that is usually made of acrylic, contains a heater and filter in addition to the integrated pump, motor, and jet system. Although a whirlpool spa does not have to be drained after each use, the water in it does have to be treated regularly with chemicals to keep it clean and clear. A whirlpool spa also has to be drained after a specific interval of time has passed to replace the old water with fresh water. The frequency of these procedures is determined by each manufacturer and is stated in the instructions for use. A hot tub is simply a spa with a vessel that is made of wood instead of acrylic. The acrylic vessel is reinforced with fiberglass for added strength. In addition to acrylic, whirlpool spas also can be made of such materials as Gunite and concrete.

Whirlpool baths are designed for use mainly by one or two individuals at a time. Whirlpool spas, on the other hand, are designed to accommodate comfortably as many as six individuals simultaneously. Spas are equipped with sophisticated control systems that enable them to be preset for use at any given time and at any specific temperature setting during the week.

Whirlpool spas and baths such as those manufactured by Jacuzzi Whirlpool Bath® (Figures 184, 185, and 186) are available in many different styles, sizes, and colors to match any decor and please anyone's personal taste. Whirlpool spas and hot tubs can be installed on a deck or patio, and some of these units are portable so that they can be moved indoors when the weather turns cold or rainy. Those that are sunk into the ground are permanent installations and cannot be moved. Although wood is a better insulator than any of the other materials used in their construction, all of the materials are acceptable options. Ultimately, the style that the homeowner selects depends more on how and where it is going to be used than on any other consideration.

Spas made of fiberglass are manufactured by molding multiple layers of that material together. These layers are then covered with an acrylic or gelcoat surface. This type of manufacturing process results in a whirlpool bath or spa that is both strong and watertight. Gelcoat, which is a polyester resin material, serves as a smooth, durable surface over the molded fiberglass layers. The acrylic surface, which is a plastic coating, is softened and then formed with the use of heat. An acrylic surface ensures that the high gloss and color will not fade or wear as it is used over the years.

Concrete spas are constructed either by pouring concrete, which is not done frequently, or by pneumatically applying Gunite or Shotcrete over a predetermined shape or form. The Gunite or Shotcrete construction process results in excellent strength and offers tremendous flexibility in terms of design.

To make a spa with the Gunite construction process, a close-to-dry mixture of hydrated cement and sand is sprayed from a nozzle over a system of reinforcing rods. The rods have been tied together to form a preplanned shape. The result of this process is a very durable spa. The difference between the Gunite and Shotcrete construction processes is that the Shotcrete is premixed before it arrives at the site so that it can be pumped while it is still wet into the preformed spa.

In both types of construction, the hot tub or spa area is first excavated. Tie rods are installed to form the desired shape of the spa or hot tub and then the Gunite or Shotcrete is applied. Almost any shape can be created using these methods. Skilled workmen are essential for both applications because the Gunite or Shotcrete has to be applied evenly to keep the thickness of the walls equal throughout the spa area. To build a spa using the poured concrete process, the area also is excavated initially. Then forms are constructed, rebar is installed, and the concrete is poured. This type of spa construction entails excessive labor costs and requires the use of heavy equipment to bring materials to the site. Additionally, the poured-concrete construction process is not always possible at all locations. Its high equipment and labor costs and impracticality at some sites makes it the least possible construction option.

Hot tubs, which are becoming very popular throughout the country, use traditional barrel-making techniques. The wood species used for their construction, which include redwood, Western red cedar, Alaskan yellow cedar, teak, and mahogany, are chosen because they are durable, resist decay, and do not react to the chemicals in the water. A top grade of kiln-dried wood that is free of any defects such as splits, knots, or decay and that has a

184. *Fiore™ whirlpool contoured corner bath for two. Courtesy of Jacuzzi Whirlpool Bath.*

185. *Half-moon Maurea™ bath provides side-by-side bathing for two. Courtesy of Jacuzzi Whirlpool Bath.*

186. *Razza™ whirlpool spa incorporates a rounded shape and sloped acrylic edges. Courtesy of Jacuzzi Whirlpool Bath.*

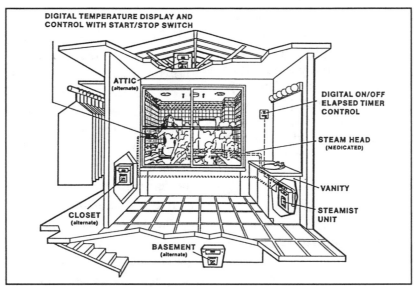

187. How any basic bathtub or shower can be converted into a steambath. Courtesy of Steamist.

vertical grain is used for hot tub construction. Some species of wood used for hot tub construction leach out chemicals into the water after the tub has been filled. For instance, redwood leaches out natural tannic acid that discolors the water. Other species such as Western red cedar and mahogany leach out some chemicals into the water but to a lesser degree. The same wood should be used for the sides, bottom, and seats in the hot tub, and all of the joints should be watertight. Handles and fittings have to be rustproof, and screws used in its construction should be made of stainless steel so that they do not rust. The seats or benches in the hot tub have to be constructed so that they do not interfere with the water's circulation in the tub and so that they can be cleaned easily and thoroughly.

The homeowner should be sure to choose a whirlpool bath, or spa, or hot tub, as well as the equipment needed for its operation, that is UL-approved, or approved by a similar testing laboratory. The installation has to conform to the electrical requirements dictated by the National Electrical Code and by local and state codes. Some of these products and equipment have the IAPMO (International Association of Plumbing and Mechanical Officials) label on them, which indicates that local codes have been met or even surpassed in their construction and manufacture. A skilled contractor should be hired to do the installation, and he should be familiar with all code requirements for these types of installation. It is essential to adhere strictly to these codes for the safe use of this equipment.

STEAMBATHS

Steambaths are beneficial in several ways, not all of which are obvious. Every homeowner is aware of the relaxing qualities of a steambath, but most do not know that a steambath can assist individuals with respiratory illnesses such as asthma to breathe more easily. They also do not know that when the steam is at a temperature of more than 100° F it can kill the Rhinovirus, cause of the common cold. In addition, although having a steambath in a house was once reserved for the very rich, it has now become available to the average homeowner. In fact, any tub or shower stall in even a modest home can be transformed into a steambath. The development of steam-generating units by several manufacturers such as one by Steamist (Figure 187) has made this conversion available to all homeowners.

Steamist's shower enclosure is made steam-tight with the installation of special doors. The steam-generating unit then blows steam into this enclosure. The generator is powered by an individual electrical circuit that is connected to an appropriately sized circuit breaker to accommodate it. The temperature control, which is located near the steambath for easy access, enables the user to select a temperature setting between 100° and 130° F while a timer sets the duration of the steambath, which can be up to one hour. A water tank is installed in the generator and a solid-state control heating element brings the water to a boil to create steam. Water for the steambath is drawn from piping attached to the bathroom fixtures' piping with the use of appropriate fittings. Generally, the water line is 3/8-inch copper piping and the steam line is 1/2-inch copper piping. The steam-generating unit is made fairly small, only 2' x 2' and 6 inches thick, so that it can be installed in a small closet or vanity. This unit does not have to be installed near the steambath. It can be placed in the attic, for example, as long as it is no more than 25 feet away from the steambath.

The capacity of the steam-generating unit depends on a variety of factors, including the size and location of the bathroom as well as what materials are installed in it. The steam-tight enclosure has to be sealed from the floor or tub to the ceiling to trap the steam in it and to allow the temperature to rise.

When a steambath enclosure has been installed properly, the desired temperature should be reached within 10 to 20 minutes. The materials used in the construction of the walls in the enclosure can affect the stabilization of the temperature in it. For instance, marble and tile walls soak up the heat so the temperature cannot stabilize until these walls have become heated. In addition, when one or two of the enclosure's walls are formed by exterior walls, the temperature in the enclosure takes more time to rise and stabilize in it. When wall products are used that have better insulating characteristics, such as CORIAN and fiberglass, a smaller-sized steam-generating unit can be used because the temperature rises and stabilizes more quickly than it would with wall products that have poorer insulating characteristics. The installation cost for this type of steambath varies greatly, depending on the extent of the work involved in the conversion. The easier the installation is going to be for the contractor, the less he will charge to do the work, and vice versa.

PART VI
Seeking Safety
in Your Home

22
Accident Prevention

THE IMPORTANCE OF PREVENTING ACCIDENTS

In 1988, 22,500 individuals died in home accidents in the United States, according to figures available from the National Safety Council. These deaths were caused by falls, fires and burns, suffocation, poisoning, drownings, and firearms, among other accidental causes. Sadly, of that total, 350 children under the age of five drowned, mostly in accidents in swimming pools and in bathtubs, and 4,500 people who were 75 years old and older died from falls. During the last five years, more than 100 children have drowned after falling or crawling into buckets left around the house, according to government statistics. Most of these children were less than a year old and, in some cases, the 5-gallon sized buckets contained only a few inches of liquid (Figure 188).

Although deaths from accidents in the home have continued to decrease overall since 1980 when there were 22,800 deaths, there was a 5% increase over 1987's total; that is, an increase of 1,000 from 1987 to 1988. This increase for the most part was due to increases in deaths from falls, poisonings, firearms, and accidents caused by electric current, explosive materials, hot substances, corrosive liquids, and steam. Disabling injuries due to accidents in the home were more numerous than any due to other classes of accidents. In 1988, some 3.4 million individuals in the United States were disabled for periods of one or more days as a result of injuries received in the home, and 90,000 of these resulted in permanent impairment.

According to the U.S. Consumer Product Safety Commission, even automatic garage doors have caused injuries and deaths. Since 1982, some forty-five children died due to door accidents, while twenty-seven children were injured because the doors failed to stop and reverse their descent when the doors touched them. A monthly testing of the automatic garage door could easily prevent such tragedies. With a little care and attention to what is happening around the house, the sorrow and pain of these accidents and deaths could be avoided. That is why it is so important to take time to review some of the safety precautions recommended by the National Safety Council and similar organizations to make every room in your home as safe as it can be.

PREVENTING FALLS

Most of the accidental deaths that occurred in 1988, a total of 6,500, were because of falls in the home, but this is not surprising. One homeowner found out how easily such an accident could happen. He had a habit of bringing his television set, a so-called portable model that actually was quite heavy, up and down the stairs during the summer to take it from his air conditioned living room earlier in the evening to his air conditioned bedroom later that

188. *This warning label is available from the Coalition for Container Safety to help prevent small children from drowning in buckets with as little as a few inches of liquid in them. Courtesy of the Coalition for Container Safety.*

night. Unfortunately for him, his children had a few habits of their own, such as leaving toys, books, sneakers, etc., on the stairs. One night the homeowner did not see one of these objects as he was about to descend the stairs and he fell down sixteen steps. He landed on his back with the television set on his chest. Luckily, he was only bruised, but he could just as easily have been killed. This homeowner abruptly decided to buy another television set to use upstairs to avoid similar trips, pardon the pun, in the future.

Homeowners who take a few precautions can protect the family, especially seniors and small children, from falls. These precautions include removing ob-

stacles from around the house that an individual can trip over and keeping objects off the stairs. Teach children to put toys and games away after they have finished playing with them instead of leaving them scattered about where a person can trip on them. Keep traffic lanes in the house clear of obstacles and loose objects, and install lighting in dark areas such as long, narrow hallways. Wait for the floors to dry after they have been washed before walking on them and wipe up any spills as they occur to prevent someone from slipping on them. When waxing floors, apply no more than two coats of wax and buff well after each coat or, better yet, use a self-polishing wax that eliminates the need for buffing altogether.

Scatter rugs should never be placed at the top or bottom of a stairway. When the scatter rugs you are using in other parts of the house do not already have a non-skid backing on them, apply adhesive strips, foam rubber, or a special spray coating to make them skidproof. When choosing carpeting or an area rug, purchase one with short, dense pile instead of the type with long, thick pile, and put a good quality, medium-thick pad under it for better footing. The longer pile may seem luxurious, but it also is easier to trip on. Arrange cords for electrical appliances so that an individual cannot trip over them while the appliance is being used.

PREVENTING ACCIDENTS IN THE KITCHEN

With so many activities taking place in the kitchen, often at the same time, it is not surprising that accidents occur there frequently. The homeowner who practices a few accident-prevention techniques can greatly reduce the number of accidents that occur in this busy room. For example, keep handles on pots and pans turned sideways on the stove or range top to prevent children from pulling hot liquids and food items down onto themselves. Use pots and pans that do not tip easily, such as flat-bottomed ones, and keep children out of the kitchen while you are cooking and even when you are cleaning. Avoid the use of utensils with sharp or raw edges that a child can run into while playing. Pick up hot pots and pans with pot holders or mitts, not with a dish towel, which cannot prevent your hand from being burned, especially when the towel is damp.

Make sure that all handles are secured tightly on pots and pans to prevent spills of scalding liquids and food items.

Sharp knives make it unnecessary for the homeowner to press down hard on food items to cut them. This prevents food items from slipping out from under the knife, causing a finger or two to be cut. These sharp knives must be kept out of the reach of children, and they must be stored so that they cannot be grabbed by the sharpened edge. It is best to use a knife caddy for their storage to protect the knives from being damaged as well as to prevent accidental cuts.

Even today's popular microwave oven requires caution for its safe use. To prevent any accidents, read the manufacturer's instructions carefully before you try to use it and then follow them strictly for safe and effective results. Never try to operate the microwave oven unless the door is closed tightly, and do not lean against it while it is in use. Use pot holders or mitts to remove cooking utensils.

PREVENTING ELECTRICAL ACCIDENTS

Electricity offers the family a world of different conveniences and experiences, but at the same time, it can be hazardous when safety precautions for its use are not followed. Purchase electrical appliances that have the UL-approved (Underwriters Laboratories, Inc.) seal on them. Never connect or disconnect any electrical equipment when your hands are not thoroughly dry, when your hands are sweaty, or even when you are standing on a wet surface. When an appliance is not in use, especially a television set, disconnect it from the wall receptacle. Always disconnect the cord from the wall receptacle before you remove the cord from the appliance. Plug the cord into the appliance before you plug it into the wall receptacle to reduce sparks and arcing of the terminal pins as well as to lengthen the life expectancy of the appliance.

Homeowners should never use a multiple outlet plug in a single wall receptacle to plug in several electrical appliances because doing so can overload the circuit. Overloads also can be caused by the use of extension cords. Generally, the homeowner should not plug in two electrical appliances such as a hair dryer and a toaster into a single wall receptacle because this can overload the circuit. Two heating elements can be plugged into a single wall receptacle when the homeowner knows that the circuit is large enough to accommodate both of them, such as when he has had an electrician install a larger circuit specifically to accommodate this heavy electrical use.

PREVENTING FIRES

Deaths from fires, burns, and injuries from fire in the home in 1988 totaled 4,100. That is why it is essential to know what to do to prevent fires in a house. In addition to installing smoke detectors on each level of the house and keeping fire extinguishers in strategic locations around the house, which is explained in detail in the next chapter, there are many other ways to keep the family safe from fires. For instance, a simple one is to store matches in cabinets and closets where children cannot reach them, and to teach children to give you any matches they happen to find. Do not ever store gasoline in the house, and when it must be kept on hand for use, store it outdoors in special safety cans that are made specifically for its storage. Other flammable liquids such as oil-based paints, turpentine, and kerosene that are left over in small quantities after use should be stored in their original containers or in safety containers bearing the UL or similarly approved label. These liquids should never be stored in glass and they also should not be stored indoors. Oily rags and oily furniture polish cloths should be stored in covered metal containers and must be kept away from the stove or fireplace.

The homeowner should never use a cleaning fluid that is flammable and he should never start an indoor fire or, for that matter, quicken an outdoor fire, with kerosene or any other flammable liquid. Even leftover grease from cooking should be kept away from the stove or range top while it is cooling and before it can be disposed of properly. In fact, keep paper, fabrics, kindling, paints, turpentine, etc., away from the stove, range top, fireplace, or furnace to prevent a spark from igniting it.

While cooking, wear clothes that fit tightly. Loose-fitting dresses, blouses, or shirts can be ignited easily if they come into contact with the flame on the stove or range top, or if they come into contact with a spark from the fireplace. The homeowner also should be aware of the fact that some household items can be explosive when they come into contact with a fire. These items include leftover flour, uncooked cereals, and dust from the vacuum cleaner. It is best to dispose of these items immediately to prevent injury or damage.

Heating equipment is the number one cause of fires in the home in the United States, according to the National Fire Protection Association (NFPA). More than half of all deaths resulting from fires are caused by wood stoves, portable electric and kerosene heaters, and fixed area gas-fueled heaters. The NFPA notes that the majority of all heating equipment fires can be prevented by taking precautionary measures such as cleaning, maintaining, and using the equipment properly, which includes cleaning chimneys, allowing for adequate space, and burning proper fuels. This organization recommends that only tested and approved products be purchased, that they be installed and maintained correctly, and that they comply with local fire and building code requirements.

When a fire starts in spite of all your best efforts to prevent one, be prepared with an escape plan that every member of the family has practiced over and over again. It is especially important to teach children what to do and what not do in case a fire starts,

to prevent them from panicking. The National Safety Council and local organizations have free materials available to teach a family what to do in case a fire starts in the home. It is essential to get a copy, study it, and be prepared, just in case.

The homeowner can supplement all of these safety precautions by following the maintenance suggestions already discussed in this book as well as those that appear in the sections ahead. For instance, make sure that the central heating system is cleaned and serviced regularly because heating is the number one cause of residential fires, ranking second as a cause of fire deaths. In addition, have the fireplace, chimney, and flue cleaned at least once a year to prevent creosote buildup, another frequent cause of fires that was discussed fully in Chapter 16. Check all of your electrical equipment regularly, looking for frayed wires or burn spots on plugs. Avoid the use of extension cords even as a temporary measure. Hire an electrician to install additional receptacles. Disconnect electrical cords when the electrical equipment is not in use and while the family is sleeping. Test smoke detectors regularly and change batteries twice a year. Most important, be aware of the possible causes of accidents in the home and remove any obstacles or problems that could cause someone to be hurt or killed. Preventing accidents before they happen is the best solution of all.

23
Taking Precautions Against Fires and Burglaries

PREPARATION TO PREVENT LOSS

A house is vulnerable to a fire or burglary at any time, but this is especially true when there is no one in it. To safeguard your house and its valuables, not to mention family members, it is a good idea to understand the importance of a security system, smoke detectors and fire extinguishers and, when appropriate, fire escapes and sprinkler systems. The installation of these precautionary measures can not only protect the homeowner from financial loss but, more important, they can give him peace of mind. Additionally, since a house is usually filled with mementoes as well as the usual amenities, these safeguards also can protect these treasured items. Let's begin our review of these safety precautions with security systems, since these days they are becoming more popular as homeowners deem them to be more necessary than ever before.

SECURITY SYSTEMS

Data released from law enforcement agencies indicates that houses that are protected by a security system run less risk of being burglarized than those without one. Additionally, homeowners of houses with a security system installed in them pay about 10% less for their home insurance policy than those who own houses without a security system installed. Another advantage of a security system is that, in addition to protecting the house from burglaries,

the system often also can protect it from fires. Some security systems even can call for medical assistance when the homeowner or a member of the family becomes ill or is injured. Other essential tasks the security system can perform include turning on lights automatically at preset times and intervals, sounding an alarm when a piece of mechanical equipment malfunctions such as a furnace, and identifying doors and windows left open before the homeowner leaves his house. Today's sophisticated security systems can not only make us aware of problems in the house, but they also can prevent problems from occurring. For any or all of these advantages, a security system is a worthwhile addition to any house.

Security systems are either hard-wired or wireless and usually they are activated and deactivated with the use of a control panel or console. Some of these systems also are interactive; that is, they can be deactivated from another location to provide access for a plumber, electrician, etc., without setting off an alarm. The system is deactivated by placing a call, perhaps from the office, to the house's security system. These types of security systems usually are equipped with some type of desktop console or panel that can sound a differently toned alarm for various possible occurrences, or that can indicate on the console or panel itself where the problem is located in the house. For instance, a kitchen window that has been left open is indicated specifically on the console display so that the homeowner can close it before he leaves the house.

Some security systems use infrared (heat) and motion sensors to detect a possible problem in the house. The motion sensor emits a signal into the area it is monitoring. If a burglar walks around in this area, his body will deflect the signal back to the security system to trigger the alarm. The heat sensor detects the heat emitted from the burglar's body and this increased amount of heat triggers the alarm. Small pets that are left in a house with this type of motion sensor cannot cause problems with the detection system because the pet's body is too small to emit enough heat to trigger the alarm.

Areas of the house are broken down into a number of zones in a hard-wired security system. Windows are outlined with magnetic tape that is applied to window glass and to sliding patio doors and French doors. Switches are connected to each door and window, and the entire system is wired in a continuous closed circuit. If an intruder breaks the glass and damages the tape, the closed circuit is broken and the alarm is triggered. The wiring used to connect this system is thin speaker wire, which can easily be hidden behind moldings and baseboards. This thin wiring is run to the central console where the control panel is housed. The control panel enables the homeowner to control the entire system as well as its various zones to arm and disarm them as needed. The control panel also is programmed to delay the alarm to allow time for the homeowner to enter and leave the house before it is activated. Smoke detectors can be connected to the console to enhance the security system's usefulness. For the most part, hard-wired security systems have to be installed by a security company since they require an understanding of electrical circuitry as well as some skill and patience to install the wiring and the magnetic tape correctly and unobtrusively.

Even though some wireless security systems are very sophisticated, they are easier for the homeowner to install than the hard-wired systems. The basic wireless system usually includes a console, magnetic window and door switches with transmitters, speaker/siren, window decals, AC power adapter, an antenna, and a module telephone cord. Additional accessories can be purchased such as smoke alarms, an indoor siren, motion detectors, etc., to customize the system to a house's specific requirements. Some consoles have an automatic telephone dialer to make local and long-distance calls to relay an emergency message. Various wireless systems also can be programmed to call for help in case of a medical problem.

Before purchasing any security system, the homeowner should assess what he wants it to do in addition to providing security, and whether or not he wants the hard-wired or wireless system. The advantage of the wireless system is that it is easier for the do-it-yourselfer to install. The wireless system's disadvantage is that it does not sound an alarm unless the window sash or door frame is opened; that is, it will not sound an alarm if just the glass is broken. The hard-wired system has magnetic tape on the glass that will trigger the alarm when it is broken along with the glass. That's its advantage. The disadvantage of the hard-wired system is that it is costly because, most of the time, the homeowner cannot do this type of installation himself. The homeowner should research this subject further before making his final choice so that the system he chooses provides the kind of security he feels his house needs.

SMOKE DETECTORS

The installation of smoke detectors is an excellent way to protect the entire family from fires, especially fires that start at night while the family is asleep. And, since smoke detectors are fairly inexpensive, it is almost criminal not to install them at strategic locations throughout the house. Smoke detectors also can be incorporated into the house's electrical system when it is being rewired, or during a new house's construction. Since most homeowners are not engaged in new house construction or an electrical system upgrading, battery-operated smoke detectors are a good alternative. They can easily be installed by the homeowner. When battery-operated smoke detectors are used, the homeowner should make a habit of changing the batteries on a regular basis, perhaps twice a year when clocks are changed to and from daylight savings and standard time. Naturally, the batteries also must be changed anytime during the year when they are tested and found to be weak or not operating. A battery-operated smoke detector with a dead battery in it cannot provide an early warning signal of a fire. That is why this maintenance procedure is an essential one. Dust and paint also can interfere with the operation of a battery-operated smoke detector. To keep smoke detectors free of dust particles, they should be cleaned with a vacuum regularly. Also, smoke detectors should never be painted because the paint prevents them from detecting the presence of smoke.

Basically, there are two types of smoke detectors. One type uses a photoelectric bulb and the other produces charged molecules of air to sense the presence of smoke and trigger an alarm. The smoke detector that uses a photoelectric bulb emits a beam of light that is deflected off the smoke particles when they enter the detector. The beam of light reflects into a photocell and this triggers the alarm. The other type of smoke detector has a small radiation source that charges the air molecules electrically. These charged air molecules, which are called ions, allow a tiny electric current to flow into the ionization chamber. As smoke particles enter the chamber, they become attached to the ions and reduce the flow of electrical current. This decrease in the electrical current triggers the alarm.

Since each type of smoke detector is capable of detecting different types of fires, it is a good idea to install both types in a house. The smoke detector using charged air molecules detects fast-flaming fires, while the one with a photoelectric bulb detects slow, smoldering fires. Since both types of fires are possible at any time, installation of the two types of smoke detectors provides for an improved advance warning system as well as enhanced safety.

The location of smoke detectors in a house is as important as whether or not they are installed. An early warning signal can be delayed or prove false over and over again because the smoke detectors were placed incorrectly in the house. Usually, the manufacturer of the smoke detector tells the homeowner where it is best to place the type of smoke detector he makes along with the instructions for use and care. As a general rule, smoke detectors should be placed close to the bedrooms, usually right outside the doors, so that the alarm can be heard when the family is asleep. Smoke detectors should be attached to the ceiling at every level in the house. One also should be installed in the

basement or cellar on the ceiling that is located at the bottom of the staircase that descends to it. This is a critical location since the furnace or boiler, hot water heater, washing machine, dryer, freezer, and second refrigerator often are housed there. A smoke detector also should be installed just outside the kitchen. It is not appropriate to place it inside the kitchen because the heat and smoke emitted from the stove will set it off frequently. This is also true in bathrooms where the heat and steam from showers and baths will trigger many false alarms.

The correct placement of the smoke detector in a house with a forced air heating and cooling system also is essential for it to function properly. The smoke detector should be installed between the return air register to the furnace and the sleeping area, and it should be at least 3 feet away from the register because the register will blow smoke away from the detector if it is too close. If the smoke is recirculated through the return air register, it will become diluted and this will delay the alarm. By the time the alarm is triggered, it may be more difficult to escape the fire and smoke than it would have been if an earlier warning has been sounded.

The homeowner who sleeps with his bedroom door closed should install a smoke detector inside his bedroom as well as outside. The smoke from a fire inside his bedroom cannot trigger the alarm until it reaches the other side of the closed door. By that time, the occupants of the bedroom could be unconscious as a result of smoke inhalation. Again, the delayed alarm eliminates the advantage of having smoke detectors installed and such a delay could be fatal.

FIRE EXTINGUISHERS

Every house should have several fire extinguishers in it, and they should be maintained properly so that they can be used quickly and effectively. Fire extinguishers should be placed in the kitchen, garage, or workshop, near the furnace or boiler, in the living room and, at least, on each level of the house. Fire extinguishers that are to be used in the kitchen, garage, and workshop should be suited to fight the types of fires that occur in these areas. There are a great many combustible materials in the living room and bedrooms, so it is especially important to have fire extinguishers in these rooms or nearby.

Fires can be ignited near a fireplace or in a piece of mechanical or electrical equipment. That is why it also is important to have a fire extinguisher in these areas of the house or at each level of the house. A fire extinguisher can help to provide a path for the homeowner's escape from the fire, but it should never be used in an attempt to put the fire out. In case of a fire, call the Fire Department immediately. Never try to use a fire extinguisher to put a fire out by yourself since this will only delay the response from the more capable firefighters. When a fire starts in a house, get yourself and your family out of the house immediately and do not waste any time trying to collect personal belongings or mementoes.

The pressure in the fire extinguisher has to be kept at the appropriate level for it to operate properly when it is needed. A gauge on the fire extinguisher indicates the level of the pressure in it. When the gauge indicates a discharge reading, the fire extinguisher has to be recharged. If it cannot be recharged, the homeowner will have to purchase a new one to replace it. This replacement should be done immediately. The homeowner should make a habit of inspecting the fire extinguishers on a regular basis to be sure that they are operating effectively and reliably.

FIRE ESCAPES AND SPRINKLERS

A house that is considered to be a multiple dwelling — one that houses at least three families — usually is required by city or town fire codes to have a sprinkler system, a fire escape, or both installed, as well as smoke detectors. These items are essential to save lives in case of a fire. Because they are so very important, fire escapes and sprinkler systems should be kept in good condition for use at a moment's notice.

The fire escape is attached to the building so that residents can step out the windows onto what is called the basket. From the basket, they can either descend to the streetwalk or ascend to the roof via a staircase or ladder to escape the flames and smoke. The fire escape has to be anchored securely into the wall of the building because it is going to carry a great deal of weight when a fire starts in addition to its own weight. The walls into which it is anchored also have to be structurally sound to hold the fire

escape securely. The ladder that ascends to the roof has to be anchored at the roofline to give it complete support.

When a fire escape is not painted regularly, it rusts. Eventually, this rust could affect the integrity of its structural members. In such a case, the ladder, staircases, and baskets would loosen and corrode after many years of exposure to the weather. All of these problems can be avoided by painting the fire escape at regular intervals. Sometimes, it also is a good practice to apply an undercoating using rustproofing paint. This is especially helpful in areas where humidity levels get very high. In some localities, the proper painting and maintenance of a fire escape are required by local and city fire codes. The homeowner in these areas who lets his fire escape remain unpainted and rusted can be cited for violating these codes.

The piping for a sprinkler system, the other essential piece of safety equipment in a multiple dwelling, is either tapped off the house's water supply line or it is installed as an independent water supply inlet line. Local building codes usually dictate exactly how this must be done for a correct installation. A main shutoff valve is installed on the water supply inlet line. This valve must be kept in the open position at all times so that the water is available at any time in case of a fire. Branch piping is installed throughout the various living areas in the building to carry water to them. This piping is attached to the ceilings in the hallways and then sprinkler heads are attached to the piping at specific intervals. Once again, local building codes dictate how the branch piping is installed and at what intervals the sprinkler heads are attached to it. Extra sprinkler heads are attached near the water supply inlet line, sometimes placed in cabinets near it.

There are several types of sprinkler heads for this system, and it is important to use the right one for each specific installation. Sprinkler heads designed and specified for residential use should be installed in residential properties. The reason for this is that residential sprinkler heads have a quicker response time to a fire than commercial sprinkler heads because they are activated at a lower temperature. For example, a residential sprinkler head usually operates in about thirty seconds, while a commercial sprinkler head operates within three or more minutes. The longer response time enables the fire to spread rapidly before the sprinkler head activates. In so doing, it causes the fire to need more water to extinguish it than if a shorter response time had elapsed. The standard for the water supply in a sprinkler system, established by the National Fire Protection Association, is only ten minutes. In effect, this means that the sooner the response time activates the system, the better, to use the water supply effectively.

The sprinkler system works automatically in response to an increase in the temperature of the space near the sprinkler heads. As the temperature rises, a device in the sprinkler head is activated to release water from each sprinkler head in the system that is located near the fire. Water sprays out of the sprinkler heads to extinguish the fire. A sprinkler system should be tested annually or at least as often as local fire codes dictate, to be sure that it is always fully operative. There is a legislative movement afoot to require the installation of a sprinkler system in one- and two-family houses as well as in multiple dwellings because such systems have been known to save lives. Some states and localities are investigating the impact of this type of legislation on homeowners, so do not be surprised if your area enacts such a law. Working in conjunction with smoke detectors, sprinkler systems can prove to be invaluable in reducing the loss of life and property. That is why it is so important to keep those that are installed in good condition.

24
Dealing with Health Hazards

IDENTIFYING AND PREVENTING HAZARDS

There are many potential hazards in a house in addition to the obvious ones. Health hazards are present frequently. These include the presence of such materials as lead and asbestos. Gases such as formaldehyde and radon also are sometimes in a house as are various rodent problems. Not every homeowner is going to be faced with all of these health hazards; however, he should be aware of them should one happen to be discovered. The homeowner should know where the problem might exist, what causes it, what types of health hazards are involved with it, and how to eliminate it from his house. Each of these problems can be resolved satisfactorily so the homeowner does not have to panic if he suddenly encounters one or several of these health hazards in his home. The solutions to these problems include knowing how to prevent them in the first place as well as knowing how to deal with them effectively and efficiently to eliminate them. Since lead is the most common and perhaps the most well-known health hazard in a house, let's begin with a discussion about it.

LEAD IN PAINTS

Earlier in this book, in the water main section in Chapter 12, lead in drinking water was discussed fully to alert the homeowner to its dangers. How-

ever, lead is not only found in drinking water. It also can be found in old houses where walls, ceilings, and interior trim moldings were coated with lead-based paints. Attempts to remove this paint such as sanding it or burning it off with a torch only expose the entire family to lead's toxic effects.

Both low and high concentrations of lead are harmful; however, infants, children, and fetuses are even more susceptible to its dangers than adults. This fact is exacerbated because children peel the lead paint off the surface and eat it. Even when they do not actually swallow it, their lead-contaminated fingers transfer the lead to other objects as they touch objects around the house. When they inevitably put these objects into their mouths, the lead is ingested along with their saliva. Exposure to lead can affect the physical and mental development of children. Children's I.Q. levels are lowered as a result of lead exposure, their attention spans are shortened, and they exhibit behavioral problems. The harmful effects of lead in the body include brain and kidney damage as well as damage to the nervous system and to the blood cells.

Because it can be so harmful, it is essential to remove lead-based paint from the house when it is found to be present. This can only be done by having a sample of any suspicious paint tested by a laboratory. There are several ways to remove lead paint from a house, none of which is simple or inexpensive to do. For example, lead paint can be removed from door and window trim moldings by carefully removing the moldings and sending them to a paint removal shop. Naturally, it is difficult to remove old trim moldings without breaking them and, once they have been removed, it is expensive to have this type of paint removal work done. That is why most homeowners prefer to replace the old moldings with new ones, a better choice when it is not critical to the house's historical heritage to keep its moldings intact and original. Paint removers can be used by professional restorers, but it is not uncommon for the lead paint to be so embedded in the wood that it cannot be removed fully from it. Again, it is best to remove the wood moldings and install new ones to be sure that all of the lead-based paint has been removed.

Walls that have been coated with lead-based paint can be covered with wallpaper, paneling, or similar materials to minimize exposure to the lead under the covering. The lead paint can be removed to repaint these walls, but there are some special problems to deal with before a new coat of paint can be applied. For example, lead paint cannot be sanded off these walls because the sanding spreads lead-contaminated dust throughout the house. Cracked and peeling paint would have to be removed carefully from the walls, again to prevent lead-contaminated dust resulting from this scraping from spreading throughout the house. All of the lead paint removed from the walls has to be cleaned up from the floors and discarded properly to prevent lead contamination in the town, municipality, or neighborhood. This type of work should be done by an abatement company that is familiar with the work and is capable of doing the job thoroughly and safely.

The homeowner should never attempt to do this work himself because he might do things that could leave his house in worse shape than it was before he started. For instance, he might decide to use his vacuum cleaner to pick up the lead-contaminated dust and peeled paint flakes from the floors. This is a bad idea, as is the use of a commercial vacuum or wet/dry vacuum cleaner. The reason is that the lead particles are so small that they pass right through the vacuum cleaner bags and are exhausted out the other end into the house. Only specially equipped vacuum cleaners with appropriate filters can be effective in this type of cleanup job. They are used by abatement companies that specialize in the removal

of hazardous materials. These companies also are authorized to dispose of this lead-contaminated material properly. These are important reasons for to have this work done by a qualified professional.

ASBESTOS FIBERS IN INSULATION

Until the early 1970s, asbestos was used in the manufacture of many building materials for residential and commercial construction. Some of the materials containing asbestos include siding, floor tiles, chimney cement, ceiling tiles, and pipe and boiler insulation. Even some wood fillers and other patching compounds contained asbestos. Today, most of these products are no longer made with asbestos, and the labels on some wood fillers and patching compounds, for instance, specifically state that they do not contain asbestos.

The areas in the house where asbestos usually can be found in its greatest abundance is in its application as pipe and boiler insulation. In this type of application, asbestos is generally found in the basement or cellar, but it is not strictly confined to these areas. Asbestos pipe insulation is most dangerous when it has been damaged or broken because the asbestos fibers are being released into the air in the house from it. These fibers are so tiny that they cannot be seen by the naked eye and even the nostril hairs cannot filter them out of the air before inhaling it. Ordinary dust masks and household vacuum cleaners also cannot filter these fibers from the air.

Once inhaled, these asbestos fibers accumulate in the lungs where, according to the U. S. Environmental Protection Agency, they can cause lung cancer; mesothelioma, a cancer of the chest and abdominal lining; or asbestosis, an irreversible scarring of the lungs that can be fatal. The symptoms of these diseases usually are not evident until many years after exposure to the asbestos fibers, and many individuals who become ill with these diseases were exposed to elevated concentrations of asbestos over long periods of time such as while at work. Unfortunately, asbestos-related diseases also have been known to appear in housewives who have been washing their husbands' asbestos-contaminated clothing for many years.

Any asbestos that is found in a house should be removed or encapsulated by a professional abatement company. This is not a job for the homeowner, mainly because inexperienced handling of asbestos can cause more harm than good. When a homeowner suspects that some type of material in his house may contain asbestos, he should call an asbestos abatement company to test the suspicious product for him. It is a good idea to test old ceiling tiles or other materials in an old house that may contain asbestos before any renovation or remodeling project is undertaken. When such a precaution is not taken, the homeowner risks emitting asbestos fibers into the air from contaminated materials as they are being removed.

One homeowner learned about this when he removed old ceiling tiles from one of the bedrooms in his house. He later discovered that they contained asbestos. He had to have an abatement company come in to clean his entire house because the asbestos fibers were everywhere in it. This was a costly project that easily could have been avoided had he had the old tiles tested before he removed them. Armed with a better understanding of the potential danger of asbestos-contaminated materials, this homeowner also had the abatement company remove other asbestos-contaminated ceiling tiles that were installed in other areas of his house.

Any remodeling project can be a dangerous one if the materials that are going to be removed contain asbestos. For instance, some insulation materials placed in wall cavities in old houses may contain asbestos. To determine whether or not they do, this material has to be tested before it is removed. If asbestos is found, a certified asbestos removal company should be hired to remove it carefully so that it does not contaminate the rest of the house. These companies have permits to discard contaminated waste at specifically designated dump sites. The homeowner would not be allowed to dispose of any materials at these sites. In addition, federal, state, and local laws forbid the disposal of this material along with household garbage. That is one more reason this job is best left to professionals.

FORMALDEHYDE IN BUILDING MATERIALS

As was the case with asbestos, formaldehyde has been used extensively in the manufacture of many building materials. Unlike asbestos, it also was used in the manufacture of numerous household products. Additionally, it was used in the manufacture of some glues and adhesives and as a preservative in some coating products. Formaldehyde also can be found in the smoke emitting from unvented, fuel-burning appliances such as gas stoves and kerosene space heaters.

Those building materials that contain formaldehyde include pressed-wood products and adhesives that contain urea-formaldehyde resins. These products include particle board, which is used as a subflooring or shelving in a house; plywood panels with a veneer made of a softwood or a hardwood; plywood panels such as those used to make kitchen cabinets and furniture; fiberboards such as those used on the bottom of drawers and as furniture tops; and exterior sheathing materials such as plywood and flakeboard, which contain phenol-formaldehyde resins. Pressed-wood products that contain phenol-formaldehyde resins usually have lower emission rates than those materials that contain urea-formaldehyde resins.

During the 1970s, many homeowners had urea-formaldehyde foam insulation pumped into the wall cavities of their houses because it was considered to be an easy, inexpensive, and effective way to insulate the house. After this type of insulating material had been installed, however, high concentrations of formaldehyde were found in the air inside these houses. Studies of this problem found that the level of urea-formaldehyde concentrations in the house declined as time passed, and these studies suggested that houses insulated with urea-formaldehyde foam insulation many years ago should not still have high concentration levels of formaldehyde in them. These same studies, however, also indicated that the levels may still be high if the insulation has become wet or if cracks have developed in the interior walls, exposing the foam to the living area.

Formaldehyde has been found to cause cancer in animals, a conclusion made after various tests were conducted. It also may cause cancer in humans. A colorless gas with a strong odor, formaldehyde can make an individual's eyes tear or even cause burning sensations in the eyes and throat. In some cases, it has been known to cause nausea and breathing difficulties. Asthmatics can be adversely affected by formaldehyde when they inhale it. These are some of the reasons for the concern about the presence of this gas in a house.

In 1985, the U.S. Department of Housing and Urban Development set standards to limit formaldehyde emission levels in prefabricated and mobile homes constructed with plywood and particle board. These types of homes have a particular problem with formaldehyde emissions because they usually are quite small and are constructed with large quantities of pressed-wood products. The HUD standards are meant to reduce the formaldehyde emissions in these types of homes to a safer level.

The rate at which formaldehyde-infused products such as pressed-woods and textiles release formaldehyde gas emissions changes. As noted earlier, formaldehyde emissions generally decrease as the product ages. Conversely, high indoor temperatures and high humidity can increase formaldehyde emissions when the products are still new. When a homeowner is concerned about the level of formaldehyde emissions in his house, he should have the indoor air quality tested. The local Environmental Protection Agency office can assist the homeowner in finding a local firm to do the test for him. Depending on the results of the test, that firm also can advise the homeowner on what steps to take to alleviate any emission levels that may seem high.

RADON GAS LEAKAGES

Radon gas is an odorless, invisible, radioactive gas that is produced by the breakdown of uranium and radium in rocks and soils. It can be found in any soils or rocks that contain uranium, granite shales, pitchblende, or phosphate. The known health hazard associated with exposure to radon is an increased risk of developing lung cancer. The U.S. Environmental Protection Agency (EPA) has stated that fewer than 5% of American homes have been tested for radon, and it estimates that there are more than eight million homes at greatest risk. Some states have already made radon testing mandatory before a house can be sold, and the EPA would like to make radon testing mandatory nationwide.

The location of a house, as well as how well it has

been constructed, determine whether or not it has a problem with radon. Radon has been found in houses built on top of landfills that were once used as dumping sites for industrial wastes, particularly those containing debris from uranium and phosphate mining. Radon enters a house through cracks in the foundation walls or in the concrete floor slab. It also enters a house through openings in the foundation walls that were made for the water supply inlet pipe but were not sealed tightly after the water pipe was installed. Radon also enters a house through the soil in the sump pit at the location of the house trap or through the soil in the crawl space. Once the radon seeps into the house, it becomes trapped in its enclosed space where concentrations of the gas may increase to a dangerous level.

There are several ways to prevent radon gas from seeping into a house. For instance, any cracks in the foundation walls or concrete floor slab should be sealed, as well as any openings around area drains in the floor slab or around the water supply inlet pipe in the foundation wall. The homeowner can do this work himself by using the repair kits that are available with an injection gun, epoxy filler, and mixing nozzles to fill and seal cracks in walls and floor slabs so that they are waterproof and keep radon gas out of the house (Figure 189). Another way to prevent radon gas from entering the house is to adequately ventilate any crawl space as well as the basement or cellar so that the gas cannot collect in these areas. By increasing the air flow in these areas, any radon gas that may collect there will be dispersed.

There are two ways to determine if there is a radon gas problem in a house. The homeowner either can call a radon testing company or he can buy any one of the various testing devices available to do the test himself. Initial testing either can be done with charcoal canisters for a three to seven day period (Figure 190) or with alpha track detectors for a two to four week period. These types of testing devices are left exposed to the air in the house for a specific period of time, as stated by the manufacturer. They are placed in basements and crawl spaces and in the lowest area of the house that is used as a living space. These tests are best conducted when ventilation in the house is at its minimum level such as during the winter when doors and windows are closed most of the time. After the specific amount

189. Devcon® Concrete Repair System permanently fills, seals, and waterproofs cracks and parting lines along concrete floors and walls in basements to eliminate seepage of water, air, or radon gas into the house. Courtesy of the Devcon Corporation.

of time has elapsed, the devices are sent to a laboratory for analysis.

When the laboratory analysis indicates that radon is present in concentrations in excess of 4 "picocuries per liter," which is the current EPA guideline for living-level radon mitigation, further tests have to be conducted to decide what course of action to take. The same testing device can be used again that was used for the initial tests; however, it has to be left in the house for a much longer period of time than elapsed for the first tests. Improved testing devices now available to homeowners give a twelve-hour average reading. Other new models even provide the average annual reading. Some of these devices also can pinpoint the locations where radon is seeping into the house. The homeowner who wants to monitor the radon levels in his house on a continuing basis can purchase radon monitors that provide current and average radon levels by simply pushing a button (Figure 191).

RODENT INVASIONS

Sometimes the pitter-patter of little feet around the house is the sound of a rodent problem, and it is a problem that can be serious. Mice and rats carry many diseases, and even dead rodents present a potential health hazard in a home. Rodents also consume and contaminate stored foods, and they have been known to cause many electrical fires because they gnaw away at the insulation covering on the wiring and expose it, causing electrical shorts and sparks. Disease-carrying ticks, fleas, and mites on rodents carry such serious illnesses as Rocky Mountain spotted fever, Colorado tick fever, and Lyme disease, among others. Squirrels can take up residence in an attic where they can create quite a filthy mess while they expose the family to possible illness.

Rats and mice tend to hide in areas where they are not going to be disturbed very often by the homeowner and his family, such as in deep closets, storage areas, and the basement and attic. In addition to their scampering noises, telltale signs of their presence in a house include droppings near walls or behind objects that are rarely moved, and packaged goods and cardboard boxes that have been gnawed open. Other indications of rodents include openings around pipes, ducts, and vents that have been enlarged, and tracks made in flour sprinkled along walls, pipes, and beams to discover them. The homeowner should realize that the presence of one mouse or rat is an indication that there are more of them in the house because rodents are communal creatures and they multiply rapidly.

Mice and rats can be killed with baits, such as those available from The d-CON® Company and other manufacturers. The baits have to be placed at 3- to 6-foot intervals in areas where signs of their presence have been found. Traps also are very effective; however, the homeowner has to be able to deal with the disposal of a dead rodent, a task not every individual can readily handle. When baits are used, be sure to keep them in areas where children and pets cannot touch them, and read the manufacturer's instructions for use to be certain that the baiting is being done correctly.

It is not necessary and, in some states, it is even illegal, to kill squirrels with poisoned baits to rid them from an attic. Usually squirrels can be driven out by scattering moth balls around in the attic or by keeping bright lights lit in the attic. Both of these methods are effective deterrents. Traps also are available for rental or purchase to catch the squirrels without harming them. Once caught, however, the squirrels will have to be taken at least a few miles away from the house before they are set free to find a more appropriate residence.

There are several ways to keep squirrels out of an

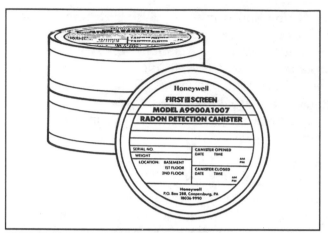

190. Radon detection canister designed to be used by trained professional contractors who can help homeowners to better interpret results and offer solutions. Courtesy of Honeywell Inc.

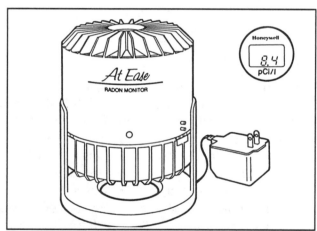

191. Radon monitor is useful for homeowners who want to monitor radon levels on an ongoing basis. Courtesy of Honeywell Inc.

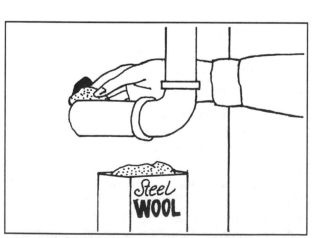

192. A free booklet from d-CON® shows homeowners ways to keep rodents out, such as sealing potential entrances around pipes, as well as how to deal effectively with those that get in the house. Courtesy of The d-CON Company.

attic. For instance, the homeowner can cover any holes with a wire-mesh or metal sheeting to prevent access to the attic through these openings. He also can trim any tree branches that hang near the attic to prevent squirrels from easily jumping from the branch onto the house. One homeowner learned the reason to prevent their access into a house when he was unfortunate enough to have a squirrel enter his living room by coming down the chimney. This homeowner had left the damper open even though the fireplace was not being used at the time. Because the chimney was cool, the squirrel had easy access into the house, in this case, the living room, where the fireplace happened to be located. The trapped squirrel panicked at the sight of the homeowner, who also panicked with equal intensity. In its fury to escape, the squirrel damaged several pieces of furniture and memorabilia before it found its way out of an opened window. Chimneys are common entrances to houses for squirrels. For this reason, it is important to keep the damper closed when the fireplace is not being used, especially during the summer when the chimneys are quite cool and more squirrels are roaming around than during the rest of the year.

There are many ways to keep mice and rats out of a house. For example, keep garbage in sturdy garbage cans with tight-fitting lids instead of in paper or plastic garbage bags that are easily accessible to rodents. Avoid creating sites for nesting such as piles of firewood, lumber, and other building materials. Unharvested crops should be removed from the garden at the end of the growing season and discarded to prevent rats and mice from feeding on them. Leftover pet foods that are outdoors also should be discarded immediately to prevent rodents from eating them. Rats have even been known to eat from bird feeders, so homeowners should limit the amount of birdseed to a day's worth for the local bird population.

There are steps the homeowner can take in his house to prevent rodent invasions. For example, stacks of newspapers and cardboard boxes should be kept off the floor and away from walls. Openings where rodents can enter the house also should be sealed thoroughly. Because mice can squeeze through a 1/4-inch diameter hole, it is important to fill and seal openings around pipes, vents, ducts, wires, etc., with sheet metal, steel wool, caulking, or a quick-drying cement (Figure 192). Floor drains should be covered and the covers should fasten tightly to prevent rodent entry. In addition, bulk food items such as pet foods should be stored in containers with covers that seal tightly. All of these simple and relatively inexpensive maintenance procedures can protect the homeowner and his family from disease-carrying rodents.

PART VII
Appendices

1
List of Suppliers, Manufacturers, and Associations

American Plywood Association
P.O. Box 11700
Tacoma, WA 98411-0700
(206) 565-6600
Wood building products.

Andersen Corporation Inc.
100 Fourth Avenue North
Bayport, MN 55003-1096
(612) 439-5150
Windows and doors.

A.O. Smith Water Products
Company
5605 N. MacArthur Blvd., Suite 360
Irving, TX 75038
Glass-lined water heaters.

Berner Air Products Incorporated
P.O. Box 5410
New Castle, PA 16105-0410
Heat recovery ventilators.

Bionaire Corporation
90 Boroline Road
Allendale, NJ 07401
(201) 934-0700
Air conditioners.

Bionaire Corporation
901 N. Lake Destiny Drive, Ste. 215
Maitland, FL 32751
(407) 660-0265
Water filtration systems.

Bossaire, Inc.
2901 S.E. Fourth Street
Minneapolis, MN 55414
(612) 378-0049
Heat recovery ventilators.

Carrier Corporation
P.O. Box 4808
Syracuse, NY 13221
(315) 432-3147
Boilers, furnaces, heat pumps,
air conditioners, etc..

Cedar Shake & Shingle Bureau
515 116th Avenue, N.W., Suite 275
Bellevue, WA 98004-5294
Shakes and shingles.

Conservation Energy Systems
P.O. Box 10416
Minneapolis, MN 55440
(800) 667-3717
Heat recovery ventilators.

The d-CON Company
P.O. Box 4130-W
Westbury, NY 11592
Pest repellents.

Devcon Corporation
780 A.E.C. Drive
Wood Dale, IL 60191
(800) 227-7950
Concrete repair system.

Jim Dunn Company, Inc.
195 La Rancheria
Carmel Valley, CA 93924
(408) 659-0598
Radiant floor heating.

Fibermesh Company
4019 Industry Drive
Chattanooga, TN 37416
Concrete reinforcement
material.

Four Seasons Design &
Remodeling Centers
5005 Veterans Memorial Highway
Holbrook, NY 11741
(516) 563-4000
Enclosures.

Goodwin Lumber Company
Rt. 2, Box 119-AA
Micanopy, FL 32667
(904) 373-9663
Many wood products including
virgin heart pine flooring and
paneling.

The Home Depot, Two Paces West
2727 Paces Ferry Road
Atlanta, GA 30339
(404) 433-8211
Home centers with computer-
aided kitchen planning systems.

Honeywell Inc.
1985 Douglas Drive North
Golden Valley, MN 55422-3992
Thermostats, boiler and
furnace controls.

Hydrotherm Inc.
Rockland Avenue
Northvale, NJ 07647
Boilers, furnaces, volume water
heaters, and baseboard heaters.

Innovis Interactive Technologies
Tacoma, WA 98477
(206) 924-2900
Computer design systems for
home improvement projects.

Jacuzzi Inc.
100 N. Wiget Lane
P.O. Drawer J
Walnut Creek, CA 94596
(415) 938-7070
    Whirlpool baths, spas, hot tubs.

Lennox Industries Inc.
P.O. Box 799900
Dallas, TX 75379-9900
    Boilers and furnaces.

Lindal Cedar Homes
4300 South 104th Place
P.O. Box 24426
Seattle, WA 98124
(206) 725-0900
    Prefabricated houses.

Marvin Windows
8043 24th Avenue South
Minneapolis, MN 55425
    Windows and doors.

Masonite Corporation, Building
Products Group
One South Wacker Drive
Chicago, IL 60606
    Building materials.

The Maytag Company
Newton, IA 50208
(512) 792-7000
    Appliances.

National Chimney Sweep Guild
P.O. Box 1674
St. Cloud, MN 56302

National Fire Protection
Association
One Battery March Park
P.O. Box 9101
Quincy, MA 02269-9101
    National Electrical Code® and
other information on fire safety
products and standards.

National Kitchen & Bath
Association
687 Willow Grove Street
Hackettstown, NJ 07840
    Free information and referrals.

National Pest Control Association
8100 Oak Street
Dunn Loring, VA 22027
    Information on pest control.

National Safety Council
444 North Michigan Avenue
Chicago, IL 60611
    Free information on safety.

National Wood Window and Door
Association
1400 East Touhy Ave., Suite G-54
Des Plaines, IL 60018
    Information about these
products.

NORCO Windows, Inc.
P.O. Box 140
811 Factory Street
Hawkins, WI 54530
    Windows and doors.

Owens-Corning Fiberglas Corp.
Fiberglas Tower
Toledo, OH 43659
    Roofing, insulation, and
    insulated sheathing.

Pease Industries, Inc.
7100 Dixie Highway
Fairfield, OH 45014
    Doors.

Pella/Rolscreen Company
102 Main Street
Pella, IA 50219
    Windows and doors.

Season-All Industries, Inc.
1480 Wayne Avenue
Indiana, PA 15701-0370
(412) 349-4600
    Windows and doors.

Shakertown Corporation
1200 Kerron Street
P.O. Box 400
Winlock, WA 98596-0400
    Shingles.

Simpson Door Company
400 Simpson Avenue
McCleary, WA 98557
(206) 495-3291
    Doors.

Slant/Fin Corporation
Greenvale, NY 11548
(516) 484-2600
    Boilers, baseboard heaters, air
conditioners.

Steamist
One Altman Drive
Rutherford, NJ 07070
    Steambath.

Thoro System Products
7800 N.W. 38th Street
Miami, FL 33166
    Waterproofing, maintenance,
decorative, and insulation products
for concrete and masonry.

3G Mermet Corp.
3963 Virginia Avenue
Cincinnati, OH 45227
(800) 847-7243
    Rustiver wall covering.

USS
P.O. Box 86
Pittsburgh, PA 15230
    Plate and structural products.

VELUX-AMERICA INC.
450 Old Brickyard
P.O. Box 3208
Greenwood, SC 29648
    Skylights.

Weil-McLain, a division of The
Marley Company
Michigan City, IN 46360
    Boilers and furnaces.

Western Spruce, Pine & Fir
Association (membership includes
the following):
Alberta Forest Products Assoc.
204-11710 Kingsway Avenue
Edmonton, Alba., Canada T5G OX5
    Grading and supplying wood
products.

Western Wood Products Assoc.
Yeon Building
522 S.W. Fifth Avenue
Portland, OR 97204-2122
(503) 224-3930
    Grading and supplying wood
products.

Wood Moulding and Millwork
Producers Association
P.O. Box 25278
Portland, OR 97225
(503) 292-9288
    Grading and supplying wood
products.

2
Free Information for the Asking

Coalition for Container Safety
P.O. Box 27381
Washington, DC 20038-7381
(800) BUCKET-5
    Free warning label and
brochure.

Consumer Information Catalog
P.O. Box 100
Pueblo, CO 81002
    Free brochures from
government agencies.

d-CON Booklet
c/o d-CON Products
225 Summit Avenue
Montvale, NJ 07645
    Free booklet.

Massachusetts Historical
Commission
80 Boylston Street, Suite 310
Boston, MA 02116
    Copy of "Historic Buildings and
the Lead Paint Hazard."

U.S. Consumer Product Safety
Commission
Washington, DC 20207
(800) 638-2772
    Free brochures on product
safety.

Index